4.11.13

C.B.S

The Chucklehead Broadcasting System

Celebrating 44 Years of Glorified Insignificance

by

Louis A. Coppola

authorHOUSE®

AuthorHouse™
1663 Liberty Drive, Suite 200
Bloomington, IN 47403
www.authorhouse.com
Phone: 1-800-839-8640

First published by AuthorHouse 3/24/2008

ISBN: 978-1-4343-4543-1 (sc)

Printed in the United States of America
Bloomington, Indiana

This book is printed on acid-free paper.

The Diary Of A Mad Technician

OTHER PUBLISHED WORK BY THE AUTHOR

Plays
Chiaroscuro (Samuel French)

Television
Checkmate (Benson, ABC TV, Prime Time)

Fiction
Homecrest Avenue (Authorhouse.com)

Glossary of Abbreviation
AM - 5a or ayem
PM - 6p or pyem
Anncr - announcer
Bite – excerpted voice or sound
Bird - satellite
BOD - Broadcast Operations Department
Bemba - silly, talkative
Cioè - namely; this, that
i.e. - id est, that is
SM - station manager
PD - program director
T B - talk back or intercom between rooms

I had a dream about a pet monkey who survived a fire by crawling inside a play box and pulling the drawer over his head. I woke up thinking the monkey survived because he was of resolute and determined character.

Scene Setter

Out-cue: "keep in touch"
Runs: 28 seconds

"Thank you so much for attending our wedding. It was good to meet both of you and to <u>try</u> to dance with your son, who is a real cutie! Phil and I felt so lucky about the entire day of August 19th. It was a spectacular summer day - we couldn't have gotten better, plus, and most important, the people who attended the wedding showed, oh, so much spirit. Thanks for contributing to that spirit."

*

"Ditto that. With little more than a week to go at C.B.S and a two-month trip looming up, it's time to get nervous. Ayn, it was great to meet you, too, after hearing about you from your husband for years while we sat in Studio D at 5 AM. I'm only sorry I didn't get to speak to you much. And I'm going to miss my favorite tech after I leave C.B.S. You helped make it a great place to work at for so many years. I remember when I first started out I'd hear stories about the wild man of the overnight. I was a bit apprehensive about working with you. Maybe you mellowed out - it must've been Ayn's influence - but I've enjoyed working with you and it was a great pleasure having you, Ayn & Ion at our wedding. Even if there's still the <u>wild man</u> in you- or especially so- I hope we'll keep in touch."

Ciao for now!

ACT ONE

CHUCKLEHEAD

1 *Wild Man of the Overnight*

(*headshot*)

Ha, ha, ha. I gotta say up front, ha, ha, I got this chuckleheaded habit of talking to strangers. Ha. Why? I don't know. Because most people're tighter than a tick's ass. Ha, ha, ha. Maybe it's an old radio-bemba habit. Everybody chuckles in radio. Hi, Sue. Ha, ha. Hey, Drew. Ha, ha. You can say that again. I can, but I won't. Ha, ha. It's 20 after the hour. What hour? Eisenhower. Ha, ha. In that case, it's 16 hundred and zeros at 3 o'clock. Ha, ha! Ho, ho! There was an accident at a nursing home. What happened? I forget. Ha, ha, ha. What's the time now? Don't know. Took a shower and my waterproof watch drowned. Ha, ha. Hee, hee. (*serious*) Or maybe I'm just reachin' out. I mean the point of going out is contact, but how many people say hello? Hello's a big commitment. It can lead to goodbye, and goodbye's one up on hello. Wave to a passing train and the engineer waves back. Wave to sailors putting out to sea and they wave back. But wave to somebody in the street and you're weird. Sometimes strangers'll talk to me.

Insert Actuality. Runs: 25 seconds

"Some jobs are like doin' time. I retired after 25 years on the job. The other day I saw someone I used to work with and a strange feeling came over me, a feeling of what it must be like when an ex-con meets a former prison mate. A moment of revulsion; recalling a detestable time and a desire to flee the scene."

:07 sec

"How do you know when cantaloupes are ripe?"
"They have a certain smell, like women."
"I thump 'em myself."

:12 sec

"I'm retired from C.B.S."
"CVS? They in business that long?"

"No. C.B.S, Radio and Television."

"Oh! Did you work with-?"

"Yeah. He'll never get hemorrhoids. He's a perfect asshole."

:36 sec

"Remember Anita Ekberg in La Dolce Vita?

"Pita? Breads. Aisle 8."

"What a pair!"

"Pears, section 2."

"Standing in the Fontana di Trevi with her dress up."

"Dressing, aisle-"

"Drove Tarzan bananas."

"Bananas-"

"Bah-nanas!"

"Organic or conventional?"

"Organic, man!"

"The bin behind you."

"More men visit the Trevi than St. Peter's in Rome and-"

"Romaine, aisle-"

"No. Rome, Rome! They kiss the stones; fill vials with water, cross

themselves, and pray to Ekberg's tits."

"Tits? Aisle. Tits?"

"Big ones."

"How big?"

"Watermelons."

"And they pray to them?"

"On their knees."

"What do they say?"

"Mama-mama-mamma..."

Some days I start out happy, and- well, like this time, which left me doing a think piece on myself. The wife and I are getting into the car in the Edgewater Whole Foods parking lot when this cream colored, two- door vintage, sport Jaguar with a low-slung phallic hood pulls up in front of us. I mean, a fabulous piece of macho machinery, like driving on four testicles with an enormous erection between Anita Ekberg's tits. The driver in his thirties gets out wearing Terminator shades, casually lights a cigarillo as the passenger door swings open and out steps Pussy Galore smoking a ball point pen, sandy blonde tresses undulating in the breeze off the Hudson River. Look at this trio, I think. Bet they're all fucking each other and the Jaguar's winning.

"What year's your car?" I ask.

"What year's the car?" he says rhetorically, in a drawl reminiscent of W. C. Fields. "1967."

Intuition says *leave it there*, but I don't.

"Back in 1967," I go, and he cuts me off in that supercilious voice, *Back in 1967,* while raising an eyebrow at his pal, Miss Paper Mate with blue lips. "Back in 1967," I continue, but I already hate him. He made me feel old. It was thirty-six years ago when I joined the Chuckler Fraudcasting System. "They had a raffle," I go, "and someone won a Jaguar like that one."

"So," he says, "you're one of the Burrow Boys."

"No. He was before 1967."

"Oh, right."

Goddamn right, I think, happy because I corrected the smug jag-off, but also angry and envious of him, the blonde, the car, their youth.

"He's full of himself," I say to the wife as we drive off.

"Yes," she says. "He's riding on pontoons."

"Riding on pon-toons," I say, aping the creep. Now I'm not laughing. I'm thinking, which is <u>bad</u> news. When I think, I get serious. When I get serious, I get depressed. When I'm depressed, I piss in the wind.

Back in 1967 I was riding on pontoons myself. *1967.* Light years ago. I remember looking in the showroom window on West 57th at the winning prize. A spruce green sapphire dream turning on a black onyx dais trimmed in diamonds, with a silver jaguar leaping off the hood, and I thought; *there are cars, God and Jaguars.*

"Now I'm history, too, like that Jag, a minor relic tucked away in the shadows of the Fraudcast Museum." Up to then I'd forgotten about being old. I fight it. *You're Aunt Jo was right,* says Ayn. *You came a long way, honey, for a kid off the streets of Brooklyn.*

I never really failed. I fell in love with the glamour and promise of show business, saw her for the whore she was, and walked. Of course I got help from the business itself, which is 98% inhospitable. What happened in Hollywood to John Barrymore and Marilyn Monroe- alcoholism and suicide- is the tip of the iceberg. So I quit college in 1960, Hollywood in '63, disc jockeying in '65, became a technician in '66- and maybe that's okay. Because in '67 I joined Chuckler Fraudcasting System, hung in for 25 years, and grew up as they say in radio parlance *on the other side of the window.* First, I went underground on the nightshift to "regroup" and obliterate my past. Then I switched to days and nearly nuked myself. In 1991 I woke up dead in a hospital bed, drained of piss and vinegar, and older than JFK when he was murdered. So I retired on disability. It ain't paradise, but even on a bad day it beats the shit out of going to that TV-radio-bemba whorehouse on 57th Street.

☺

2.   *Parallel Strangers*

Twenty minutes later, the misses and me are at Englewood Library returning Mother Goose books- we're heavy readers- when Smiley Face jumps up at me like a pop-up character in a kid's book.

"What's this? It's too soon for Halloween."

"Is it too soon," says Ayn, "to ask what you're talking about?"

"Haunts. First the Jag, now Smiley Face on 50 book covers on the piano display."

"He's high on himself. Good for him."

"He was smiling when we met at C.B.S in 1970, smiling when I retired in '91. Lots of people were smiling then."

"Not me."

"And he's still smiling in 2006."

"It is sort of infectious."

"Like jock itch," I go, my face between two books in an airhead grin. "Two chuckleheads frozen in time. Maybe he's secretly crazy. But aren't we all?"

"Yes. Only with you it's no secret."

"Hey, I like to be silly and it's misunderstood. We're all misunderstood sometimes, even you." She gives me the "mois" look. "Yes, you, almighty articulate one. Now take C.B.S, please."

"Drop the book, Henny, or take it out."

"They've got the best writers and newscasters," I go, leaving the check out circle, "yet we'd often say-"

"For people in communication we don't communicate."

"And 'read my lips, asshole!' Forty years and still smiling. He's a human beacon."

"A lighthouse."

"You'd think his cheeks'd be tired by now."

"And your jaws."

"My drawers?"

"Jaws. Like in mouth?"

Bob Reefer's autobiography is titled, 'Things I Didn't Say On TV and Still Won't Say In My Book'. It's a non-tell telltale about the life of a tattletale. He drops names, but no profanities. Even gave me a non-mention several times. Likewise in autobiographies by Woolly Crankcase and Ms. Leslie Helmet-Hair. I worked with them separately many times and got even more non-mentions. Their books should be anthologized in a tome called *Face Time*. Someone added up face time on a TV show and the Air-Hog, Radio-bemba Award went to the hostess who had 6,982 on-camera minutes to her male partner's 3,119. The counter's the same chucklehead who knows how many sperms go up the fallopian tube.

Of the three books, only Leslie Helmet-Hair quotes expressions from the trenches like, *those assholes in New York*. In public, Smiley Face and Crankcase are Mr. and Mr. Clean. But the dirt on Crankcase is that he loves ribald humor, and playing bass in drag."

"Uncle Woolly?" says Ayn. "You're lying."

"What's the diff? It's too funny to pass up. In his book, 'A Reporter's Wife,' a caption under a picture taken in the oval office says, 'That's me enjoying champagne and a raucous story with the President, his Press Secretary, the Vice President...and in the foreground is producer Ben Givinghead.' In the trenches 'raucous' means a fuckin' dirty joke."

"So much for the people's right to know," says Ayn as we exit the lobby overlooking Engle Street, "You're picking on them because they represent your opposite self. The person you left behind."

"Reefer reminds me of Billy Taylor, David Frost's music director. I worked with Billy at WLIB. Goof up, he'd smile like Reefer and move on. No inquisition under the lights. Gil Noble was also at LIB back then, and cool, too. He was a reporter who wanted to be a DJ. In Billy's PR photos he's always smiling. I go why? He says, that's what I sell. He was born in Virginia. When I go, beautiful country, suddenly he's not smiling, his eyes narrow, and he says quietly, you think so? Later, I learned, Virginia had 500,000 slaves- the largest number in the 15 states; bred them to sell south. At Harpers Ferry the government under Buchanan murdered John Brown."

"Apples up," says the misses. "That's the key. Minor to major. Laugh the world laughs with you. Cry, you cry alone."

"Taylor and Reefer should co-anchor The Billy Bob Apples Up Blues News- a crying out loud review. Just a black screen with eyes, lips and teeth. Reefer and I are the same age."

"Maybe if you smiled more you wouldn't be on disability."

"What'd you mean earlier by they represent my opposite self?"

Ayn takes one of her pain-in-the-ass fuel gathering kundalini-tantric breaths, and lays it out. "Their smile is the light in your heart, which you hide under a bushel. You get a perverse pleasure out of running away."

"Listen," I go, dodging the point, "the Hard News is that Smiley lacks delectable vindictiveness."

"You joke, but envy his success." *That I do.* "He walked through the door. You didn't. You can still go through it. And don't give me the-at-my-age stuff. The library has a writing group, a lecture series." *They pay?*

"An honorarium. What's the difference? You'd be you, not a substitute."

"The pay's good subbing. There's no pressure."

"Please. You've been kicked out of three districts."

"Four. I don't speak their language. I lacked discipline. I try to discuss writing, my play, my book, journalism, people I've met, and get nowhere."

"It's the wrong forum. Go where you'll be appreciated."

Fear keeps me from acknowledging her real meaning, which is performing. So I cover with, "Your friend in the English department at Tee Hee High said, 'don't talk to students too much.'"

"Meaning don't try to make pals. The trick is when you walk into a class don't smile."

"I can't work that way."

"What way can you work? You wrote that union newsletter and they kicked you off. You go too far. Like the drummer in *Music Man* said, *'ya gotta know the territory'*. Know why those news anchors are successful, why your friend Cholly's a millionaire? They know the territory."

"At Chuckler a union protected me," I go, still skirting her meaning while in the back of my mind a telling word is forming itself. "Subs have no recourse. Kids and parents call the shots." I keep running my mouth to bury that word but it persists. "Teachers want an easy day and secured tenure. They leave work, and then don't check it the next day. Kids see that and look at subs as a holiday." Forget that nonsense. The word, man. It's important. Echoes of *'ya gotta know the territory'*. "Another mistake," I go, shoving the word down, "was talking to teachers. In the faculty lounge one sub, about age 75, says, 'kids are liars and teachers hate us.' I thought he's exaggerating. He wasn't. I asked one principal, if I send kids to the office would I be shooting myself in the foot? He says, 'No. We want to know.' Next day I send in two kids. Guess what?"

"Ouch!"

"In both feet."

While Ayn shakes her head says, "You couldn't get me back teaching. No way," I see clearly that inescapable word, clue to my troubles. The Greeks said, it's in the knowing, knowing the terrain, knowing thyself, what's permissible, what isn't. What you can handle, what you can't. This is for you, that's not. I go, "Didn't you teach in Paterson under Joe Clark?"

She nods yes. "He carried a baseball bat." *Now there's a man who knew the territory.* "He was an 8th grade teacher at an elementary school and moved on to principal at Eastside High where he became the man everybody read about. He'd chained the doors, which was a fire hazard. When he talked with that bat in his hand, it always made me nervous." *Somebody had to get serious.* "I know. He was dealing with drugs and guns. He was a military man and took that approach." *Spare the rod and spoil the child. Where's he now?* "Southern Jersey, I think; head of a disciplinary school."

"Maybe I'll give lectures with a bat in case nobody laughs."

"I enjoy when you read your work to me. Others will, too. Why deny who you are? What did Swami say when you gave him advice? 'What the hell you are doing, selling me my own medicine?'"

I hadn't thought of Swami Das in years. Now he loomed up big as life; bald, coconut-brown skin, clad in yellow robes. Swami, man. Where are you, where are you now? Long dead and buried. Goddamit! Dead and buried, but still sitting on top of my head. From his pink lips comes that word like a cue ball striking the pack, boom! The letters explode every which way, and then reshape themselves. *Stop the nonsense, my friend. Say the word. Admit it.* OK. I've been 'reckless'.

"Teaching is another trap," says Ayn, real serious. "In your words, at day's end you're Willy Loman peeled like an apple, thrown away like rind, and you just want to take the pipe. Your friend Julie is right. You can't teach people anyway."

Julius and his wife, Mary, two lives dedicated to art. Cézanne is his God. Mary bows to wood sculpting. I envy their life in art. The idea makes me cry. Jesus and Mary. She talks too much. Poor Julius can't get a word in edgewise. Ha! That'll be the day! "We crucify ourselves," he says. "Some things you have to compromise, but never your work, which is who you are as a man. I decided long ago never to pursue anything to make money. And I succeeded. At 87 I don't have a penny. Just an attic full of paintings. Big ones. So I consider myself a successful unknown penniless artist because I've been able to do what I wanted all my life, which is paint. My work is a well-kept secret. Hidden sometimes even from me." *Where does it all come from; life, art?* "Who the hell knows? Listen. There are enough lies in the world. It doesn't need yours. By the way, what's it all mean anyway? We haven't advanced very far as civilized human beings. I don't care what people do. It's the killing that bothers me. We still kill each other. Is that civilized? The world's full of lies. What's left if we lie to ourselves? Yet people do it every day and live with it. I'm not surprised just amazed."

Like many women, Mary's patient eyes are full of quiet curiosity and consternation over the human dilemma. On the church, she concluded long ago it was a waste. She was in trouble, went to them for help. The priests sat her in a pew while they disappeared behind the iconostasis for a chat. "I'm bleeding," says Mary, "and they're talking, but I'm not aloud to hear. That's when I realized the priesthood was just a good ole boy gang. You know the ribbons on the chests of soldiers? It's men's jewelry. Know why Indians greet each other with prayer hands? Keeps them from hitting each other."

Ayn's talking to my back and suddenly she rings my bell again. "Go through that door. Nobody will kill you!" *Nobody?* "Read your stories. You might have fun. You told me audiences aren't hanging juries. They come to be entertained. Smiley went through that door because he has better things to do than lick his wounds. He's focused and determined. They can't kill you deader than you've been killing yourself."

"I'll treat show biz like an old bitch mistress whose come back."

What I learned in my 20's I should've picked up in elementary school. What I learned in my 30's I should've picked up in high school. What I learned in my early college days I should've been picked up for mental vagrancy. I got my BA at 55, and had a bash. Dr. K, a psychologist friend, coined the invitation based on when I should've graduated, four years after high school. *My*

1959 College Graduation Party in 1990. Now in old age I wonder, *Who am I?* Those early years seem to belong to some other foolish man. Maybe Ayn's Billy-Bob Beacon is a lighthouse calling, *This way! You don't have to be a wreck lost at sea.*

In the '70's Reefer exhibited his paintings on TV, showing a sensitive side of himself not generally seen by the public. God knows when that work-a-holic found time to paint. Maybe on the red eye from DC to NY- that would explain the palsied style. Then, like the California side of me fell off the map, the artist in him disappeared. So, I'm left with two Bobs; broad stroke pragmatic Bob who never confuses his public image with the private one, and Bob, the mysterious painter.

"I've got nothing bad to report on Reefer."

"That's refreshing news," says Ayn.

"He never met anyone he couldn't have fun interviewing even on death row."

"That didn't last long."

"His charm is offensive. He's like Townsand and Curealt, the original 'May I, Thank you, Pardon me' boys. That nobless oblige 'Gone with the Wind' crap's not foolin' me."

"Nobody fools you. But you."

"Absolutely. How can anyone work 50 years anywhere and not hate somebody?"

"Pills and lies."

"How'd you know I was gonna say that?" *Intuition.* "Uncle Woolly says, 'it's our right to know.' So Bobbo, give us the dirty truth about those assholes in New York."

"There's one less since you retired."

"Absolutely! Bob needs us to write a sequel."

"All expenses paid in Venice."

"Absolutely. We'll dot the i's and cross the t's in a gondola; seal it with lunch at Harry's Bar. In fact, who needs Bob? Send the advance C.O.D. care of Café Florian,

Casanova's old hang out. The cover'll be Smiley in a miter holding a crosier titled Mr. Etcetera!"

"That's your dad's epitaph."

"How about Hot Air?" *No. That's yours.* "I got it. Fifty Fuckin' Years Before the Mass!" *Fair. But drop the F word.* "We'll research stolen Venetian art like the Four Bronze Horses of St. Mark's."

"What's the organic link?"

"Organic? Oo! Let's see. Media and horses both give out horseshit! No? The horses were stolen. News steals people's lives."

"A stretch, but better."

"We'll hang out on the Lido; watch tourists feed pigeons in San Marco. Maybe we'll mention Reefer's art, but only if he agrees. Maybe he'll tell us the name of that noted correspondent who lost it when he didn't get the Evening News job."

"Who was it? Probably him."

"No," I go, saddened by what business does to people. "When Uncle Woolly got the job in 1963, Mr. X became embittered, extended his already extravagant liquid lunches, and his marriage failed. His colleagues say he never rose above it. They say he came wobbly legged out of Le Biarritz on West 57th in mid-afternoon, staggered into the street, hailed a cab, and narrowly missed getting run over. My guess, it was Harry Breezener. He didn't understand, a job doesn't define a man. The man defines the job. Anyway, if DaVinci had a code, so does Bob. He never names names on iffy topics, or uses vulgarity. We'll translate what he means when he says, 'he's an unpleasant producer,' or 'the overnight hours were grueling,' or so-and-so was 'uncomfortable to be around.'"

"What do you think he means?"

"Cock-sucker! Asshole! Son-of-a-bitch! And nights're a motherfucker!"

"Lacks imagery."

14

"How about Uncle Woolly behind a clothesline holding a laundry basket wearing a poke bonnet with a nicotine mustache. Tootie Fruity, Randy Rooty! And don't tell us the commute's a bitch?"

"That's a given," says Ayn. "Tell us the juicy insider stuff."

"Like Reefer's Naked Birds from a train. We'll team Woolly with Cesar Romero, a drag queen. They say, he'd come down out of the Hollywood hills in a dress."

"With the mustache?"

"Lookin' for actor Randolph Scott in gingham n' hemp skivvies. Then, lickin' a pretend roll-your-own while Ayn's beside herself, which is hard to do, being in two places at once, I go, "Leastways, that was the gossip 'round the Tinseltown cor-ral. I never give credence to actor talk, sufferin' as they do from tunnel vision and the me-mees. But when I did the rope trick and worked with Lucy, I hear-d it from the horse's mouth."

"Cut the manure. Heard what?"

"Why, when I was a mere striplin' on my pappy's plantation on Avenue U in Brooklyn-"

"Tell me before I kill you."

"Jack Donahue, Lucy's director, was an ex-hoofer who knew Romero from their dancing days. While he's directing I see he's wearing a wide link silver bracelet. 'A copy,' he says, 'of Cesar Romero's.' Beautiful. Lucy dated Romero a few times, but he never came on to her. "One night we're dancing," she says, "he stops, says with tears in his eyes, 'Lucy, I'm strange.' I thought, God, no. Please! He starts crying. I go, life's full of strange things. Then we're both cryin' but for different reasons."

"God! Another fantasy buried."

"When I want to see that bracelet I watch Sinatra's Ocean's Eleven. Romero comes into the funeral parlor looking for the money the gang stole from casinos. He pauses, his arm at his waist and the bracelet's on his wrist. Ta-ta-ta-tah! The swishbuckling Evening News with Crankcase and Romero in babushkas; Randolph Scott in gingham riding his horse Hawse. Tootie Fruity! I can hear Reefer. Is gossip all that necessary? Only if you have a potty training disorder. Question: 'Mr. Romero, you sleep naked or in your underwear?' You don't sleep in your underwear? Whose do you sleep in? Uncle Woolly's! Instead of Cesar it should be Seize-him!

Reefer says, 'most heart attacks happen at 3a.' Mine was at Las Cinco de las Tardes when Garcia Lorca's bulls were running."

"How apropos," says the wife, sliding down the railing.

Calling after her, I go, "Y'know, Lorca died the year I was born."

"You're him, my pot sticker, reincarnated in Las Cinco de las tapas."

"No. My tortilla. He liked boys. Let's work him into Reefer's bio." *Good idea, my batata. Less Bob is more Bob.* "We'll put him in the anniversary Wheel-dex. Today in 1936 Franco's fascists and a passive Church shot Spain's greatest living poet. Congratulations! Now back to Bob. But first this: in Spain people are more alive dead?" *Oh?* "They celebrate El Dia de los Muertos- All Souls Day, dress up, and in Catalan they say, 'per moure l'esquelet' to move your skeleton and dance on graves."

"I should've been Spanish. Why'd they kill Lorca?"

"He was iffy, a communist, and an influential writer. It scared 'em. He made enemies denouncing the church and Queen Isabella. He said, when they drove out the Moors it marked the decline of Spain."

"What's our transition back to Bob?"

"How about, Back to Bob."

"Should be more organic."

"He paints naked vegetables."

"Is he naked or the veggies? Either way he's got my vote for the Chucklehead Museum." Tripping down the grassy knoll, Ayn lands with a bound, and laying a finger aside of

16

her nose, she says, "Write your own screed, Ernesto. Why should I be sole beneficiary of your dissatisfaction and self-denigration?" *True.* "You did lots in your life." *I did?* "You had the nerve to leave a negative home environment; used the army to get into radio; acted and taught Karate in Hollywood; joined the biggest entertainment conduit in the media; met Sonny and Cher-"

"I never met them."

"You said she was better looking in person."

"What I said was, a friend said he met Cher in the street and he told me he told her she was better looking in the street."

"So, we'll change him to you and leave it there. Moving on." *That's organic.* "You bought a house; raised a beautiful son; finished college; published two books and you're writing a third." *I am?* "Another of your theorographies, only you're talking it away. Get your skates rolling and weave a pearl around it. To me you <u>are</u> one of the Burrow's Boys. You're a thinking writer with integrity. And when you say writers and artists, don't say them, say we."

Not knowing whether to curtsy or shit, I go, "Reefer's the Sinatra of News."

"And you're the stranger in the night."

3.   In the Dark Everybody's Equal

Nosies (reporters) coming to work at 4a (AM) call it the 'Lobster Shift.' To me, in at midnight, it was the Dracula Shift. Either way it turns you into beef jerky. In the '70's Reefer came in at 4a to anchor morning TV, and we'd rub elbows now and then- we were too tired to shake hands! Sometimes he'd come to radio to record an audio track. When passing each other in the halls, or cafeteria, it was groggy howdies, and chin rubbing wondering what in hell we were doing in the middle of the night when decent folk were fast asleep. Reefer was looking for TV face-time, and I was the Tar Baby wallowing in self-vilification.

One morning I stayed after my 7a out time to donate blood. When my boss Mortin, Director of Tech Operations, saw me in the hall he covered his eyes and tried to drive a Number 2 pencil through my heart. A born kibitzer, he'll die laughing at his own jokes. He's 6' 2" and weighs 240 pounds, so when he jokes I laugh in self-defense.

"Good to see you," he says, "but that's only one man's opinion. Ba dum bump! What're you doing among the living?"

"I'm here for the blood drive."

"Giving or taking?"

"Where do I go?"

"Upstairs. One of the TV rehearsal halls."

"You giving?"

"Every day at the office. Ask Ida. But approach slowly. She's not used to seeing you."

"I'm not used to seeing me."

"Then we're all lucky."

That night I go into the newsroom to ask the rotunda, Mal "Roundy" Terkel, editor/producer hourlies and News Roundup (NR), if he gave, or plans to give blood.

"No," he says, "I give plenty working with technicians."

"Mal," I go, imitating Dracula, "we technicians are the victims and C.B.S news is sucking our blood!"

"No wonder the stock's anemic," says Mal, ripping copy.

"You're a prince," I go. "But only when you're smoking your corncob pipe and eating cheese from that delicatessen in your attaché case."

"So that's why you're here?"

"Got any bread to go with it?"

"Bread's fattening. We've got a fine selection: provolone, aged three years; Cello Straveccchio, five years; Camembert, Danish Fontina, Granapadano, that's a heavy, harder cheese, slightly tart, but terrific."

"Any muenster?"

"We don't carry rubber."

"Should you be eatin' cheese?"

"Why? You got something better?"

"Dairy causes mucous."

"So do you but I live with it."

"What's that green mildewed thing?"

"Aged provolone, you jerk. This is Gouda, and that's Goat, and if you say, it's 'bad-ah' or 'you're kidding,' I'll kill you."

"Well," I go, girding for the shoulder punch, " you have to take the ghouda with the bad-ah. My wife says-"

"Wife? Who'd marry you?"

"A woman who takes the good-ah with the bad-ah."

"Go away."

"My wife says goat cheese is healthier than cheese from cow's milk because goats're cleaner."

"Compared to technicians, yes."

"They won't eat if they're sick or their food's got additives."

"Some of us aren't goats," says Mal, underscoring leads in red. As I reach in his attaché case to check a label, Mal slams the lid just missing my fingers. "Bad idea; unless you want a stump for a hand."

"What's the blue bottle?"

"Phillip's Magnesia."

"That's to help the colon push out all that gourmet goop."

"No," says he. "I take a spoonful after working with techs. It cuts the crap. Now if you'll excuse me. Some of us actually work here."

"Really? Doin' what?"

"I'd tell you, but I don't have time to draw pictures."

"You're nasty, Mal. I'm gonna call insecurity, and tell 'em you're nuts!"

"Let's put it this way. My craziness does not preclude your craziness."

A bloody footnote. I never gave blood. They insisted I sign a disclaimer that I wouldn't sue if I got Aids from the needle.

Work the overnight long enough and life does you one better than the Girl From Ipanema. In time, changes were taking place in society and me. When the Equal Opportunity Act passed I thought, *Great! Day timers deserve everything they get.* Didn't bother me because on the Dracula Shift in the dark, we're all equal. Besides, I'd rather look at skirts than pants anyway. Was I in for a surprise. One night a black female desk assistant shows up in pants, remarks about my wide brim black fedora the size of a bat wing umbrella. *It does nothing for you.* Or was it the other way around? A week later around 2a she slaps a white newscaster. I don't know why. Maybe she was trying to keep him awake.

While I'm holding down the fort in the AM, the battle of the sexes was raging in the PM. The men had closed ranks against encroachment of their territory by the Maids of Orleans. Soon, All Quiet On the Western Front erupted into skirmishes of Liberte, Egalite, and the so-called Fraternite gave way to Sorority. Nights started looking like a holiday.

Rumors trickled down about sporadic entanglements over issues of etiquette and language use. Somebody in TV got trapped just holding the door for a woman. A tech was caught with his pants down when one of "them" walked into the men's room. On an hourly newscast a cue was missed because a tech said, 'she's a wrap.' I figured I was safe working AM in the AM and

FM 'em all. But it was awkward adjusting to that first female wave. Looking to prove themselves, they played hardball and the men bobbed and weaved to avoid an equal rights dispute. Buzzwords like "chick" and "broad" went underground, or if uttered inadvertently, an apology followed. In the presence of women the rough and tumble colloquy between men turned into dancing on eggshells. Later on, when everyone relaxed, if you logged a verbatim conversation with expletives you couldn't tell the women from the men.

One night, a supposed brother, a boozy creep daytime tech suffering from insomnia and joint-ritus, can't pass a bar without stopping, rings me up slurring words and talking like I'm a fellow conspirator. What an asshole! I go, you pulling my anchor? He says, "No, man! I mean, person. Everybody's paranoid. Now women want to be on top on the job and in sex too." Fair enough, I go. Either way, it's win-win. Figuring he's going to bend my ear, I put him on the overhead speaker. "Ya there, pie-san?" I go, No! "If the bitches sh-show up at n-night watch your ass not theirs. Ha! Don't shay, 'newsman.' That's out! Sh-shay 'newsperson.'" Sounds awkward. "N-never shay, 'girl.' NG. Fahget honey n' sweetheart. Even the generic <u>he</u>, n' <u>sh-she</u> is ver-boten. Sh-say 'Ms.', 'm'am', 'lady', and 'Mah-dam-me'. Woman's out, too." Why? "It's got the word 'man' in it. In sports they want into the lockers. 'Magine that? A guy can't even fart in peace. What's the world comin', too? Say the wrong word and they cry, hiccup, dis-criminal-ization! Sexual hair-ass-ment! Even callin' a ship 'she' is sexist. Man a-live! I been thinkin', once women get into the union there's gonna be trouble closing letters Fraternally Yaws. The fuckin' word labor'll have two meanings. One clit-wit reported me to the front office 'cause I said, 'What's your background? Pluggin' in a tampon.' Moe-hammed Ali's right. It's a man's world created by men not women. That's why it's called man-kind, not womankind. His-tory not shis-tory. The word woman really means woe to man." You got that right, honey. "Hear what I'm sayin', Mr. Pie-san?" When I ask if any of them are good looking, he says, suddenly sober, "Wha's the diff? Never shit in ya livin' room." After I go, "I don't. I use the bathroom," I hear a click and the line goes dead. Well, I thought, there's another good reason for working nights. Little did I know that a new day was dawning on the nightshift.

4.   My First Boss

Diary, 1991. Sometimes I think about life before Chuckler. I wonder what might've been had I remained in California. Joe Hyams, columnist for the LA Herald Tribune, summed up my Hollywood sojourn in the movie Play Misty, based on stories I told him about Eve and me. More on her later. For practical reasons he left out previous incarnations. Now for those same reasons, I re-rack the tape. There'll be lots of rewinding and fast forwarding. So grab your socks.

In my last year of high school in 1953-54, I went nights twice weekly to Announcer Training Studios on 42nd Street in Manhattan to learn how to be a Chucklehead. Of course back then I was just 17, about to step out, and radio, only 27 years old, was already giving way to Television and looking for ways to reinvent itself. For me, those early radio years were full of mysterious and intriguing names like announcer, news reporter, and disc jockey. At the top of the list was an imaginary dance hall called Martin Block's Make Believe Ballroom. My mom gave the school a down payment; I supplemented the rest working part-time, and took the old BMT from Kings Highway, Brooklyn to the Great White Way. The whole place was magical, like when I first saw Venice. Pure fairy tale. My fondest school memory centers around James, a thin rail of a black man about 38, from the southwest. He had country ways and I liked him for it. On breaks we'd go to a 42nd Street cafeteria-bar just off Broadway where the grill danced with ham and eggs, home fries, onions, franks, and cryptic orders of 'BLT hold-da-mayo!' Food didn't interest James. He saw it the way gays look at Monroe, with a dubious eyebrow.

"All that energy chewing," said James. "Takes lots of effort moving my jaw. Chewin' and swallowin' tires me out. Same with women. I can only swallow but so much. I married, once. Now I nibble short of starvation. I'm more interested in death. I'd like to try it, once." He always ordered a cold glass of hundred proof buttermilk. He'd douse the head with salt, drink, smack his pink-white lips, wipe away the milk mustache with the back of his hand, lick it, and screw up his face from the tangy salt. Pretty soon I had to try it myself. Buttermilk with salt is a sour milk smoothie, which even now excites the juices in my mouth.

Over the years I've wondered what became of those classmates. One student had nasal problems. He couldn't breathe properly because the air passages in his nose were blocked. Some people can't see beyond their nose. He couldn't talk past his. No air entered or left his nose. He sounded like he had a perpetual cold. He tried draining his sinuses, but it was only a temporary fix. He was our sinusitis poster boy! He was dia<u>gnosed</u> with a "deviated septum". He went for surgery and I went for the dictionary. While they were breaking and realigning his septum, I learned that devious meant straying from the normal path, and tricky. So I dubbed him Devious Septum. He loved it, even used it in class for a pen name. *This is Devious Septum with the news.* Because he was a mic hog, some guys called him Devious Septic, as in full of shit. His nose was always bandaged. When simulating air work he sounded like he was talking through a pillow.

"The swellin'll go down, the doctor says. Then I can breed n' talk naw-mal." When the bandage came off, he read copy, and everybody cried, "Put the bandage back on!"

Two decades later, in a recording studio off Broadway at West 44th, I was working with Danny Davis, comedy writer for comedians like Jackie Vernon and Charlie Manna. We were doing a dry run for a proposed talk show. While Danny's interviewing impressionist David Frye, somebody taps my shoulder, and says in a nasal voice, "Long time no see." Years condensed into a yesterday I'd almost forgotten. "It's me, the Maltese Fawl-con." *Right. Hello.* "I'm here in sales." *Good for you.* "It's a living," he says ruefully. "I do a weekend air shift in Patchogue." *Long Island. Gets foggy there?* "Now and then. Rolls in from the ocean. Funny seeing you right after a drainage and re-alignment. Shades of 1954. 'This is Devious Septum and the news.' Ha, ha. Oh, my nose hurts. Bleeds easily. They say I'm allergic to radio. All that electro-magnetism bombardin' my capillaries. Remember the Weehawken kid? Had a Bob and Ray sense of humor; ironing anchovies. He's a radio dispatcher for the Palisades police." *Not a lot of room there for humor.* "He slips one in here and there. Well, you're busy and I gotta run. Ciao!"

On graduation in June of 1954, dumb and 18, I hopped a bus for Selma, Alabama, chasing an ad in Broadcast Magazine without first sending a resume. I sat back of the bus until we crossed the Mason-Dixon Line. Then the driver said, 'you have to sit up front.' I refused and he wouldn't drive on. Then a levelheaded black woman whispered to me, near as I remember, 'thank you, son. But it would be best for everybody here if you do like the man says, or we'll never get home.' I wonder what I'd've done if she'd been Rosa Parks?

Altho' I couldn't put two nickels together, hadn't cracked a book, or had the vocabulary to say *discrimination is amoral,* I felt it intuitively. At rest stops I saw signs on water fountains 'White Only' and 'Black Only.' I drank from both and noticed something peculiar. Their water tasted like our water, and I didn't die. What wasn't potable was man's thinking.

Selma, 1954. A Ticking Time Bomb. I walked from the Selma bus depot to the radio station asking directions on the way and found myself in the black district. *White marble eyes in ebony faces watch me from windows and porches, kids look up and wave hello. A man in bib overalls pulls a soda bottle out of a sidewalk freezer in front of a grocery store, looks me over, and yanks the cap off with his mouth. In the box cold sodas float in ice, but I don't have a spare nickel. 'Just keep on the way you walkin'. It on the right.' Sad silver dollar eyes unaccustomed to a white boy strolling by and probably wondering what else was on my mind.* I remembered my Brooklyn Eagle paper route on East 14th Street. All 14th Street below Neck Road was black and scared me. I'd toss the Eagle and pedal away fast. I'd put off collection day for two days before starting my rounds. *First house. Oh, God! Inside. Upstairs. Jesus! A long shadowy hall.* Heart pounded. Knock-knock. *Eagle boy!* I said, and stood back ready to bolt. The door opened. I looked up into the face of a real black man with no knife in his hand. "You the Eagle boy?" he said. "Lord! Yawl look more like a Memphis sparrow. Ha! Here y'go son with sumpin' extra for kitty." Thank you! A whole quarter was mine. It was big stuff to me. "Who stole home yest'day, son?" Jackie Robinson? "That's right. Ain't it sumpin'! Jackie Robin-some bases! Mm, mm!" Afterward, I thought, what was the fuss? Delivering and collecting got easier with each stolen base and nobody killed me. But we all wanted to kill the umpire.

The radio station reminded me of a tacky bus depot. It had nothing to commend itself except a microphone (*mic*) and transmitter out back. A secretary told me the DJ job was taken. I didn't understand then or ever the extreme competition and jealousy in the *broadcast fraternity*. I took 'no' for an answer, which in part would define my future. On the way back to the bus station I waved to the man at the soda box, decided to hitch a ride north. Next thing I was seated in the jaws of an 18-wheel leviathan roaring down the highway spitting fire and smoke. I held on at every turn afraid I'd fly out the door. On the way I learned that truckers talk to each other by blinking their lights, i.e., one for hello, two for passing, maybe three rapid blinks signal, 'Police Ahead.' We pulled over for a break on a graded shoulder so steep I thought the truck would surely tumble down the embankment. The truck leaned right. I dozed leaning left. After that I stuck to passenger cars only.

D.C. Tiny. The White House looked like a picture post card; but the streets, north, south, east, west were a Chinese puzzle. I checked into a YMCA, went to see Marlon Brando in *On the Waterfront*. Later, at the Y I made friends with Big Tiny, 600 pounds and twice as amiable. He slept on the floor because no bed could hold him. He laughed about himself. "When I step on a fortune telling scale the card says, *'One at a time, please.'*" Tiny showed me a promotional picture of himself sitting in a refrigerator. Stuffed was more accurate! Sporting a broad smile with chunky limbs hanging out, he looked like a giant turtle with a Calvinator shell. The picture was captioned, 'The Ton In One Refrigerator!' The curious thing to me was how, under all that weight, he kept a cheerful disposition. Blacks amazed me, too. They carry the horrific weight of oppression yet still laugh heartily. *Silver dollar eyes floating in a tub of sweet sodee pop in white country with ice water in its veins.* Later, Selma exploded. Maybe Tiny did, too.

Boot, Fort Bragg, Feb, '55. *I know a gal in Fayetteville/ She won't do it but her sister will/Sound off! 1, 2! Sound off! 3, 4! 1, 2, 3-4! This is my rifle, this is my gun. This is for fightin' n' this is for fun!* I joined up for school and the

GI Bill. What was I doing in North Carolina? Playing out the scenario of the nameless, poor and uneducated.

"You candy-asses think, I'm going to sschoo-well! The bayonet's yawe school-well! First lesson, kill the goddamn enemy! The bayonet's the backbone n' balls of this man's army! The bayonet kills few men, but scares many. "No bastard," said Patton, "ever won a war by dyin' for his country. He won it by makin' the other poor dumb bastard die for his. If you're going to win any battle, make the mind run the body. Not the other way around. The body'll give up. It's tired, morning, noon, and night. But the body's never tired if the mind's not tired. When you were younger you played all day, and the body never tired. Make the mind take over not the body." If yawl hope to get yawe sorry ass back to civil-eye-zation when I say, fix *bayonets, fix 'em!* This is the U-knighted States Army of Ah-meerica! Best killin' machine the world's ever known! Only big balls survive! Lemme hear clicks ring out. Fix bayonets, ho! Rifles port. Ho! Parry n' lunge! Ho! Pull back! Turn. Parry. Lunge! Pull back! Hesitate, you're dead! Soldier, kill me! Too late. You thought about it. Gettin' past me is your passport to school. Fail here, you'll repeat basic. Where you headed, soldier?" *Film school, sergeant.* "Gonna shoot the enemy with a camera. Comes a bayonet in ya ugly face, what-cha gonna say, watch the birdie? Forget tanks and planes. Come mop-up time, it's the bayonet door-to-door. Fuckin' mano-a-mano! The difference is balls. Bayonets should be fixed when the firefight starts. Ready! Lunge! Ho! Rifle butt out! Bust that son-of-bitch's jaw! If the bayonet sticks in his bones, kick it free! Fire a round. Blow open his chest. When abolitionist John Brown was captured at Harper's Ferry, Lee's commander lunged at Brown with a sword that bent like a limp noodle. 'Cause in rushing to get dressed he strapped on his dress sword. Always check weapons twice. Hold that rifle up like your dick! Yawl have one? It does get hard? In combat ya either hard or dead! It's fuck or get fucked! Kill or be killed!"

I cried. I don't want to kill anybody. The devil was dancing until God came as an NCO- a kindred spirit from Ohio- and pulled me together.

My other problem was saluting. Was it with the right or left hand, or should I bow? Sometimes I'd use both hands. On bivouac I got one 2nd Looey so confused even he forgot how to salute, threw up both his hands in disgust, saying, "Private, you're the goddamn enemy and I give up."

Signal Corps, Ft. Monmouth, April '55. Mobile film crews in the field are expected to know the 35 Wall Sound Camera like their M-1 rifle, i.e., take it apart, reassemble it blindfolded, and shoot on the run.

The top student got first pick of assignments and chose a seemingly boring post: *Recording Specialist in the White House.* After Nixon I can only imagine the conversations that well-mannered, quiet, mid-western farm boy overheard: the Kennedy brothers' attempt to kill Castro; the Bay of Pigs fiasco; the Cuban Missile Crises; LBJ's Gulf of Tonkin ruse to justify war and feed the munitions industry. McNamara and LBJ sold a fish story to Senator Fulbright. *Shoot at us we're going to shoot back!* The alleged provocation, said an eyewitness, was a *non-event, shooting at whales.* America swallowed the bait hook, line and sinker. McGovern: (It was) "the biggest fraud ever perpetrated on the American people." Now it's the neo-con, pre-emptive, first strike horseshit.

Gore Vidal's 'Dreaming War,' dateline, 2.1.50: the State Department concluded America had a choice, support France in Indochina, or face extension of Communism in Southeast Asia, and the west. So, they spawned the domino theory. By 1955 America was paying 40% of the French cost of the war. American money and lives marched in Vietnam for 25 years to the tune of 58,000 dead Americans and thrice as many Vietnamese. Why?

It profits not egoistical leaders and their greedy-eyed financiers to admit that it's always a game of chess *and never dominoes.* Ike warned: Beware, the military industrial complex.

My choices: Texas, or the Pacific. In Texas I might've stepped in shit and come up smelling like James Dean in *Giant,* or become a politician, and said, "Recession means that people's incomes, at the employer level, are going down, basically, relative to costs, people are getting laid off."

July '55. I sailed out of Frisco's Presidio, embarcadero to the sea, on a rusty tub bound for the Sandwich Islands, dreaming of grass skirts and bare-chested girls. Olive drab against a gray warehouse on a rickety wharf- dismal Alcatraz somewhere out in a foggy bay; herded on a tanker gray as the water, grayer still the wide Pacific, anything but pacific. *How many 18-year-olds had sailed it never to return?* Human cattle in humid cargo holds, dimly lit sleeping areas greasier than an August afternoon in the Dewey movie house, Brooklyn: admission ten cents, plus a free comic book. Windowless, hot, stuffy, floors gummy from soda, red lights over exits, but no escape to Coney Island Avenue. Duffel bags piled by a wall: partially visible RA numbers and US define enlisted men from draftees. *You RA? Dumb shit!* Soon, nothing matters. What is eaten is regurgitated. Everything reeks of vomit. Arms, legs, and heads hang limp in mid-air like stored marionettes in spidery hammocks swinging side-to-side as the ship drones on, churning sea and stomach. Time's a clammy face slack jaw moaning, *Mama! Get me off this floating toilet!* Boots suck at steel. Shadows grope, slip, and slide windmilling to the latrine, or stagger topside, but leave it in the stairwell. *Fresh air! Don't look at the horizon! The only thing risin' is my stomach!* Lifeless bodies sprawled fore and aft until five days later crowding the rail: Diamond Head! The Aloha Tower! Grass skirts dance on a pier for Matson Line tourists. As soldiers hoop and cheer in imitation, arms waving, hips grinding, my stomach does the hula over the side.

Signal Corps switches signals again. No openings in Journalism school. Then, no openings for a Film Specialist. So why offer me Hawaii? They stick me in a maintenance unit repairing PA systems and tank headsets in a hellhole fictionalized in *From Here To Eternity*. At Schofield Barracks, home to Prewitt and Maggio, I find my own "Fatso," a lanky, pop-eyed top sergeant from North Carolina who likes leaning on people. I didn't join up to be a lamppost. Quotas be damned! Screw me once, your fault. Screw me twice, my fault. So, I start signaling the Signal Corps with my middle finger. The lesson I'm forever learning is never accept less than what you want and always dot the *i*'s and cross the *t*'s.

"Yawl mus' love extra duty," says the Top, eyeballing me as I stood at attention in fatigues way too big. "KP n' cleanin' the cesspool. That what y'want? Ya say no, but I hear yes." Map-like eyes; hot, boozy breath in my face. "Button y'shirt! Yaw outta uniform. Gawd! Yawl look like ya been dipped in shit, deep fried, and pulled through a keyhole backwards. Come this weekend when yawe compadrees're chasin' wah-heenies in Why-kee-kee, you'll be cleaning the crapper with a toothbrush. Tighten that bed! Got more damn wrinkles than an elephant's ass!"

I bought a 45-RPM record player. After lights out I'd listen to George Shearing on low volume. The mellifluous blend of Shearing's piano and Cal Tjader's vibes were a balm. When the Top shut it down, I shut down even more, which got me extra duty policing the quad for cigarette butts, full field inspections at 4AM with push-ups, guard duty at a deserted warehouse with an M-1 and no bullets. Maybe the Top thought if I had them I'd shoot him. Then I was assigned to taking ID photos at the Inspector General's office- a long way from film. Every other photo was a disaster. Evenings I marched around the quad with my rifle and imagined the pockmarked walls of buildings were strafings from 1941 Japanese warplanes. *Attack! It's real! Attack! Holy shit! Eat dirt!* The barracks darkened one-by-one. The moon and stars brightened over the quad, Prewitt played funeral taps for Maggio.

Then I caught a break. **This is KTAH,** *Armed Forces Radio, Tripler Hospital Medical Center, located in the hills above Pearl Harbor.* KTAH was staffed by a handful of well-spoken, tailored soldiers. The Top was Master Sergeant Doogan, but they reported to John Seehaas, civilian head of Tripler public relations with a GS12 rating equal to his retired rank of marine colonel. The staff played records of stateside programs, read news and hospital releases, conducted tours and produced staged showcases all interlaced with live deejaying, and that's what I wanted.

I introduced myself to Mr. Seehaas, a buttoned down man always in suit and tie; stolid; intimidating not given to small talk or idle levity. I knew to hold my tongue and keep my distance from this silver fox of Dutch/ German origin with snow-white hair, a pale face tinted in rose, possibly phlegmatic, a small nose, thin firm lips, sharp chin, and steel blues. With a stroke of a pen he could change my life. He was my Oz. I choose my words carefully. Only repeated myself to emphasize my desire to work at KTAH. He shuffled papers, half listened, and my heart sank momentarily when he said, "There are no openings." Then he added, "But, you can fill in on weekends," and I almost kissed him. With my foot in the door all I had to do was wait for somebody to rotate stateside.

The staff was all draftees anxious to return to college. To keep up I taught myself grammar. Soon I caught mistakes, even mine. One guy rushed the news late for a date in Waikiki saying "the president in a communa-keek". He meant "communiqué". I stored it in my word bank with others from *30 Days To A Powerful Vocabulary.* One day I connected an adjective to a noun and voila! I was a painter with a pallet of words.

Recordings were on vinyl and acetate discs recorded at 78, 45 or 33 1/3 revolutions per minute. All big as hubcaps. Years later I thought *ET,* the movie, stood for *Electrical Transcription.* Discs were 5 to 20 minute copies of stateside programs. An hour show had 4 discs segued on cue. The biggest problem was adjusting turntable speeds to match the RPM's. Forget and Doris Day sounded like a chipmunk. The format mixed live deejaying with: Don McNeil's Breakfast Club; Dinah Shore; serials and dramas like Cecil B. DeMille's Lux Radio Theatre; The Lucky Strike Hit Parade; Bob Hope; Jack Benny; Burns and Allen; and Detective Johnny Dollar. *I was sittin' in this one-armed joint downing two fingers of red eye playin' footsie with myself when she walks in; Grade A on the hoof with looks to kill. A hunk of feminine pulchritude with a back porch swing that broke a lot of necks. She spelled the beginning of the end.*

In a month I got my wish. Seehaas cut orders reassigning me to him as a Broadcast Specialist 703. Others brought more to the table than I did; middle-class college types, but Seehaas took me, an uneducated 19-year-old with heart, and changed my life.

5.   The Falcon

Aside from on-air chores I helped produce live entertainment for GI's in the hospital auditorium. Mr. Seehaas would book USO shows, local club acts and performers passing through to points east.

One morning I was sent to Ala Moana Harbor to greet a magician who'd just sailed in and was *scheded* to perform at Tripler. Magic is right! There was this tall, slim, handsome mustachioed man in white pants and blue blazer with ascot, topped by a captain's hat standing mid-ship of a 100-foot yacht surrounded by a bevy of beauties in shorts and swim suits. *Shiver me timbers!* I thought, ogling the gammy crew from stem to stern. *Avast, mates! And blow me down!*

Actor-magician John Calvert had starred in film as Michael Waring, The Falcon, a popular detective series of the '40's. Later, I learned he had bought that yacht from Henry Ford, who'd built it for his son, Edsel. Now it carried John's entire magic act around the world. Some act! He'd have no trouble reading my mind. I don't know what was up his sleeve, but I knew what was up in my pants. If he'd said, pick a number, I'd've chosen the redhead on the end, or the juicy blonde at his arm and said, "watch us disappear." Imagine? Cozied up on a yacht full of women bound for Japan, Singapore, and Australia. Hawaii, he said, was just a layover. The whole trip was a layover! Is it weigh anchor or lay anchor? Arr! *You'd have to be tying me foreskin to the mainsail every night.*

John was a terrific magician, but the real magic was how he got to be Pasha of a floating harem! A stark contrast to the tanker I came over on. John said he was going around the world. I thought, *Aye, mate! Every night! Avast and shiver me timbers! Set sail for the Labia Majoras! The Grand Galapagos Penus and the Mammory Islands! Arh!* Talk about cabin fever! I'd get my sea legs in bed. The big question was not, is John getting any, but how much and how often? He must've walked on three legs! Of course it was a soldiers fantasy. He was a fine sailor with a great pair of sea legs, a different pair every night. I saw myself buried at sea wearing a white flag on my third leg. When they set sail from Ala Moana to points east my heart was aboard AWOL and I'd rechristened her the Clitorus Mundi. *Arrh! Heave to yee fee-lines and blow me down!*

6. Murder On the Prurient Express

Then came Lady Day and a standup comic. She sang jazz and blues. He talked it. In 1957 Billie Holiday's star was descending, she would live two more years; Lenny Bruce's was ascending, he would live 9 more years. She was queen of the minor key, wore a gardenia, sang with quivering voice about loneliness, lost love, and Strange Fruit hangin' from the poplar tree. He was a dime-a-dozen comic in black suit and tie; a tad iconoclastic; Strange Jewish Fruit, his heritage on his sleeve destined to crucify himself on a porcelain gallows at the end of a needle.

In the 60's Lenny Bruce danced across America holding a mirror to its face and shook up the status quo. For expiating his devils and society's through cathartic, scatological monologues: Jew, nigger, kike, wop, dago, mick, spic, dick, fuck, shit, piss, ass. By ridiculing taboos, politics, and religion-, which divided more than healed-for all that, and his brazen use of drugs- Lenny Bruce was ostracized and hounded to death. As in all injustice, shame belongs to those who looked the other way.

In 1957 Lenny Bruce was in Honolulu in the Tom Melody Review, direct from the Melody Club in LA. A stripper named Honey was on the bill. Later, their marriage evolved into mutual disrespect. But at the time Bruce was a typically wired, jittery comic doing jumpy one-liners laced with rococo riffs on taboo topics. I was working the wings at the Officer's Club when Lenny grabbed a base newspaper, and paraphrased what was written giving it a risqué twist. I was next to emcee Tom

Melody, who'd been watching Lenny like a hawk. When Lenny picked up the newspaper Tom gasped, *No, Lenny. Don't do it!* He turned officer names in the paper into jokes and insinuations. Melody's remark was prophetic. Bruce went on to cross the line of taboos speaking no-no's, things known to be true, but not voiced in public. Lenny was a sidewalk Henry Miller, in love with his own lyricism. *A spade's a spade, man.*

Another time Red Foxx blew into town, a very risqué comic but no social threat because he was contained in a second tier black nightclub circuit. After his TV sit-com hit, Foxx led two lives; one for mainstream audiences and the other for nightclubs.

Lenny Bruce, the nightclub "messiah of smut", introduced character and attitude into stand-up comedy, which had been the playwright's providence. He decried duplicity on any level even his own. For Lenny the brevity of "he said, she said" became the basis for concise self-expression. He carried the joke technique into current events and later applied it when he read his court records to audiences, his monologues were moving in the direction of character and dialogue with a second performer. One solo shtick he did in a Waikiki club in 1957 was his characterization of a penniless pot-head trying to get the most out of a joint. He'd exhale and chase the smoke, fanning it back into his mouth while keeping an eye out for the cops. He'd blow smoke up his sleeve, inhale it, and catch his nose on a cuff link. Then raise his lapels, blow smoke inside his coat and re-inhale it. *Love my clothes!* Then he tried to split a joint with somebody in the audience by going mouth to mouth. *Wait. You kosher, baby? Jesus! Oh, let's not go there. Jesus could've used a little shit stuck up on that cross with those fuckin' nails. Maybe he was on something. He had that look. Who looks that way with nails in them? Com'on. You got nails in your hands, your feet and you're gonna tell an asshole thief on the next cross, This day thou shalt be in paradise? I don't think so. Maybe paradise is drug talk. Hey, wanna try some paradise? Two sheckles. Hey, buddy! Get the fuck off my cross! Okay, you Romans. Do me. What, my feet too? What feet? Those are mine down there? Weee!*

Fifty years later I still see iconoclastic Bruce with Tom Melody yelling, "Not that one, Lenny!" Gripped by a daemon out to burn the glossy Hollywood vision of America, he was also a confrontational, standup rabbi; drug-driven by compulsions to cleanse himself and the world. A tall order even for God, it seems. Washing dirty linen in public cost him dearly. If Hollywood decimated us, TV completed the burial.

Bruce died in 1966 with his conviction still on the books for *Giving an Obscene Performance in 1964 at Café Au Go Go in Greenwich Village, New York.* He'd used over 100 "dirty words" undercover police later testified. Imagine? Two Laurel and Hardy detectives were tea-totaling ringside while waiting on Lenny to come out and hang himself. *Art, my dear Stanley, is in the eye of the beholder. Ollie, is a bee holder somebody who holds bees? No, Stanley. That's a bee keeper. You're a beholder and I'm a beholder. Ollie, I'd rather be gone. This is dirty business. Indeed, but somebody's got to do it. Not to bother your cranial vault, Stanley. This night promises to be a question for the ages. You mean old people? I mean everybody for all time. Drink your tea, Stanley. Now, let's unholster our digital counters and practice. Everytime I say bleep in a sentence it's a dirty word and you press the button. What the bleep is happening, you bleepin' bleeper? How many? How many what? Words. You didn't say start. Close enough. The larger question is, Where do First Amendment freedoms end, and obscenity and decadence begin? Between the bedroom and the toilet. Any fool knows that. Yes, Stanley. And you're not just any fool. Right. I'm a bee holder and belong to everybody. You see, people can't go around saying everything what's on their fornicating minds.*

Why not, pray tell? Because candidness in a duplicitous society is divisive. Oops. Show time. Lenny comes on, and a minute into his shtick the cops've got writer's cramp. *86, 87, 88. I got 90.* Shit, piss, cocksucker, spic, wop, kike, goy, nigger-nigger! *That a double entendre? No. A double negative. What's putz? Yiddish for golfing. Asshole, that one or two words?*

Fellini's *Satyricon* depicts Bruce's kind of people; amoral, apolitical, asexual worshippers of hermaphrodite. Bruce married a stripper-lesbian, smoked weed, and engaged in manáge á trois. He put his finger on the pulse of society, proclaimed the body devoid of humanity, and was hounded to death for saying the emperor has no clothes. His bio should be called *Murder On the Prurient Express.* The poor guy wound up alone and dead in a hotel toilet. Artists are bleeders of the cosmic conscience.

On December 23, 2004, New York Governor Pataki gave Bruce a posthumous pardon, calling it "a declaration of New York's commitment to upholding the First Amendment". But there is no pardon for those who betray the basic human right to free speech, and work. Lenny was no angel. Kitty Bruce, his daughter, in the Fort Wayne Journal Gazette, 12.5.04: *My father's life was worse than you can ever imagine.*

One thing escaped Lenny until the end, but he probably knew it intuitively. Like a wild-eyed nightclub Jesus Christ, he went down jobless, harried, crucified at the end of a needle, and maybe for a moment before darkness enclosed his Judaic mind he saw himself as messianic in cyclopsian head gear- two black leather cubes strapped by phylacteries, one to his forehead, the other to his left arm, each containing parchment inscribed:

Mah neesh-ta-no ha-lei-loh ha-seh mee-kol ha-lay-los?
(Why is this night different from other nights?)

37

Schneider, Alfred Leonard, Alias Lenny Bruce, 1925-
1966
American Super Jew laying tefillin for the sins of man

I'm in a barbershop. I ask the manicurist for a date. She says, I'm married. I go, Tell your husband you're going out with a girlfriend. She says, Tell him yourself. He's shaving you.

☺

7.   *Mah Neesh-ta-no!*

One night while closing the station I see an Amazon in a hospital gown hobbling down the hall on crutches, one leg in a cast. Under her hospital gown it was the Battle of the Bulge. Her curves had curves! She was lost in the labyrinth of Tripler corridors. *Follow me,* I go, showing her the way back through the radio station. I even tried the stairs with her leading the way, but the leg was a problem. *How about piggyback? You carry me.* Piggy came later on the couch in the station lounge playing radio. That's where you turn her knobs and she watches your antenna rise. I'm in my army issue, she's in her gown, her broken leg over my shoulder, the soft skin of her other leg sensual against mine. *Oh, honey! Oh, baby!* As I'm kissing her breasts big as Diamond Head, my hand up the Manoa Shute, the door opens, the lights come on, and in walks Seehaas on tour with an Inspector General. I jump up and salute. They salute. I salute again. *As you were,* says the IG. *That is, at ease, soldier.* I mumble I'm showing her the station. *We have tours during regular hours,* says Seehaas. *Lock up on your way out.* While dressing I see Seehaas through the control room window explaining the set-up. Next day Seehaas comes by the station. I apologize, thinking, *it's all over.* One stroke of his pen meant Schofield. He turns from the door, says, "You have temperament, son. You can't have talent without temperament."

☺

8.   Hui O Mokomoko to Hollywood

Joe Hyams (or Jo Heims) also forgot to say what a great actor I was, because after discharge I faked my way at the University of Hawaii. It helped being an ex-GI. Later, I taught Kenpo Karate for Ed Parker in LA, and I couldn't fight my way out of a paper bag. Make it two bags. I'm not talking windbags, but real fighters like Mike Yung and Ed Parker.

Manoa Campus, Spring, 1958. When Mike Yung first said Kung Fu I thought, Column A, Egg Fu Yung. Column B, Kung Fu. As for Martial Arts, "Martial" was a guy's name and "Art" was Rembrandt.

"Haole, you got room in the shade for one Chinaman?"

That's how we met on campus at the University of Hawaii, like one of those sudden sunny Hawaiian rains; me flaked out in the shade on wooden steps at a side door of the barracks that served as the campus canteen. I was starved, living on dime "crust" sandwiches- peanut butter and jelly stuck between discarded ends of old bread.

"Sure," I go, as this lanky guy walks up, arms swinging freely, a book in one hand, and sits. "How you like my Hawaiian sun? Strong, eh?" *Yes.* "See that wahine? *(girl).* Miss Cherry Blossom. One knockout, eh?"

Next thing I know we're walking to his home in nearby Kaimuki. On the way he punctuates his thoughts with fishhook hands and claws.

"I show you something you never see before." *What? Food?* "Have a seat, haole." He points me to the steps of his mom's one story wooden house with a porch. "Be right back." I sit, stretch out, catch a breeze from Waikiki, and he's back in a skosh with a food tray of tea, rice, and chicken. I want to kiss him but instead flush red.

"Chicken teriyaki," he goes, smiling, further narrowing dark almond eyes into slits. "Japanese. Not Chinese, but good. Chinese teach them to write. All the same ideographs. We read the same paper, but we can't talk to each other. No common language. Very funny. Yes?" He rolls his shoulders, grins sheepishly while fish hooking his hand in downward moves. "Chinese," he continues, "invent many things: fireworks, paper, kites, dominoes, printing machine, Mah Jong, Kung Fu. Columbus used compass to discover America, invented by Chinese. Silk is Chinese, too. How they get worms to make a shirt with pockets, I don't know. Amazing! We invent acupuncture." *What?* "Needles in the body like a pin cushion to heal pain and sickness." *Needles?* "Yes. Fine needles, sterilized. They puncture the skin at meridian points in the body, and it cures illness by releasing blocked energy. How you like that, haole? Very complicated. Chopsticks big acupuncture needle. Stick in mouth cure hunger pain. Also, very sexy." He opens a paper packet. "Chopsticks joined like legs of new bride. You split them you know you got one virgin."

There was something engaging and curious about Mike, an intangible affinity seemingly struck by chance, yet there was design in it. Italians call it *simpatico*. My yoga teacher, Swami Das, used to say, *You can't meet someone without knowing them.* It's the wheel of life.

Mike spears some chicken and says, "Second chopstick is a spare." We dig in. "You good with chopsticks. Most haolies can't coordinate fingers."

When Mike talks his body flows like a river, the Yangtze from eddy to white water. When expressing himself, he closes one eye, scrunches up his shoulders, and tilts his head like a boxer sparring. His pigeon English mixes Hawaiian, Japanese, Chinese, and Philippine-with pronouns and verbs missing here and there. His Hawaiian accent is a lilt that hangs expressions in mid-air. "You guys. We go walk?" *You guys* include both sexes and your dog.

Mike squats and eats, forearms resting on top of his thighs.

"What do you think of Chinese people?"

"Right now I love 'em better than Italians."

Mike laughs in a splash of running water split by a rock. "Fork and knife waste food. My people not like to waste food. Very bad. In the old country food was hard to get. Waste adds up at the end of the week you can feed somebody for two days. No knives at the table. Meat is cut in the kitchen and the bones saved to make stock. Fork chases pea in dish like spearing fish in the river that flies away. Chopsticks pick up a grain of rice. Eat soup with chopsticks." He raises the soup bowl to his chin, sips and shovels its contents into his mouth. "Chinese spoon not shallow Western spoon." He takes up a porcelain utensil shaped like a gondola with a gondolier standing at the back. *Why's the bottom flat?* "To rest on table when soup is hot. Spoon also doubles as shoehorn. Ha!" Suddenly frowning, he goes, "My people think too much." *Long history.* "We give Marco Polo spaghetti. Eh, mama mia! How many kinds of pasta Italians have?" I shrug. "We have mee fun, chow fun, lo mein, hand-pulled noodle, bean thread, cellophane noodle. Invented by a paranoid looking for poison. Chinese invented abacus, tea, rice, ice cream, wheelbarrow. Chopsticks originated in the Shang Dynasty 1400 BC to replace knives. A knife at the table is dangerous. Then, chopstick became a weapon." He tossed one into the grass like a dart. "Even a toothpick is lethal like a splinter in the eye. A thousand noodles only tip of the iceberg. When Chinese think, I don't ask, what you thinking? I'm afraid of the answer. The Chinese invent for fun and to find out what the next guy's thinking. 'I make paper boat.' 'I make noodle with tail look like mouse. I light tail.' Bang! Exploding noodle! 'I no like that noodle in my soup.' 'How you make it?' 'More important why. Your money or I stick noodle up your okole!' (*butt*). Eat. Teriyaki good, not Chinese."

Mike moves like a fighter who's never flatfooted. His words jab and punch at me at times rapidly depending on how I follow him. Suddenly, I'm sailing with boyish wonder on the China seas, blown overboard and ashore on stories of people who defy gravity like birds and insects. It was a strange fighting style called Kung Fu (Gung, anglicized), a revelation.

"Chinese culture societies teach Martial Arts. You need minimum of 25% Chinese blood." Mike shapes himself into a grasshopper, jumps to the step above me, hands like mandibles. Scrambling down on all fours, he whirls about screeching "Yip, yip! Monkey Style." Then, he shoots straight up closing his legs like scissors, his body absolutely still, his arms chest level with one extended in front of him with a bent wrist and forked fingers. "Snake Style, venom in the fingers like fangs." Bam! Mike flashed past me; the wind from the snap of his hand popped my ear. "Bet you never see that before, haole?" *I still didn't. Do it again.* "There are five styles: Crane, Dragon, Leopard, Tiger, and Snake- arms moving, but not moving. Eyes, temple, nerve points, acupuncture meridians; carotid vein in the neck." He pauses to scoop rice into his mouth. Following some silence, he chuckles. "I show you some-ting new, eh, lo fun?" *What's lo fun, a Chinese noodle?* "All you know about China from Chinese menu. Marco Polo was first lo fun, foreign devil." *You gave us noodles, but we gave you Lasagna.* "Chow fun, flat noodle." *And ravioli!* "That wonton!"

Martial Arts (MA) is a surreal mix of boxing, judo, jiu jitsu, weaponry, aerial combat, and a strange thing called chi. Training is West Point discipline with the philosophy of Lao Tsu. Mike used to laugh saying, "The lo fun goes to China one year and writes books explaining Lao Tsu when even for Chinese it takes a lifetime to understand. Practioners of MA study calisthenics, philosophy, psychology, ethics, herbs, logic, calligraphy, healing, acupuncture, and reflexology."

In the '50's Martial Arts started moving east to west through Hawaii to California. Ed Parker was a Hawaiian, who introduced Kenpo Karate to America. Other names come to mind like Bobby Lowe, Professor Chow, Hui O Mokomoko, and private Chinese societies like the one run by Sifu Lau Bun in San Francisco. They put down the foundation for the phenomenal rise of Bruce Lee.

One night Mike takes me to a Kenpo School in a wooden building in Honolulu for a look at empty hand fighting. Behind drawn shades, shadowy praetorians in the bowels of Rome's Coliseum rehearse for a turn in the arena. The master was Professor Chow.

Bodies grouped eight across and several rows deep; they punched and kicked the air with ferocity. Groups and crowds always unnerve me, likewise uniforms. Everybody wore black gis (*gees, uniform*). "1, 2, 3, 4," shouts Professor Chow in a call and response. "KEE-AYE!" the class shouts back, striking imaginary opponents. In the blur of movement comes a whip-like snap. Mike explains. "When the lo fun copied Kung Fu, he mistook the sleeve snap for chest pounding."

This was Hawaiian Martial Arts 1958-9. It reminded me of bayonets in boot camp with a blood curdling, animalistic scream, intended to focus the mind, dispel fear, and scare the shit out of the enemy. It put me off at first, but later, the philosophy behind Martial Arts changed my mind. *The master's hands are never soiled by blood.*

Mike rarely talked about himself, but he'd flash his hands and feet like *a human windmill!* A mutual friend,

43

Henry "Box Head" Yoshino- a jazz and classical flute and reed musician- told me Mike boxed in college, and was a *tough street fighter. Messing with him would be one big mistake.*

One sunny day on campus Mike Yung introduces me to members of Hui O Mokomoko following their awesome Kenpo Karate exhibition. 'Hui' in Hawaiian means syndicate (group), and 'mokomoko' means scrapping with hand and foot. I decided to join them, but first I had to pass an interview held outside their gym, a street level basement in a Buddhist Temple minutes from downtown Honolulu. I sit nervously under a wide wooden stairs leading up to the great temple hall. Before me sat a senior committee of brown belts led by three black ones, all in burgundy gis. *Where you from stateside? You play sports? Why you want to study Kenpo? Character number one. Principles of Kenpo like all Martial Arts: reverence for life, brotherhood, and self-control.*

Hui O Mokomoko practiced Okinawa Kenpo codified by Prof. Chow, which is closer in form to Japanese Karate than Chinese Gung Fu. Moves are strong, angular, and economical, using hands, palms, claws, elbows, knees, and feet. Chinese Gung Fu (Shao Lin) is more circular like the Tai Chi symbol. Circularity is more natural to body movement than angular or straight-line thrusts, which can be stressful to joints and muscles. Mike Yung: *To get around the law that forbade people bearing arms, the Chinese practiced fighting using farm tools and disguised it in dances. They studied insects, animals, and reptiles, how they move and fight, and adapted it into fighting techniques like Crane and Praying Mantis. Chinese always thinking. Soft like water; strong like wave. Magic using logic; balance; knowledge of pressure points and skill to strike accurately with minimal wasted energy. Moving a thousand pounds with a feather. My mind does not see you where you stand but 20 feet away. Catch the center, the in-between moment, and turn the energy against itself like a ball thrown into a horseshoe. Find a fulcrum you can move the earth. How you like that? Look. Hidden Hand style. Arms behind the back come up following the body's contour, shooting out from the rib cage like one dart. Sticky Hands style, clinging to the opponent like clothes on his back. Boxing is confrontational; Kung Fu is stealth. It was handed down among aristocrats who had time and money for lessons. Poor people learned by becoming monks in a Shao Lin Temple. Know why there were so many monks? Food was scarce. A monk with a begging bowl was not a beggar, but a respected holy man. On Chinese New Year watch the Lion Dance, the footwork dancing over the firecrackers.* Two decades later Ali would echo Mike's words, *float like a butterfly, sting like a bee.*

Hui classes were held behind burlap-covered windows. Three black belt Hawaiian-Filipinos taught class, two were brother and sister. They wore heavy, burgundy colored jiu jitsu gis designed for grabs and throws. Later, Parker introduced a light cotton gi to facilitate quicker movement.

"Use one big basin," says Ruby, explaining how to dye a white gi. She was a black belt, brown-skinned, 5'5", 105 pounds, with long black hair in a ponytail. "Borrow the kind. Fill it with warm water. Put in two packs of burgundy dye from the supermarket. Get one big stick, stir to make da kind dissolve. Throw in the gi, turn every ten minutes so the dye works into the kind. Soak overnight. Hang up in morning to dry in shade."

In French class it hits me. I forgot to hang out my gi. Kenpo was at 6. I quick dry it at a Laundromat. While dressing under the temple stairs I smell whiffs of kim chi (*pickled cabbage*) cooking, which can get stinky. Five minutes into the workout I hear, *Phew! Smell like one chicken crawl under the floor and died.* Somebody's cookin' kim chi, I go. *Wrong!* The hot drier and dye in my gi didn't agree and I smelled awful.

In ability, Ruby equals any man, which I find out when the class pairs off for one-on-one. I find myself alone because nobody wants to dance *with a skunk.* Ruby helps out and partners with me. That's when I learn never get cute in karate when you're a novice. We do defense-offense exercises, kicks and arm blocks. Ruby kicks, I block. When it was my turn I fake a forward kick, she goes to block, I pivot on my support leg, do a sidekick I'd been practicing, and nick her gi. I thought it was neat.

"Oh!" says a surprised Ruby unamused. "What that, haole (*whitey*)?"

"Something I've been practicing."

"Some-t'ing, eh?" she goes, dropping into a horse. "We free-style." She beckons me forward. Now everybody is looking. "What else you got?"

"Nothing," I go, backing up. "Just that."

"You one trick-fighter, eh? You wanna play? Come. We play."

I duck behind bodies that scatter and temple pillars. Ruby tracks me like a bloodhound staying between the exit and me, hands at her sides other times dropping into a fighting horse. Two guys shove me at her holding their noses. I take off my gi top and wave it like a truce flag. *Look out, Ruby! Rotten Egg style.* I give up and apologize. She smiles, "Okay, haole," then whirls with a flying kick that whispers across my chest. My jaw drops and everybody laughs. *Skunk Man style stinks!*

Ruby says, *Somebody can get hurt. Learn basics, then play.* That night I was invited to stay after class for *free-style* boxing. A "hit" occurs when an opponent's gi is grazed. They followed the discipline of "control".

☺

9.   A Hui to Hooey and Clickety Clack

My days in Hawaii were numbered. Mike had told me about his friend Ed Parker, a Hawaiian, who was making a name in movies and teaching Kenpo in Hollywood. I put it on a back burner. I was in school, doing DJ work, and failing in both. My grade point average slipped below 2.0, and my DJ show from the Menehune Lounge in Waikiki went sour.

Menehune(s) are Hawaiian leprechauns and they were certainly busy behind the scenes in a Hui, or group, formed to bolster a failing nightclub owned by an elderly Caucasian couple. Fresh money bought the club a face-lift, a new all-jazz venue, and me doing a nightly two-hour remote over KIKI from a perch above the main floor. I also emceed the stage show. Record distributor George "Cubby" Chun supplied the music with staples like Sinatra, Nat Cole, Mel Torme, Peggy Lee, Billie Holiday, June Christi, Anita O'Day, George Shearing, the Modern Jazz Quartet, and the 4 Freshmen. Cubby favored Peggy Lee for smoothness and musicianship. Fifty years later I think how right he was about Lee- a voice of fermenting passion, bone hot, skin cool, every phrase and tiny gesture a smokey innuendo of sexual eloquence. In the song Fever, she strips me naked.

I met George in a Honolulu music store when I purchased drumsticks for lessons I was taking with haole Bob Groya on St. Louis Drive. Later, George invited me to play sidekick on his KIKI radio jazz show. He was sly and got around my off-the-wall monologues, wind chimes under haiku, and longwinded selections from T.S. Eliot. He'd open my mic on a dead pot (no volume) and play a record on air while I *waxed eloquent* to four dingy walls. God love him for a sneak.

KIKI radio, 250 watts of Poi, emanated from an outhouse pretending to be a quonset hut in a poor industrial-residential area of Honolulu. It was constructed of prefab W.W Two military surplus with a corrugated metal roof overhung by palm trees and a hung over chief. The station manager-owner, Angelo Riossi, was also a beer distributor and brassiere salesman, which suited the chief because he liked to drink it by the cup.

It was a dimly lit, four-room cheese box with a lounge, small office, a studio, and a step-up control room reminiscent of a tacky train station with furnishings from a bus stop liquidation sale. The studio was empty except for a floor mic literally on the floor- no stand. Interviews were done like a luau. The on-air people sold their own time, and operated the console. There was nothing consoling about it, or the clunky turntables with Stone Age electricals.

KIKI was turnstile radio, a Laundromat of the air. Drop coinage in the boss' hand and wash your laundry in public. I had an 11 PM slot, but got bumped by a jock who sold more time. I'd go on saying, the call letters should be BYOBB; bring your own brown bag, including toilet paper.

Goose necking over the console was a bi-directional ribbon mic, dead on the side taped 'X'. The hot side had a dent and that's what I went by because sometimes the tape was gone. Some people thought the 'X' was the side to talk into. The same people who see a door that says, "Pull" and they push.

The mic was too heavy for the old boom and required holding and adjusting to keep it from dropping against the board. When talking the mic had to be held gingerly because the boom springs creaked like a game of peek-a-boo with the door of *Inner Sanctum*. It was like being on a crowded beach holding two ice cream cones while hitching up bathing trunks with a stretched out elastic belt to keep them from falling below your ass. The mic hit the console so many times it smelled of spilled coffee, the VU meter (*volume unit*) had no glass cover, the needle was bent, and always registered two decibels.

Also, the mic's on-off toggle switch popped. I'd keep the volume on zero, open the mic, raise the volume, and reverse the procedure going off. Another way to mask the pop was to have music in the BG. Between holding the mic, turning it on, flipping a page in the commercial book, cueing a record, and starting a turntable you needed more arms than Vishnu and Lakshmi. Sometimes listeners heard a crash followed by a feint, *son-of-bitch!* What'd he say? *I fell in a ditch.* On the positive side you developed quick hands and learned to do several things simultaneously. I could self-combust, crash, and burn all at once.

Aloha nui loa. This is Pat 'Diamond Head' Paterson, the host with the most, sending you 250 watts of love. Pat was a silver-tongued mulatto from Paterson, NJ, who played romantic music and whispered sweet nothings to listeners. He'd start his evening "Love Nest" by sounding a pitch tuner, then say in earnest the purplest prose imaginable, written tongue-in-cheek by local DJ's. *From Lihue to Lahaina, Maui to Molokai, from Waikiki to Waimea Falls, Manoa to the Pali, it's your Love Nest Casanova, your imu of love, the host with the most. Leis of love, and garlands of kisses.* One night I walk in, hear Pat on the speaker, but no Pat's visible in the control room. The boom mic is broken at the neck, a pitch tuner's on the dash, a disembodied voice says, *I'm your love ghost.* Then, two brown hands with white palms reach up from under the console to cue a record. *Your host with the most. Sending rainbow hugs. Garlands of kisses.* At the start of the show he adjusted the mic; it broke off the boom, and hit the console with a bang heard *from Lihue to Lahaina, from Waikiki to Waimea Falls.*

Mike Yung stopped by during my lounge program to say Ed Parker was in town. Ed and I met the next night in my Hui class when he came by to greet his childhood friends. They'd all grown up in Kalihi, a district of Honolulu- not far from the Buddhist Temple where the

Hui practiced. They'd studied under Professor Chow. Ed was Mormon, shrewd, and educated at Brigham Young. On graduation in the mid-50's, he opened his first Kenpo-Karate Studio in Pasadena, where he lived with his wife Leilani and their children. He opened a second studio in 1959 on La Cienega Boulevard in Hollywood. Parker was the father of American Kenpo, which makes Prof. Chow his Hawaiian grandfather.

One night at the Menehuni Lounge, I'm asked to introduce pianist Joe Castro. *This cat's great. Just blew in from Vegas by way of LA. A terrific jazz pianist. Let's welcome, Joe Castro!* In my head I was saying, *all I know is he split the mainland after a fallout with some chick named Doris Duke. She banned him from all her mansions around the world including Pacific Heights.* That night Joe slept behind the bar with the menehunies.

The new managers stipulated that if the club failed, the liquor license reverted to them, which was what they really wanted. Meanwhile, George got me a civilian job in the musical records section of a department store where he set up records he distributed in town. The manager was an attractive Philippine-Hawaiian; thirtyish, levelheaded; and I messed up. A haole jeweler went to LA on business and asked me to fill in as the store's PA announcer. I jumped at the chance without seeing the bigger picture, or clearing it with my boss. I thought I could do both jobs and shot myself in the foot. The announcements were simple. "Prices have been reduced! Extra discounts on items already marked down. Terrific low prices!" I adlibbed *lo-lo prices,* and learned the hard way that in Hawaiian "lo-lo" means stupid. They thought I was drinking Okole Hau.

"They're not ready for you," says George, shaking his head. "I don't think you're ready for you!" At age 22, he predicted I wouldn't make it until my 30's. At 31 I joined Chuckler Fraudcasting.

Around this time I started doing comedy with a haole character I'd met through a college girlfriend turned stripper. My short lived comedy debut combined a fortuitous meeting and my last stand in Hawaii.

☺

10.   The Colossus of Roads

In the elevator, quiet, head slightly bowed; you'd never know. I held the door for him as he trotted up, smiled, said thanks, and got in. You'd hardly know he was there, but I knew. Even though the three of us were preoccupied with foolish youthful thoughts, I knew I was standing next to a colossus. Sally on my left, also a U of H dropout, turned stripper; between us her personal beautician, an alimony escapee out San Luis Obispo and my new comedy partner; and behind me *the* Colossus.

We'd all come our long separate ways- *and a cold coming it was* - to share an elevator, and later a stage of a local strip joint where that week the colossus was featured. Strippers would bump and grind; Sally would come out doing her gammy dance as Autumn Lee, beautiful long auburn hair flying about naked shoulders; in between more bumps and grinds the hair guy and I would ape the Thousand Year Old Man; more bumping and grinding and then the Colossus in key light dancin' on his last legs.

It was sinful! In 1960 Joe was tapped, milked dry to within an inch of life by government and handlers. But in his prime, Joe'd made bundles at the gate and for side betters, thrilled America in a post-depression era, even added a twist with the Bum of the Month Club.

Joe was past his salad days. Lines in a puffy brown face, red maps for eyes contrast with our smooth, resilient, tight skin. The face spoke of another time flatter than

Canvasback, a cartoon character who entered and left the ring on a stretcher. Joe was tempered, forged in the heat of pugilism. Yet Joe remained gentleman Joe. Never hit below the belt, or had a bad word for anybody. He was laconic, and when he spoke his thoughts were understated. Later, a ref wrote a summation of what pugilists endure: *Only The Ring Is Square*.

I knew what Joe was thinking in that elevator. He was sizing me up, but I held back 'cause in a clinch I'm mean. In truth, 5 to 1, Joe probably thought less of his glory days than his fans, and more about his mother and his boyhood down south among the poplar trees. Although as a man he'd been in and out of the limelight more years than he could recall, Joe remained country to his soul. Standing next to him in that small lift, I sensed he was never full of himself. He seemed just like his media image, humble, plain and unassuming. A good guy. But look out for that right. I nodded to him again for want of words. He nodded back maybe for the same reason like he'd done over decades for VIP's and countless oglers. The same look, the same humble nod; more said in mime than words.

As the elevator started up, I thought, there were three of us. In fact, there are a lot of us, but only one Joe. They called him the best, if not the greatest, of all time. He was living proof that the meek shall inherit if only occasionally like the night his belly burned hotter than Pele on the Pali.

So there we were, sardines in a can in a new apartment house off Ala Moana harbor where I said aloha to John Calvert on his 100-foot floating harem. Sally pressed 4. I faked a one-two with the floor buttons and uppercut 6 for Joe. One of his shoulders twitched. If he smiled I don't remember. It was a brief ride with living history; temporarily quartered in the Arms of Ala Moana while touring in a song and dance act.

Sally was from small town America, tall, sensual with great willowy legs. Joe had great legs too, once. You need legs to do what they did. It was all dancing and balance. What Sally did with her bumps and grinds, Joe did with his hands and feet. Lotsa bobbin' and weavin', titillation and going for the jugular of primitive instincts. But for the moment in that elevator we were just passengers sharing a ride. Sally and I were Jack and Jill dropouts, and Joe was the sleeping colossus in the beanstalk. *Fee, Fie, Fo, Fum! I'm schmelling the blood of a Nazi Hun!* I never forced conversation with Joe, or did a corny one-two. I left him to his privacy. I just gave him a chucklehead nod, and stole glimpses of him when he wasn't looking. If glimpses were stolen physical relics, the Brown Bomber would've disappeared long ago like ruins of Pompeii. When we got off, Joe started out too. He must've been deep in that boxer's world of one-too-many. I prefer thinking he had Sally on his mind. "No, Joe," I go. "You're floor's two up." *Oh. Thank you.* That moment 45 years ago is still vivid.

We met again backstage at the *Tacky Tiki Club,* capacity 250 mixed bloods: Hawaiians, Philippinos, and Buddha-heads, campus jargon referring mostly to Japanese, or anybody who raised the grade curve by studying hard. Most talk was in a foreign language or pidgin English, which is the same thing. Comedians had to fight to be understood. Sally had no such problem. Her body spoke Esperanto start to finish. Funny. No one understood Joe's body language; worn out, abused, the common language of boxing usury. But Joe's dead now. Buried in Arlington.

The band starts playing. Boom, rat-a-tat-tat. Out come strippers; off come clothes. Sally's long hair flying about her face and drawn sensually between her willowies; our shtick comes between veils and pasties; then the band strikes the introductory music for the main man. Out dances ex-vaudevillian and second banana Leonard Reed. Joe comes up beside me in the wings with cane and top hat. I adjust his necktie. *Knock 'em out, Joe.* He nods and steps out to applause, a tad awkward but all smiles, not a phony bone in his body. Few realize they're looking at a colossus shucking n' jiving, bowing n' tap dancing to meet tax debts.

Hawaii was still stretching itself as a new state. Caucasians were haolies, probably still are, who came from the mainland or stateside or USA proper, trailing the taint of Captain Cook. Maybe in that strip joint Joe looked Hawaiian, one of the natives who had made it big stateside in Martial Arts. *No fingers, elbows, knees, or groin kicks? Right. Only fists covered in balloon gloves big like pillows.* Asians had a different slant on the fight game that was beyond the Marquis of Queensbury, as the world would soon discover through Ed Parker and Bruce Lee. Meanwhile, Joe seemed vague and far-off- *a geek in a nightclub hole eating crow.* It was a job, which is fair enough. What wasn't fair was Joe, a champ on the ropes, reduced to a museum relic in a road show.

"Moshi, moshi."

"Hi. Arrigato."

"What you do last night?"

"I see Joe Rouis at Tacky Tiki Club. Maybe next time he take off clothes, too. Ha. His legs not like Sally! She something, bruddah! They have one ugly stripper. When she take off clothes people yell, Put back on! Ha, ha!"

"Dat funny! Ha, ha, ha."

"I see one stripper stateside. Built like one brick shithouse. She come out already naked."

"Hi? She get right to point. Then what she do?"

"She get dressed on stage. First put on stockings, then bra, panties."

"Ah, so! That silly!"

"No. Very clever. When she finish she all dressed ready to go home."

"You take home?"

"I go backstage. She say, fuck off, chink. I'm a dyke."
"Dyke? What dat? Something you put finger in?"
"Lesbian. Woman who like woman."
"Ah, so! Then why she dance for men?"
"I ask same question. She say for money, you fuckin'
coolie, and 'cause I one cock teasin', son-of-bitchin' ball
blaker! Ha, ha, ha!"
"I don't tink dat very funny."

Neither was Joe's story. The ex-colossus tap dancing
for dollars in a dive on Ala Moana Boulevard near Waikiki.
It was a real-life epilogue to Rod Serling's *Requiem For
A Heavyweight*, top hat and cane in place of an Indian
headdress. Marciano knew when he cried in his locker
room after knocking out Joe that it wasn't right. Joe
had been exploited for money, run into the ground by
handlers and boxing itself, right up until the last drop of
blood on Rocky's gloves. In economics they have a loftier
term utilitarianism- the good is measured by usefulness,
or "utiles", one good, one "utile". Of necessity Joe morphed
into a yodeling *utile* on tired legs in need of money owed
for back taxes. No one considered the debt owed Joe for
what he'd done for America and freedom; or his ensuing
military record. **1938.** He'd returned after a defeat for
unfinished business with the *Feuherer's mensch.* In a
packed Yankee Stadium, eyes on a postage stamp ring,
ears the world over glued to radios, everybody on the edge
of their seat waited anxiously for the rematch that had
come to symbolize Freedom verses Tyranny. Americans,
north, south, east, and west forgot their hungry bellies
and dumb prejudices, and pulled together for the Brown
Bomber as though he were battling Hitler himself.

At the opening bell an impatient Joe *came out of his
corner like God's thunder. Knocked the Hun,* said a buddy
who was there, *punched him from pillar to post.* They
say one of Joe's body punches was so devastating it
elicited a scream of pain *never heard before or since,*

almost feminine in pitch. Later, Schmelling confessed *I'd been hit so hard I couldn't recover.* Two minutes into round one, Joe's knockout punch rocked America and the world. *The elation was greater than all the New Year's celebrations that ever were wrapped in one.* When the Hun went down, jubilation was seismic. People danced, screamed, laughed, and wept. The knockout sent a message of freedom to tyranny everywhere that said, *Hitler your days are numbered!*

Then glory faded. America moved on. When Joe was on his last legs, his government and fans became forgetful children who slight their parents, unappreciative and unmindful of their duty. Joe's life ended ignominiously, two-stepping in top hat and tails when he ought to have been a national treasure sitting next to Abe in the Lincoln Memorial.

Joe Louis, Billie Holiday, and Lenny Bruce all had destiny in their pocket, but Joe- well, Joe was visceral, forthright, and untainted, the New World spirit, right up there with the American eagle.

Between the business of boxing where Only The Ring Is Square, and the unconscionable US Internal Revenue Service where only The Square Get Ringed, they hit Joe hard in the 12th round of his life. Shame on you and those who knew better but did nothing.

Among my father's belongings is a plastic wallet-size calendar put out in 1947 by Empire City Savings Bank, Two Park Ave., NY. It reads:

IN WHICH OF THESE GROUPS WILL YOU FIT
HERE IS WHAT FIGURES SHOW WILL BE THE FINANCIAL CONDITION OF AN AVERAGE GROUP OF 100 PEOPLE:
AT AGE 65: out of 64 still living only 10 are self-supporting
54 are dependent on others
BE SURE TO BE INDEPENDENT AND SELF SUPPORTING
START NOW TO SAVE AT LEAST 1/10 OF ALL YOU EARN

But Joe's dead now. Buried penniless in Arlington Cemetery with full military honors. The funeral ironically paid for by Max Schmelling. When we met in Hawaii, Joe was already the Indian in a headdress.

I, too, was in my last rounds in Hawaii. The comedy team fizzled out after Autumn Lee danced off to Australia on the arm of a rich dude. The Menehune Hui was full of hooey. My gig folded from lack of business. I never got my last paycheck, a drop in the bucket of misfortune compared to Joe. Instead of going *"lo-lo in lei land"* I did a reverse Castro, split for LA, found my own Doris Duke, and went-

☺

11. *Lo-Lo In The Land of La-La*

Diary: 1961. Scene 1. Reality check at the Employment Agency.

"What do you do, sir?"
"I'm a disc jockey."
"When did you last work?"
"Two weeks ago."
"For how long?"
"A week."
"As a DJ?"
"No. PA announcer in a department store. I deejayed before that."
"How long?"
"Three, four weeks."
"Which is it, sir, three or four?"
"Three."
"What else?"
"I drove a taxi one summer."

"How long?"

"A month. I was a waiter in college for five months."

"Then you're a waiter."

"No. I'm a disc jockey."

"Sir, we go by what you've actually done; your real work experience. Not what you're planning to do."

Decades later, LA streets, once familiar, melt together. I took a room in Hollywood on Fountain Avenue near Rossmoor, dropped in on Ed Parker at his La Cienega Kenpo-Karate Studio, got a warm Hawaiian welcome, and then did a walk-about. Hollywood was drab after lush Hawaii. But then I was alone and broke in a desert city, squatting under a thermal canopy that kept all the fetid air and carbon monoxide from escaping. Right off the plane my eyes burned. The noise and vastness of the airport scared me- strangers jostling one another without an "excuse me."

Hollywood and Vine was nothing but low-lying buildings with no hint of Allen's Alley. Grauman's Chinese Theatre was a washout baking in the sun, but at night it lit up like Christmas. Schwab's, a drug store-deli, on Hollywood Boulevard at Laurel Canyon Drive, a rendezvous for aspiring actors, was a distant cry to Junior's in Brooklyn, Katz's and Ratner's in Manhattan, restaurants serving authentic German-Jewish food: borscht, flanken, blintzes, thick pastrami on rye with mustard, schmaltz, and free sour pickles. Hollywood PR promoted Schwab's as the place Lana Turner, beauty pin-up of the '40's, was discovered at the lunch counter drinking a soda. After that wannabees flocked from all over settled there all day looking to be discovered who couldn't get discovered if they carried a sign that said, put me in a movie and I'll pay you.

In the '20's and '30's movie money built a bunch of orange and lemon groves into a town based on fairy tales and the illusion of a cinema aristocracy. But its "reel" legacy is the ruined lives it left on the cutting room floor, countless numbers driven to alcoholism, dope, and suicide.

Oblivious to that reality, I sent out audition tapes for DJ jobs. Gave one to Joe Hyams whom I'd met through Ed. A month later and no offers, low on cash with holes in my shoes, I bought a used pair at the Salvation Army for a buck. They fit okay at first, but were too small. My feet started to swell up with pain. I had to sit every other block. I visited Pasadena Playhouse, found tuition was high, joined Desilu Playhouse (DP) and enrolled at LA City College. There, I met a serious Paul Winfield who lived in Watts and acted in a group called the Attic Players. I still remember his excellent class performance of the avant-garde *Oh, Dad, Poor Dad. Mama's Hung You In the Closet and I'm Feeling So Sad.*

Desilu in 1960 was spread over 60 acres of prime Los Angeles real estate. Foremost for me was Desilu-Gower in Hollywood where I studied acting and worked with Lucy. It was formerly RKO where Shirley Temple grew up. Streets I walked to get to Desilu Playhouse (DP) were Gower, Las Palmas, and Selma. Actors hung out in Nickodel's on Melrose.

When Desi first arrived by car in Hollywood in the late '30's under RKO contract, he turned right off Sunset Boulevard on to Gower, saw the RKO sign, turned in at the gate and wound up in Beth Olam, a Jewish cemetery. A gateman sent him back down Gower; left on Melrose, left at the first corner, and left at the Paramount gate. That's how I walked to DP where my performances were consigned to Beth Olam.

At first specific zoning ordinances and fire codes had to be met, along with notarized permission from residents on Selma before they could open up a double door audience entrance. He promised to sound proof the wall facing Selma, guaranteed security for crowd control, and quality seats for every family. If Desilu succeeded he pledged to buy their homes at market value, which he did turning them into production offices.

DP, just inside the main gate, was in the Little Theatre, a musty, one-story wooden building set against a backdrop of warehouses containing TV sound stages, and storage areas for sets. The Little Theatre had a proscenium arch, dressing rooms, and seating for 200. Some nights while alone studying a script, I fancied I'd heard spirits of departed RKO players. After working The Lucy Show I had the feeling of being orphaned out by a ghost family with no sense of allegiance, or fellowship. Lauren Bacall wrote, when Bogey got sick, their friends dwindled to a handful. Years later when Lucy's crown was slipping, C.B.S dropped her. In the end we're all strangers at the gate. Adolph Menjou once said, *Every actor for himself.* At an audition at Paramount Casting I went up for a butler part in a Jerry Lewis movie, and crossed paths with the future Bones of Star Trek, Deforest Kelly. I thought, *Forget him. I can butle better.* Joe Hyams laughed when I told him. To me it was a silly line. Wrong. Years later I heard Stan Laurel say in an old movie, *I can butle.* In *My Man Godfrey,* zany Lombard asks Powell, the Forgotten Man, *Can you butle?*

Lucille Ball started DP as an acting school/repertory company with a select group of actors who studied, received a stipend, and were free to work elsewhere. DP was a tribute to Ginger Roger's mother, Lela, who ran an acting school at RKO in the '30's when Lucy was a novice. Maybe those were the spirits I heard in the wings. While at DP I did *Here we Are; A Hatful of Rain*; and minor roles in *Julius Caesar* directed by Wally Matthews, featuring top character actors Steve Marlo, Ford Rainey, Karl Swenson, and Joan Tompkins. Other character actors were Tony Barr, John Hoyt, and Marvin Kaplin. They were bricks and mortar of movies with stage credits running the gamut from the Tyrone Guthrie Theatre to the Goodman to Stratford-On-Avon and Orson Wells.

Sadly, most were over-qualified for mundane Hollywood and languished in bit parts.

One night a teenager with an odd name gave a helluva performance in a scene from *The Miracle Worker.* Later, Darby Zarby starred in movies as Kim Darby. Occasionally writers like Ray Bradbury popped in. DP was for actors what Terry Robinson and Jack Lalanne Health Clubs were for the public, a place to stay in shape. At DP in 1963 I first saw a funny play called *The Wonderful Ice Cream Suit,* which took over 20 years to make it to film. There was actor/director Joe Sergeant; a movie dialogue coach who'd been with Sandy Meisner, a contemporary of Lee Strasburg and Stella Adler. I first heard of Meisner when my college buddy John Phillip Law split Hawaii for the Neighborhood Playhouse in New York. Members of the DP were always coming and going God knows where. Acting's a gypsy life. If you're rich you can wait out dry periods. One actor begged for work so much he got water on the knee. To cure it he stood on his head and drowned from water on the brain. Musicians have it rougher with cross-country one-nighters. Lucy and Desi started *Desilu* so they could be together and live a normal life.

Evenings I'd walk to a local TV station to see Henry Morgan do a West Coast version of the *Tonight Show,* which I fancied would take over, but didn't. Morgan was one of the first casual radio hosts of the '40's to personalize commercials. He had short-cropped hair, a pinched nose, and a loopy sense of humor combining balderdash with tongue-in-cheek. Nothing's funnier than talking through a pinched nose with your tongue in your cheek. His trademark was a Mickey Mouse wall clock in the background. His style was right of Robert Benchley and left of hokey Ernie Kovacs. A typical guest was loopy PR mogul Jim Moran. They say he dug up a New York street in Con Ed clothes with pump guns, police horses, and then melted away. One night the short walk to the station took an hour. I hobbled in late on sore feet and had to watch standing in front of an off-stage monitor. A man puffing a cigar came up, nodded hello, and we laughed together at Morgan while I shifted feet. The guy next to me puffed his big cigar, checked his watch, and its Danny Thomas waiting to go on. Strange, to have been penniless in busted shoes standing mute next to a famous comedian. Why didn't I ask him for a job? *Help me? You won't be sorry. Somebody helped you. How about a pair of shoes? Socks? Anything? I butle better than Deforest Kelly.* If there are no accidents in life then that encounter was saying *sell you. Nobody else will.* But I did the Christian thing and gave him his space. Timidity and low self-esteem'll kill ya faster in *no business like show business.*

In 1961 Ed had two Kenpo studios (gyms), one in Pasadena on Walnut, his main office, and the other on the edge of Hollywood on La Cienega Boulevard. Later, it was moved to Santa Monica. La Cienega dissects Sunset and Hollywood Boulevards, and veers left at the base of the Santa Monica Hills. High up to the right was the word HOLLYWOOD, a tacky beacon with one fallen letter. The sign always impressed me as a nametag for dysfunctional people in case they got lost.

The La Cienega Kenpo-Karate studio was 14' by 40' covered with 3' by 6' zabatones or tatamies- straw mats encased in green vinyl with a raised rice paper pattern. A foyer gave way to an office on the left and a few steps straight ahead was a narrow lounge and three-quarter wall with a rectangular window looking into the gym. Instructional placards lined the walls, and at the opposite end full-length mirrors covered a partition separating a changing room with showers and a rear exit to a parking lot.

Nights following class, Ed's cadre worked out under the supervision of Wu, Parker's friend down from San Francisco ostensibly to teach Tai Chi. Curiously, they weren't doing Tai Chi or Kenpo, but Chinese Hung Ga, a style using long, sweeping, circular arm moves and kicks. When they left I turned off the light and rolled out my Salvation Army sleeping bag.

I hung out across the street at Murray's 5-star greasy spoon. I'd fill up on bread and hot milk eaten straight from the pot, which earned me the nickname *Schissel-* 'pot' in Yiddish.

Whenever it rains I think of Noah's Ark. That first January in LA, rain fell in biblical proportions. Streets were rivers, intersections lakes; mudslides buried homes, others slid down hills. I bought a raincoat at an Army and Navy Store, but I really needed a raft. Then the roof started leaking. I put out buckets and towels. My usual at Murray's was out. *Every schissel's catchin' leaks, kiddo!* Water streaked the instruction placards, turning black letters into tears of mascara that slid down the wall and were sucked up by dry straw in the mats. Ed and I mopped and bailed for days. Nights I slept on the desk in my raincoat. With heaters and fans going 24/7, the studio turned humid and smelled like a wet barn. One morning I wake up to a surreal scene. *Ed,* I go on the phone, *it looks like a Dali hot house. Mushrooms everywhere. Between the mats. From seeds hibernating in the straw just waitin' for water.* Mats were leaned against walls, or put outside after the rain stopped. *Forget Kenpo,* I go. *Let's sell mushrooms to Chinatown.*

I phone a friend I'd met in summer school in Hawaii. Di's parents lived in a Bel Air mansion near Jerry Lewis. Her home exemplified sprawled out living at its extreme. A bungalow could fit in their living room - which included a movie theatre- and there'd still be room for dancing to a full orchestra. The kitchen had commercial-size appliances: stainless steel refrigerators, sinks, and assorted pots, pans and utensils that hung like glistening stalactites over a butcher-block table the size of a bocce court. At the time, Di was ensconced with a Mexican-American artist who'd won art awards. They lived on the second floor of a private home overlooking Echo Park Lake, visible on occasion when the blue smog lifted. They were fun, generous, and I often slept over on a bed in a storage room full of pictures, pallets, paint tubes, easels, and frames. Di had a friend at an employment office. He got me work as a guard-time card keeper at the back door to the Wilshire Hotel. Until my first check I scrounged leftovers from trays busboys brought back from the dining room. One day I'm walking home eating my usual day old bakery bread and drinking from a quart of milk when I realize, *I just got paid!* I toss it all in a garden. At Murray's it's *Ham and eggs, home fries, and toast.*

12.   The Russian Rock Bath of La Brea

1962. While at LA City College I dated a classmate who lived with her parents on a quiet, tree-lined street in Watts. Later, Mike Yung came to town, and we visited his cousin's grocery store in that same inner-city district before it exploded. One afternoon we were talking in my office at Parker's studio, when a Mexican-American walked in wearing a thick mustache, in his 30's, about 5'4", maybe 200 pounds.

"I want to learn karate."

"Why?" I ask.

"I'm a masseur at the La Brea Russian-Turkish Steam and Rock Bath. We get weirdoes. People who ain't straight, drunks, and they grab me durin' a massage."

"Grab you where?"

"My leg," he says, rolling his eyes. "While I'm massaging them. I just move their hand away. I'm not that kind of guy. When they're drunk they come on strong. I mean some of them are weight lifters, and wrestlers. Last night a drunk grabs my leg, I slap his hand, he gets mad, and starts chasing me around the table, whipping the towel at me. Lucky, his girlfriend came in." *Girlfriend?* "A guy. They laugh and go for a steam. It's not funny to me. I'm getting grabbed 2, 3 times a night."

Later, Mike went with him for a free massage. The next night we went together. I wanted to see the place for myself. The bath house was tacky, dimly lighted, had a massage room, two steam rooms, and a changing room with stalls and draw curtains. While Mike and I flipped a coin to see who'd go first for a massage, a man came in wearing a wedding band. He picked up soap, a towel, and went out.

"He's married," I go. "What's he doing here?"

"AC-DC," says Mike.

The masseur says, "After the massage if you want a steam use the room on the right. The other's the Bridal Room."

"Keep your ass to the wall, haole," says Mike, swinging off the table. We entered the room on the right wrapped in towels and were quickly enveloped in steam. I made out a figure seated on an upper tier, a ghost on ceramic tile. As we sat down in the middle of the room, a fat guy came in wrapped in a huge towel, and several others followed rapidly. They sat around us at a respectful distance. Then the lights went out, there was movement in the dark, and when they returned a second later everyone had changed position but us. Again, the lights went out. I started to nudge Mike, but held off. He might think it's one of them and let loose a punch. When the lights came back on, the fat guy on our right was on my left, and the two guys on my left were on Mike's right. Mike looked at me. I looked him. The lights flickered. Mike got up. "Come. We go, haole." Out in the massage room the masseur says, "If you stayed in there you'd be married by now." I asked about the muffled voices and noises in the steam room on the left. "That's the daisy chain. They go belly-to-back and choo-choo around the room. See how they wear the towels? Toga-style is a Roman Senator. He dictates. A mini-towel's a princess, likes to receive it. Turban style's a Queen Bee. No towel's a cow who likes gettin' jerked off." Just then a guy walks by with a towel folded over his wrist. "He's a waiter," says the masseur. "With him, it's a la carte."

13.   The Chinese Box

Wu Who? Wu Shu! Parker met Wu Shu in San Francisco during one of his periodic visits to Sifu Lau Bun (Lew Ben) for treatment of bone spurs in his heal. Woe to Ed for wooing Wu who was knowledgeable in Kung Fu, Hung Ga style, and Tai Chi. According to Wu, the two men struck a verbal agreement to share their knowledge, with Wu teaching Tai Chi out of Ed's studio. When I came on the scene, Wu was an unhappy camper. Parker, allegedly, had not kept his word. Judging from my experience with both men, I'd say neither one had played with a full deck. Following the adage 'does Macy tell Gimbel' let alone build him a better store, Ed was reluctant to share his turf. As for Wu, it's likely he always had in mind teaching on his own. Also, their philosophy was different. Wu was open and Ed was closed. By letting me sleep at the La Cienega studio I became Ed's eyes. He'd ask casually, *Anything going on after class?* Later, he used the same approach on me by letting a destitute student sleep in his Santa Monica place. No doubt the guy, along with other "da-votees", told Ed what he wanted to hear, and then some, about how I ran the place. Did I open on time? What I said in class and out. Did I do Tai Chi? Count off in Chinese? I was Ed's buffer while he established a new cadre to promote and run his business for nothing-, a

Gestapo claque of high school kids doing his dirty work. It was his way of doing business.

By then I was mostly sleeping with Eve anyway. While her divorce was pending, I hung my hat in a pad back of her house in Benedict Canyon, which I shared with Steve, friend, student, and professional pianist. At the time, Eve and I were looking to open a Karate school in Ventura.

Before the Wu split I wrote and designed a Tai Chi brochure under the impression it was to promote classes taught at Parker's. Woe to me when Wu took off with Ed's cadre, plus over a dozen advanced students, and established the first public Chinese Gung Fu Academy on Hollywood Boulevard. It was a store with large windows separated by a center door. My brochure hung in a corner of one window. Wu never paid me for it, nor did I receive money from Parker for helping to develop his tri-fold, produced by artist-cameraman Jim McQuade. Jim was genteel, soft spoken and intelligent. I suggested he *make room for women, kids, and movie stars.* A mock-up cover was a pencil sketch of four-on-four men, the on-coming group attacking with raised clubs and the other defending with their backs to the viewer. Photog Jerry Stout, a gangly 6'2" student, shot the pictures. On the floor he was all elbows and legs moving in a distracting way. Block too soon and a whip around fist or foot'd hit you. Comical, but effective. Like batting in baseball, if you watch the pitcher's body and not the release point, you'll get zonked. Eve and I posed for photos at La Cienega with Nancy Kovacs defending against Bronislau Kaper, and Chick Sullivin teaching my kids class. In one pic I'm taking on an attacker. Today, that brochure is Martial Arts memorabilia.

One day Parker stormed into La Cienega. *"Who's here? Anybody in the back?"* It was the day Wu split. Ed checked the showers, returned, and said, *"If I didn't have a family there'd be bodies on the floor."* They say, a little knowledge can be dangerous. It's true in Martial Arts. Ability and balls don't always come in one package. That day was dangerously close to *show down at the Kenpo-Karate Corral*. And when the dust settled it would've been Ed walking into the sunset.

Ed gave me a brown belt and I became his major-domo in Hollywood. I never aspired to black belt because to me, a non-fighter, brown was less provocative. Frankly, it's the man, not the belt, that holds up his pants. Ed had one reliable student left, brown belt Chick Sullivin, who was promoted to black and started teaching. A barber by trade, Chick stood 5' 8", weighed 170, had black hair, and moved sharply. He ran a two-seat barbershop in the burbs. One day he's trimming me when his dog jumps up on the other chair. *Down, Kenpo*, says Chick, which made me laugh. It was like a dentist calling his dog *Tooth*, or an actor with a dog named *Hamlet*, or a priest saying, *Be back, Sister Mary. Pope has to poop.*

My proudest moment teaching occurred in my kid's class when the Raven walked in, a shy 9-year-old with bright red hair and freckles. His parents lived on the beach in Malibu. Raven had a bully problem at school. With each lesson, some on Malibu Beach, he gained confidence and assertiveness. While sparring I even let him knock me down. Soon I had to be careful. One day he walks in smiling ear-to-ear. *Monday*, he says, *that bully goes to push me. I fake right, go left, kick him in the shin and he falls down crying. Now when he sees me he walks the other way.*

☺

Toadies Above and Below the Mat. Every master has an inner circle of copycats who exemplify his attitude and philosophy. Not all of them are forthright, but neither is the master, sometimes. Within this group of "da-votees" there is a pecking order, back-bighting, and ready criticism of other fighting styles. Parker, God love him, was foremost a businessman dedicated to survival.

Toward that end he played students against each other in a merry-go-round of Pavlovian spoon-feeding. He'd dole out just enough knowledge to keep everyone licking his hand and talkative. There was an in-group when I arrived and another one when I left. Rich Muntgomry and Rick Torez led the first group under Wu. The second group consisted of bootlickers centering on a runty nameless character and a renegade 17-year-old Tom Bleecher. They were Ed's new eyes and ears. Soon it was shades of Wu, except I didn't screw Ed. I liked him. I knew I was out of favor when he declined my help in relocating to Santa Monica and Cotner near highway 405. *Stay by the phone, and forward any messages,* he says curtly. *Give out the new address.* Years later I read Lee Iacoca at Ford Motors kept a black book on his subordinates. I call it pragmatic paranoia. I became expendable because I was salaried, and neglected business in my infatuation over Eve.

In Hawaii in 1960 my mind was already on Chinese Martial Arts; the mother, full of legend, body awareness, and a philosophy of right living. While teaching and doing exhibitions I'd count in Cantonese and sprinkle my talks with words like Kung Fu, Tai Chi Chuan, and showed on an elementary level how the styles differed. The "da-votees" mislead Ed into thinking I *put down Kenpo! Talked in Chinese!* Ed was wary of a Wu repeat. In fact, he was already re-building a new cadre while working on a second book, *Secrets of Chinese Karate,* an examination of Chinese Shao Lin Temple style. With a few exceptions, toadies were laughable. They were ignorant of China, never heard of Tai Chi or Kung Fu, words they couldn't spell or pronounce. *That King Cong? Gone Phooey? Tie Kick?* Kenpo Karate was *Campo Car Rate!* In Martial Arts they were babies learning to walk and say 'mama'. One day Ed agreed to give me a percentage for teaching privately, but later reneged. Shades of Wu.

In the end, Ed's wife Leilani summed it up. At the time I was standing by Ed's Cadillac, trying to heal our rift, when Leilani leaned across Ed in the driver's seat, and what she said was the last I heard or would ever see of them. *If you want to talk to Ed, call before you come over; make an appointment. You don't walk in on a Macy's executive without calling first.*

I like the way you handle the students, Ed once complimented me. *You keep your distance and don't let them get familiar.* Ed was shrewd; giving me the Hawaiian treatment that was more comment than observation. It was part of his carrot and stick business style. Students under a master often languish with mixed feelings of veneration, fear, and dreams of inheriting the ultimate secrets of *the flower.* What Eugene O'Neill called "everyman's pipe dream" in the end smokes the dreamer. As Ed pursued privately the secrets of Shao Lin always refining and redefining what he'd learned to suit him, he rarely let anyone get too close. Ed once observed of me, *You like the Chinese because of the aesthetics.* True. *But I also appreciate China, the mother of it all.* Had Ed been forthright and into Lao Tsu, things might've been different between us. To a degree, his *Secrets of Chinese Karate* also summed up his personality.

Around 1963 Mils Crenshaw came to town from Salt Lake, worked out with Ed, and received a black belt. They were friends since their Brigham Young days in the mid '50's. Mils had a kenpo studio in Salt Lake. Before Wu's break I crossed paths with Martial Arts aficionados Sweeny, Torez, Muntgomry, and the spunky Tracy brothers all Parker black belts.

Tom Bleecher was a special kid, age 17, when we met at Parker's. Good looking, blonde hair, stood about 5'9" or 10", with all the requisites of a potential California surf bum. He was clever, unafraid to talk with adults, and wiley. So it's no surprise that he became a writer and ex-husband of Linda Lee, Bruce's widow. Now that Parker's gone he might be married to Leilani's daughter. Back then Tom lived in a bungalow in back of somebody's home, possibly with a divorced parent. One night he took me to a party in a canyon home off Sunset around Chevy Chase and Loma, or maybe Monte Leon Drive, that belonged to choral master Roger Wagner. The grounds were manicured and the house and furnishing were right out of Home and Garden, mixing Italian rococo and French provincial. The party was hopping with high school kids, definitely too young for me. So I hung back and enjoyed watching them. Then Tom, the rascal, led a group to an upstairs phone, dialed a random number from a directory, and using a child's voice, he alternated between fear and panic. *I'm, I'm 9-yrs-old. And, and my parents left me, and, and didn't come back. A movie theatre. The balcony, I think. Help me, please. I'm scared. It's dark and I'm scared. I used my last nickel. Please help me.* While others muffle laughs, Tom gives out the house phone number, hangs up, and waits for the call back. When it comes, he lets several rings go by, picks up and says in a groggy, adult voice. *Hello. What's that? A lost child? Not here. No. This is a private residence. Better find that child before a pervert does.*

Sterling Peacock was a Mormon who defied his last name. In free-style he was a veritable blue jay. His technique was still, unflinching, and Spartan. When we met in 1962 he was a strong boned, 6', 190 pound brown belt about to turn 18. He had boxed in the golden gloves, which accounted for his stamina and quick reflexes. It was near impossible to get in on him. He stood his ground quietly, let his opponent come to him, and then it was wham, bam, thank you ma'm. Always balanced, his moves were tight and lean. He was the Hemingway of Kenpo. For fun he stood straight as a board, hands by his side, and would fall flat on his face. At the last second he'd bring both arms chest level and cushion the impact with his palms. For an encore he'd dive in the air headfirst and break the fall the same way. I said, *Terrific. Now do it with a hard-on.* A year later he left to do missionary work for the Mormon Church. It was the last I saw of him, a Kenpo kid with integrity.

Closer to me in age and temperament was schoolteacher and fellow brown belt, Dan Inosanto. I found Dan soft-spoken, calm, talented in the arts, and forever curious about Kung Fu. I told Ed, *of everybody, Dan's the trustworthiest. And most important, he's an educator.* Regretfully, Dan lived in the burbs, maybe Inglewood, and I had no wheels, or we'd've hung out more. He had a wife and family to look after. So it came as no surprise to me many years later when he joined Bruce Lee.

In the Catholic Church devotees are "i pecori" – *sheep.* A poor Shepard makes a poor flock, they say. I once asked Wu why Muntgumry, an ex-Parker black belt, and generally quiet, had grown opinionated? *He was always talkative with me,* says Wu. *I don't teach through paranoia.* How Wu actually taught did not reflect well on him when a *duh-votee,* also an ex-Parker brown belt, had a fatal accident- snapped his neck doing a hanging rope trick. But then some students have their own mind.

14.   1962: They Call It Judo

While teaching karate I'd count off in Cantonese with a twist. *Yut, yee, sum, say! I teach you pay!* While shuffling left in the horse I'd forget to say reverse, and watch them bang into the wall. Or, I'd sneeze, *Ah-chew!* and say, *you guys punch so fast I'm catching a cold from the wind. Karate is very fast. Watch.* They'd look, I'd do nothing, and then say *Wanna see it again?* That was in 1962. When asked if I had a black belt I'd say, *No. Suspenders.* It didn't ingratiate me with Ed, a serious businessman.

I set-up an interview for Ed with Bob Crane, an LA morning jock out of Connecticut. Later, Crane starred in Hogan's Heroes. Deejay Crane had quick hands and a juggler's sense of timing. He worked out of a combo studio over-seen by a master technician in a pivotal control room who handled commercial inserts and cut-a-aways. Because Crane improvised, the engineer's union allowed him to operate his own board. In a typical interview Crane would sneak in nutty phoners, and sound effects off records marked in crayon. He wore split headphones, one half tuned to cue, the other monitored off-air. He could split his focus that way, too. While talking with a guest he'd cue up and slip in an effect from his arsenal of politicians, stars, laughter, boos, cheers, etc. *Karate is to judo what boxing is to wrestling.* And you're to me what I'm to you, you dirty rat you. Explain that? *It's the science of dirty fighting.* Leave my lawyer out of this. By dirty fighting y'mean dirty filthy or dirty sneaky? *Anything goes: fingers in the eye, chokes, groin kicks.* You'd be a hit at a masochist party. *In Karate we use hands and the feet.* You're a black belt. I have a yellow one. Do you have to register with the police? *No.* Oh. They register with you. My producer says you can break a board with your bare hand. I hope he didn't mean my control board. Oh. You came prepared. Have board, will travel. *Boom!* Wow! I have a lease. Maybe you can break it. Show me some hand moves. (*Ed complies)* You can get a speeding ticket with those hands. I'd hate to be the cop to give it to you. Ever get mad? *I count to ten.* In normal or karate time? You married? *Seven years.* Bet the wife goes to bed with a crash helmet in case you turn over in your sleep. What's her favorite song, *I Get a Kick Out of You?* (*Ring)* Hello. (Voice: Your guest's a brute! An animal! *(fay)* Can I have his phone number?) Where you from, Ed? *Hawaii.* No wonder they say, *Keep Your Eyes on the Hands.* With you it includes the feet.

On the side Crane made pornographic, home movies with a partner who was mentally unstable. Crane acted in the films with women whose spouses or boyfriends became upset when they found out. Crane tried to dissolve the business, which antagonized his partner. In 1978 a decade after his success in TV's Hogan's Heroes, Bob Crane was on tour in Scottsdale, Arizona. He was found murdered in his motel bed from a blow to the head by a camera tripod. The case was never solved.

☺

15.   The Eve of Success

Life is a series of bad jokes, bonehead moves and near misses. Lots of people study Martial Arts for the wrong reason, which is how I met Eve. Her analyst recommended Karate as therapeutic exercise for releasing aggression and marital problems, but he hadn't considered that by flipping two letters marital becomes Martial, which is the wrong way to go. Pillow fights are a better idea, but then Eve would put bricks in hers.

One day I'm on the floor exercising when in sails this knockout red head rigged from stem to stern. I could smell the ocean and feel the hot wind off her body and the draft between pulling me toward her. Ed signs her up for private lessons, demonstrates the horse and how to hold the arms with elbows close to the sides. She drops into a stance with her lovely legs and arms turned out. Ed touches her lightly where necessary to bring everything in line. She had fare form considering the great form she was in. But in bed who's thinking two left feet? If she'd walked in an hour later Parker would've been gone and I'd be teaching that body. *Your breasts, may I adjust them? There. Now spread your legs. Good. Toes in and heels out. It opens up the acupuncture points so the chi can flow through the clitidian, I mean, meridians.* I felt the chi rising in my loins. As I head for the front office, Ed gives me a wink. I watch them reflected in the window facing the street. You can't stay in business long thinking what I'm thinking. But then Ed was married, not me. A lesson later Ed gives her to me because of a conflict with his Pasadena classes. That's when the books flew out the window.

One day Eve invites me to supper at her home. At the time, 1962, her husband Marton Lieds was a corporate showbiz lawyer at a talent agency with a dozen last names long as your arm. Later on, I learned he'd been a Chuckler lawyer and then vice president of Desilu Productions. When Desi was first building the business end of Desilu he remembered tightfisted Marton from a New York encounter. After a show, Marton gave him a petty cleaning bill. Desi figured *better to have that son-of-bitch on our side.* Marton brought with him several network cronies to manage the cash flow. So there I was, going to supper at his home, knowing zero. Later, when Joe Hyams asked me to set up an interview for him, he must've assumed I knew Marton's background.

Eve and Marton lived in a terracotta roofed palacio right out of *Sunset Boulevard,* only modern and not spooky. Dean Martin lived nearby on Mountain road; Jerry Lewis was further along in Bel Aire; Pickfair, once the domicile of Mary Pickford and Douglas Fairbanks Sr. was back over the hills near the Marian Davies Estate; Howard Hughes was a skip and a hop away, buttoned up in a bungalow back of the Beverly Hills Hotel- a reclusive, hypochondriac germ freak walking around with his feet in shoe boxes to keep them from touching the floor.

Marton is 5' 6", medium build, in his late 40's, and friendly out of deference to Eve. *I did some boxing in my youth,* he says over aperitifs in their recreation room, palm trees in every window. Fighting is the last thing on my mind. On learning I am an aspiring actor he offers anecdotal business advice. *Your life's in the hands of corporate administrators for whom everything in life hinges on a decimal point. At C.B.S in the '50's there was Hue Robenson, a vice president in charge of programming who was followed by Jay Aubree, the smiling cobra. Two unscrupulous men. Aubree dropped the final axe on the television programs like Playhouse 90. We had a TV pilot in the can for the new season. Contracts were signed, actors and technical crew committed to housing leases. The star was John Bromfield, Corinne Calvet's husband, handsome, laconic, and monolithic. He couldn't act- an ex-football player built like a brick shit house. For a dramatic high point the villain ran and Bromfield would tackle him. The pilot cost thousands to produce. In August, Robenson says, I have a better story. It didn't matter that money and people's lives were committed. In this story, he says, the hero's a Spanish aristocrat who rides out for justice on a big black stallion wearing black clothes and a mask. Nobody suspects him. He duels the bad guys and gallops off leaving his trademark. A "Z" slash with a sword that turns to fire. We paid off everybody and went with The Mark of Zorro. That's the acting business. I'm proud of one thing. As Robenson was leaving I said, You're a cold-hearted shit.*

After dinner, in the living room over San Bucco and coffee, Eve says, *Mart, help him get a Screen Actor's Guild card. He's got character. He's not your typical Hollywood hopeful.* I flush. Martin's reply was wiser than I knew. *Better to get a Screen Extra card.* But extras can't do lines. *You'll work more often and get to see why directors say, 'that's a take.'* He was speaking of on the job experience and steadier employment. But I tended always to put the cart before the horse. Then, too, I had become smitten by Eve. Later, Joe Hyams summed her up as *the kind of woman who'd get you to rob gas stations to keep her-* a metaphor for Man Eater.

If an affair is meant to be, words are secondary. When Desi met Lucy, he said, his opening lines were the corniest in history. "Miss Ball?" "Why don't you call me Lucille? I'll call you Dizzy?" "Okay, but it's not Dizzy." "Oh? How do you say it, Daisy?" "No. Daisy is a flower. It's De-si." He admits it's a wonder she went out with him at all. "Do you know how to rumba, Lucille?" She says, "No. I've never learned." "Would you like me to teach you how to rumba? It might come in handy for your character in the movie you're doing." There was no rumba in the movie, but Lucy didn't know that. Probably didn't care. She had a man. "We're all going to El Zarape," says Desi, "a swingin' Mexican restaurant on Sunset. All the kids from New York are going there for dinner. They have a great Latin band and I thought maybe you'd like to come and get to know the kids a little better, if you dunt have anythin' else to do?" Lucy says, "I 'dunt' have 'anythin' else and I'd love to." That conversation lead to a 19-year marriage, the multi-million dollar Desilu Studios spread over 60 acres of prime land in Hollywood and Culver City, 29 annual productions, and by 1960 they were bigger than MGM.

I won't bother recounting my first words with Eve, even if I could recall them. Let's just say that after her lesson I took her to Murray's for Kara-*tea*, which graduated to baccia mi. Years later when I met Ayn the openers were sterling, too. "Hey." "Hay? You a farmer?" "Yeah. I'm lookin' to plant some seeds." "Till me another one, Farmer Gray." And I did.

Eve set the tone of our tempestuous relationship. Either we were kissing or punching each other. At times I couldn't tell the difference. One evening we're driving to Dan Innocento's for supper- we were both brown belts under Parker. I'm behind the wheel clocking 70 on the LA Expressway. Suddenly Eve's off the map and a flaming banshee. One hand's on the wheel, the other's blocking her slaps and kicks, the Mercedes is weaving between cars and lanes. I pull over thinking, every goddamn night's *Wine and Roses* and *Lost Weekend.* Bloodshot eyes. Imaginary demons. I turn the car around and drive her home, the first bar in Beverly Hills. I was too broke and embarrassed to tell Dan what had happened. They should rename LA, Los Anus, City of Lost Assholes.

Let's re-rack for Captain Karate. Although in 1961 Martial Arts (MA) was a sampan on the American horizon, I felt it was a potential gold mine for Hollywood. MA was already popular in Asia. With the exception of jiu jitsu in *Bad Day at Black Rock* starring Spencer Tracy, Hollywood was totally into guns, cowboys, fisticuffs, and thin plots. MA could open up new vistas of legend and folklore. It was imaginative, and full of the Samurai and Bushido mystique. To work, it needed a new culture awareness, a new type of action hero, one of color, but America of the early '60's was not ready for heroes of color, Asian or otherwise. When Ed and I worked *The Lucy Show* they called what we did *Lucy and Viv Learn Judo*, but it was really Karate. Meanwhile, I heard talk of Bruce Lee, which placed him in Hong Kong and later Washington. The Hollywood in-crowd, always curious and with money to burn, added Karate to its list of spurious, extra curricular activities that included séances, spirit contact, and an eastern religion called Bahai, named after it's prophet. How I came to it I forget- probably the free h'or d'ouvres- but the last meeting I attended was in the Hollywood hills at the home of conductor-composer Russ Garcia. Apart from his beautiful wife, and panoramic view of LA, what sticks most is the simple yet elusive idea that *all the leading world prophets have taught the same thing, love and compassion.* Anyway, MA intrigued people like Jose Ferrer, Nick Adams, Nobu McCarthy, Macdonald Carey, George Hamilton, Blake Edwards, Nancy Kovak, Robert Wagner, Warren Beatty, and Bronislau Kaper.

Sidebar: Bronislau Kaper was born in Warsaw, 1902. He'd started at MGM in 1940. He wrote musical scores for *Gaslight* (1944), *Them!* (1954 considered a science fiction classic), and he'd just finished *Mutiny On The Bounty* (1962) the year we met at Parker's. At the time I knew nothing about this debonair 60-year-old Polish Romeo and European romantic as evidenced in his music. His Polish accent heightened his charming manner. When we met, I go, *Bronislau's a long name. What do they call you for short?* He goes, *Bronislau is my nickname.*

Broni, like his buddy Jose Ferrer, loved women. One day I arranged a photo session for Ed's new brochure involving Broni, Ferrer, Hyams, and actress Nancy Kovac whom I'd met at an Argosy Magazine shoot. When she walks in late, Jose's jaw drops and he tries to split. *If I'm seen in a picture with <u>that woman,</u> even for a brochure, Rosemary'd never believe me.* Meanwhile, Broni is pulling Nancy to the mat. *Yoga, my dear. It is wonderful for the back. Very relaxing.* While prying him lose I'm looking over my shoulder to make sure Jose doesn't escape. *This shoot's dead,* I think. Jose's in the john changing to street clothes. Broni's back topping Nancy. *My dear, you will love this position. It is from Richard Hittleman. Now it is from Bronislau, to you and free.* How he worked her to the mat so fast I don't know, but it piqued my interest in yoga as pornography.

Following a Karate exhibition, we were at Broni's Beverly Hills home for lunch when I ask, *what've you written?* He sits at the piano and plays a medley: *Green Dolphin Street* (1947), *Invitation* (1952), and *Hi-lili*, which sounded like a renaissance folk melody. I go, You wrote those? He goes, *Guilty as charged. They are from my movie scores. The last one Hi-lili, hi lo is from Lili, 1953. It won me that little illusive gold statue on the mantel called The Oscar.* Then I ask, How do you get to write music for movies? He says, *First you need musical talent and then the skills. The requisites for stealing.* He chuckles. *Hi-lili*

*I wrote in fifteen, maybe twenty minutes. It came quickly.
Sometimes I write all day and have nothing to show. The
process opens the door, and voilá, suddenly something
beautiful. That, my friend, is the exception to the rule.*
Broni died in LA in 1983.

16.   The Manchurian Groaner

One day in 1962 a 5' 9" julienne of a string bean
actor shows up for private lessons. Henry Sylva (*Hatful
of Rain*, Broadway) is Spanish but looks Eurasian, has
almond eyes, high cheekbones and the attitude of the
descomisado he played in *Viva Zapata*. As the butler in
Manchurian Candidate, Sylva was prepping for a karate
fight scene with Sinatra. Each time we'd meet it was
always the first time. Sylva was a verbal tightwad and a
minimalist in facial expression, more Asiatic than Latin,
and gave the impression that each smile cost him a
hundred bucks. Or, maybe he was always playing to a
camera and paranoid Frank. Anyway, the two were evenly
matched broomsticks with middling coordination.

John Frankenheimer was part of the New York
television clique of directors and writers that included
Sidney Lumet, Rod Serling, and Blake Edwards who
went west, when in the late '50's TV dramas with
sensitive subjects were dropped in favor of sit-coms. Joe
Hyams confided to me that Parker had *auditioned for
the butler part and scared the shit out of Frankenhiemer.
But don't tell Ed*. Probably Ed blitzed him like he did Rod
Taylor (Hitchcock's *The Birds*). According to Ed, Taylor
fancied himself a pugilist. *So I say to Taylor*, vis-à-vis
Frankenhiemer, *throw a punch*. With me as a dummy,
Ed does an arpeggio of lightening blocks, punches, and

elbows ending in a backhand to the groin guaranteed to ring bells.

To Frankenheimer, Sylva was safe as an actor and gloss figure that made Sinatra look good. Parker was overwhelming, 6', 200 pounds, big-shouldered, had a white mane forelock, and flinty eyes. A prototype waiting to happen. Jack Palance, Anthony Quinn, Wallace Beery, and Victor McLaglen (Oscar winner, *The Informer*, 1935) all in one.

In cinema, the hand is quicker than the eye. Film editors are masters at laying out fight scenes that move so fast viewers have no think or focus time. But a second look at a fight will show flaws, mismatches, and stand-ins wearing wigs and dresses. In Red River, John Wayne has a showdown scene with diminutive Monty Clift. To even the odds, John Ireland cripples Wayne by shooting a gun out of his hand.

In 1962, Blake Edwards directed *Experiment In Terror*, marking the start of Martial Arts in American cinema. Parker was a stunt man for the film and his cadre appeared in it. Blake studied with a Parker aid. One day I heard Blake say to the aid over the shower wall, *Come with me to San Francisco. You can teach me karate during breaks.* There was silence followed by gagging, a fake cough, and I nearly blurted, *Take me!* Later the aid says, *I'm chewing a toothpick and almost swallow it. The cough's something I saw in a movie.* Wu and the cadre were anxious to see their scene and we went to a Westwood showing. Detective Glen Ford goes to Chinatown for clues to a killer terrorizing Lee Remick by telephone. The big *scene* comes when Ford walks in on their work out in a Chinese Physical Culture Society. It moved like figures at a railroad station from a passing train. It was their stop, they wanted to get off, but the train kept going to hoots and hollers. In later movies, Blake would spoof Martial Arts with Peter Sellers as loopy Clouseau battling his Asian valet.

Otto Preminger once told me he didn't give a part to an actor who read with sensitivity because he *drops his voice. If the audience can't hear a line the scene is lost. I have three weeks to rehearse. I have no time to teach.* Ditto Frankenhiemer, whose focus was on completing a movie on budget, not discovering talent. In the final cut, Sinatra and Sylva bull through a half-assed karate fight like flatfooted bantamweights with bad form. In Hollywood, truth and art are coincidental.

Sidebar: Around that time Ed gave private lessons at different times to Robert Wagner and Warren Beatty. *They were getting ready,* says Ed with a twinkle in his eye, *in case push comes to shove over Natalie Wood.* He got a kick out of mimicking Beatty. *He has a habit of crinkling his eyes. I come inside to demonstrate a block, he pulls off and squints like something's in his eyes. It was nerves. But he also wears contact lenses and is afraid of getting hit in the face. He makes a living with his face.* All along Ed chuckles, squints, and punches weakly, head held back.

One day Joe Hyams came in for a private lesson, but had something bigger on his mind. *Ed, feast your eyes on this.* It was the first of four settlement checks from a counter suit he'd won when Cary Grant sued him for libel. Ed's eyes widened. It was a quarter of a million dollars.

When Nick Adams was starring in *Saints and Sinners* for MGM TV, Ed visited him on the set and I followed along. The sound stage looked like a madhouse, people crawling all over like ants at a picnic; cameramen, boom men, gaffers, sound men, lighting techs, set movers, stand-ins, script girls, an assistant director, the director. The logistics alone were mind-boggling. The madness came together when the director yelled, *Quiet on the set! Ready and Action!*

On a break Nick waves to Ed and comes over. A bit player who had screwed up a scene several times stops by. *Get your lines down before coming in,* says Nick. *Too many goofs get you a reputation as unreliable, and then nobody'll hire you. Time's money, pal. I went over my lines at five this morning on a plane from Vegas after being up all night.* Shooting resumes on an office set with a portly actor reminiscent of Charles Laughton in voice and body. I forget his name but I'd seen him at DP. He was an actor with great stage presence, impeccable delivery, stood foursquare in his space, and I sensed a character with history, i.e., he'd been somewhere and had somewhere else to go. He did not use stage technique, but played the camera the way Nancy Coleman once explained to me her method in film. *Play big on long shots; small on close-ups.* The man was what acting is all about. Commanding attention.

Around noon we joined Nick for lunch in the old MGM cafeteria where many film stars had dined, laughed, cried, come and gone. Was this the room Gable entered, I wondered, after a long seclusion following Carol Lombard's death in a plane crash? They say she was Gable's kind of woman; beautiful, smart, and elegant with a fishwife's mouth. Her death devastated him and he just disappeared. Then, one day he walked into MGM's cafeteria, and the place went silent. They say, you always know when Gable's in a room. It lights up. He goes to his usual table. Then, one by one his colleagues stood up and applauded. The King was back! What were they cheering? Life and the guts to go on. God! Maybe I'm sitting at the King's table. Gable died in 1954, after filming *The Misfits*.

At the table were Ed, Nick, Joe Hyams, Robert Vaughn, who would make a bid for president in 1966, and Hershel Bernardi of *Peter Gunn* fame. With that last name, I wondered, is he Italian? Somebody says, not with Herschel for a first name. Maybe half Italian. Bernardi, a gifted raconteur, had us in stitches telling Sholem Alechim stories. Later, he would do a one-man show based on Alechem's work. Robert Wagner stopped by to say hello. He has the marble face of David, I think. If he laughs it'll crack. Suddenly, I imagine him toe-to-toe with rival Warren Beatty, two guys who trade on looks, squinting, heads held back.

"Oh, yeah?"
"Yeah!"
"Says who?"
"Says me!"
"Oh, really?"
"No. O'Reilly!"
"You're cruising for a bruising!"
"You're begging for a wooden kimono!"
"I'm using that in my next picture."
"What, a still?
"I'll still you."
"Your mother wears combat boots."
"Your father's mustache! Step outside."
"Now you're a director? Learn to act first."
"I got a part for you. Down the middle of your head!"
"Take off your contacts!"
"The face is off limits."
"Yours is off the wall!"
"Kiss my ass!"
"I don't do X movies!"
"Sez you."
"Sez me!"
"You and your mother."
"Leave Natalie out of this."

Later, walking to a sound stage, Robert Vaughn tells an anecdote about a dinner he had at the home of Natalie Wood and Robert Wagner. *They hired a British butler who was so proper and elegant, he scared them. They'd ask for something and then get it themselves while he stood looking very British, very proper, and very bored.*

At dinner they asked for breadsticks. The butler arches an eyebrow, says, 'Very well. Bread sticks. Will there be anything else?' 'No. That's it.' Over dessert, Natalie whispers, 'Bob, ask him to pour me coffee.' Bob says, 'You ask. You want the coffee.' They smile at the butler standing by. He looks down his nose at them. Bob says, 'It's okay, honey. I'll do it. He starts to pour, the butler clears his throat, says, 'Serve from the left, sir. Pour from the right.' And looks off like he'd been waylaid on his way to Windsor Castle. Bob whispers to me, 'We're thinking of asking him if we could have a night off.'

17. Eddie Albert's Stained Glass Nose

Diary, 1963: *The Lieutenant, MGM TV.* Playwright Arthur Miller: the end is prefigured in the beginning. John Dewey: the first five years determine a life. The Greeks cut deeper. Hamartia or *fate,* a character flaw. Frankly, the older I get, the more I see it in my own life.

Joe Hyams helped me get a job on *The Lieutenant* TV show that featured alternating leads each week: Gary Lockwood, Rick Jason, and Robert Vaughn. I directed a fight scene between guest Eddie Albert and a soldier. Later, Eddie starred with Ava Gabor in their TV hit *Green Acres.*

Eddie was genuine, down to earth, and unassuming; just the nicest guy you'd ever want to meet. I doubt he had a violent bone in his entire body. We had a preliminary script meeting at his Pacific Palisades home between LA and Santa Monica Beach. Eddie lived in an unpretentious ranch style home set among trees and shrubs, the very personification of Eddie himself; cool and laid back from the main road. Margo, his genteel wife, served refreshments on the patio. It was my first job. I was nervous, but Eddie was polite and receptive.

Karate is fighting with an economy of moves. *Is it Japanee Samurai?* Same ethics. Comes from China. *Well, okay. What do I do?* When I showed him a sequence of moves, Eddie gave me a look I'd seen him do in movies, a sheepish smile like he gets the drift but not the meaning. Once he moved I foresaw trouble. A far cry from agile Douglas Fairbanks Sr., for whom there was no such thing as a wild stunt, Eddie lacked coordination, which could be dangerous even to himself.

On the way out, Eddie shows off his hobby. Thank God it was passive. When not acting, singing, or playing guitar he designed stained glass panes framed with backlight. Several of them were mounted on his den wall like mini versions of church windows. *Exactly,* he said, taking us to his worktable where he had bins containing shards of glass varying in size and color. Using narrow lead strips that folded on two sides with a silver binder in between, he joined the glass shards by soldering them together. *The trick is to pick the right colors and apply the correct degree of heat without cracking the glass or making a mess. That one on the wall is my favorite. I was working and accidentally knocked over some glass. What you see framed is the pattern the glass formed when it broke on the floor. I just sealed it with lead and voilá! I love it!*

Scene: Chattesworth, Ventura, MGM's location for exteriors. Rolling hills, rock outcroppings, copses, ravines, and tumbleweeds. During *The Lieutenant* shoot I became friends with an attractive lady, age 24, an extra who did stunts, stand-ins, and rode horses. She reminded me of the sister in Gene Autry's Phantom Empire with the Radio Riders on Radio Ranch and the Phantom Riders who lived underground. The Radio Riders were kids whose motto was *To the Rescue!* I wanted to be a Radio Rider. When I wrote to Gene Autry my mom said, *In the real west cowboys don't ride horses. They* *pick spinach in the field in the hot sun.* A decade later in Chattesworth, directing Eddie by a ravine, I expected to hear the Phantom Riders thundering out of their secret cave raiding spinach fields. The only thunder I heard was Eve in her Mercedes.

I don't recall the extra's name. So I'll call her Jean, after Autry. She'd grown up on a horse farm in Nevada. She put me at ease on the set, and offered me friendship. Sometimes I get mad at myself for letting it all slip away. *Look,* she says pointing into the distance. *Those riders following the wagon? The camera's in the wagon. The riders are extras, stand-ins, doing long shots for the stars of Gunsmoke. I did that the other day.*

While Eddie was open to direction, his opposite was locked into the John Wayne round house school of fighting. Gary Lockwood, an ex- stunt man, saw my problem and said in an aside, *When it's not working I take control. Otherwise your reputation ends up on the cutting room floor.*

The two men would be fighting by a ravine down which they'd fall and continue battling. I demonstrate karate blocks, punches, and a mule kick. *A what kick?* Hit Eddie with a claw fist. *A what fist?* A tiger's paw. *A John Wayne's better.* Shove your palm under his chin. When Eddie grabs you from behind, elbow him in the gut and turn to hit him. Eddie blocks, shoves you down, goes for you. You mule kick. He falls back. You tackle him and you both tumble down the ravine. *Lemme hit him a John Wayne!*

Roll! Action! At the bottom of the ravine the stunt guy comes up with a John Wayne to the face, catches Eddie flatfooted, and he drops like a sack of potatoes. Great! Only Eddie's not getting up. *Cut!* He's holding his nose, but not unconscious. *You okay? Gee, I don't know. I'll get an ice pack.* The bridge of Eddie's nose was bruised, and slightly bleeding, but not broken. Meanwhile, the next scene sets up and the producer says, *Tone down the fighting. I got a directive from New York. Limit violence and no blood.* Lockwood yells from the ravine. *That's Mickey Mouse bullshit! A fight without blood's worse than a dry hump!*

Gary was right. Thinking back to that shoot makes me anxious and claustrophobic. Eve was right, too. I was never "your average Hollywood hopeful." I'm a Radio Rider on the cusp of glory with spinach in my hair. For a while we all live forever.

The last day of the shoot, Eve meets me as I come off the back lot of MGM, Culver City. In the lobby of a wooden building that serves as a gateway, I was among extras, the assistant director Eric Von Stroheim Jr., and the tech crew. I introduce Eve to Jean. I wanted us to be friends, meet later over supper, and swap ideas. Suddenly, Eve flies into a jealous rage, everybody freezes, and I'm shocked. I wanted to disappear. Mr. Karate, pussy-whipped by a crazy redhead with a Mercedes Benz. I'm sure what happened was not new to those film veterans, but it destroyed me. I wouldn't understand it for years.

Looking back, I'm proud that I did the show, worked for Parker, and didn't kill Eve, or anyone else I met in the entanglements accompanying her peripatetic, drug and boozie nightlife. What I perceived as a godsend was a shrike. Beneath every caress was a kick in the balls. From then on I turned inward in a slow, living suicide that by degrees destroyed my Hollywood career, and eventually my dreams of being a disc jockey. To do anything in life, wrote ex-slave Fredrick Douglas, you have to assert yourself or you will be beaten down and judged less than a man. I never wanted to judge or hurt anybody. As a kid I remember crying because I regretted bloodying a bully's nose. Winning is less important than self-assertion. *Take charge, pal, or you end up on the cutting room floor.*

In 2005 Eddie Albert, age 99, succumbed to Alzheimer's. His son held his hand to the end. I would've. Eddie was that kind of a man.

18.   Captain Karate

I arrived in LA with no keys. The more keys you have, the wealthier you are. Soon I had two keys, one to Parker's place, and the other to a Volkswagen with a drawback canvas top purchased from a newspaper ad. A fun car while it lasted. I'd go to Venice in Santa Monica, park on a side street, sit in the back, and write. I created Captain Karate, stunt man/fight scene choreographer and problem solver. I anticipated by 10 years what became known as *Chop Socky potboilers.* Meanwhile, Bruce Lee, four years younger, was moving toward Hollywood. Where I was Marco Polo knocking at the Great Wall, Bruce was China itself.

I designed Martial Arts jewelry, turned the gi into pajamas with a black belt. I had bed sheets with snake and dragon prints, slippers or "kicks" with tiger heads and fists, chopstick darts, metal stars, spikes, snake rings, and "Tiger Palm," an herbal ointment for healing skin. On Eve's patio in Benedict Canyon I strung up a punching bag connected by elastic to the ground and the roof eave designed to sharpen reflexes. Its unpredictability when struck sharpened reaction. Blink and it would hit you. I split the Tai Chi Chuan double fish head symbol into his and her halves by separating the yin-yang symbol along the curved inside line. The result was two tear drops that I called the Tai Chi Lover's Pendant. The idea enervates me to this day. Back then I knew in my gut that Kung Fu would capture the American imagination. Eve was already into it.

"How'd you bruise your leg?" I go at the outset of a lesson. *Bumped it.*

"On what?" *My husband.* I think, stop, but she looks and smells too good. So I head for my own Barrymore *bus accident.* Sinatra licked Ava's shit, shooting guns from a car in the desert. *Welcome to the club, kiddo.*

That first night in the Canyon, on her couch after dinner with Ray Charles on the phonograph; Strega in black coffee; a fire in the hearth; light flickering off her beautiful alabaster face with salmon Latin lips, unapproachable like a Goddess. Do I dare kiss them; chance offending her? What would it feel like to kiss that face, those sensual lips? Would lightening strike me? Would a detective hired by her husband snap a picture through the window? But a hard dick has no fear. Strega in the blood overcame nerves. I move in and she doesn't resist. My God! We're embracing. Oh, God! Ambrosia lips; tongue of nectar; *A Rainy Day in Georgia.* Eve in my loins; breasts of pink carnations; rose petals falling all around. The desert guns of Sinatra and Ava pale in the Canyon hills, and I'm a bloody Barrymore bus-capade waiting to happen.

One night Eve and I were at a Beverly Hills party hosted by some cuckoo group therapy pal - a highball happy screwball who buried two husbands, and was working on a third, an accountant at Paramount. Eve was torched when we showed up late straight from supper in Malibu. She melted into the boozy crowd like it was family while I stood apart. I'd catch glimpses of her; a tumbler of straight scotch in one hand, bottle in the other, and laughing like her pending divorce was nonexistent.

When men heard I was in Martial Arts it aroused curiosity in some, and machismo in others. The latter were mostly creeps who thought karate was Japanese ballet. My ass is in a chair by a window for easy egress. I'm thinking like Bette Davis, What a dump! Waiting on

Eve to toss in the towel could go to sunrise. In the back of my head, I began realizing I was fighting a losing battle with a punchy broad with two personalities. What drew the crowd was her sexuality and Rita Heyworth looks. Later, I characterized our relationship as shades of Lucy and Desi, only Eve was Desi. She never knew when to go home. We'd be dressed to go out. I'd say, *Let's not close the bar* and she'd go ballistic. *We're not out the door and already you've ruined the night. Goddamn killjoy!*

Nights were always main events in restaurants or one-arm joints from Beverly Hills to Chinatown to Rosarita Beach. She'd dance, back peddle, and sidestep her devils with pills and booze. No amount of coaxing from the corner helped. She'd fall on her face before quitting. Between rounds she'd hit the john for a second wind, pop pills, and come back fresh as a daisy while I'm holding up my eyelids with swizzle sticks. *Night is when the devil finds you. So keep bobbin' and weavin'. Get caught flatfooted he's gotcha. Sleep? What's the guarantee you will wake up?* She dreaded, *Hurry up, please. It's time!* Or, *Last call! Going home? I am home! Tell you what, Mr. Bar Tenderfoot. I'll buy the place.* She was Doris Duke, Rita, and Ava combined. One barfly was reduced to tears when I said, *The lady's leaving with me.* Nights were *Who's Afraid of Virginia Woolf* ending in the last scene of *Streetcar Named Desire.*

The beach ball in front of me is holding a cheese cutter in a stubby hand; a four-eyes with jalopy blues magnified by thick lenses. He hadn't seen his dick in years.

"Have a seat, Sancho," I go.

"Why?" he says, rocking on his heels. "You wanna hold hands?"

"It's a shorter distance when you fall."

"Look. R-rock steady." Before he raises his hand I have it by the wrist.

"Ah," I go, sniffing the cheese cutter, "Gorgonzola. 1957. I believe." Then I imagine puncturing his panetone belly with two snake fingers and seeing him jet backwards around the room like a deflating balloon.

"You don't look tough."

"That's the secret," I go releasing his wrist.

"What secret?"

"Of appearances."

"'Pearances?" he says leaning in. "What, a Chinese riddle?"

"Take yourself. You look drunk."

"But I'm not."

"Exactly."

"It's an a-pearance," he says, slurring words. "Underneath I'm sober-er-er than a Jewish church mouse." He wobbles like he's going to fall on me so I gird myself. "You're the one's drunk!" he says. "That's why you're sittin'. Can't hold your booze. I can hold mine. See?" He slaps his caldron belly. "I'm only giving the 'pearance I'm drunk."

"Don't fall on that cheese cutter or you'll end up circumcised twice."

"Know what they do with the f-foreskin fr-from circumcised Jews? Plant 'em and they grow up to be Italians. I box, y'know. Numbers. Yes. Squeeze n' crunch the suckers till they cry. Numbers don't lie. It's pipple who don't add up. One plus one equals three. What you see *ain't* what you get. Poople think I'm Eye-talian cause my name's Marciano, but I'm no spaghetti bender. I'm a Jew from NYU. Ha! A black guy goes to a doctor cause he's turned white from the neck up. The doctor goes out, mixes a prescription, returns, says, Drink this. The black guy drinks it, says, Jesus! It tastes like shit. The doctor says, It is. You're down a quart." He laughs and stumbles into the crowd.

Meanwhile, Eve's swimming the room like a somnambulant doing Tai Chi, or a snake looking for someone to bite. She comes to me. "Let's push hands." It's a Tai Chi exercise with two people facing each other palm to elbow, wrist to wrist, rocking back and forth feeling each other out for the center of gravity. "Let's push off instead?" I go. "Too early," she says.

A guy looms up, smoke in one hand, drink in the other. "You're the Karate man," he goes, measuring me. "Last time I looked it was the 20th century, not medieval Japan. Bathrobes and swords went out with samurai and incense. What's it called, those knitting needles they stick in themselves?" *Acupuncture.* "Puncture's right," he goes inching closer, his stinking cigarette in my face. "You one of them masochists?" *No. I'm a sadist.* "Come again?" *I shove cigarettes up people's asses to stem the meridian flow of bullshit.* "In a bar what're the odds you'll meet a guy in a kimono carrying a Samurai sword? I got a kimono. Never wear it. The sleeves keep knocking over drinks, catching on doorknobs and pot handles. On stairs you can hook your foot in the hem, trip, and bust your ass. Show me something." *Come to a class.* "Can Karate take Joe Louis? Is it faster than a bullet? One good thing about kimonos. They're big. You can hide a hard-on." *Yeah. Lots of things except a big mouth.*

Eve comes up, bats her lovelies at him. "Do you know Tai Chi?" He says, "Never met her." She says, "Lucky. She's a deceptive lady." He says, "Aren't they all." Eve starts to show him push-hands, which he takes for dancing. As he leans forward to grab her, she bends at the waist, he falls forward, bangs his head on the windowsill and gives himself a freebee map to the stars. As I head out, the accountant's standing on the kitchen table playing sword swallower with the cheese cutter. He mimes slicing himself across the crotch while singing, "Don't know why; There's no meat behind my fly; Cockeyed Rabbi." An old Brooklyn joke.

We got home around 5, rose at noon on another of many long days and nights filled with uppers and downers, Librium and Spancils, Milltown's and Rob Roys. When Eve insisted on going out, I threw her car keys into the ivy garden overlooking Benedict Canyon Road. She called the police. When they arrived I was hiding on the roof. I recall thinking, *I'll leap on them like Lenny Bruce imagined himself doing from a bar top to a couple of anti-Semites. Only instead of yelling, "Shazam! Super Jew," I'll go, "Shazam! Captain Karate!" Fortunately, I understood that they were* not the "reel" Keystone Cops, but real LA police. Then my mother's face appeared, soulful and calming. It's my father's face that gets me climbing roofs. Between them it's a whiz-bang Yin-Yang effect. So, I stay quietly in place and avoid headlines I'd never live to read.

NINJA NUT SHOT IN BUTT!
KARATE *IS* SLOWER THAN A SPEEDING BULLET!
CAPTAIN KARATE PLUNGES FROM ROOF, BREAKS FALL WITH HEAD

The cops leave. Eve searches the ivy for her keys. I drop down at her feet, scare the shit out of her, she screams, runs into the house, and returns holding a spare set of car keys. "Ha," she goes. "Ha," I go, grab them, fling them into the ivy, drop into a horse, and go, "You want to mess with Captain Karate? Mucho Hombre con Cahones Grande!" She shouts, "I'll crush your cahones grande!" I laugh; taunt her, "Toro! Toro!" while dangling two sets of car keys in her face. Enraged, she charges me. I mimic largos, farols, veronicas, and a pase de pecho. "Olé! " She snorts, "It's No-lay, Jose, esta noche!" An hour later we're in her candy apple red 1960 Mercedes-Benz, 280 SL, top down, wind in our faces, flying down to Rosarita Beach into the arms the mariachi and a thousand violins.

☺

19.   *Lucy*

Scene: Malbu. June 12th, my birthday. I'm broke, but feel like Marco Polo sitting on a firecracker called Martial Arts. Over cocktails at a Beverly Hills piano bar, Eve looks ravishing. Her red hair, hazel eyes and rosy cheeked, white skin blend with the yellow twist and golden Rob Roy at her scarlet lips. A couple of drinks later we're in the Malibu Pier, our favorite seafood restaurant. On the way we had a quickie on the beach road around Las Flores. The clear water in Malibu, unlike Santa Monica and Venice, reminded me of Hawaii. Looking out at the ocean from Malibu, nothing behind me exists. The Pier was casual dress, a far cry from crust sandwiches at the U of H snack bar. The ambiance was subdued, and romantic with a captain's table and chair décor, and side booths illumined by sconces and candle centerpieces.

As usual Steve Golden, my student and friend, was at the piano, and winked as we came up following the maitre d' to our table. Before Eve, Steve and I would hit the jazz spots like Rumson's Lighthouse, Hermosa Beach, and some LA jazz club featuring Herbie Mann and a little known but funny jive talking trumpet player Jack Sheldon. As we go by the piano Eve says something to Steve, and slips money into his lapel pocket. He nods gratefully, pink spidery fingers on white ivory never missing a note. Steve's over six feet tall, has black hair worn in a pomp reminiscent of Artie Shaw, and likewise has a jaded perspective on work, women, love, and audiences- they're loud, boorish oafs always asking for repeats. Steve's speech is laidback, lazy west coast jazz jargon tinged with humor drier than a martini. Gigs on the road are bummers. Guys are "dudes" and "cats," gals are "skirts" and "chicks," and cars are "wheels" and "shorts." When he first walked in for lessons he says, *Man, teach me a shin kick. I get people bugging me at the keys; spilling drinks on my threads. Ya dig? My cleaning*

*bill's outa sight, man. Can you fix me up with a steel tip
shoe? Dig it. One kick'll keep the creeps away.*

One of our mutual friends is a bass player I'd met
in Hawaii when he came over with Anita O'Day. He'd
recently backed her at the Loser's Club, which had a
billboard outside announcing Loser of the Week. On April
15th the Loser of the Week was *Everybody*. Well, one day
during Steve's lesson said cat shags in talking like the
Loser of the Month.

"Been turned outa my pad. Catchin' zees in my
Jag."

"Oh, man!" says Steve. "The pits!"

"Where's your bass?" I go.

"Back seat of my short, man." He points outside to
his jaguar parked at the curb. "The neck of my ax is
sticking out the rear window. I'm living out of my glove
compartment."

"Man, that's the pits. How'd you find me?"

"The dregs, man. Your mom, man. Say, I hate to tap
you, man, but can you lay some skin on me?"

"Dude," says Steve, "I'm tapped out. Barely coverin'
my bones. Ya dig?"

The guy goes, "Oh, man. I hate to hock my ax again.
It's my bread and butter. I'm naked without it. Lucky
I don't play piano. I'd never get it in the back of my
short."

"Dig it, man," says Steve. "You should've taken up
flute. A definite downer living in your short in your
shorts."

Approaching Steve, I go, *How's the love life, dude?*
Arching an eyebrow, he goes, *Gone south, man. Didn't
want to do it sideways.* Then he lifts a leg indicating a
steel tip on his shoe and plays *Something to Remember
You By*. Like I say, he's a wry martini with an olive.

The window next to our table was a reverse painting
in chiaroscuro, reflecting us in flickering candlelight on a
backdrop of beach and white-capped black waves. Lovers

scamper in the sand, two bugs running up the window, overlaid by a shimmering waiter with our usual Rob Roys. Eve pops a pill, smiles, offers me one, I pass, and she salutes me. *Happy Birthday, darling.* Our eyes meet over rims of gold liquid, lemon twists, murmuring voices, tinkling silverware, and a lonesome piano. *Thanks.* I'd almost forgotten. We touch glasses. *Cent'anni!* Will we seize the moment; rise above death, which comes in quiet waves pulling time from us like grains of sand? The couple returns, fireflies in the glass, and disappears below. Eve, a dark-eyed, luscious rose full of candlelight, moonbeams and stars. It would take years to find words to explain what happened. Reason gives way to passion and existence is a tweak of desire to be more than water dissolving in sand. The lovers are back, pants rolled up, dress held high, demi-gods kicking the receding waves then back pedaling as new ones roll in. *Catch us if you can! You sudsy-headed fogy.* They fall into each other's arms- Kerr and Lancaster in *From Here To Eternity*- hot loins simmering at the hem of a chuffy ocean.

What are you thinking? asks Eve. Thinking? The balloon man whistles far and wee. Inclining her head with a fetching look, she says, *Oh, so serious. Let's not be serious tonight. Let's be happy, careless idiots.* She hands me a gift: a set of heavy gold cuff links and a large, gold snake ring with sapphire eyes. I look long at her, candlelight dancing in her eyes and I'm lost for words. Everything I wanted was there with Eve in Malibu off the Pacific Coast Highway not far from another haunt of ours at Topanga Beach. We were on the brink of a new perspective in the fight game ready to hit the screen. It was a unique moment, like being born.

Let's open a Karate studio, says Eve. Where? *North LA. A Thousand Oaks or Ventura.* It was a great idea. Yet something told me, stick to being a DJ. Eve was always on the go, an alcoholic pill freak. *We could split off from Parker in a franchise. Or, go it alone.* I reach across the table to take her hand and find it holding a black velvet box. *A down payment on us.* I want to keep its contents secret, frozen in time, like this night in Malibu. Was I a DJ, or Captain Karate?

Eve had taken one of my ideas to her Beverly Hills jeweler and created what I called the Tai Chi Lover's Pendant. She split the double fish along the inside curve and turned it into two pieces. One half was silver, the other black onyx with a diamond for each fish eye. No dollar value can be placed on an original idea that works. The pendant was a glimpse of a potential future that would take guts to carve out. The diamond fish eyes flash in the light. Every step in life's a decision, a battle to hold on. Mix in soft silken hair, feminine heat and it's catching waves in your mouth.

Steve broke the spell with *Happy Birthday*, as our waiter came up with a cake. The whole joint started singing, I made a wish, blew out the candles, and Steve segued to *The First Time Ever I Saw Your Face.*

I wanted a foot in the movie business and Karate was my stepping-stone. In 1963 I had hold of something old from the east but new in the west. I stood behind Ed Parker introducing MA to America through Hollywood, an exciting alternative to anemic westerns and trite gangster stories with guns and roundhouse punches. MA had the stuff of legends, and Ed was becoming one himself.

I often wonder where I might've ended up had Eve been healthy. Me, too, for that matter. I was fighting my way into Hollywood. Life is such that when you don't know what you have people will take it from you. The Greeks call it *thay-say-fane.* They will eat you alive, and you won't know it. Parents do it to their children, public schools continue the job, and society and business complete the burial. Intentional? Yes. Human nature weeds out the weak. It's our MO, the horror that Joseph Conrad and Eugene O'Neill wrote about. The truth under self-deception is urban cannibalism in the guise of cocktail talk.

Christ! I couldn't see two fuckin' feet in front of me. One night, Eve and I were standing at the bar of the Chianti Ristorante, serving northern Italian cuisine; one of those small, inconspicuous, but elegant, shirt and tie restaurants. Call up for reservations. Walk in off the street, better have deep pockets. That night the Chianti was busting at the seams with the Hollywood set. Eve and I we're wedged in at the bar sipping cocktails while waiting on a table. I was so infatuated with her that we might as well've been alone on a desert island. I don't know what I was drinking, probably that gasoline with the fancy name Rob Roy. I was upset and fulminating over her life-style, which was dragging me down. *How the hell're we going to run a Karate business if every night we're closing some bar and rolling in at sunrise?* After we're seated, she asked if my anger was posturing. *What're you talking about?* We were standing next to Marlin Brando. *No. He was standing next to me.* He was just back from shooting *Mutiny On the Bounty.* We had that in common. Soon I'd be jumping ship myself. But for now, my balls were duty bound to the vaginal colors, but in the back of my mind was the slow realization I'd signed on with a female Blye. I could've cared less about Brando. Just like when I ran into Steve McQueen in a Westwood Ristorante. I looked in his face and never saw him. Why should I? At the time, I was with Nancy Kovac. I could've cared less. In my gut was Karate and Kung Fu, which Hollywood couldn't even spell, let alone pronounce. Cully Jimson. That was me. A Joyce Carey character wavering between prison, poverty, and art. A cuttle fish among sharks. Now it's all far off like Hawaii itself, but at times it comes back fresh as an island sea breeze.

In 1962 the University of Hawaii was just building the East/West Center. Its concept is what Ed Parker brought to Hollywood via Martial Arts. I'm proud to say I helped take that first step eastward on *The Lucy Show*, episode, 'Lucy and Viv Learn Judo', which aired February 25, 1963. It marks the start of Marshal Arts in America. Dick Martin, of *Laugh-In,* was featured in that show. He was easy going and curious about Karate. I go, *I have an epileptic student. He's dangerous because I can't tell when he's practicing Karate or having a fit.* Later on, Karate became comedy shtick. *Hear about the soldier who had a Karate black belt? He forgot, saluted and knocked himself out.*

Ed Parker got a call for *The Lucy Show* and I was to be his assistant. We were to play ourselves as in real life. The storyline had Lucy coming to Parker's Studio-Gym for self-defense to protect herself from burglaries in her neighborhood. Because comedy requires quickly understood images, the writers called the episode "Lucy and Viv Learn Judo" instead of Karate not to confuse it with carrots, diamonds, or the carotid vein.

How I got on *The Lucy Show* had its Hollywood twist. Desilu called Ed in December, 1962 to shoot in January. My mom sent me some money. I flew home for Christmas and surprised her with the news, the best gift I ever gave my mother. I remember landing in New York in the snow, being greeted by my family in huge winter coats and scarves- we were young and together then- and my crazy old man looking like a cross between Walter Huston and Khrushchev in a big, black furry Russian wool hat. For a second I thought I'd landed in Moscow.

Show business is *full of letdowns.* Returning to Hollywood Ed tells me Desilu hired someone else. My heart sank. How would I explain it to my folks back home? Late in the afternoon on the first Monday of the show's rehearsal I was glum-faced in Murray's. He says, *Listen, my fine-feathered Schissel. You and I, we're paisans, Jews and Italians. You hold on. Hear me? What you want you'll get if ya want it bad enough.* Next thing

Parker plunks himself down next to me. Murray says, *Comin' up. Water with a shot of 2 cents plain.* Ed drops a script on the counter, smells my coke and says he's off the show. *They want a more experienced actor.* I'm sorry to hear that. On the title page of the script was my name. Ed says, *It was your script before they hired the other guy, who, by the way, has two left feet.* I go, now they'll have four. Murray brings Ed's drink; he lifts it for a toast. I go, to what? *To us,* he says. I go, right. To us. *Never say die.* Then, he smiles, and says, *Meet me at Desilu-Gower tomorrow first call 7AM, unless you have other plans. The other guy was bad.* I start to punch his shoulder, think again, and slap the counter, yelling, *Professor Murray-ority! One schissel with honey!*

The Lucy Show was done live on three sets with three cameras before an audience seated in bleachers. A fourth camera rolled on a continuous sound loop to match everything. Desi's initiative here revolutionized TV. But Christine Costello says, *it was Charles Barton, director of Abbott and Costello, who first used three cameras to keep spontaneity alive.*

On the show I pull Lucy by the arm in a dizzying circle, throw her down, and punch her. She looks up wide-eyed and in awe. America's first reaction to this strange fighting style, more Karate than Judo. Ed breaks some boards with his hand. Lucy tries it and gets laughs just looking from the board to the audience, to say, *my poor hand.* She measures the board with those big blues Desi loved. Then, strikes it, and screams in holy pain. The crowd roars, she blows on her hand, shakes it, and milks the laughs. I wait for the down curve of laughs before moving.

Afterward, I spent hours at Desilu looking through photos for a good shot of the four of us. Any picture that didn't enhance Lucy had a big black circle stamped on her face. Finally, I find one and Ed says, *I see you got one that makes you look good.* I thought it was the best picture I could get under the circumstances. The real mistake was not getting it autographed by everyone. Now, they're all gone but me.

One time I was behind Lucy when a blonde extra cut across the set pushing a baby carriage. Lucy yells to the director, "Hey, Jack! Who's it this week, blondes? Last week it was redheads!" The blonde kept walking and never looked back. Messing with Lucy was a no-no.

Vivian Vance's performances as second banana to Lucy are second to none. After the show, she wild tracked tongue twisting commercials on camera without a mistake. She was genuine, and appreciative of a book I gave her (and Lucy) called the *Art of Love* by Eric Frome. *Oh, honey,* she goes, *I read it every night before bed.* When I said, in college I minored in psychology before dropping out, she said, *That's very good, honey. Go back. Finish your degree. The world needs more psychiatrists.* In the late forties Vivian had been hospitalized with a nervous breakdown.

If anybody needed help it was Eve. She was a touchy-feely, Jekyll and Hyde tinderbox; at night a nocturnal dipsomaniac with moonlight devils only booze and drugs could silence. When the moon was out Mother Teresa turned hellion. Drink and pills made bearable the overhanging darkness, but the side effects were erratic. Every night in giro- *on the go,* swilling Rob Roys and straight scotch. Worst of all it hurt me with Parker. I dreaded evenings in the Casa di Escobar downing Marguerites, or our latest haunt in LA's Chinatown. She'd latch onto the maitre d', the bartender, anybody who could talk her to the next drink. It pained her to hear T.S. Eliot's *HURRY UP, PLEASE. IT'S TIME.*

☺

20.   Chinatown, LA

Sundays Eve and I studied Tai Chi at the China Press offices. While there I met wiley Professor Ark J. Wang who ran a trading company at 300 Ord Street, New Chinatown, LA. His Martial Arts business card read: Karate, Tai Chi Chuan, Gung-Fu, Lion and Dragon Acting, WAH QUE STUDIO, General Conditioning, Self-Defense. Instructors: Leon, Wing, and Jung. Classes were repetitive with little practical application and no division according to ability. He showed his instructors moves piecemeal and let them practice unsupervised. More on that to come.

A student's life is a rich man's game. To learn, one must take several classes weekly, which is costly. In old China it was taught to the upper class because they had money and time. Rich or poor, then and now, the trick to advancing is to gain the master's confidence, and then get invited into his inner circle as an apprentice. For a master the big question is, who to trust? For example, what went down in Hawaii between Ed and Professor Chow, others did to Ed.

Chinatown, LA was pre-Disney, a hypnotic fantasy village of warrens and courts packed full of book and postcard stalls, restaurants, bars, variety shops, pagodas, water fountains, a wishing well, herbal dealers, glittering red and gold boutiques of Chinese sundries- good luck charms, jewelry, and incense to burn for Qwan Yin, Lao Tsu, and warrior gods. Inside the main entrance to Chinatown was an import store with gold lions guarding the entrance and two red pillars supporting a Romeo and Juliet balcony encircled by dragons. From within I often heard moon harp music. Years later I fancied that it might've been in such a place in Hong Kong where Bruce Lee died in 1972. Was it the family daemon, revenge of a peer by way of the silken embrace of Betti and opium, or the Chinese elders striking back for breaking the Kung

Fu code of silence? There have been great advances in forensics since then. Exhumation and examination might prove one of several scenarios: a brain hemorrhage; substance abuse; poison. Allegedly, Lee was acquainted with a dealer from whom he may have bought drugs. It is further alleged Lee used cortisone and hashish to relax and alleviate back pain; anabolic steroids, a deadly equagesic tablet possibly ingested at Betty Pei's. Taken together, the drugs interact with chilling results. Place of death suggests mistress. Documents in Lee's belongings point to steroids and marijuana. Myths of heroes are better than reality, perhaps necessary even if false.

The Chinese man in white linen sitting opposite us was a mysterious, skinny version of Detective Charlie Chan. He orders pan-fried noodles, cracks a raw egg over it, and douses it with vinegar for *easy digestion*. Eve reacts to this Asian sphinx like he was an old friend. All I want to do is kick his skinny ass. But I was in Charlie Chan's territory. He was no friend, but a dealer, and we'd only met recently in Tai Chi class at the China Press. He was in his 60's, wore a silk shirt and tie, rolled an ancient piece of green jade in one hand, and kept a cigarette burning in the other- smoking it like it was Monroe's tit. He remains a stranger to me, but not to Eve who seems to share something in common with him. I couldn't figure it out unless it was a hollow leg. They both drink like fish. But Charlie Chan was pushing drugs out of his Import Store with the moon harp balcony. Their conversation eludes me because of the general din of chatter and music, and a certain resistance I'd developed to furtive Asian eyes based on Menehunies in Waikiki. Also, his Confucian homilies and adages put me off. *The hero dies once, the coward many times. People who sleep on hill not on the level.* I see him in a Chinese straw hat with pigtails: *One never knows what the truth might be.* Maybe he was trying to find out if I was her lover or an undercover cop? To me he was an elusive Chinaman who had more going for him under the table than on it. Ostensibly, he dealt in antiques, cheap artifacts, and herbs, but in truth he dealt in bootlegged booze and drugs. Eve was addicted to both. While her looks held most men's attention he was suspiciously aloof. I wanted to turn him upside down to see what fell out of his pockets. But giving into that impulse meant a nightly battle in Hollywood bars with me ending up in a hospital, DOA. Then, curiously, they both stepped out in tandem for the john. Around 3AM the family fun ended.

Eve and I left Chinatown through the back to a side street where we'd been parking lately. She got defensive when I said she was too drunk to drive. I had to run around to the passenger seat or she'd've driven off without me. In a fast u-turn she backs into a parked car, pulls out, goes through a stop sign, remembers to put on the headlights, and halfway down the next block we pass a patrol car. *Pull over,* I go. *If he comes back and you're behind the wheel-* She slams on the breaks. We switch places. A mile from Chinatown she grabs the steering arm. *I hate you! You son-of-bitch!* I pull into a deserted supermarket parking lot while looking out for cops. *Don't tell me calm down! I am calm! Get out of my car! Get out! Out! Out! Out.* It was a repeat performance of the drive to Dan Inocento's house. *Turn off the radio! It's not on. Then turn off the silence!* A car drives by. In the middle of more curses she says, *I love you.* Did I hear right? What's this? To me, love was a word in a foreign language. All I could do was sit and wonder. I think it's what boxers say in clinches to soften up an opponent for a knockout. I love you, kiss me, and then, boom! I go, the sun's coming up. Brilliant. But it was setting for me, except for the surprising 'I love you'. Another crazy, twisted night. They never end with her. Now it's hit 'im in the gut; one, two, I love you. Two nuts in a candy apple Mercedes dangling on a naked Christmas tree. Are we the first decoration up or the last one down? Is she Christmas Eve, or All

Hallows Eve, blotchy-eyed with mascara running down her pumpkin face? She gets out of the car and checks the back for damage. Kicks the bumper. I try to get her back inside. She hits me with her purse. *Ain't love grand!* Get in the car. *No!* Get in the car! *No!* The cop car's liable to come back. *Good! Lock me up and I'll throw away the key!* I get in the car hoping she'll follow. Suddenly I hit the accelerator, peel out, circle the lot, and head straight for her. Eve doesn't move. I jam on the brakes just short of her. She's unflinching lit up in the headlights, like a grotesque Breugel. I lean across the seat, open the passenger door, she gets in, says, *I love you.* I go, *I love you, too. Let's go home before the sun comes up and we melt.* Today, that scene'd be on a TV show called *Security Camera.*

One day while waltzing around Wah Que's, I looked in the mirror and saw a kid playing with a wooden sword who never grew up. No money, no job, a screwball girlfriend, and I'm a cardboard warrior living in the 12th Century Mung Bean Dynasty. I went for a walk.

Chinese weapons are fascinating in shape and purpose. One of the more dangerous is suon-gai-kwin, or nunchuks; essentially two sharp black jacks connected by a chain swung from the end or the middle- a combination sword, knife, dart, and club- a windmill with a shifting axis, the ends whipping about seemingly in self-flagellation. To go against it is to walk into an airplane propeller. In the west it was fencing, wrestling, boxing and guns. World War Two introduced Japanese jiu jitsu, but what was this Chinese madness?

I liked Sifu Wong, at first. I doubt the feeling was mutual. He had the affable public persona of a businessman, but underneath he was a hard, suspicious man with base interests. One day I realized I hadn't seen the nunchuk kid around. He had an accident. Automobile? *No. While playing* with *the suon-gai-kwin, he accidentally gave himself a bloody gash in the forehead.* Wong was wrong to let him use the real weapon instead of a rubber mock up in an unsupervised situation. It amounted to leaving a loaded gun in front of a child. After all, it is Martial Arts, although most of the time it's a pretend dance concert.

I lay low on the john floor of my studio apartment shared with pianist Steve Golden, in a bungalow in back of Eve's house off Easton Drive. Steve was out. Me, too. Out of my mind. Eve and I had a bigger than usual blowout. She called the police. Murmuring footsteps approach. Eve feeding them drunken nonsense. Fists pound the door. But I lay low under the sink not daring to breath. No Immaculee Ilebagiza playing footsies with Tutsis courting a machete, but close enough for my blood. *Hands try the knob. Somebody goes round and tries the sliding glass door. Locked. Thank God. I lay low, Brer rabbit ears perked, eyes darting from window to door, praying they go. Would they force entry without a search warrant? Could they have gotten one so fast? Only in B-movies. I was dancin' with myself in this one-arm Kenpo joint on La Cienega, playin' hello with my dick, when she walks in. Grade A bitch on the hoof. A hunk of feminine pulchritude with looks to kill. Parker points her to me. It was the beginning of the end. Voices recede. I lay low on the john floor hardly breathing, downing two fingers of red eye pussy-whip. A roach crossing the shower mat makes more noise than I do. The lucky bastard escapes through a crevice. Good thing Steve isn't around to open the door, or say, Told you, man. The chick's looped. You're Loser of the Week, dude.*

21. An American Lie

November 22, 1963; late morning. The radio's on in the background in the studio in back of Eve's house, which

I shared with Steve. I'm shaving and Steve's making his bed and joking about the fake bullhorns I'd bought with Eve in Rosarita Beach, Mexico. I'd put 'em up over the kitchen counter and he'd take 'em down.

"Tacky, man," he was saying, "dumb and tacky. Y'dig dumb?" Then, suddenly he stops cold, points to the radio, and raises the volume.

President Kennedy has been shot.

Years later everybody remembered where they were that day. Mal Terkel was in the newsroom next to editor Mort Danke, talking about granapadano; Stan Blather was 50 yards on the other side of the grassy knoll holding a yellow grapefruit bag; Reefer was in Houston covering a non-event; Ayn was teaching 5th grade, *a slow class, in a Catholic school in Crafton, PA. We were laughing, about what I don't remember.*

The President of the United States has been shot in Dallas.

"Oh, man!" cries Steve, face like a mouthful of vinegar. "There are some rank cats in this world."

Something wonderful went awry that day. It was not JFK, the rich, charismatic politician with more charm than substance, who died, but youth, vigor, and a myth. Ten years later, LBJ, out of office and nearing death, said the 'conspiracy' word, but gave no names. Even if the old codger had, then what? Revolution? "They" sealed up the evidence until 2038. Doubtless "they" will find reason to extend it. Was it Bay of Pigs payback; the military-industrial complex; the Castro brothers; mafia revenge to an ungrateful president? The mob swung Chicago and Virginia votes for JFK. *They shot the wrong Kennedy!* Whoever, whatever, that Dallas day the White House, where we had been resigned to old men, went dark, and with it a glimmer of invincibility, the death of hope, children underfoot in the oval office, and touch football on the White House lawn. Even in Camelot *there are rank cats.*

☺

22.   *A Few Good Questions*

Eve's car starts up. She's heading for the bars. I run out of the house, dash across the patio, leap a row of bushes, and land in front of her as she's pulling out of the carport onto Easton, a side street with a downhill grade to Benedict Canyon Road. She hits the brakes. I bang on the hood. She waves, *Move away!* Accelerates, and I jump on the hood. *Eve, wait! Don't go!* She swings a hard left onto Benedict Canyon, and I fly off like a dry leaf onto the road, rolling and twisting in the wake of the Mercedes. I roll quickly to the side. No bones broken. No on-coming cars. Down the road her tail disappears around the bend leading to Sunset Boulevard. My right hip stings, but it's just an abrasion with minor bleeding. Later, Eve would bathe it, kiss it, apologize, and we'd screw like crazy. Limping back to my pad I remember, I have a private Karate lesson in Bel Aire.

"But Maria, my gi's in the bedroom."

"Miss Eve, she say, no mas entrare." Eve told her Mexican maid to lock me out. Shades of Joe Castro and Doris Duke.

"Tu sabe, Maria" I go. "It'll be forgotten manana. I just want my gi."

"Make mucho problemi por me,' she says, holding her baby in her arms. "Si, si," I go, chucking it under the chin. "Solamente la uniforma." The kid starts bawling. I fake leaving, and then make an end run into the house, a distraught Maria and the bawler on my tail making with the vayas and subitos. "Please. I need job; my baby." "Don't tell her." "Come back when Miss Eve here." "When'll that be, when the cows come home?" I phone the student. Car trouble. He picks me up on Benedict Canyon Road and Easton. I borrow two dollars from Maria. Gracias. Between Eve and me, we owe her plenty. Funny. The wetback had more ready cash than us, plus a house in Mexico.

Mulholland Drive runs above Bel Aire, a gated community with heavier money than Beverly Hills. My college student lived at his parent's home up in those hills, on a cul-de-sac. I lived in a cul-de-sac, too, an army surplus sleeping bag on the floor at La Cienega. It was my pupa stage.

The drive to his home was a reprise of background scenes from old Bogie movies and Sunset Boulevard, which starts off with William Holden floating face down in a swimming pool. Eve had a pool, too. Jump in, you break your balls. It was bone dry, full of weeds and fissures. The four hundred thousand dollar house sat on unstable ground at the edge of a hill in Bel Aire Heights and was looking to lay a wet one on Beverly Hills. Shades of Sal Mineo, Natalie Wood, and James Dean in *Rebel Without A Cause*. Only this house was modern with a walk-around fireplace in a glass enclosed living room. I grab Eve and bust semen rolling on Italian terrazzo. Top of the world, Mom! No spinach here! Just two coconuts in a grade B cliffhanger fraught with dangerous sex. I don't know who was more cracked, the house or me. Any second we might slide down the canyon in one orgasmic tribute to tinseltown and the San Andreas Fault. Eve gets out some tools she'd brought and we start ripping off gold plated knobs and faucets, which she considers part of her divorce settlement. Ah, California! A far cry from Autry's Radio Ranch; Roy Rogers, Dale Evans, dude ranches, and the Sons of the Horseshitting Pioneers.

"That's the Beverly Hillbillies house," my student points out as we drive up the winding road. Hollywood cornpone! Christ! Can you get any dumber? Yes. Me. Falling off the hood of a Mercedes. The whole town's full of rubes. The lucky ones are rich. A couple of young, hot shot Parker students, California Turks in tank tops with keys hanging from their asses, tried to sell me a tract of land in their real estate development. *For just seven hundred and fifty pesos, dude. You can own your own piece of California.* Where? *The Mohave Desert outside Barstow.*

The kid's home sat on a summit like a Japanese pastoral watercolor, with distant hills and dales shrouded in mist better known as LA smog. The house was pseudo-Mediterranean, with a terracotta roof set amid pines, sycamores, chestnuts, oaks, and beds of oleander and trumpet flowers. From the pool out back you could see Bel Aire, Brentwood Heights, and Westwood; in the middle distance was Pacific Palisades, and further out Santa Monica Bay and the Pacific Ocean; all of it visible year round ten percent of the time.

A domestic places a tray on a poolside table, cold lemonade with mint in tall smoky glasses. As we loosen up, the turquoise pool sparkles, liquid diamonds in the hazy sun. Like Sal Mineo in *Rebel*, the kid seems lonely. Or maybe it was me, on top of that drive, with nowhere to go but down. I had plans to open the kid up, get him in a group for contact, but for the moment all I want is to swoop down from that aerie nest to pluck Eve like a worm, from her candy apple short. Our cadences echoed into the murky hills and vales. I adjust his horse. David Niven says in the '30's, Hollywood had no smog; the air was sweet with fragrant hibiscus, jacaranda, orange tree blossoms, oleander, and eucalyptus. By 1963 it was history. All that remained was in old movie background scenes.

Screw her, the bitch! I pack my stuff, split for Chinatown, and rent a tacky room until my money runs out. I end up in the street lugging my valises until my arms nearly drop off. I sit on a curb, lost. The last place you want to be lost in is Chinatown, LA.

I had a business card from Wong. His gym was closed, so I hauled ass and luggage to his China Imports Store on North Broadway. I implored him, said I was down and out. He gave me an enigmatic Asian 'so sorry' smile. He wouldn't even store my bags in the back of his store until I found a job. I had been his student, albeit an independent one, but still he might've shown compassion. I was desperate. Begged his help again. So sorry. Well, I wasn't going down on my knees. Foolishly, I left my gear outside his back door that faced a parking lot. I figured it'd be safe there, but when I returned everything was gone. Wong said he knew nothing about it. I think he did. To him I was a *Lo fun- a foreign devil.* He may have been a Grand Master, but to me he was a Grand Rat. I knew if I went after him, one of us would be in big trouble, most likely me. To the cops, Wong was a businessman. I was a homeless vagrant, no money and no keys. Also, I had an unpaid traffic ticket, which is a felony in LA and leads to jail if you have no cash. I learned that the hard way when I was stopped for a traffic violation, was told I had two outstanding tickets, wound up fingerprinted and in jail. I still owe Steve bail money, *50 skins, man.* A similar thing happened to a noted musician friend of his who wrote movie scores. Steve's mom bailed him out.

Once, Eve dropped me off in Beverly Hills near Roxbury Drive, not far from Lucy's house, if memory serves, and a short walk to Parker's studio. Also, she was in the middle of a divorce. Evidence of a third party would "compromise" it. So, I'm walking along, when a car pulls up, a man in plain clothes gets out, says, Show me your ID. *Fuck you! ID yourself.* I'm Detective B___. What're you doing here? *What the fuck's it look like? I'm walking.* Get in the car. *Fuck you! You get in the car.* I thought, maybe he's a private dick hired by Eve's old man. *I work for Ed Parker. You want me I'll be there waitin' on the mat.* He jumps on the short wave and I continue walking. Get in the car? Like some gestapo. Not me! I wasn't about to mention Eve either. The guy yells after me, Come back! *Ya want me? I'll be at Parker's Karate studio, La Cienega.*

I manage the place. I'll meet you there on the mat in ten minutes. Fortunately he was a no-show.

The Big Kahuna, Ed, and I reached a friendly impasse. But the real wedge was Ed's new Pasadena Studio, snivel mouth cadre that had been *sucking up* to him since the Wu split. *He counts in Chinese!* True. *Talks about Tai Chi!* True. *Says Kenpo and Japanese Karate're angular, inferior styles.* False. *Says the mother of Martial Arts is King Phooey. And he's late opening up.* I let the cards fall as they may. What I should've done was open a place of my own with Eve.

There were several possibilities. We'd looked in Canoga Park, and Ventura. I knew enough to step out with or without Parker's blessing. What held me back was Eve's wildness and Karate. At heart I was a Deejay. Karate was an afterthought, a new direction, and not a lifestyle suited to my temperament. Parker once said, *I don't want to be teaching Karate at 65.* I was thinking in terms of black and white. I saw myself competing with sifus, which was beyond me. It was like saying, why teach elementary school when there are college professors with PhDs? It meant people coming in off the street challenging my authority. All excuses for not committing myself. We all start somewhere. Mike Yung might've joined me. There was the possibility of networking with the Hui O Mokomoko. Even to this day I find myself peeking in dojos, or showing moves to young people. So, what stopped me? Lack of business savvy and confidence-especially in a partnership with mercurial Eve. Had she been as I first saw her when she talked on my behalf to her husband, things might've been different. In walking away I was setting a pattern of letting people kick me in the ass. Years later, Tilley, an art student and friend, saw it, *How many times are you going to let people kick you in the ass? Frankly, you don't need others to kick you. You're doing it to yourself.*

My life's a bunch of hits and misses, mostly misses, and it gets me mad. Am I afraid to hurt others, afraid of success, or both? Could it be my father sitting on my head? It was easier to walk away and concede the turf than stand and fight. For years I dreamed of LA; Karate; Eve; my friendship with Nancy Kovack. I'd see myself literally fighting my way back, banging heads to get to a position of respect. My soul called out in dreams, don't deny me. *What're we doin' underground on a detestable job?* It's a period of gestation. *Gestation, my ass! Pushin' buttons, and listening to bullshit? Get real!* Maybe Karate stood for something; maybe it was fortitude and character building. And maybe your Aunt Phyllis is the good witch of north. Maybe this is what my old man meant when he said, If there's one thing I can give you it's my will power. *It was a passing moment of lucidity. All he ever did was knock us down.* On the flipside, had I stayed with Martial Arts I might've ended up like Ed Parker with a massive heart attack at the Honolulu airport, or Bruce Lee in a coma in Benedict Canyon. *All subterfuge. Put the past in a box, put the box in drawer, and move on. If, as Homer wrote, sleep is the twin of death, then its fraternal brother is the nightshift. We're extremists, judgmental, full of escapist illusions, and unable to fit into a world of fruitcake religions.* I wanted to belong yet I couldn't accept a society that speaks out both sides of its mouth. We go to the theatre for intimacy, but outside we're strangers. It's the era of "He said, she said"; hidden cameras; mics up the okole- *ass.* Love thy neighbor. If he denies you, kill him! In the same breath we hate, maim, kill, and then create clinics, hospitals and the Red Cross. We make animals pets, and then lop off their heads. We need space ships to rocket clear of our rotten selves. We envy birds not for themselves but for their natural talent of flight. To show our love we clip their wings and cage them. I look back trying to sort out the pieces. Julius: *One doesn't necessarily have to be the best at one's craft to set up a shingle. Some of the worst people do it. You just have to know how to sell it. That's the real, dirty work. And it "ain't" hard to do. We're all gullible. And by the way, oddly enough, sometimes it's fun.* Mary: *I was never one to speak up when I was young. I still listen and watch. I'm saving myself for when I leave this world and go upstairs, presumably, to meet Him. I've got a few questions I've been saving.*

Back in the early '60's Karate had its frauds and masters. Ed often pointed out books and pamphlets that showed bad form: fists bent at the wrist; a horse too wide; feet turned out. Mas Oyama, a master noted for killing a bull with a punch, was from the Japanese school of Martial Arts. His knuckles were so calcified from hitting hard materials that he had trouble opening and closing his hand. Venerable masters like Nishiyama and Nakayama come to mind one replacing the other around 1963. As for me, well, in short, *I seized the moment but sunk to the occasion.*

I was again penniless with no keys, like the day I arrived in LA two years earlier. I had the shirt on my back and a Tai Chi pendant around my neck, which I wasn't going to hock. More than clothes, I lost all my notes and illustrations of Captain Karate. I felt a tremendous emptiness, an overwhelming sense of loneliness. I started searching my pockets, but for what I didn't know. This pocket, that pocket, and back through them again. I must've looked like a pervert feeling himself up in the street. What did I want? I was devastated, a man without a key. Lost in LA with no keys was bad enough, but in Chinatown it's deadly. Keys mean something. They say who you are. Without keys, you're nothing. The more keys you have, the more you're connected. I had worked up to three, almost four keys until a moment ago: I had a car key; a key to Parker's studio; a key to the place I'd shared with Steve; and now nothing. Something pinched my thigh. A small silver suitcase key was poking my leg through a pocket hole. I stared at the key for a long time. It would never unlock anything again and neither would I. What kept me from falling apart, I don't know. Maybe it was that little silver key and the pendant. You come into the world with nothing and leave with nothing. I wanted to die. People swirled around me like giants, cars were steel leviathans grunting and honking, grating, irritating, and fraying my nerves. Everybody had keys, even low lives, but not me. All I had was a dead-end suitcase key. Key, keys, keys! Substantial keys that opened locks of consequence. Keys, so many fucking keys, that said, *I open this or that; things; objects; property; deposit boxes full of money and jewels.* All I had was a little silver key, a suitcase key pinching me like an old friend, pulling me out of my funk, telling me to get my ass up out of the gutter and moving. Luckily I was not prone to violence. How'd Ed put it? *If I didn't have a family, there'd be bodies on the floor.* My only family was back east. I wasn't going to disgrace them. God knows some people deserved to be taught a serious lesson. I'd started to put that impulse in my writing, but now it was all lost somewhere in Chinatown. In a couple of days I'd be dirty and picked up for vagrancy. Jesus! What the hell was I doing to myself? I had no fight. I never could fight people. I wanted desperately to get along, to achieve things without hurting anyone, but I was dreaming, a pitiful adult with a child's fantasies of good and evil, of love and compassion. That was Captain K, but he would use Karate, if necessary, where in my own life I was timid and non-confrontational. Somewhere along the way, one has to honor oneself.

Against better judgment I telephone Eve. What follows is sad and funny. At a clothing store Eve buys me a beige corduroy suit for $10. One half was faded white from being in the sun on a window dummy. Now it was on another dummy, Mr. Yin-Yang with hazel fisheyes.

Come night it was bars, numbing booze, and to bed at dawn. Sooner or later we'd end up doing a candy apple swan off Mullholland Drive. Occasionally we'd sit home in Benedict Canyon by the fire, drinking strega in coffee, and listening to Ray Charles. Blind, he found every piano note, while I had two good eyes and couldn't find my fly.

One night Eve tries to kick me. I block by lifting my leg with my foot turned in and she gets a nice gash on her shin. Another time, in the company of Pietro, she catches me off guard with a punch to my nose. I absorb the impact by leaning back.

"You broke it," I go, checking myself in the bureau mirror.

"It's an improvement," says Pietro, cackling perversely. I resented him because he was with Eve without my knowledge. Maybe they were getting even because I was close to Nancy. She and I were simpatico from day one when we met to do a photo shoot on Karate for Argosy Magazine.

Pietro was a Runyanesque character with sparkling snake eyes verging on lunacy. While he acted like life was a game, there was an edge to him that signaled danger- a New York Italian with vague connections. He never said. I never asked. *Curiosity killed the cat. Hear too much, next thing you can't leave.* He was Nancy's friend and I took him at face value; an interesting face, too, I found on getting a closer look when he escorted her to supper at Eve's place. He was southern Italian, a gypsy, white teeth in the ruddy face of a gigolo with something primitive about him, lusty even, a good time Harry. I sensed he could turn on a dime and somebody'd end up dead. Maybe that's what appealed to Nancy.

"You think it's funny?" I go, shoving Eve into him thinking, *ya don't like it start swingin'.*

It was a B-movie moment and corny. But then dying is corny, when you think about it. So's your ass in a cut away tux. My nose wasn't bleeding. I nursed it with ice from a bedside water carafe. It may also sound corny but a man has to be careful of the company he keeps and the cues he takes from a woman. Pietro existed because Eve encouraged him. She was always latching onto men like a lost lamb with no fear of the consequences. A snake stuck in a hole asks a rabbit for help. The rabbit says, *But you'll bite me.* The snake says, *Help me get out and I promise not to bite you.* The snake gets out and bites the rabbit. *Why'd you bite me?* asked the rabbit. *You promised not to.* The snake says, *I can't help myself. It's my nature.* To me, bars are that hole. People like Eve and Pietro are the snakes.

I was in my mid 20's. Eve was 10 years older, and Pietro was in his 40's. She'd been married to several millionaire husbands. They'd both been around the old elephant. Pietro had been in lots of brawls over women. *One time after a breakup,* he told me, *I'm on 2nd Avenue. The bitch comes boppin' along, and starts swinging. I'm bobbin' and weavin', tryin' to get away. Then the cunt's purse must've had rocks in it. I keep walkin'. Then, on my mother's grave, the bitch jumps on my fuckin' back. On 2nd Avenue! People're lookin'. The last thing I need's to get picked by the cops. Publicity I don't need. I'm already popular. But I can't shake her. On my mother's grave! I grab her; turn her upside down- Swear on my mother! - stick her head-first in a trashcan, wipe my hands, and walk away.* Exactly what I wanted to do to them. Seeing them upside down in a trash can makes me laugh and calms me. Besides, I'd seen bruises on Eve, so doubtless other men failed to knock sense into her. Luckily, I've always known when the edge was near. A woman sets the tone of a relationship. Either she's with you, or you're Mr. Castrato.

Fast forwarding several years. I'm strolling along 1st Avenue at 55th Street when along comes Pietro with a strawberry-blonde on the cuff. Sporting summer pastels, they look like characters out of O'Henry, who just blew in from Bermuda for a high stakes game. I wonder not only where they're going, but also where they've been, and why, but I don't ask. As always, he's cool, and she's no bimbo, even if a tad too blonde. *Hey, paisano. Ciao, ciao! Meet Peaches.* She bats her lovelies like she's sending me an urgent message in Morse code, which I chalk up to the midday sun. After the *paisano* stuff, I'm told Peaches writes. *Some pieces for Cavett; Channel Toiteen.* Where does he find 'em, I wonder? Nancy was out of his league, too. Just then a fella strolls by and Peaches says, *Hey, Pee-pee. Ain't that the same guy from before? Who is he?* Pietro doesn't look, his half moon eyes traveling up the street in the opposite direction. Peaches says, *Is he an actor, maybe?* Pietro doesn't answer. His lazy eyes are busy inspecting the nearby roofs and balconies of buildings like he's looking for FBI agents with binoculars. Then he smiles at me and says, *Looks like a bean shooter to me. A pants cannibal. Fahget 'im!*

23.   The Last of Eve

Racking back. One day three Los Angeles policemen walk into Parker's place. I got nervous. Were they the cops at Eve's house when I was up on the roof? I brace myself. Turns out they want lessons. So I give them a demo. Using one cop for an opponent, I go, *punch with your right.* He gets inventive like I did with Ruby. In a real fight, combinations are thrown. As I block his right with my right he shoots out a quick left to my exposed ribs. Instinctively, I cover with my left and catch his fist in my palm, and that cinched the deal. Funny. There I am, Captain Karate, *Roofus* the Ninja Nut, booking cops and not the other way around.

Several classes later, I put Eve in with the cops for contact practice. Nobody connected the dots. Eve had a lot on her mind; divorce, dreams of singing lost at the bottom of a glass. I was starting to see she had the spotty memory of a drunk and the alcoholic's dry mouth, thirsty tongue smacking against parched lips. *It was me, honey, up on the roof. I threw your keys in the ivy. We go 12 rounds nightly after supper. Hello!* Some people fight and have so many tantrums they can't keep track. They develop a short memory on personal behavior.

During a break Eve surprises me by telling the cops she has a .38 Special. Bad news. I don't like guns in unstable hands. The good news? She has no bullets. The bad news? They invite her to the police target range with buckets of bullets. *Boom!* The Special kicks like a mule. Nothing like the monster M-1 that could dislocate your shoulder.

Early one Benedict Canyon morning, I wake after sleeping on the living room couch. Eve had locked me out of her bedroom the night before. The reason doesn't matter. Pick one. Bow legs. Flat feet. A full moon. She was a pazzarella, and I couldn't see the forest for the trees. We had a tiger by the tail, Karate, but booze and pills confused everything. In *Tropic of Cancer* Henry Miller examines a vagina with a flashlight: *So this is what makes the world go round.* Yes. And it had me spinning.

Eve opens the door for Maria who brings her a breakfast tray. I slip in behind thinking I'm smart, but I'm dumb. How dumb? Stay tuned.

"Buenos dias, Maria," says Eve fluttering her mariposas.

"Buenos dias, señora. Y tú, señor? Huevos, café?"

"Nada, gracias, Maria." I go, closing the door behind her. On turning back to Eve, I find I'm looking straight into the barrel of a .38 Smith and Wesson Special, the one we'd used on the police pistol range; a black steel hole over a breakfast tray bigger than God Almighty.

"I've been waiting for you all night," says Eve.

Slowly, I raise my hands. Speaking in flat tones so as not to excite her, I go, "Okay. You're right. I'm going." *No sudden moves,* I think. *Don't go forward. Don't turn. Just step back nice and easy.* On my third step Eve lowers the gun, puts it under her pillow, withdraws an empty hand, and I'm on her like a bat from hell. I reach under the covers, flip her and the breakfast tray into the air. She goes flying; eggs, coffee, and toast into the curtains lining the glass doors on the other side of the bed. I grab the gun, sleek, hard, black steel, look from it to her, and say evenly, "This is goodbye." Outside I toss the gun into the thick ivy, and split directly for the airport. *Any luggage, sir?* No, I go, standing at the counter in my yin-yang cord suit. I write a check against insufficient funds, fly to New York, re-pay the airline with a loan from my mom who says, *"Arlecchino! Go back, I'll shoot you myself."* I never saw Eve again.

In 1972 we were reunited in *Play Misty for Me,* a psycho thriller written by a secretary named Jo Heims, suspiciously close to the name of my friend and confidant Joe Hyams. Clint Eastwood played me; a laid back DJ who read poetry at night (he forgot wind chimes in the background) and Eve was Eve, a knife-wielding nut. *If it's not you,* a friend says, *it's extraordinarily coincidental.* In Hollywood, if you've got talent but don't know it, people will take it, plagiarize your life, and steal your dreams.

ACT TWO

ANÁMNĒSIS
(to remember; a preliminary case
history of a medical patient)

1. That's the Ticket

Devious Septum: From the Manhattan School of Radio and TV Electronics, under the directorship of Marvelous Marvin Matusoff, an industrious C.B.S/TV engineer, to the boonies to Disney to Harlem.

Marve taught me to crack a book, use flash cards, highlight facts to separate chaff from wheat. His school offered an eight-month intensive in radio and television electronics leading to a Federal Communications Commission First Class Radio Telephone Operators License (FCC). Sometimes called a First Phone, or Ticket, the license would open up more jobs at directional radio stations mandated by law to have licensed engineers on duty when broadcasting to keep the signal centered. To get a First Phone the FCC gave a test consisted of 90 multiple choices, plus 10 schematics and 75 were passing. You had to understand DC/AC voltage, amperage, impedance, magnetism, and motors. More than half the class failed in the first round. They couldn't do the math or figure out why 9 lamps, a radio, a TV, a toaster, and dehumidifier plugged into one extension cord from one outlet would blow a circuit. To them, *conduction* meant the guy who runs a train, and *induction* was a draft notice.

Broadcast stations transmit signals in patterns assigned by the FCC. "Non-directional" transmitters broadcast in an unrestricted 360-degree pattern. "Directional" stations send out signals in specific directions based on location and proximity to other stations operating on similar frequencies. Some might transmit north with nothing southward, or in a figure-8 with the tower at the center where the circles join. Put another way, signals are like lawn sprinklers governed by pressure, and direction. A chief and a First Phone assistant monitor the signal to keep it from drifting, or overlapping other transmissions like emergency SOS calls.

To low budget stations DJ/First Phone holders were expedient. They did air work and kept the signal on target. A typical help wanted ad read: "Yestdy. 1ˢᵗ Ph Combo; Car Nec. Res/aud tpe, Bx 9, Aligatr Ally, Flda."

While a combo-deejay, I did some crazy things. John, chief at WBNR, and I were at the tower taking readings. I go, What kind of power we got? He smiles, hands me a fluorescent bulb, says, *Stick it up in the air.* The bulb lit up. Don't know why I didn't. Then, I got cute with the power unit and narrowly missed entering the *Twilight Zone.* Early one Sunday the power wouldn't kick in. So I climbed on top of a generator. Thinking it's a car battery with loose connectors, I grab the cable at the terminal to jiggle it, got a buzz, and let go. Sometimes you can't. It's electro-magnetism. I was almost a fried UFO over Duchess County. Where I was just not thinking, there were many First Phony graduates of four-week crash courses who thought air waves were women in uniform, watts was in LA, and 'grid leak' was incontinence. Down the pike one blustery, rainy night my ticket came in handy when a 50,000-watt directional tower buckled faster than a quarterback blindsided in the pocket. More later.

Diary, 1964. Two students helped me a lot. The first one I met in Kelly Park, Brooklyn. I was determined to get a license and prove to myself that I could handle academics. The summer before school I boned up with basic books on electronics and math. Sometimes I'd study at Kelly Park on Avenue S where I grew up and hung out with my old pal, park director Heshie Plotkin. His aid was a Brooklyn College student good in math and he voluntarily tutored me.

First day in class I'm sitting next to Ruben Rivera, from Puerto Rico, in town for a license. In those days PR's were scorned as mañana people. *Mañana, my ass.* Ruben aced every test. We became study buddies, updating class notes, and quizzing each other during breaks. My test scores were not far behind his.

I found a love for math- did it without a slide rule- and was excited by the mystery of electricity, magnetism and light. Initially, wrote Physicist Feynman, they were discovered separately, but are connected as different aspects of the same thing, i.e., electromagnetism. Maybe life and death are different aspects of the same thing. On a clear night, we've all felt the stars resonating. Maybe man is one lonely aspect of an electromagnetic universe. The question is what's sensitivity got to do with it?

Ruben was levelheaded. That kept me tolerant of Eric, The Red, our first teacher. Impatient to cover a proscribed amount of material, he'd forge on whether you got it or not. He'd discourage questions with condescending answers while curling the ends of red handlebars, which gave him the look of a conceited cat. *In Puerto Rican,* said Ruben, *we say, Rrr-radio-bemba, when someone runs his mouth. The really dumb question is the one you never ask because you never get the answer.* I repeated questions until that *Rr-radio-bemba's* turgid answers were clear. One time he got so annoyed, he threw down an eraser, and said, *Jesus Christ! Somebody must've sold your mother a wooden mug!* So I repeated my question. On a break, Ruben laughed when I said I knew the answer the first time. It was payback. Don't mess with my mother! In that, Spanish and Italians are muy simpatico.

I won't say Ruben was confident, but he had a return plane ticket to San Juan dated the afternoon of the final. No way would he repeat that course. *Is the plane gassed and ready?* I'd tease him. *The motor is revving up, Chico!* He got the last laugh during a hands-on. We built amplifiers. He finished first. When I pushed a signal through mine it whistled and blew up. Test day I took all the allotted time from 8AM to 3PM, answered easy questions first, then hard ones; he whipped it by noon, waved 'adios,' and by the time I finished he was halfway to Puerto Rico. Ruben Rivera, one of those brief, simpatico encounters that last a lifetime.

I bounced around radio, did comedy in the Borscht Circuit, went from WBNR to WANV to KEZY to my swan song in El Paso, Texas. Stepping off the plane I was hit with a blast of hot air and a sizzling tarmac that could fry eggs. The Program Director took me to supper at a Juarez dog track. On the way I saw blocks of shanties with surprisingly huge TV's. Later, the Station Manager (SM) suggests I change my name to *Louis B. Louis* a la *William B. Williams of WNEW*. He was into sanitized ethnicity. Two first names separated by a meaningless initial. Then he says, *While VP at NBC, I denied work to a young Ernie Kovacs.* I thought, *keep that distinction to yourself.* I lasted a month. They wanted a news-oriented jock. Next I answered an ad for a Princeton job. The SM gave me a network caliber audition: five minutes of news; re-write of copy and a PR release; a sports piece followed by an ad-lib on what I'd read. Seeing I can string two sentences together, he wants to hire me. *I'm not a newsman,* I go. *I'm a personality jock. I'm afraid I'll say the wrong thing and get fired.* He says, *We'll work together and find out what sort of animal you are.* Meanwhile, Big John, the chief engineer from WBNR was now an assistant at WLIB, Lenox and 126th Street in Harlem, where nobody's Sound on the Goose. Over lunch I tell him I'm broke, tired of bouncing around. It was Tinker to Evers to Chance. John introduces me to his Chief Greenspan, who tosses me to owner Novak for an interview. *All you do is run the control board for AM and FM.* Fair enough. *The pay is $120* a week. Fair enough. Beats Princeton by $15, plus it's Manhattan. I never had a problem at LIB or in Harlem, even though I'd walked the streets sticking my nose in the Apollo where I saw a young Flip Wilson, listened to *stepladder street talkers,* and Jomo Kenyatta with a machete hanging from his belt. Legal, I guess, 'cause it wasn't concealed.

Bend over with a machete in your pants you get a cheap circumcision.

Re-racking. After graduation I got a gig in Beacon, New York playing middle-of-the-road (MOR) music and writing news at WBNR, a one-story building with a transmitter outback on two acres off a main road near town. Next to the building was a junk car with a busted bumper, flat tires, weeds, and vines growing up through the fenders. When it was time for me to move on I forced the issue by painting in big red letters on the side of the junk car WBNR MO-BILE UNIT. Funny PR to a UFO like me, but not to my MOR bosses.

Devious Septum: Help Wanted: Morn DJ; C & W; Sum news & spell chief; 1st ph must; res, & aud tape to WANV, Waynesboro.

Virginia. Just outside of DC, says the station manager (SM) on the phone. How far outside? *Less than an hour.* On foot or by car? Tell me in hectares. He goes, *Heck, I don't know. We're a new station. There's one other station in town.* I think, a two-horse town. *We've been broadcasting three months. The town's a mix of southerners and northern transplants working for Du Pont and GE.* What's the pay? *We're looking for a morning man. Somebody personable.* What's the pay? *The what?* How much a week? *Oh. $110 to start.* I'm a personality morning man. You want a personality? *Yes. A morning man. You don't have to knock their socks off. Just keep 'em interested. If I might, here's a tip on how to get on. We're a small town, not sleepy, but southern. It would be wise to keep northern humor minimal.* I figured, no confederacy jokes, but he means smart-alecky city humor. I go, *Can I phone in the show? You can mail me the checks.* It wasn't a far-fetched notion. Just ahead of its time.

I took the job, but not the advice. Came on like Sherman with the competition, only this time the North lost. During my show I'd phone the other station, ask for the time and weather, turn it around, and put it on the air. Eventually, they got wise and clammed up. I go, Somebody might go out improperly dressed n' catch knee-monia. *True. We hope it's you!* Click. I even disguised my voice. Yawl know where I can get me sum good grits? And, What road do I take to get to Hungry Mother State Park? My boss says, *When I heard you call them I nearly drove off the road. Don't push it.* Did I listen? No. When not bugging them I'd do my "Peruse da Nooze" bit: fake news, cockeyed sports scores, wrong time signals, and silly want ads. "Castro convertible, 72" wide, 6 months old. Excellent condition, owned by a virtuous little old lady who doesn't toss in her sleep." "For Sale: Farm tools: A pitchfork slightly out of tune; a Lock and Load Rake. Animal butcher and tanner. Must be sensitive." I'd wander off mic to a kitchenette. I go, Management's cheap. For air conditioning the boss runs around waving a wet towel. Later, the SM said, *Going off mic people'll think something technical is wrong with the station.* I'm usin' sound texture to create depth, make listeners lean in to hear. *The only leaning in will be to tune out. What good is it if you're funny but can't be heard?* Right. *Also, pace yourself. Leave some pickings for tomorrow.* He was in my corner, even suggested the novel idea of *a lavaliere- a lapel mic like in TV.* Back then lapel mics were relatively new technology. Radio and recording studios used heavy, ribbon mics. *With a lapel mic you can talk hands free and walk around- within reason.* He added the last part on seeing the glint in my eye. *Make all the coffee you want.* No, I go. I'm off coffee during the show. *Why?* Keeps me awake.

One morning a listener calls up for weather. *Sorry. No weather today. The other station's not talking to me. But there is weather out there like it or not. We expect a continuation of more weather tonight into tomorrow with temperatures more or less. Why don't you call the other station? Ask for weather and temperature and get back to me.* Then, I get the bright idea to tune them in on a radio set by my mic, and go live with their weather report. After that, they started wearing split cans, me in one half and themselves in the other, recording my show to catch me putting on their show. I go, *I hate headphones.* Can't stand to hear myself. That's why I listen to them. Later, my SM says, *On approaching the railroad track nearby, I hit the accelerator, took the rise in one fell swoop, landed with a bang on the other side, yelling, don't do it!* Crossing frequencies is illegal. It might interfere with emergency calls. Fat chance. But there it was nonetheless. The FCC fined us; I was suspended, and fired out of fear of license revocation. But I was the talk of a two-horse grit circuit. A restaurant sponsor said, *Go to Memphis. They'll love you.* I didn't, but he was right. I was a step ahead of Hee Haw and the booby hatch.

Frankly, I wasn't thinking. Back then there were lots of things I wasn't thinking, or doing, that I should've been thinking about and doing, and am probably not thinking about or doing even now, which I ought to be thinking about and doing, but don't. My style was studied loopiness, but at times I'd get trapped in the loops. I hated losing the Count Basie gig.

THE NEWS-VIRGINIAN
Friday, October 8, 1965
Jaycees Set Count Basie Appearance
Count Basie and his world famous jazz band will appear in Waynesboro Oct 22...in a two-hour concert... sponsored by the Waynesboro Jaycees... WANV Radio personality LC will serve as master of ceremonies.

Show business is a gypsy's life, Georgie Jessel once told me, in sharp nasal tones. *It's so big, kid, you can stick it in your hat.* As Jessel got into his chauffeur driven antique Cadillac with a roof of painted flowers, I said, *In radio you're at the mercy of format changes, jealous program directors, and spineless management.* Jessel rolled his eyes, foggy with age and drink, one slightly closed, and said, *Right, kid. And when all the crap clears at the end of the day you're left standin' naked in front of a fickle audience. Show-biz! You're forever with your hat in your hand. Great life for a masochist.* Then Jessel, ex-vaudeville comedian, a once vibrant song and soft-shoe hoofer fish-tailed into the night, under a canopy of flowers squeezing the neck of Chevas Regal.

Most news is morbid or below the fold- back burner crap of puerile interest. A steady news diet breeds paranoia, like going to a doctor several times a day who shoves a mirror in your face, and tells you his patients have Alzheimer's and big casino. It may be sticking my head in the ground, but I'd rather go to a party than a funeral.

Back then I didn't appreciate the importance of an independent press in a free society. I took America and my liberty for granted. Later on I understood its value and necessity for holding leadership accountable. Freedom is not a given. It must be protected and fought for at every turn. In cutting Burrow loose, C.B.S showed it's eye was veiled. Bailey liked money too much- invitations to ground breaking ceremonies, and sitting on boards of prestigious organizations like the Museum of Modern Art- to jeopardize his elitist standing. The death of broadcast news began in the late '50's when Bailey, and other network moguls, passed the word down to VP underlings like H. Robenson and J. Aubree, to kill all sensitive subjects that might alienate advertisers. Subsequently, the high point of TV drama, exemplified by Playhouse 90, Westinghouse, and Kraft, was suborned and killed. Next came integrity in television journalism with Ed Burrow's demise, circa 1963, which opened the door for the whores of broadcast news and mindless TV. Integrity, ethics, and truth in news went out the window. Bailey to Burrow: *Thou shall not come between Madison Avenue and me. We're an entertainment entity not a bully pulpit. Our survival depends on advertising dollars. Dirty as it might seem, that money pays our overhead, our mortgage, puts food on the table and our kids through college. I will not jeopardize that for a principle involving news nobody will remember the next day. It is a fairy tale to think a broadcast station can ever be a free forum as long as it's life depends on advertising and a government license.* To recoin words out of the life of Frank Lloyd Wright, *a great business takes a great patron.* Burrow is up there with Jesus, Joan of Arc, Gandhi, and all the great artists.

Henry Miller thrilled and confused me. I took him at his word. To be quiet all day, no newspaper, no radio, no gossip, completely lazy, not caring about the world's fate is man's best medicine. Such thoughts are dreams. My mistake was trying to live those dreams on radio, where the common denominator's do-re-me. I thought, what touches me, touches others. But defiance of the status quo is tantamount to messing with gravity. Commercial radio and high school rock concerts are not bully pulpits for a half-baked Colossus of Maroussi: When you're heart is right language and flags don't matter. To be out of touch is the best gift you can give yourself. Newspapers foster lies, greed, hatred, suspicion, fear, and envy. We don't need journals and the Evening News. We need love, and our hands in the earth. To say, to hell with what our neighbor is doing will renew our lease on life. Forget wireless phones, palm pods, the *Internet,* suicide bombers, terrorists, roadside bombs, battleships at sea, Stealth planes, oligarch driven politicians, lawyers, packaged goodies, gadgets, electric razors, veggie cigarettes, saran wrap, aluminum foil, and the almighty buck. An O'Neill pipe dream? Yes. People strike to uphold the right to spend a life in the role of someone other than who they are.

John Brown, 19th Century, Abolitionist and martyr, wrote a funny piece called *Sambo's Mistakes,* in which he touched on reading for education and enlightenment. *I have spent my whole life devouring silly novels and other*

133

miserable trash, such as newspapers of the day and other popular writings are filled with, thereby unfitting myself for the realities of life, and acquiring a taste for nonsense and low wit, so that I have no relish for sober truth, useful knowledge, or practical wisdom.

While the nightshift shielded me from daylight reminders of hopes and dreams, it was also the ultimate self-put down. Shackling myself to the thing I disliked was like an AA victim tending bar. Better to be insentient wood drifting in the coral at Punta Melones in Culebra, Puerto Rico.

One morning at WANV, while "perusin' the Nooze" I hit on a missing person story and chase it on the air. News is generally straightforward with little wiggle room for first person, and zero tolerance for opinion. *Maybe he's got amnesia. My boss does. Every payday. I get it the first of the month. Brr. It's cold out there. It's cold in here. I asked the boss to raise the heat and he lights a candle. I had to buy the matches. First day on the job I go, Where's the mic? And he hands me a megaphone. So, anybody out there, phone me, if you have a clue about the missing man. Meanwhile, I'll call the other station. See what they know. Not much generally. Hi. This is- Click! Surprise! Maybe the missing person heard me and left town. I would. How could he just disappear? Ring! WANV.* (Me with deep voice) *Why don't you disappear? (Click) Thanks for calling, mom. Maybe the guy's hiding in Hungry Mother State Park. No. I just like saying Hungry Mother State Park.*

"Trilbee suffers awful from disturbances," one caller says. "Harmless. Just now and again he wanders. Yes, sir. Something sticks in his craw and he wanders. Say, yawl got me on the 'hair' waves like the others?" *Yes, sir.* "The wife says, you're a kick in the pants." *Thank you. What's Trilbee look like? I wouldn't know him.* "You would. He's 6', 5", 300 pounds; legs like See-quoias. Always in the same clothes, summer or winter, red bib overalls and a slicker. Bald as a baby's butt. Laughs at nothin'. Ain't lost 'cept to his self, or I'm a monkey's uncle. Ha. My wife said, have a banana! She's an elbow in the ribs."

So I'd play music and return mid-stream of a phoner with someone along the chase route who would then lead me to a neighbor *down the road apiece.* That way I inched along gathering information. "Seen him out back. Thought it was a deer. Nearly shot 'im. He was wearin' an anti-Bambi antler hat." Another phoner. "Out my window nothing but snow n' my doghouse. Mildred up the road might know." *Hello? Mildred Up-The-Road?* "Hello yourself, ONE-VEE. What's the weather?" *Hot under the collar cross-town. Why don't you call 'em and get the weather for me?* She calls back, and I put her on live, giving the weather, all for a dime. The subject, namely Trilbee, momentarily lost in the spontaneous talk.

Back then radio news followed print form. Stations were formatted and electronic news had yet to invent itself with terms like "anchor," "satellite feed," and "feed the beast." What newspapers placed in quotes became a "sound bite," and "actuality," i.e., exploitation of character witnesses as dramatic re-enforcement of a story. *Tell or talk stories* became *show and tell productions.* The beast was, is, insatiable!

"Morning to you WANV," says the policeman on the other end of the phone. "If you want the weather you got the wrong station." *I'm calling about a missing person.* "Trilbee? Ain't missing any more. I just had grits with 'em at Granny's. Great with butter." Who, Trilbee or the grits?

The FCC fined WANV for crossing frequencies. I was suspended, fired by the owner, and lost the Basie gig. I received some consolation from the SM. *Your missing person story was inspirational. Tracking human interest live on the air. Had me glued to the radio.* As with Karate, I was breaking new ground- a jazz musician, improvising fresh ditties with no thought of marketing, and blew off my career in far-out licks that went nowhere.

2. The Last of the Great Spoonfeed

Devious Septum: This is the Station Manager, KEZY in Disneyland, Anaheim. Heard your audition tape. We want you for our morning man.

Diary. The SM was an S & M paranoid SOB melon head who hired me over the Program Director's head. The PD, *Prize Dickhead,* was not only jealous of me, but secretly resented that I'd been hired directly by the SM. PD's are jacks-of-all-trades, masters of none. They do partial air-shifts and then ride herd the rest of the time. Years later, a C.B.S writer told me *never let a PD think you're more talented than he. He'll hate you.* This Texas bred PD was a Top 40 radio-bemba chucklehead whose talent was taking out breath spaces between phrases in commercials to save time. One morning I'm on-air, pause between bits, and he pops a soda can. I wish I'd popped him. From a time salesman I learn 17 other guys had wanted my gig. Four weeks into the job I emcee a high school rock concert in an open-air theatre packed with a thousand kids hot to trot. Rock singers Dick and Didi were on the bill. Later, I saw them on Dick Clark. After the first act I come out wearing a grand piano cover for a cape. *My problem,* I go, *is I think I'm a bat. Woo! And everywhere I go people keep trying to nail down my wings. Wee!* I told Borscht Circuit jokes, broke them up, and let slip a harmless risqué one that killed the golden goose, i.e., you can think the word underwear, but don't mention it unless it's in Spanish. It didn't matter that rock lyrics were explicit and the show smacked of sex. Just don't mention it. That two kids in the wings were making out like bandits. Don't mention it. A female singer in hip huggers had a naked midriff starting under her breasts and ending above her crotch. I didn't mention it. I alluded to it. She dances off, I go out in my Steinway cape and say, *Did you see the voice on that one?* After a pause the place breaks up. I do another joke with an unmentionable, and as I come off the principal with a gyrene haircut, says, *You're off the show! We can't have that talk here.* Not thinking I'm in hawkish Birch country, I go, *You hear the lyrics of those rock songs? Who was the singer wearing hip huggers, a singing nun? You've got kids kissing in the wings. Should we keep lying and hiding the truth, then when they're 18 give 'em a gun and send 'em to die in Vietnam?* His reply? Yes. Washington was doing it. He covered his tenured ass, reported me to my SM, and the PD fired me. "The SM hired you," he gloated. "I resent doing the dirty work."

Some colleagues argued on my behalf, but the SM only agreed to $200 severance pay, accompanied by an uncalled for connection to my Italian heritage. *You should get married and raise a family. Sinatra's in the news again. A shady, disreputable character, don't you think?*

A time salesman steered me to his aunt Ann Levitas, an account executive with Foote, Cone, and Beldino advertising on Wilshire in LA. She gave me a lead to a station in San Jose. Somewhere outside Salinas I got stuck in a dense fog, made a turn, and nearly drove into a barn door. I started crying. The fog, the night, losing my job was overwhelming. I scratched all the way back to within striking distance of LA, and screw up again. Misplaced words, a joke. Jesus! What's wrong with me? I had those kids. They liked me. So did my colleagues. The scary thing was that I had control of them. If I said, *March around the building,* they'd've done it. Maybe that scared the principal. I begged him *don't call the SM. The job means a lot. You can roll with it. I can't.* He didn't care. A KEZY staff writer: *Did they laugh?* Had 'em in the palm of my hand. *Then that's all that matters.* Don't know what matters, never did. Alone crying in the fog of Big Sur and Henry Miller looking for pubic hairs with a flashlight.

I turned east and went home. Since then I've wondered how many Anaheim High School boys, Class of 1965, died in Vietnam? If any, I hope I gave them a laugh before they gave up the ghost. Part of me gave it up, too, in California's desert.

Devious Septum: This is WTHE, your Station for Wonderful Country, 1520 on the radio dial. 10,000 watts of Long Island country music.

> To Whom It May Concern:
> Louis B. Louis worked here at WTHE for a six-week period. While here he proved to be completely mature and able to exercise good "radio" judgment, especially in his presentation of a warm, friendly radio personality. Our format calls, however, for a "rock and roller" Deejay, and Lou's most engaging quality – the ability to sit back, relax, and do a low-keyed entertaining program – is, paradoxically, at odds with our format.
> Given an opportunity to work for a station whose format were more of an "easy going" nature, Lou would indeed prove himself to be an asset. He is quick witted, and handles live copy in a personable, sincere manner. His ability to get along with his fellow announcers is above par, and his punctuality is beyond reproach. I'm sorry to see Lou go from our organization. We shall miss him.
> His credentials include a 1st Phone License, which is more than important in this business. If you'd like further information, please contact me, the program director.

Frankly, I was the PD's summer vacation replacement. August, 1966.

3. The Other Side of the Window

"Yeow! This is O'Jay. Sweet as o-range juice! Don't believe me? Just squeeze me. Yeow!" "I'm Bill McCrary." "This is Gill Noble." "I'm Shelton Lewis. Now the news." "I'm Earl Bostic with your Gospel Caravan." "This is Leon Lewis. My guest is Percy Sutton." "This is rrradio-bemba! Your radio mouth high fivin', jivin', rockin', jockin' Fat Jack Walker, yaw pear-shaped talkah!" "Hello, I'm Billy Taylor and this is jazz." "Aqui esta Santiago Grevi. Una ves mas! Moda como e!" "I'm Ed Williams. I'm Del Shields, you beautiful people, with jazz on FM."

Diary. 1966. Tom Tracee was LIB's Music Director. One day I step into a lively discussion. *Honey,* says Tom, summing up, *the white man's politics is a motherfucker! Now, my dears, I'm taking orders for Obies. Who wants what? Bill? 'Ribs.' Shelton? 'Chicken with rice n' black-eyed peas.' What else's new? Mm, mm! And you, Gil? 'Eggs Benedict with champignon.' The hell you say! Get down brother. You're still uptown. 'I'll pass.' Workin' on that stomach again! Looks fine to me, baby-cakes. Now what'll it be for the cute white boy? 'Scuse me, the brother from downtown come uptown to visit. You stayin' long enough for lunch?*

One day on a walk-about lunch break, I stopped to hear a street talker on a ladder just off 125th Street- a fiery guy named Jomo Kenyata with a machete on his hip. I lost track of time and had to run back to LIB to relieve the board man. Later, newsman Shelton Lewis says, *Ya got guts. You could've been taken for FBI. And if you run in Harlem, nobody thinks you're late for work. They think you just pulled a job.*

Ed Williams, LIB's jazz jock, interviewed singer Oscar Brown, Jr. I'd first heard Oscar sing in 1962 in LA in a jazz concert featuring Miles Davis' back. Oscar sang folksy jazz, somewhere between Josh White and Bobby

Troup, with a sprinkling of Raffi. In 1967, after a failed Broadway show, he had *no desire to return to New York. Frankly, I don't even want to go on the road. I'm going back to Chicago to stay. Sometimes, brother, you make more progress by standing still.* Will you do TV? *Man, TV's nothin' but stone comic book.* Oscar Brown, Jr., died, 2005.

Some said Leon Lewis, PD, was soft on whites. If so, I needed it. Like Malcolm X concluded, blacks must learn to get along with blue eye. Leon was affable, articulate, open minded, and gray at edges of his mustache. To me he was friendly like everybody at WLIB. My time there was the sincerest and most exciting of all my radio days. If I could re-live it, I'd stay there and produce. But like Adam Clayton Powell III said, *all I want is a piece of the pie.* The media pie was downtown.

One day I hitch a ride downtown with Leon. On the way he detours for a Harlem history lesson called *Striver's Row. Ever hear of it?* Swinging west off Lenox around 138th, I see buildings that rival the best anywhere. *The style is neo-Italian Renaissance, Georgian. Starting in the '20's it attracted ambitious as well as successful African-Americans in medicine, dentistry, law, and the arts: Thurgood Marshall, W.C. Handy, Noble Sissle, Billie Holiday. Joe Louis had a tavern at 555 Sugar Hill, which runs from Edgecomb to Amsterdam, 145th to 155th. It got the name Sugar Hill 'cause to live there you had to have lots of sugar in your pocket. It was sweet and expensive even then. Living here put one in an exclusive society that said you'd arrived socially and economically. Between Striver's Row and Sugar Hill lived Duke Ellington, A. Phillip Randolph and Hazel Scott, Basie, Strayhorn, Fletcher Henderson, Jelly Roll Morton, Fats Waller. There's a renaissance going on. People're coming back and renovating.* If I'd been blindfolded and driven there I'd swear it was blue-blood Brooklyn Heights. The architectural style, stones, oak doors, was no different. *Right. They share that rich, brownstone look; high windows with arches, herringbone brickwork, and workmanship that died with the passing of those last waves of immigrant European artisans.* By the '70's quality gave way to expedience, and sheet rock. *Look. That wrought iron gate. It's a servant entrance. Some buildings go back to 1890 and David King, Jr., a developer. They have the first modern plumbing. Look. That old sign on a corner, 'Private Road, Walk Your Horses'.* How about that?

Eddie O'Jay was WLIB's dynamic morning man-fast paced and demanding. Unlike Bob Crane in LA, no dispensation was given to O'Jay to operate his own board, but he needed it. He was spontaneous. It was anybody's guess when to open or close his mic. He'd jump in over a song a la James Brown. *Yeow! I feel good! Got my mop n' bucket n' I'm off to the Hotel Theresa to make me lunch money. Yeow!*

Whimsical jocks like O'Jay and Fat Jack needed to operate their own boards. But union contracts specified jurisdictional rights over electrical equipment, including wall light switches. In those days techs ran the show, talent talked, and gave hand cues for what they wanted, which could be touchy business with fast jocks. Blink you could miss an O'Jay hand cue for pertinent comments, like *YEOW!* and *Got to, got to! Mm, I feel good!* Goof ups turned into the *yeow of doom,* and *you'd feel bad!* In time the union allowed an on-off mic switch in the studio. The master control tech just left the board mic hot (open), which relieved some of the pressure of having eyes in the back of the head. Once, a little thing like who controlled a mic switch could start a strike. It boiled down to work and money. With a mic switch at his fingertips, O'Jay was a kid in a pastry shop; jumping in and out, doing his radio-bemba 'thang', honking his ball horn four hours straight, wired start to finish.

Yeow! I feel good! Honk! Ooo wee! Some pretty little thang called soundin' sweet and edu-ma-cated. Honk! Quit it Squidget. She called me, not you. She be talkin' highbrow, and sayin', Oh, Eddie, darling, play Merry Christmas, Baby. And I'm lookin' at my tech and all he knows is White Christmas. I'd like to play Jelly, Jelly. Honk! Shh. Squidget! But you ain't foolin' me. Yeow! I know you're going out the door right now with your mop and bucket. Yeow! Honk! Honk! I'm O'Jay. Good as o-range juice. Squeeze me fool and find out. Honk! Not you Squidget. (signals hit record; tech misses cue) Honk! Y'got that right, Squidget. The brother's day dreamin'. (on TB) I could drive a truck through that hole. Don't nonchalant me! I'm competing with downtown. Soupy and your brother jocks. ABC, MCA. They cut 'em some slack, not me. I can't afford screw-ups! Get it together!

After working several hours with O'Jay, I came away nerves frazzled like Little Richard's hair; a spastic walking down the hall. *Yeow! Got to, got to! M-m! Squeeze me, fool! Sweet as o-range juice! Honk! Honk!*

O'Jay was an intense cat about 5' 6" weighed maybe 170 pounds. David Braithewaite was a cool tech about 5' 9", about 300 pounds, and built like a line blocker. His mind was on going to *Motown. That's where it's happening!* One morning Braithewaite relieved me on the O'Jay show. I go, *Watch 'im. He's frisky. All over the map. Fuck 'im,* says Dave, and misses a tight cue coming in a little loose. O'Jay's yells, *Wake up!* Dave non-chalants another cue and O'Jay goes ballistic. *Don't lemme come in there! Hear what I'm sayin'?* Dave snaps back on TB, *Bring it on, brother. I'm right here.* O'Jay slams down his headphones, runs out of the studio, Dave gets up casual-like, says, *I'm gonna sit on that fool's head,* opens the control room door, stands foursquare in the entrance, which is two steps above the hall level, and waits. O'Jay barrels up foaming at the mouth, sees Dave towering over him like a Pittsburgh Steeler, stops short like Road Runner, and returns to his studio. Less is not more. Big's better. *Yeow! I feel good!*

While at LIB, I tried acting and comedy in the Borscht Circuit.

The Lincoln Center Rep Company was doing *After the Fall* by Arthur Miller, and directed by Elia Kazan, in a bubble theatre in Greenwich Village near NYU. At first I thought the play was about the falling out of bosom buddies Miller and Kazan- they had shared the same bed in Hollywood with Marilyn Monroe, circa 1950- after Kazan caved in to the McCarthy *House UnAmerican Activities Committee (HUAC)*. Miller refused to cooperate with HUAC, but Kazan named names, and many comrades ended up blacklisted. To Kazan, *work was his life. Principles don't pay the rent.* But *After the Fall* is a holocaust story; *even the Jew has his Jew*, with a touch of Monroe thrown in. Twelve years later he and Miller were back working together, principles giving way to expedience.

A college buddy from the University of Hawaii, John Phillip Law (*Love Machine*) was in the Rep group. Backstage he told me they rehearsed above Ratner's in the East Village. Next day, I went to the Broadway office of Robert Whitehead, the company's producer, to ask about joining the group. Later, I talked with Kazan in the rehearsal hall above Ratner's. Both times I was told the cut-off age for supporting players was 28- I was 29- and the company was set. If I couldn't get in the group I was going to get in Salome Jens. I looked around. The actors were on a break. A guy was singing and playing an upright in a corner by high, murky windows. I'd seen him before, maybe in a Hollywood one-arm joint. As I get closer, I recognize Ralph Meeker, alias Mike Hammer. I go, *What brings you to Rome, y'gutter gunsel?* He fingers some high keys, says, I ain't packin', gumshoe. I go, *I'm revoking your detective license, and your gun permit. I*

143

catch ya snoopin' around Salome Jens I'll toss you in the slammer. Nothin' personal. Say, I thought the snakes of tinsletown were more your kind of people. Running a lick, he goes, Well, ya thought wrong, gumshoe. The best part of LA is Frisco and Vegas. After the *Kiss Me Deadly* caper in '55 things went sour. Y'see, my fine cultured, and friendless flatfoot, the idle mind's the devil's playground. *Tell me about it.* I just did. When nothin's doin' in dreamtown y'sit around a turquoise pool exercisin' your elbow- *capeesh?* - goin' stir crazy waitin' on a phone lead that never comes. *Tell me about it.* I just did. If New York's Rome, then Hollywood's Pompeii waiting on Vesuvius.

What I most remember about the Borscht Circuit was sinking feelings of futility and loneliness. During a return gig at Goldberg's Bungalow Colony, before a packed house, suddenly in the middle of a joke I went blank. A lady down front smiled, but no words came. Was it fear of failure, of saying the wrong thing? Heshie's stroke? No more joke writing on the Coney Island boardwalk. Or, was it the lost memories of youth that my childhood friend Artie Resnick had written about in his song *Under the Boardwalk*? Walking out through the audience, I go. *Thank you. I'm sorry.* I walked out. Outside in the night I stumbled along a path. Where's the moon? What happened to the stars? They were there when I ran in to the music. Where was <u>my</u> lucky star? She's run off again behind the moon with Rob Roy. Suddenly, it was the Salinas fog all over again. Nobody cares! Nobody! Only Heshie, and he's dying. Eve, that bitch! Parker and his da-votees! That damn gyrene school principal! Joe Hyams, or secretary Jo Hiems, or whatever he calls himself, he named it. *Eve could get a man to rob gas stations to keep her.* Heshie, I need you. Make me a joke. *Life's a joke, kid! Don't let it kick you in the ass.*

Mrs. Goldberg offered me food, consolation, but I'm shut down mind and body. Keep the money. I couldn't even relate to a singer in another show I'd done at a big hotel. I came off the stage trembling, bumped into a redhead. *You were good,* she says. But I ran out the back door and down the road. Don't remember driving back to the city. Later Heshie says, *Putz! What're you saving it for, your old age? Ya should've gone with her. Worried about what you did in the morning.* I still get mad thinking of those wasted days. *We'll see what kind of animal you are. Under the Boardwalk, she was so fine. She'll get you to rob gas stations.* I didn't talk about what happened or why I'd become a tech. I'm working for money. *We'll figure out what kind of animal you are. Under the Boardwalk.* The sort of animal that isn't mean enough or sufficiently tough with others or myself. You must be both. Nice guys finish last in everything.

Summer of '67. White stations downtown were 'diversifying'. Music Director Tom Tracey guffaws. *Oh, baby-cakes. De-versifying, my black ass! The white man's politics are a motherfucker. M-m! Lemme 'splain somethin'. Ofay's outré. Comprende? They want access to the ethnic food. Dig what I'm saying. The man wants your contacts, your black book, baby-cakes. He can't go to Harlem with the rest of the girls without gettin' his white ass shot. We're his bulletproof vests. In other words, baby-cakes, make the man pay for what's in your black book.* So the gang broke up to work for the man. Gil Noble and Ed Williams joined ABC; Billy Taylor and Tom Tracy went to WNEW; Bill McCrary joined Channel Five; Leon Lewis became a talk host at WMCA, and I kept going to Earl Bostic gospel shows. Ebony was African-American, a maid in my hotel on Lexington at 49th Street. *If I get pregnant I'll send the child south.* Five-foot-nine, oh so fine, under the bed slats was like *Under the Boardwalk.*

Chuckler Production Technicians Wanted

I answered the Broadcast Magazine ad and joined the man in August of 1967, as part of the first wave of hiring when local radio went all news. Yet I still see my old friends; Billy Taylor and Ed Williams doing jazz, Noble in the news booth, Braithwaite foursquare in the doorway waitin' on O'Jay. That sweet, mellow last summer of '67 at LIB before the split downtown and to Motown. I wish I could bring it back. Fat Jack talking his talk, O'Jay honkin' Squidget, Bostic with the Gospel Caravan, Santiago Grevi, y una vez mas! The wind rustles the grass, leaves fall, new ones appear. Then Swami happened and Ayn was not far behind.

The grape on the vine was orient and immortal which never should be picked nor was ever sown. I thot it had stood from everlasting to everlasting. The dust and stones of the street were as precious stones; gates were at first the end of the world. Green trees when I saw them first thru one of the gates transported and ravished me; their sweetness and unusual beauty made my heart leap and almost mad with ecstasy. They were such strange and wonderful things. The men! Oh, what venerable and reverend creatures did the aged seem. Immortal cherubims! And young men glittering and sparkling angels! Boys and girls tumbling in the street were moving jewels; I knew not that they were born or shall die. But all things abide eternally as they were in their proper places. Eternity was manifest in the light of day, and something infinite behind everything appeared, which talked with my expectation and moved my desire.
Thomas Traherne, d, 1674.

4. First Impressions

Diary: August, 1967. Entering Central Control (CC) local radio on day one, all the techs were neatly dressed in sport coats, shirt and tie, and pressed pants. They were calm, business-like, talked in low voices like at a funeral parlor. One man leaned on an ampex tape machine working a crossword puzzle; another was checking stocks in the times with a magnifying glass. They were all mello with soft, clean hands, and keys hanging from their belts. To recoin Ouspenskaya in a French Revolution movie. *Turn out your pockets, citizen! Voilá! Keys! Pour vous, la guillotine!* Soon I discovered 'citizens' on both sides of the window needed a French haircut. The mean age of newly hired was 30, while those on the job ranged in age from 50 to 64. Some had started out as "apprentices", the name given to neophyte engineers in the '30's. Thursdays a secretary handed out paychecks. One day she was selling dollar chances. First prize, a sports Jaguar. The winner was a newly hired tech from MCA who cried the blues. *I gotta pay capital gains. I live in Red Hook, Brooklyn. Where am I gonna park?*

September '67. The first 90 days were a probation period in case new employees didn't work out. One tech was dismissed for screw-ups. But his personality was too open, as I would learn later for myself. If techs have one talent, it's being cool and circumspect. This tech belonged on the other side of the window. A combination of actors Hal March and John Cassavetes, he pranced about like a 'tumler' (*emcee*) on cruise ship who never knew which way the wind was blowing. They got him so paranoid, he'd date and initial all his work, which was like signing his own death warrant. Screwed up cartridges were traced to him even if someone else made them. C.B.S dismissed him. Last I heard he was deejaying in Patchogue, LI. One foggy day walking on a road, he was fatally struck by a car, and initialed the ground in blood.

Hardly a month on the job, Director of Engineering Greene (he hired me) shows me a union letter requesting my dismissal for not paying dues. I felt betrayed. *Why didn't they talk to me first instead of notifying you? It's an oversight. Nobody explained dues procedure.* He smiles, says, *Walk a check over to their office after work. That should resolve the issue.* It did. Still, it was a heartless show of managerial skills on the part of technicians elected to represent workers. Messing with a man's job is bad business. All things considered, our union protected us from kangaroo courts, arbitrary firing, and later, harsh cutbacks of the '80's. Complaints must be written and substantiated, or a worker is at the mercy of liars and character assassinations.

The first on-air talents I met were sports announcers Pat Sumerhill and Jerry Koleman, deejay Wally Kling, announcers Art Heinus, Bill Gillian and Hale Syms. We'd bump each other at crazy hours of the night. Art Heinus hosted music 'til dawn, sponsored by an airline. We'd wake him up periodically for commercials, breaks, time signals, and public service blurbs. His voice was deep and sounded like his balls were in his pant cuffs. He went to Frisco to anchor news. At 6AM we'd all belly up to the bathroom sink, shaving and slapping ours faces with cold water to stay awake. One day I saw Summerhill in the Black Crock lobby and he invited me for a drink in the Ground Floor Bar. Pat lived in Saddle River and traveled back and forth by helicopter. I thought it was awesome. In college he majored in Russian History, which I thought was a degree in football tactics. Pat was no sport. When I had to pay for my own drink, I thought, *You know what you can do with that helicopter.*

"I used to open for FS on TV," Hale Syms told me, "back in the '50's. Sinatra asked me to be his announcer. It was tempting- the high life and all, but I declined. I'd've been lost in his entourage. I have no regrets being a staffer." According to an ex-Vegas dancer, Frank also asked comic Shecky Greene to join him. *Stick with me,* he said, *I'll make you a star.* Shecky says, *if bein' like you is what it takes to be a star I don't want it.* After the last show that night at 4a, Frank's bodyguard, Andy 'Banjo', who played a tune on his head with Joe Fisch on billy club, accosted Shecky. On the way down Shecky broke Fisch's nose. Shecky can't prove who ordered it, but says, *drop a dime in any scar in my head, it'll play a Sinatra song.* No sweetheart himself, Shecky was a drinker. *One morning, he climbs on a gambling table and pees.* If Hale had said yes to FS, maybe today his own head would be an oldies jukebox playing saloon songs from the king of the minor key.

☺

5.   *A Night Watchman*

Diary: Contrary to what *they* say, the moon's for owls and bats, not humans, even though we think like night predators. The cumulative effect of repressed emotions and sleepless nights had, as they say, unintended consequences, i.e., *a deleterious and debilitating effect on* the *body politic.* Zorba, the Greek: *Days are men. Nights are women. Nights belong in the arms of a woman. Don't mix up the two.*

I tried to blend in with the skeletons- a token few feeding the beast 'til the big boys arrive. Nights were peaceful from 1968-73. Hourlies ended at midnight and resumed at 6AM. I'd kick back for z's, walk the deserted halls, shoot the breeze in the cafeteria with a Nigerian cashier and Oscar *Mez Ami,* the half-breed cook who was once cabin boy on a pirate ship, and a sous chef on the Staten Island Ferry. Enter the film developers, two savvy guys with a penchant for Chinese take-out at 2AM. When not developing 16mm film in stainless steel vats of chemicals, they hung out in an adjacent lounge chewing the fat, usually yours. They were cool and detached, which I liked. Their usual greeting was, *Say, hump?* Advances in videotape and the electronic camera sent them packing and a piece of me went with them. To that sentiment they'd say, *Hump this, asshole!*

One night I get the bright idea to write. I start running off at the pencil in a notebook mixing cathartic feelings with drawings, memos, news clippings, and a theory that *prolonged exposure to artificial light can cause cancer.* Sometimes I'd take notes on note-takers chasing targets.

Bloody bullshit! Shouts a tape-ops nosie slamming down the phone and throwing his pencil in the air frustrated by PR flack run-around. So I toss cotton swabs at him. He throws his pad at me, and I counter with my notebook. He knocks over his chair. I kick mine across the room. Nights'll do that to *the body politic.* Tape reels and ballpoint pens go flying. One sticks to the ceiling. *Bet y'can't do that again. No? Two at once!* Boom! Soon the ceiling looks like a porcupine's ass. *Best way to stick 'em is underhand.* Then we try tacks and razors, which prove too dangerous unless you want medical leave with one eye and a cheap nose job. A Desk Assistant looks in. *Phone's off the hook. No shit, Dick Tracy!* He ducks out under a barrage of whatever moves. *We better pull the crap off the ceiling, or it'll be acupuncture with lead poisoning. Worse. If Roundy Terkel comes in, gets hit by a Number 2 it'll be the Hindenburg all over. Shards of granapadano in a pink cloud of Philips Milk of Magnesia.*

From 4a, that's how AM's written in the newsroom logbook, lower case p means PM. From 4a to my out-time at 7:30a I work in Newsfeed, a closed circuit broadcast of secondary news to affiliates. Over the years I suffered a few glory-bound, simian asshole producers fueled by the Burrow legacy, and the Protestant work ethic- a day's work for a day's wages. I didn't think it applied at night. My work ethic is army rooted in Escape and Evasion, or my *Disappearing Act.* Lesson 1: Goofing off with complicity, or CYA, the cover your ass coffee run. *I'm going to the john. Coffee anyone? Yeah. I'll have a cup from the urinal. Gotta be better than the cafeteria.* Or, *Mark the edits on the verbatim sheet. Leave the reels on the console.* Then I'd split down the hall leaving a note on the lounge door, *At Film Developers, Back in 5,* with no time reference as to when I left. But producers have to produce. They're driven by the fear of getting it wrong or not at all. Their worst nightmare is a silent news wire. Then it's manifesting something out of nothing like producing me vertically.

Newsfeed producer Roi was a pleasant lady. Her father did a West coast TV cookin show. At first she wanted to par-boil me, but then forgave me on learning that I was not a total flake, but going to college during the day. Unlike some producers, Roi never tried to make haute cuisine out of a smorgasbord of leftover news. Some of her colleagues never heard of an out take, and thought the more tape cut the less likely you'd be perceived as unproductive. Feed the beast whatever. One guy who came through newsfeed was a tall Welch with tousled, sandy hair, dispassionate eyes, and glasses sliding down his nose. In 10 years he would be running C.B.S News and his colleagues'd be running from him. Right off I put him straight. Don't break my balls. To his credit he knew in an argument everybody loses. More on him later. Then came Terry "No Nonsense" Mortin, who had a slight paunch, lively Irish blues, and a landing field down the middle of his head. He took one look at me and decided to let sleeping dogs lay. He moved on to the desk and became his successor's bete noir. Jay Swoope was kin to Herbert Bayard Swoope, the eccentric publisher, but I didn't hold it against him. Of all newsfeed producers, Jay was the wisest. Before asking me to work he'd bow, buy me coffee, kiss my hand, rub my feet, and wake me gently by daubing my lips with Que-tips dipped in maraschino cherries. Every morning Jay showed the final show draft to editor Terry, the terrier, who'd proof copy and program content, and often find something wrong. Terry'd scrutinize a piece like Sherlock Holmes closing in on Professor Moriarity. To me, he was a leprechaun. To the Swooper, he was a leper-be-gone. Terry'd curl what was left of his sideboards between fingers, squint an eye, and go, *The narrative contradicts the actuality. Get* it together, pal. Or, *The difference between this show and the shithouse is the shithouse's cleaner.* Actually, I said that. It's a line from my middle school woodshop teacher. I use it whenever possible. Another favorite was when nosies over produce, I'd say mysteriously, *Ya know, y'can only plane the edge so much before you run out of wood.* Be that as it may, Jay'd return to newsfeed fuming. *He's a goddamn stickler for relevancy, timeliness, attribution, and facts.* Imagine that? *A real pain inna ass!*

Nights got darker when hourlies went 24/7. What a dumb, asinine, sadistic thing to do to me. I thought of myself more as a night watchman than a tech. It meant more bodies, more work, less air to breath, and forced me to ratchet up my E & E act. I got on best with nosies who said, *Make this bullshit cut n' kill the overhead.* Right on, laddybucks! I'd make the edit before the last bloomin' lumen faded in the corner of his eye.

6.   Good company.

Diary, 2a. The Studio E door bangs open. It's my new pals, the two Johns, film developers. One's tall and the others short.

"Hump!" says tall John. "What're you readin'?"

"He's eyes are bloodshot," says little John, "from jerkin' off."

I minded less the jerkin' off part than the hump. Humps were on the other side of the window.

I go, "Hump this, asshole!" Which resonates with them.

"Kiss off," says the taller, boisterous John.

"Here, here!" says the shorter, slyer John.

They had a knack of hoisting you on your own petard while making you laugh. They invite me to join them for Chinese food in their "suite" at the end of the hall, the developing rooms for 16 mm TV film.

"Bring the mag," says little J. "We'll have a slide show while we eat."

Food was one of their ways to set you up for the hoisting. Next thing I'm down the hall eating, and talking about Clueless, summer of '73.

"Right," says big John, slurping up noodles. "The blonde. She'd walk by and I'd go, Come in. Close the lights and let's see what develops."

"He thought of that one himself," says little John. "Ha, ha."

"In her book about her time here," I go. "She says a copy editor, he's out there now, was a pencil freak. Always cutting and slashing her copy. Give 'em the Gettysburg Address, he'd cut four score and seven years and write in 87. It's tighter! She says he was sexist."

"Me, too," says big John. "When it comes to broads."

"She means nasty."

"I go for whips."

"Let the man talk," says little J. "Can't you see he's got needs?"

"To prove she wasn't paranoid –

"She let 'im fuck her!"

"She gave him copy," I continue, "written by her male co-anchor whose writing's impeccable. He thought it was hers and slashed away."

"The guy's got needs," says little J.

"I got needs, too," says big J. "Look at this centerfold. Get a life, hump! Ya think too much. God! She's built. Forget those humps! What do you do durin' the day? Sleep with magazines? The old lady and me have a day school. She teaches. I drive the bus. I'm not waitin' for those humps to tell me film's obsolete."

"It's already history," says little J. "Videotape's cheaper and faster. I'm working on an MBA. On my next job I want to be a certified thief."

"Forget those news faggots," says big J. "That editor wanted to fuck her but the only led he's got's in the pencil."

"Here, here!" chimes little J. "Your problem? You're pathological, pussy whipped, and don't know it. That's why ya got all them unfulfilled needs."

"Pathological?"

"Dysfunctional," says little J. "Workin' nights jerkin' your puddin'."

"Jerk this, hump," I go.

"Way to go," says big J.

"Am I right, or am I right?" says little J. "Come clean."

"Easy," says big J, kicking his leg. "People with needs're sensitive."

"Frankly, what keeps me alive is my mother's face," I go.

"That's powerful stuff," says little J. "Mine gives me agito."

"I think about going back to school," I go. "I minored in psychology."

"Sick people do that," says big J. "They look for answers in Psyche 101. It's cheaper than the couch. Ever go to a shrink, hump?"

"Yeah. Once. I go, Doc, every night I have the same dream. I come to a door with a big sign. I push, push and I can't go through."

"What's the sign say?" asks big J.

I go, "Enter."

"Got ya on that one, hump," chuckles little J.

"Hump this both of you."

"But the door is real," I say, thinking don't say too much, or you'll never live it down, but I go on. "Opportunities come and I kill 'em. When I was teching at WMAL/TV in

DC, I'd watch the scenic designers of a kids show, long to be part of it, but afraid to ask 'cause I felt if I got it I'd ruin it. The one shrink I went to, the head of his couch was threadbare. I quit. I didn't want to be part of the parade."

"I got a few doors myself," says little J.

"Maybe I should leave you two pussies alone," says big J.

"The biggest door," I go, "is at my father's house."

"Here, here!" says little J.

"Notice he didn't say his mother's house."

"That's very astute of you," says the shorter one. "See how the needs are comin' out. You married? No? What're you waitin' on?"

"He's fuckin' artistic. Artistic assholes got needs."

"LBJ had needs, too," I go. "They say 12 mood swings a day, ranging from elation to futility."

"It didn't stop that old bull," says little J. "He grabbed a feel whenever. You got too much idle time. People inna third world, don't have our problems. They don't know from idle time. They're to busy scrounging for food. What we toss in the garbage they live on for a week."

"You're right," I go.

"Don't encourage him," says big J.

"In America everybody dreams," says little J. "It's an inalienable right. We're eatin' Chink food, jerkin' our puddin', and getting' paid. It ain't happenin' in South America. Here people dream and nobody stops 'em, no matter how crazy. A one-arm guy wants to be a paperhanger. Who's gonna say no? If he wants it bad enough he teams up with another one arm guy. In Guatemala they'd beat him to death with his good arm. We got newscasters with speech impediments."

"Kill the light, hump," says big J to me, pulling up a chair for his feet. "and tell us about Hollywood."

"Here, here!" says little J. "Give us your version of Sunset Boulevard."

"They're filming the Jesus story. Hundreds of extras milling about the prison gate. The Romans are releasing one prisoner. The crowd cheers, the gates open, silence, a man walks out, and a voice yells, "Barab-ass! I'm sso glad it'ss you!"

☺

7.   No News Is Bad News

Diary, September 1967; Local Radio, 5a. Watching hotshot newsman Tony Troller in a control room was a how-to lesson in chasing a story by speed dialing, and close quarter survival with a caffeine wired leopard. He'd multiple dial, trolling for targets, put each on hold, and back track for the first hello. With Troller it's hump and dump. You're loved 'til the orgasm's over. But he's a thinking hump. To avoid coming up empty, he works out advanced scenarios to counter possible alibis, and alternatives to counter alternatives. His one regret? He can't report his own death. Twenty-five years later when the phone rings, I think, *It's Him.*

Once on a stakeout we break in a restaurant. Troller orders black coffee- *Milk causes mucous, and lacquers the vocal chords.* - And drops in 12 sugars. Just watching I got an insulin shock. Even relaxed he was hyper, his face slightly oily, just enough to be sleazy. They say no news's good news, but to him no news's bad news, and a recurring nightmare. *I go to air and there's no news. Or the on-air light goes on and there's no mic.* I think, I have a dream, too. I go to work and there's no Troller.

8.   Too Soon Fades the Gleam

Diary. Overtime's blood money, especially coming off the Dracula shift when your ass's draggin', and you have to face the 9-to-5 caffeined, nicotined, gasolined, codeined, fructose freaks jacked and ready to feather their nests with other people's bones. Occasionally, I pulled some OT to cover an AMIA- an asshole missing in action. Every phoned in sickout is a Tony nomination: *The train's late; I was stuck in traffic; I got squirrels in the attic.* With the hanky over the phone and pinched nose: *Gee. Hit me out of nowhere. Threw up all night. Ah-chew! Abdominal knee pains. Maybe it's knee-monia.* Questioning sickouts is a no-no, especially by other techs who expect similar courtesy when they call up. A generic reply is, *Feel better.* Once I called in and said, *I busted my leg.* Next day the only one who noticed was Ida, the spidah, the tech scheduler. So, w*here's da cast?* She says. I go, *What cast?* She says, *Ya broke ya leg. Where's dah cast, Mr. Pulitzah Surprize winnah?* I go, *Oh. Luckily it's just a sprain.* I had to limp around for a week. One caller says *the cars actin' weird. Something with the gears. I'll be late cause I'm driving in reverse.* Sickouts are paybacks for selling your soul. The company considers it *marginal losses.* Now they're called personal days, as opposed to the rest of the year which is impersonal.

This is how I first meet Jalanzo, one of my alter egos. He's a Central Control (CC) supervisor, a Runyanesque character who puts "the" in front of nouns and sees life through a prism. When nosies burst into CC foaming at the mouth with five bells, looking to "crash and burn", and take him with them, he raises a hand, and says, "What's the fuckin' flight plan, pal, the abridged version? We don't want no fuckin' Post Mortem with the Cock Sucker's Inquisition under the fuckin' lights." On Jalanzo's heels came another unique old-timer.

It's the end of my shift. I'm in CC droppin' off a show. The phone rings. Jalanzo punches it up on the overhead, says, "CC. What can I do ya fawe?" A voice like a boson's whistle rings out, *Cee-Cee?* Jalanzo says, "Last time I looked." The voice counters like he's talking to all the ships at sea. *Be-lay that crap! This is the Commander speakin'.* Jalanzo winks at me, says, "No shit? What the fuck's up?" *I'll be an hour late. My dog Bull Halsey had a seizure. Son-of-bitch's been bangin' into furniture all night. Over and out.* Jalanzo tells me to cover him. Now I'm having a seizure. I go, *Can't. I have a doctor's appointment.* And duck out.

☺

A stakeout, or remote, is a hurry-up-and-wait field assignment. It can be a solitary vigil, or a mob scene, where you spend hours, rain or shine, waiting on a grunt and a groan from the asshole of the moment. In real estate, location is everything. It's no less true at stakeouts. In the rush when the target appears you can end up lost in the suburbs. The part I detest is lugging around on my back an armoire full of electrical crap to cover all situations. On top of it sits another dead weight, the predator nosie who looks you in the eye, sees only his reflection, and expects you to hit the floor running, which is tough to do from a reclining position with an armoire on your back.

I grab some gear and head for 49th Street and 7th Avenue. Some nut's threatening to jump out a window of the Palace Theatre building. My job? Hook up with a nosie and play tech. The Palace is a famous vaudeville and burlesque house. Across the way is the Brill Building with its own history of sidewalk lotharios, whistling tune smiths, tap dancers, and jugglers for whom the gift of life is not enough. *Man,* said Bertrand Russell, *will never be satisfied, not even in heaven.*

The rabble's milling around Duffy Square, eating popcorn, chestnuts, waving pretzels at a guy hanging from a window above the Palace Theatre marquee. The stainless steel man can't make change fast enough. Only the eight foot bronze statue of Father Duffy, head full of bird shit, is looking away toward 42nd Street, where he was pastor in the '20's of Holy Cross, the "actor's church". As a kid when I'd go to the Palace, there'd be Father Duffy in military dress and puttees, helmet at his feet, bible in hand, sentinel of the Great White Way.

Suddenly, a voice is in my ear sharp as a knife. I think, *Father Duffy, say it ain't so?* It's Intrepid Troller that loco from local, an unrelenting oral-anal, verbal-compulsive screed-head, up-your-ass radio-bemba.

"I'm network now," he says, giving me the elbow. "It's rare when a tech shows up before me." Yeah, I think, including the victim.

Troller at network meant trouble, likewise several techs who'd recently transferred from local. All busy bodies. The good news? I worked nights and wouldn't see them. The bad news? It was a military buildup, before the attack and spill over. Right away I'm looking to lose 'im. Tough to do because he's cross-eyed. You never know when he's looking at you.

"The Jumper jumps," he mumbles. "The crowd gasps."

Already the poor slob's tagged, 'The Jumper', a non-person. Soon to lead The Re-Act-Merry-Go-Round, overlaying a loop of crowd noise. Most stories have more lives than a cat. Tell 'em, tell 'em again, and repeat it. Stories can be passports from obscurity to prime time. Good ones're plums, bad ones're dogs. Next thing I know, The Jumper turned into a non-story. He was a window cleaner who stepped back to admire his work, and one half of his safety straps broke off from the hook. The police pulled him in.

Back at network I researched Father Duffy. There was a real story. Father Duffy was curé of the city. He loved the gleam of Fifth Avenue in the October sunshine. Laurette

Taylor on the stage gave him great joy. "She was Irish Canadian, you know." In the war to end all wars Father Duffy was Chaplin of the *Fighting "Irish" Sixty-Ninth*, whose "ministry of presence" in the face of bullets and gas in Lorraine and the Argonne made him legendary. One night his troops were being relieved in France in the June moonlight of Lorraine, by another Irish brigade out of New York, when two brothers recognized each other. They yelled, swore, and poked each other. They were quieted down lest they draw attention and enemy artillery. As the regiments passed in silence they began humming, *Give my regards to Broadway*. The melody spoke for all of them as it faded into the distance. *Remember me to Herald Square; Tell all the boys on Forty-second Street that I will soon be there*. Father Duffy, guardian of the Great White Way at the crossroads of Broadway and 7th Avenue, died June 26, 1932.

9.   Some Remotes Are Beautiful

November 1967. Camped cheek to jowl with media creeps outside the main gate to the mayor's mansion off the East River. The real story is the loose-knit, hungry mob waiting on the target. If I move, I lose my spot. All morning I'm hanging tough holding a mic tethered to a mobile truck a hundred feet away. Suddenly, the word ripples over the crowd. Target on the move! Front door! Main gate! Bodies rush forward, tape recorders roll; mics go hot. I'm crushed up against a black Iron Gate. Any closer I'll have African tribal marks on my cheeks. Someone steps on my foot; a knee hits me in the ass; an elbow jabs me in the ribs; I get twisted around, and find I'm drifting backwards. As the target comes up to the gate, an NBC mic snakes under my armpit followed by a short-bodied human roto-rooter. Gabe Prezmen, the midget, yells out a question. What timing, coming out of nowhere like a race horse shoving its nose across the finish line. I point my mic over his head at the target. Thirty seconds later, the flack disappears into the mansion, and the Roto-rooter is gone. No grass grew under his ass.

One night I shamble in to I find a note in my mailbox. *REMOTE: 9a photo-op/press conference; Radio City Music Hall.* Are they serious? I'm on permanent remote five nights a week. Well, "removed" is more accurate. The fact that I'd be up midnight to noon doesn't bother them. It's not like working 9 to 5 and staying till 10p. The MO in BOD is plug the hole with a body, any body, even a recalcitrant one coming off the overnight drained to the gills. Mal points out, "There's good news and bad news." "How's that?" He says, "The bad news you know. The good news is that it's a press conference with Sophia Loren. Suddenly I'm wide-awake. Maybe I'll get close enough she won't be remote. On the other hand remotes are tricky. I haven't done one in ages. I'll need special gear. What gear? The Nagra, a mic, cable, audiotape. I've got all night to work it out. Gather it and test it. Right. Wrong! The equipment room's locked. The night crew has the key. True but wrong. They quit at 7p. The supervisor's in at 6a. Wrong! He's in at 7. The clean-up crew's got a key. Wrong. Nobody's got a key, not even security. Why? Too many past robberies. The maintenance supervisor's in at 7a. That's plenty of time. I'll work a little faster. Wrong. His train's late. All I need's a couple of pieces. I'll grab 'em off the pegboard and shelves like at local. Wrong! Techs have everything useable locked in individual equipment bags. The humps! I hadn't used a Nagra recorder in years. It's like riding a bike. You never forget. Wrong. No test time. The supervisor waltzes in at 8, goes for coffee. 8:15, I'm playing catch up with 45 minutes to get it together and haul ass cross-town. How? Cab. Beg, borrow and steal this and that. No time to test or back up anything. *Rule number one, says the supervisor. Make friends with other techs. They'll help you in a pinch.* Fair enough. *One other thing. Radio City's audio system may use a Kennedy Plug.* What's a Kennedy plug? *A splitter, a T-plug specially designed to cover JFK.* Maybe it's the plug he pulled on the Cubans in the Bay of Pigs. Fair enough. Except the supervisor can't find the plug. So he jerry-rigs one in a cab on the way to Radio City. Fair enough. I get a seat eight rows from the stage. Fair enough. The first four rows are cordoned off and empty. Why? To make room for Loren's tits. A fellow tech helps me hook up. Fair enough. I roll for a test. Next thing I know, Loren's talking. Fair enough. My input and output levels match. Fair enough. So I keep rolling, settle back, and drift off. *"Ronzoni sono buoni."* A voice calls out, How do you like American men, Miss Loren? *How delicate she looks.* Loren throws her head back. The paparazzi laugh. What'd she say? It's on tape. I drift off. Wake to laughter. What'd she say? What was the question? It's on tape. Miss Loren? Blah, blah. *yes. I love spaghetti. In Italy we put bread in meatballs.* I love breaded breasts. The volume indicator peeks red now and then. I'm getting her voice, not her smile, big almond eyes, full Latin lips. Whose breasts are bigger, yours or Ekberg's? The tape flapping on the take-up reel wakes me. Loren's gone like a dream, and I think remotes can be beautiful.

☺

10. On The Nightshift In My Night Shift

Racking back to the '70's, I'd see the Smiling Reefer around. He'd pop up from DC to do weekend news. Even Ms. Helmet-Hair used to come up from *the Beltway* for newscasts wearing sling-backs and a "cement do".

Smiley, like all the Morning Show alumnae dating from 1954, never made a dent in the NBC ratings. The roster of failed hosts includes Uncle Crankcase, Jack Parr, Will Rodgers Jr., country singer Jimmy Dean, Dike Van Dick, Wally 'Sticky Face' Aces, Sue Clueless, and Helmet Hair. Fifty years later, the morning slot's still in the basement.

In the '80's, Smiley Face shared weekend news chores with Helmet Hair and China Doll Chun. My encounters with them were scattered *hellos, thanks,* and in Bob's case, *Catch yawl next time around.* A number of years later China Chun had a short stint co-anchoring the Evening Snooze with Blather. Somebody stabbed her in the back by airing part of an interview she had done with the First Lady that was off the record, and it contained a profanity. I suspect the real reason is Blather did not want to share the program with anyone. Also, there was competition between them over who covers what story, i.e., the Oklahoma bombing.

China had her own news program in the late '80's. Rumor had it she was unhappy with the show, the time, whatever. She got out of her contract saying she was leaving because she was *trying to get pregnant.*

Later, a story circulated that a gay tech tried a similar excuse on his boss. *I'd like to go on leave. I'm pregnant.* His boss says, How do you know? The gay says, *I haven't shit in a month.*

☺

People are more alike than different and often predictable. How hard is that? Ergo, *welcome to the club.* I brooded for years after Hollywood. If I weren't working holidays, I'd sleep and forget. I shunned a harsh world because it hurt too much. Maybe I was hiding from my extravagant and licentious father in whose Byzantine mind nothing was extreme, too baroque or rococo. I had no governor on my thoughts or my heart- that was always my failing, and I was predisposed to self-destruct under pressure. The question was why? One thing I know, I'm The Hopeful Masochist who loves 'no' for an answer. My journey? Getting beyond it.

It was the yin-yang of my parents that kept me vacillating: timidly creative, an inhibited exhibitionist, and mercurial. "Sonny boy," my father once said, "You in-ah you night clothes all you life. A turtle in a shell afraid to come out." Fortunately, my mother's eyes always pull me toward better things. Another time he said, "If there's-ah one thing in this mighty world I can-ah give you it's-ah my will power." Yet he always undercut me. Mom's eyes steer me and Pop's the erratic propellant. My younger brother summed me up after a late supper. He looks at the C.B.S building, and me, and goes, *How can you do this to yourself; work in this sausage factory, after what you've done?*

Fear. Mental suicide. The death of initiative. Lost dreams in Benedict Canyon. Cassavetes was right. They kill the heart at 21. I felt sorry for myself, deadly thing self-pity. 'Why did I fold?' Did my father take the fight out of me? Did I equate success with a desire to kill him for what he did to the family? Is going through that proverbial door a metaphor for him? Going through it involves the unknown, taking control, outdoing him. On Bette Davis' pillow were the words, 'No guts no glory'. I could've done a lot worse than being a tech. It gave me security, a good living, but the price was my life. I was you, mama, hiding from the old man in the attic, only my attic was the nightshift. In our own way, Mama, we both folded under pressure. It destroys me to say it. No guts no glory. For that reason, when I write each word breathes life into both of us and we live as we were meant to; openly, creatively, and without fear. I refuse to let it all be in vain. That's the route of my anger. The fight we didn't make; the stance, Mama, that we never took; a backseat attitude that denied us the joy of the good fight. Maybe in the next life we'll be toreros forced to face the moment of truth. Can't hide behind a muleta. Life will come at us, we'll go forward, sink in the sword, watch the stunned bull drop down on its forelegs bellowing saliva, bleeding and pissing in the dirt. Maybe it's gross, but that's life. So, here are two ears to us, Mama, to Homecrest Avenue, and to the good fight. Win, lose, or draw. Olé!

Funny, I've got a suite at the Wellington Hotel, Langston Hughes' old stomping grounds, a stone's throw from Carnegie Hall and never go. I sleep through holidays, deaf and dumb to life. Nights are interstices for gathering up broken pieces. New Year's Eve, 13 blocks south thousands of *wildepeople* wait for the ball to drop at midnight. Instead of joining life, I kill it thinking if they panic there'll be lotsa IHOP specials. My friend and teacher Swami Das: *there are no failures, only experience.* With me it was either, or. *When you lose something, don't lose the lesson.*

I never seriously considered changing careers. I always thought I'd go back to performing. I put half my DJ skills into tech work. From day one I operated shoulders down like I'd been decapitated. Cut! Splice! Punch buttons! Open mics! When the novelty ended I realized I'd compromised myself. While one half of me despaired, the other half saw that a little creativity in news goes far, if you can get around office politics, and have a high threshold of shame. News is extrapolated not subjective. Just rip and read. Like doctors and blood, anchors and news weren't going out of style. It's cheap drama. There's a geek in a hole on every block. Dig, get re-act, and tag on an opener and closer. Squirrel *evergreens* from out-takes. Slow days are *thumb-suckers from the wheel-dex of anniversaries.* The homeless get more face time than actors.

I admire nosies because they earn a living doing work they love. I envy their commitment, discipline, and practical pov. As a DJ I mistakenly saw them as competing for airtime, and would lock the assholes out of the control room. One nosie repeatedly banged on the door before I let him in to announce an impending tornado; important news to boaters, and beach resorts. One nosie kept coming in and out during my show. I chased him into the hall and kicked him in the ass. So laying low at night, out of the loop, made the bitter pill of teching easier to swallow, and for the most part it was child's play. With time, I came to appreciate that news and I weren't totally at cross-purposes. We were info-tainers coming from different angles. One thing they had that I lacked was grit. They never wore their heart on their sleeve. Their work ethic taught me self-control, focused writing and thinking, and that if you love something sink your teeth into it and never let go.

For working nights I received an inducement called differential, or a compensatory pay for killer hours, but no amount of money is worth it. Studies suggest that overnight work is disorienting and debilitating; worker's dip in energy and attention span starting around 5a. To recoin Alfonso Bedoya in *Treasure of Sierra Madre*, I don't need "no stinking" study to tell me that. I dipped the moment I walked in the door. After a decade I have heart trouble to prove it. Frankly, all work should stop between 10p and 7a and the workweek should be thirty hours with two-hour lunches. Where are we going anyway?

When news went 24/7 it entered the commercial market place, created the stoic anchor backed by production teams that turned flat bread into Venetian twists riddled with Byzantine redundancy. Early on Pat Weaver started a show called *Monitor* that offered stories separated by advertising like pictures in a magazine. Years later it turned up as 60 Shminutens, which operated seven years in the red until it found an audience. A blind man in Nova Scotia given seven years could find China. TV proves there is a place for epigones.

Two distinct attitudes divide nosies and techs. Nosies look at their job as a career and techs see themselves as laborers. To nosies, tech work's a no-brainer. To techs, nosies *glorify insignificance.* There is truth in both positions. The difference is that a career is a labor of love, while a job is a labor of effort. With the rise of TV in the '60's, radio lost revenue and was reduced to music and news. Techs were limited in their contributions to the air product, which no longer offered involved productions. News was straight forward. So one side of the window was eager while the other side became indifferent. Techs had grown up contributing to comedy, drama, classical music concerts, and big band broadcasts. Teching news was- well, humiliating. The work process turned into the plough pulling the horse. Writers had their favorite techs and vice versa. For my part, I hated everybody, especially those who thought they were doing God's work on earth. My favorite nosie was anyone who admitted that news 24/7 was bullshit. From them I learned to chill and that everyday can't be Sunday. I don't say this sarcastically- well, yes I do. News people are hungry, territorial dogs always foaming at the mouth for a good bite and airtime. The tough thing is that news is timely, like delivering ice in August. A nosie has to move fast or it melts.

TV news stars? Right. Star is an anagram for squealer. Anchor is a silly name. When there's a mistake, I think, *the anchor sunk.* What's a female, an *anchorette?* When two anchors say goodnight, is it *Anchors Away?* If a stringer's drunk while doing "investigative reporting" is he a strung out stringer who's a sloshed sleuth? A whip-around is sado-masochist reporters handing it to one another. In a newscast the cast should be from the neck up. What do you do? *I'm a news producer.* You produce news? *Sometimes it produces itself. Other times I coax it along. Putting disparate elements together: actuary-people talking; crowd noises; natural sound; music; and mixing them into a cohesive bird's-eye view of what happened.* Then what we hear never happened the way we hear it?

Right. No simultaneity of events unless you can be in five places at once.

☺

11. Non-Sequitor Days, Differential Nights.

The public thinks the broadcast newsroom is Mount Olympus, the Vatican, and Hollywood all wrapped up in one, but it's really a brick shithouse full of pretentious *holier than thou* electronic assholes who masturbate info with solemnity and due process, suggesting they are the Almighty's vicars and their words are *From God's Lips To Me.*

Back in 1967, however, I was like General Macarthur, *I shall return.* To deejaying. My problem wasn't lack of talent. I could easily ad lib a couple of shows a week. What I didn't grasp was the extent of jealousy and chicanery among my colleagues, and that "show business" is two words. The second one conditions the first. I was all show and no business.

☺

Devious Septum: Coming up, Chink n' Cholly and The Hoy Vey Café, but first...

C.B.S MEMORANDUM

From: R.E.G., Jr. – Director of Engineering Services.   Date: November 28, 1967

To: L.A.C Please see attached.

I will add my thanks to this also. It's nice to get this kind of memo about my people from the other departments.   REG: lfw

C.B.S MEMORANDUM

From: JD News Director   To: R. E. G   Date: November 19, 1967

A great job by all in getting out the product. Yeoman service performed by all techs, but especially L.C., who was inundated with tape and phoners, and stayed the course. Thank you, and thanks all.   JD: mnl

That was my first 'thank you' from the brass. Then I was victim of a nasty piece of newsroom back stabbing. I came in one morning at 4a and the CC tech says, *record a cartridge off ampex 3.* So I slip start a cart to tighten it, record, and he says, *Somebody's doing a hatchet job on you.*

It was Teddy Tape-ops using me to cover his screw-ups. During idle time in a production studio off the newsroom I'd been reading a book written by a Hitlerian skinhead full of misguided opinions and racial slurs. I made the mistake of discussing a passage with Teddy Tape-ops. It was nonsensical Nazi phrenology that claimed the size, bumps, and density of a black male's head was similar to a bull's. *Blacks,* said the author, *have thick skulls, which means less room for brains and they're bovine.* Hitler and Goebbels suggested the same crap about Jews.

One morning I witnessed an embarrassing moment. Editor Lew Mazer walked in ticked off about sloppy run-down sheets, leaned over Teddy Tape-ops' shoulder, and in a patronizing voice gave him a typing lesson. *Punct-u-ation clar-i-fies thought,* he goes. *For that reason your type writer has different keys. Watch me.* Taking deliberate aim, he strikes each key with a stiff finger. *This key is for comas. This one's for periods. The key at the end pressed down turns lower case into caps. It's all there on your typewriter. A-maz-ing, isn't it?* Teddy Tape-ops swallowed it with a "Thank you". Apparently, he was from the "e e cummings" journalism sch o o

1

,

☺

169

12.   Artists Starve Talking Heads Get Rich

In fall of 1967 I had a working relationship with a young reporter Ned Bratley. He'd been a schoolteacher, or principal, in Philadelphia before joining C.B.S. A passive-aggressive, he turned his teacher skills, and his blackness, to reporting and spun gold out of courteous impertinence. Reporters give the illusion of intrepid investigator, but hard questions stop at the wallet. Edword R. Burrow is a prime example of a broadcast journalist who paid the price of the forthright inquisitor.

Bratley would come in the studio in the wee hours; carton of milk in one hand, script in the other, plunk his 5'11", heavyset frame down in a chair before a table mic, and we'd go to work. Some sessions were over before they started, others were stop and go, particularly when the written word read better than it sounded, and phrases needed reworking. One day out of the blue I go, *One ice cream soda says you'll goof the read.* I'd wager on hunches: his walk, the tone in his "hello", the look in his eyes: *G' morning. What's good about it?* Oh. This read's three ice cream sodas. It was all in fun to lighten things. The sodas were to go to kids in a Harlem school near WLIB. Until schedule changes and lies split up our work relationship, my hunches were so good Ned had me in the hole for 38 ice cream sodas. But he cheated and would only bet on his terms.

Once while piecing him together in the control room we talked about boxing versus Karate. Why, I don't recall. Maybe because Ned fancied himself a boxer. *Karate,* he says short-sightedly, *can't stand up to boxing.* Depends who's fighting. First, they're different styles. What's missing in Karate is contact. *That's critical for sharpening reflexes and building stamina.* Right. But boxing has the Marquis of Queensbury rules. Uses fists only. Karate uses fists, elbows, knees, and feet. It's the science of dirty street fighting. I decided to leave it at that, sensing some tension. Probably we should've gone to a gym for some grab-ass. Men need showing before they recognize each other. Maybe we'd've both learned something. But we were on the job where familiarity can be dangerous. So I chose not to do what Parker did to Rod Taylor (*The Birds*) when he voiced the same sentiments in 1959. *Okay, Rod,* says Ed. *Throw a punch.* Soon it was biff, bam! Thank you, Ma'm!

Our sometime contact ended when I moved crosstown. But along the way his opinion of me was tainted by creepy, four-eyed Teddy Tape-Ops- He didn't know a lower case from a capital! - who had characterized me as incompetent and bigoted. Ned was part of the Shelter Island clique.

One day I corner a tech, also a "Shelter Island weekender". His Italian last name in English means 'little chicken'. He was the "lucky bird" who won the 1967 Jaguar and cried over capital gains. *Tell your buddies,* I go, *to stop the bullshit.* He makes with the Mars look, like he doesn't know what I mean, and says, *Deliver your own messages.* I look dead in his eyes and go, *I'm asking you, paisano, to avoid bigger problems. Capisce? The last thing any of you want to do is step on the toe of somebody in a tight-knit Italian family. Tell 'em. Or you can kiss your Jag goodbye.*

Meanwhile, at my request, our shop steward arranged a meeting with the technical department supervisor who was riding me from hearsay. The steward demanded proof where I'd failed in my job and insisted on written complaints signed and dated. *Otherwise,* says JK, *we go straight to the union. This is not a Gestapo society. We don't railroad people.* The supervisor backed off and never bothered me again.

After a Paris sojourn, Bratley returned reporting for TV. One day he comes into my turf to record a track. At first, I sense recognition, but it passes like a breeze.

Fuck you, I think, and Teddy Tape-ops. Never screw with a man's job. Back then I was on probation and could've been fired. Ned went on to become a seasoned reporter. We all grow up given time and a patron. But he never wrote a book. Ya paint, paint a picture. Ya write, write a book, and not a compilation of your life as a "company" reporter. Maybe I'm too harsh, but then Ned was never a cozy guy. Sadly, artists starve and talking heads get rich. The best part of him was 38 ice cream sodas he'll never collect. In 2006 Bratley, 65, died of leukemia.

☺

13. A Deafening Silence

Dateline. Local AM radio. August 27, 1967. *The silence,* said the CC tech, *was deafening. No buzz. Nothin'. We were a dead body in a casket. Like we never existed. It was eerie. I could hear myself breathe. The VU meter's bouncing. The master pot's up. The monitor position on the board was on off-air and nothin'. The return signal was dead. I figure the receiver amp blew. The phone starts ringing. What's going on? Get off the line so I can find out!*

At 4:20 PM, Sunday, three weeks into the job, AM radio went dead. Other stations were still on except WNBZ. The CC tech scrambled to trace it down, this line, that amplifier, and then a call came from the Chief Engineer on duty at the Chuckler Island tower. *Transmitter's down! Nothin's standing. This is Gus. It's raining, foggy. I heard a tremendous crash. Maybe lightening hit the tower. I don't know. An earthquake. Keep the line open.* Gradually, the puzzle was assembled. *I'm loggin' readings in my raincoat ready to head out to check the tower, when I hear a roar and boom that knocks me on my ass. Out in the rain; debris all around; no tower; no lights. Unbelievable. 541 feet of steel pushing 50,000-watts collapsed- Son-of-a-bitch! – like a busted matchstick. Thank God it fell the other way. Eerie in the rain. I could hear the feed from local like the last words at the end of the world, but no tower to transmit. I'm at Rubino's- Absolutely incredible- drinkin' straight scotch; lucky to be alive.*

Airplane Hits AM Tower

Monday's headline went on: Single-engine Piper Cherokee out of East Hampton lost in a heavy rainstorm looking to land at La Guardia Airport hit a radio tower and then crashed in Long Island Sound, killing two persons, possibly six. When the tower went down it missed hitting the power transmitter building a hundred feet away. The plane was on an unauthorized flight. All planes at East Hampton airport were officially grounded due to severe weather conditions. The Piper Cherokee out of La Guardia was returning from East Hampton when it went down.

I had a First Class License so they sent me out to Chuckler Island to assist the chief in a minor capacity. He'd been in over-drive 38 hours. The rain had let up when I drove on to High Island proper, near Orchard Beach. I drove around police barriers into a parking area, and I could see from my car a gnarled, capsized steel tower with a few feet at the base still standing, and metal parts strewn about. In the mist and dark the sight was a surreal mangle of steel. The wing of the plane must've clipped the tower and then spun off into the sound. To me the chief was brilliant. He had jerry-rigged a low signal off a support cable, or guy wire, running at a 45-degree angle from an anchored spot in the ground to a height of maybe 10 feet of what was left standing. It looked like the fat part of a baseball bat with the handle shorn off. The bunker-like transmitter building had adequate living quarters and a power generator. *One for the books,* said the Chief. *We're pushin' minimum watts. Radius maybe .2 miles. Can't get in the city, but you can hear us on a car radio across the road if no taxis are using two-ways. We're down but not dead.* I go, *Chief, we stand a better chance of pushing out a signal by grabbing hold of the Manhattan feed and transmitting off my dick.* He says, *Maybe. But your balls better be grounded, son.*

Within days the station was operating off a borrowed 10,000 watt, 200-foot tower on nearby High Island that, ironically, belonged to my former employer, WLIB. It all happened hours before our station was to go from music, news and talk to an all-news and information format. Weird timing. Like a kamikaze sent by God, or the competition all-news WINS radio. LIB had recently upgraded to new towers in Jersey's Meadowlands, and gave C.B.S temporary use of their old rat infest transmitter in Long Island City, Queens, a dreary place by day, and at night it resembled a wayside haunt for ghouls.

I spelled the chief, took readings, adjusted for drift, slept, and fudged a few. My watch was uneventful, boring really, so it didn't matter. People should have similar knobs on their heads to keep them honest. Nights car radios around City Island heard Art Heinus with "Music 'til dawn brought to you by" - *Crackle! Zzt! Car 2. Pick-up 2. Rubino's Ristorante. Zzt!* - The airline bringing you - *Zzt! One calamari to go.* Guess who that was? Like the tower I was down but not dead.

☺

14. Settling In 'Cross-town

Diary. Spring, 1968: A tech position opened up across town at Network Radio. I showed up early for the interview, browsed around the studios, familiarized myself with the board, and during the interview I casually mentioned one board pot doing two jobs. Mason Eschar, Supervisor Of Technical Network Services, agreed it was awkward.

Essentially, I was saying I already know the control board. I got the 5a shift, and then the overnight. Back then network news stopped at 11p and resumed at 6a. Before settling down on a new job it takes what techs call the baptism of fire. Mine came teching my first overnight hourly. Enter Mal "Roundy" Terkel, a Sherman tank with eyeglasses slipping down his nose, the editor-producer of hourlies and the News Roundup (NR).

Mal. Tell me something about the hourly I don't know.
Tech. Our pencils don't have erasers.
Mal. Explain that in English?
Tech. Your side goofs you walk away. We goof you come down on us like a ton of bricks. The guy stopped, restarted, and we didn't catch it.
Mal. We?
Tech. Your tape-ops guy... and me.
Mal. Did you play the tape down?
Tech. Yes. I leadered a false start and your guy didn't play it down, or he'd've caught it.
Mal. You play it down. We play it down. We protect each other. The one time you don't check things it'll come back and bite you in the ass. Run every tape down before air, and check them against the cue sheets. It's simple. Don't complicate it. Tapes come out to me, we send them back, and in between anything could go wrong. It's that kind of business. We cover each other's ass, and protect the air show. Now let's move on. Don't hesitate to tell me anything. That way we clear the air. Leave a copy of the Trouble Report (TR) on my desk so I can short circuit any bullshit that comes up later. Keep it simple and don't get paranoid. Nobody's perfect except management. As for your eraser comment, sit in my chair and you'll know. I have to answer to affiliates, notes from upstairs, phone calls from listeners asking what happened. I don't like egg on my face. If I don't know we all look like amateurs. We're a news network, responsible for news content, in

competition with other stations. Don't forget the TR. Now go back to sleep and don't quote me.

That was "Roundy", a *post mortem* minimalist. Another time.

Mal. Take off the top. For you it's marked in red crayon with arrows.

Tech. You know, depressed people have a disturbance in their melatonin circadian pattern with abnormal cortisol secretion?

Mal. Put the tape up, or I'll disturb your defecation pattern.

Tech. Our bodies try to establish a moment-to-moment balance. If a person on the nightshift encounters a man with a tape in a dark room, the eyes relay the threat to the brain-

Mal. What brain?

Tech. And the brain registers fear or anger.

Mal. You should've put all this on your work application.

Tech. I did. That's why they sent me to you. They figure you haven't suffered enough producing news all night.

Mal. Wrong.

Tech. Working nights decreases melatonin and fucks up sleep. Seasonal changes affect melatonin secretion and can cause a bi-polar disorder. Peaks in January, July; troughs in April, October.

Mal: Troughs?

Tech. Lows. Desynchronization of biological rhythms that happen in spring and the autumn equinox are related to seasonal illness. Problems in my limbis system caused by neurotransmitters to my hypothalamus provoke neurochemical responses which send messages to the front lobe of my pituitary, which responds by pouring out adreno cortico-tropic - a hormone - into the blood stream that travels to the adrenal glands, near the

176

kidneys, which pours out cortisol, which converts nor-e-pinephrine into the epinephrine, and both enter the blood stream readying the body for the "flight or fight" response.

Mal. And editing does all that to you?

Tech. To you, too, only you don't know it. Since you walked in my heart's been pumping faster, my lungs're taking in more oxygen, and my liver's releasing sugar to provide energy for my tense muscles. You bring in a tape and right away the pupils of my eyes dilate, and my body's sweating to cool down cause you're bringing violent activity.

Mal. You're nuts, you know that?

Tech. It's not me. It's my neuron receptors.

Mal. Neuron or moron?

Tech. Studies with rats prove anticipation of threatening or frightening or complicated tasks-

Mal. Like putting a tape on a machine

Tech. Yes.

Mal. And pressing a button.

Tech. It's simple to you, not to me. The ability to cope is influenced by the output of gluco-corti-coids.

Mal. I didn't know that.

Tech. Case studies show childhood stress effects neurons at the DNA level, causing changes in protein synthesis and synaptic excitability. Cortisol is secreted in timed bursts throughout the day, synchronized with a 24-hour sleep-wake cycle. It has both periodic ultradian and daily circadian variations. A rapid rise occurs with peak secretion between 5 and 9a. In depressed people it's 24/7. If disturbed, the normal boundary of our sleep-wake alternation or circadian rhythm gets lost. It needs 24 hours to complete. After 2AM there's little cortisol output. So it's not us. The nightshift's responsible for our mental indisposition. It screws up our inner circadian clocks, which like wristwatches run fast or slow-

Mal. In your case backwards.

Tech. And need adjusting. Seratonin gets mixed up with melatonin.

Mal. Good old Sarah and Mel.

Tech. Dawn and dusk get turned around in a place where the sun never sets. The clock or pacemaker within controls sleep-wake cycles adjusting to day and night, the position of the sun. Healthy people adjust to day cycles. In short, my problem's circadian desynchronization.

Mal. That would've been my guess.

Tech. Sleep disturbances are rhythmic and suggest that moods are temporal disorders in which the timing of biological rhythms is altered. The body's alarm clock is programmed to go on and off based on human circadian rhythms. Working nights ruins our sleep pattern. Depression sets in. Outside cues like light, temperature and darkness establish order in the body. Circadian rhythms can be shifted using pulses of light. Bright, artificial light suppresses melatonin, the sleep chemical. So does sunlight, which is two hundred times brighter.

Mal. If light suppresses melatonin you should be awake. What the hell am I talking about? Cut the tape.

Tech. Light synchronizes our circadian body clocks. Artificial night-light delays by six hours body temperature rhythms and cortisol secretion. Exposure to bright light resets the body clock. Bright artificial *newsroom* light manipulates biological rhythms causing pathological disorders. Look, on the console, a therapy light box. Put your head inside, turn on the ultraviolet light, and it corrects perception and moods. It feels great when I take my head out.

Mal. No doubt. Take your head out of your ass you'll feel even better.

Another time.

Tech. Techs are facchini.

Mal. As in fuck-offers.

Tech. Porters, who know right away when they're handed a load of shit.

Mal. So do I. Take the top off this-

Tech. I got a theory. Techs're like dude ranch horses who can spot an amateur by the way we're spurred. Dudes jam those spurs in until the blood runs. Play it again. I forgot to time it. What was that out cue? Right now you're diggin' into me with that tape. But ya don't jerk the reins.

Mal. Stop jerkin' me off. Roll on Wash, and edit the tape.

Tech. All my talk's in vain. Put the tape down. It's like a pointed gun. You're very insensitive, but I like you.

Mal. I'm thrilled. What you really like is your weekly bucket of oats. Now, you crazy, procrastinating screwball, put the tape up or I'll shove it up.

Tech. Oh. A triple threat. Jewish, violent, and anal. In the future, come in on tiptoes, and wake me with cotton swabs gently under the ear.

☺

15.   The Salty Bird

Jalanzo. How's ya pork, pal?

Tech. Good. Here's a TR. One goof on an hourly.

Jalanzo. I see you like to fuckin' write.

Tech. Mal said to explain--

Jalanzo. Hold y'horses, pal. I'm tryin' to read THE so-called writin'. You relied on those cocksuckers, an egregious mistake. They'll fuck you in the ass every time. Comprende? Always protect your ass and the air product. Unless y'got a fuckin' thing for the unemployment line. This is your fuckin' catechism. Five fuckin' minutes to air, say, I have no other fuckin' business than that which concerns *the* fucking hourly. A-fuckin'-men! I need you for a half hour OT. The Commander's late again. And don't make with the doctor crap. If it ain't the dog, it's the wife. Always a fuckin' Federal Case. Nobody says, I'll be late my ass is draggin'. Or, I'm bangin' the old lady onna kitchen table. That'll be the fuckin' day!

THE Commander was as I imagined him in the image of Admiral Bull Halsey: closely cropped gray hair; sharp, flinty blues; maybe 5' 5"; solid muscle; magnetic presence; and a W.W. Two Vet. To him anybody who doesn't serve his country is a faggot Vichy.

"Relieved of duty, Bunky," says the Commander entering the studio. "You the new overnight man? What? Ya don't have a life?"

Suddenly, he reaches out, clamps my thigh in a vice grip, and grins. Jalanzo backs in laughing, holding the door with his ass.

"Relax. Enjoy it, Bunky!" says the commander. "Move, it hurts worse."

"Welcome to *the* fuckin' club!" says Jalanzo.

"News," says the Commander, letting go, "The goddamn glorification of insignificance."

Later on I go, *Jalanzo, the Commander's got a grip like a carpenter.* He says, *Naw. He's a fuckin' pee-nano player. He and the wife play fuckin' duets. Her grip's even stronger. Got him by the balls with the fuckin' pinky.*

The Commander's other quirk was shooting bunnies, but only when there were three or more people in the room, making it hard to detect who blew one off-everybody quietly blaming the other person. He'd fake some business, rattle reels, shoot a bunny, and go. I still see his beady, sadistic blues looking through the small window in the door like a gas chamber executioner watching the condemned choke. He was Duke of the Dump in chinos and a beret, in and out like a mouse. The first time it happened I woke up thinking, the condensers are burning up.

☺

16. Black As the Pit

Wanted! Network Anchor. News Moses! A telegenic tailor's dummy. Texas Twang a plus with sub rosa attitude: *From God's lips to me.* Rise Abov Police Blotters and Ambulnce Chasng. Remembr: *The potty doesn't make the man, the man makes the potty.* Bottoms Up to the Winner. C.B.S is EOE, an Equal Opportunity Evader.

Nosies have two orifices from which they blow wind. Sometimes it's hard to tell which one is speaking. When President Tush went for a colonoscopy the doctor got confused. He'd heard so much shit he didn't know which end to stick the tube. Before checking in Tush handed over the power of the presidency to Lon Chaney, man of a thousand faces, That's like me telling the King of England, I'm checking into a hospital take over. Tush's popularity in Washington is down, but when he goes home to his ranch in Lawford it goes up. He's got three swimming pools. One pool has hot water, the second cold water, and the third's empty. It's for his friends who can't swim. Tush says, I'm a dwarf. Condy Rice says, You're 5'9'. He says, That makes me the tallest dwarf in the world.

If nosies say, I've zilch to report. They're history. God forbid they should tell the truth. "These inconsequential stories are making today's news. Blah, blah. In closing, remember to vote for Electronic Asshole of the Year. He/she/it must be an anal-compulsive whose toilet training went amok resulting in a love of the scatological: shit, piss, ass. *My shit's bigger than yours! Mine smells better.* Because nosies suffer traumatic poop separation, they're anal-retentive, horde, and hog everything. *I made the call. It's my interview. Bullshit! Be nice I'll give you my outtakes.* To them cutting tape is like playing patty cake with their own excrement. Better than sexual foreplay.

Their mom's said, *Sweetie-pie. This is your turd. Isn't it lovely? Never let anyone take it from you. Make Mommy another.* They grow up singing Brooklynese like Streisand; *We're having a potty!* The people have a right to know who's shitting whom. That's the way it is.

Diary. Despite discovering *it's what you do that counts not what you're planning to do,* I always felt drawn to the arts. Sooner or later somehow your "calling" will surface, and in my case it was writing. In time I came to understand that I had to remake and nurture the little boy in me until he caught up with the man. There were many bleak periods, blind allies, lots of emotional pushing and shoving, despair, but, *Out of the night that covers me, black as the pit from pole to pole, I thank whatever gods may be, for my unconquerable soul.* (Henry, Invictus)

☺

17.   The Door

After TV reached its stride in the 1970's, the Equal Opportunity Act forced the introduction of minorities and *Women in News!* But it was ten years slow in coming. To women, equality on the job included language. "Male chauvinist" terms like news_man_, and anchor_man_ had to go. In sports, women demanded equal time in locker rooms. They also pushed for equal pay. Things were so dicey early on that the Equal Employment Opportunity Commission put a notice in the newspaper to educate people, mostly men. It said, help wanted ads in columns that were classified "on the basis of sex will be considered as a preference based on sex and in violation of...the civil rights Act of 1964" which prohibits "discrimination based on sex, unless sex is a bona-fide occupational qualification." It went on, "separate headings 'Male and

Female' remain for advertisers who wish to advertise positions where sex is a qualification." It stopped short of the bedroom.

In 1983 or '84 Mondale chose Geraldine Farraro as his VP running mate. Anchorette J. Muller prayed for women in politics. *Don't screw up, or you'll set us back 10 years.* A Congress Woman, somewhere out west, had to bow out of a race for VP nominee. As she gave her withdrawal speech on TV, JM says, *Whatever you do, don't cry, please.* She cried. Men, you see, don't cry, not publicly anyway. They play hardass all the way. A writer/ editor once told me while ripping copy, *You should've been a journalist.* Maybe. I had the goods, but not the stamina. Women were right. You had to keep up with men. I had trouble keeping up with both.

Producers are androgynous creatures that excel in getting ducks in line. They're buffers between talent and a fickle public. In a symbiotic relationship, they support, advise, decide, hold the talent's hand, and even wipe their ass. As a friend and TV producer once said, *Knowing what to pick and choose is a talent, too.*

There are greater rewards on the talent side of the window than in uninspiring technical work, unless you're queer for quasars. Techs are unsung heroes, the backbone of fraudcasting. They make it all possible. Over the years I saw lots of "talent" come and go, and often wondered how they survived. Guts and guile, I guess. To me, switching jobs was scary. Tech work was undemanding, steady, had great "bennies", and was safe. When you grow up poor those are big plusses. Still, the other side of the glass had its appeal. It's a fun way to go, if you don't mind being re-born every day. I did. If I'd had a realistic grip on life then I might've pulled off the news rope trick, which is essentially standup comedy with a straight face. But I layed low wisely concluding that I was a wild hare forever destined to be on somebody's shitlist, even my own. If *'man'll never be happy not even in* heaven,' then rich or poor, it doesn't matter which side of the window you're on. The answer was not money, but following one's intuition. An Italian game show title said it aptly *Rischia Tutto!* Risk it all. To do less is death.

I was happiest when trusting my intuition. There were setbacks, sure, but I never failed because it was my heart's *necessity.* What I found out on the way is best illustrated by a rustic, Appalachian anecdote. Miss Bertha lives in the back woods. It's her birthday. She's the object of every man's affection for miles around. A caller comes knocking. Bertha says, *Who dat?* The caller says, *Jedariah. I brung you a box of candy fah ya birthday.* She says, *O, dat's nice. Put it down outside dee door on da porch. I can't see nobody. I'm too tired to entertain.* Soon another caller knocks. Bertha says, *Who dat?* The caller says, *Daniel. I brung you a teddy bear.* She says, *Put it by the door on dee porch. I can't see nobody today. I got me a rambubuncious headache.* A few minutes later there's knock. *Who dat?* The caller says, *Mose. I done brung you a hard-on.* She says, *Oh. Bring dat right in. It's perishable!*

That's life. You don't want to leave it at the door.

☺

18.   HIPPO

A college buddy once said *if you want to find somebody who folded in a chosen profession look in the peripherals of that business.* I lived at the Wellington behind Carnegie Hall, a stone's throw from C.B.S and Duffy Square. My day ended when everybody else's started and the whole day was mine. I had a cockeyed idea that by working nights and sleeping days I could out run my devils; kill the beast yearning for attention, but always met disaster. Invisibility and detachment, I thought, would allow time for healing, re-evaluation, and building a nest egg. But I was like an alcoholic hiding from booze as a men's room attendant in a bar. The mid '60's were eventful years in America, but I lay low in the heart of the new Rome, mind drawn like a shade, deaf and dumb to life and love- a beaten man and didn't know it.

In time life began to pass me by. Some news filtered down to me of sit-ins and techs on dangerous remotes. **The SDS Barricades Itself In Columbia University President's Office.** Irv, a fellow tech from local radio, was on stakeout at Morningside. He was up on a truck when a bullet whizzed by his ear. Shades of Mario Savio and the UC, Berkeley free speech movement, which that school administration tried to characterize as a *civil rights panty protest*. Like abolitionist John Brown a century earlier, the sit-in citizens wanted to live the words of the Constitution, the Declaration of Independence, and the Emancipation Proclamation. In this country, said Martin Luther King Jr., we've learned to fly with birds and swim with fish, but can't walk the earth as brothers. There is in this land a *poverty of the spirit*. Amen! Spiritual people are dangerous because they are willing to die for an idea.

Lesbian and Man-Hater Valerie Solonas Shoots Andy Warhol. *The bastard had my script, S.C.U.M. He and that phony fuckin' no-good lying publisher stole my work!* Warhol was right. Somebody nobody knew would be in the limelight about every 15 minutes.

I continued to lie low nights, as counter-culture beatniks morph into Frisco's Haight-Ashbury feel-good hippies, a great love-in of flower power, children offering roses instead of bullets. It was the Time of the Great Spoonfeed. People were sick of spoon-fed lies from doddering oligarchs and politicos. With JFK's demise the lights went out in the White House and in our hearts. It was the death of youth; mine, yours, the worlds. And the selfish, old fucks were back. JFK's legacy was Irish-

American eloquence, an infectious smile, charm and wit, vigor; the personification of hope, a Greek God in a double breasted suit with a Boston accent. He was Prometheus Bound after all, and America was tied to a rock, its heart and liver exposed for the world to peck at. Camelot was a fanciful notion promoted after JFK's death in apposition to the truth. The real "Camelot" was Ike's underwriting France in Vietnam; the Bay of Pigs; sending 15,000 advisors to Vietnam; Berkeley College kids gassed by low-flying helicopters for yelling at buses of inductees, *Don't Go to War!*

1964: LBJ Runs His Presidential Campaign On A Peace Platform. *If I can get your help, if I can hold your hand, if I can have your heart, if I can have your prayers, and if the good lord's willing I will try to continue to lead this nation, this world to peace.* And if you could stop bullshittin'! **1965:** Watts Riots in five days of horror. **Malcolm X Shot in Autobahn Ballroom, Harlem.** A threat to Hitlerian Muslim leaders, he spoke of espousing the blue-eye. Malcolm and Dr. King, left and right of Gandhi. Hello, Stokely Carmichael. Ciao, Jomo Kenyatta walking Manhattan with a machete on his hip. Enter Bobby Seal, Huey Newton, and Eldridge Cleaver, and the scary, gun carrying Black Panthers. I wanted to go into their office-store off 125th Street, but didn't, thinking, they'd shoot me. **1966: Student Protesters Go Up Against Police and National Guard:** *Zeig heil! Zeig heil!* **Ronald Reagan Runs for Governor** on self-serving speeches. Mr. Self-righteous, indignant over youth asserting itself against an old fogy establishment. An actor with an emotional range from A to B, he was for accumulation of goods beyond basic necessities. *America, you must produce twice weekly your weight in garbage or you're un-American.* His words were posturing. *Free speech advocates have no appreciation of free speech.* That's one for the Gipper. *The ringleaders should be taken by the scruff of the neck and thrown off-campus.*

They should've kicked him off the Berkeley stage for perpetuating communal lies that feed materialism and the military industrial complex.

1967, April 21. Svetlana Alliluyeva, Stalin's daughter, quits Russia for America. Why? *For self-expression* and because *it was impossible to exist without God in one's heart.* **Israel's Six-Day War** brought jokes: Arab Rifles 4 Sale, only dropped once. The Jews are giving back the Gaza, but keeping the cabanas. General Westmoreland asks for a million more troops. Hoover tells Johnson, No. It'll *endanger America's security.* **LBJ Signs Appropriations Bill, Largest in History of America.** $70 billion for defense, $1.6 billion <u>less </u>than he wanted, and forgot his War On Poverty. In March youth faces down the National Guard with Flower Power. **Hope flares in 1967** with Eugene McCarthy; youth shaves its head, cries, "Clean for Gene" who fades from the scene with the rise of RFK. **Adam Clayton Powell**, 22 years a Harlem Representative, is denied his congressional seat; House Democrats strip him of his chairmanship of the Education and Labor Committee for extravagances with taxpayer's money. An Associated Press survey said, at least 50 other representatives had done the same thing. Powell's, *What's in your hand?* Was answered with, *What's in your pocket?* To him it was a lynching northern style. What's in your pocket, brother? *When the octogenarians pass on,* Powell remarked, I *might be Speaker of the House, run for president.* Imagine? *A White House half black.* I might make *Rap Brown Secretary of Defense.* From his hideaway in Bimini he exclaimed *Keep the faith, baby,* which got turned around to *Keep the baby, Faith.* **July-August:** Racial Riots in Newark and Detroit, a city with a population of 1.7 million and 30% black. Violence erupts in 114 cities in 32 States: Estimated 88 dead, 4,000 injured, over 12,000 arrested, property damage in the tens of millions. H. Rap Brown: *Violence is as American as apple pie.*

1968: Martin Luther King Shot On Balcony of Memphis Motel. Dead at Age 39. Bus Boy Shoots RFK In Ambassador Hotel Kitchen. *Finally,* someone said, *they shot the right Kennedy.* Meanwhile **Priests Immolate Selves. Thousands of Vietnam Protesters March Against America's Dumbocracy Where the Old Lead and the Young Die. Women's Lib Is Born Out of The Counter Culture. Nixon Promises Peace But Didn't Say When. 1969:** UC, Berkeley, **Protesters & Drop Outs Take Over Campus Parking Lot & Build the People's Park:** a love place, dedicated to a future of non-violence and mutual respect. **Vietnam Tet Offensive.** Countless dead on both sides leads nitro popping, peace loving liar LBJ to say, *I will not seek re-election.* Next to signing the Civil Rights Bill it was America's best moment. Although he was beautiful in South America on greeting the descamisados in that Texas drawl: *Moochose crotchius amigers.* It ranks right up there with JFK's *Ich bin ein Berlin.* **Man Lands on the Moon! Teddy Lands in Chappaquidick:** Mary Jo Kopechne lands in the morgue. Eleven hours later, Teddy reports to the police, and goes free. **1970: Kent State 4 Students Killed By National Guard! 1973:** Nixon dodges Watergate; Peace comes to Vietnam, over 50,000 American graves. **Yom Kippur:** Egypt and Syria invade Israel. In 24 hours 1,000 Israeli soldiers die, hundreds of tanks, scores of aircraft destroyed. Arabs Seize the East Bank of the Suez. Drive Armor into the Sinai! Syria Advances 10 miles into the Golan Heights! 270,000 Israelis against 1,080,000 Arabs. Shades of Tannebaum Gate, 1947. Nixon gathers his inner circle, meets resistance to aid the Jews, tells Kissinger, *Itemize arms and materials Israel needs and double it! Whatever it takes, save Israel. Now get the hell out and get the job done.* As US planes land, Israeli pilots fly into battle, and turn the tide. **Women Demand Equal Rights On Job! Toss Constricting Bras In Ash Can!** G'bye garters, girdles, high heels, eyelash curlers, falsies.

Up Yours, Not Ours! America nose-dives; regurgitates a belly full of lies, murders and war dead. *Sicilians,* says Lampadusa's Leopard, *romanticize death born from the harsh land, and unpredictability of life.* There's death *even in Sicilian sherbet,* the way it's eaten *giving death the tongue.* In Russia's southern mountains tribesmen write love poems to their swords and yataghans. My knife, sword, protector and lover. *To Allah in Valhalla! This is my rifle, this is my gun, one is for killing, the other for fun.* It's all fun, the despicable, sensually grotesque, ultimately sadistic killing of one another. Tho' I'm Brer Rabbit licking my wounds, I hear the running feet of Kurasawa's Samurai pounding the earth, hands on sword hilts, legs wind milling in high grass, a doom-eager world bent on suicide. I lay low, Mifune in Sanjuro, under the C.B.S boards, in the jaundice light of VU meters, my soul a screaming Munch.

☺

C.B.S Memorandum
FROM: TROLLER, EXECUTIVE NEWS DIRECTOR   TO: MR. P,
VP BOD   DATE: 11/10/1970

As usual, great work all around by the technical staff this morning on the De Gaulle death broadcasts. A special word, if I may, for technician LC who was buried under dozens of NEWSFEED tapes by two NEWSFEED producers, instead of the usual one. LC came through with a fine product for the stations. Again, thanks.

Scene 1: Studio E, 2a. November, 1972.

Mal. (entering) Y'sleeping or unconscious? With you it's hard to tell. And don't say you're reading. There're no pictures. (*Tech shows union letter*) Oh, the gloves're off.
Tech. I'm not walking.
Mal. You've no choice. Put this up. Lemme time it, if you please, sir.
Tech. Always polite when y'want something. How about what I want?
Mal. Be polite, maybe I'll give it to you, darling.
Tech. Oh, sweetie. You put it up. I have to rest my feet.

Mal. I'm gonna rest one of mine up your behind. Put the tape up.

Tech. You're like management. You don't care about the workers.

Mal. Since when did you fall into that category?

Tech. Picketing's an embarrassment.

Mal. Nothing could embarrass you. You're never awake long enough.

Tech. I'll go back to disc jockeying. (*cues tape on ampex*)

Mal. At your age? What as, a Geritol jock?

Tech. Yeah. I'll play Guy Lombardo, Lester Lanin, and Phil Harris: Smoke, smoke that cigarette-

Mal & Tech. And if you smoke yourself to death, tell St. Peter at the golden gate he'll just have to wait, cause you just gotta have another cigarette.

Mal. Hit the tape. (*times it*)

Tech. I'll do nee-use from nursing homes. No shows at breakfast. Who remembered their names? Look. Job ads for DJ's in *Broadcast Magazine*. "DJ Yestrday. Great fishg & swimg. Board shift. Commish all u sell."

Mal. Hold on. The cue's coming up. Good. Rack back. You were saying?

Tech. "Ground flr Op, aggressive staff; S. M., M. O. R., T. R. to PD."

Mal. They might expect work for their money. What's the pay?

Tech. Doesn't say. They're located in Okeechobee-

Mal. God Bless you.

Tech. Florida. "Ground floor; aggressive?" What's that?

Mal. Dodging alligators. What're those other letters?

Tech. TR means tape/resume; MOR, Middle of the Road music; SM-

Mal-Tech. Small market.

Tech 2. (*pokes head in door*) Hit the pavement! Strike. We're outta here.

Mal. Take off the first sentence.

Tech. I'm outta here.

Mal. You son-of-a-bitch. You'll be back and when you do-

Tech. Just kiddin'.

Mal. Measure the outtake. Never mind. I'll do it. Where are you assigned?

Tech. (*imitates Sullivan*) To-night on this shoe, for your entertainment-

Mal. Sullivan Theatre, Broadway? They're dark. But high public visibility. (*HE exits*) Stay warm, kiddo

Outside, under the C.B.S canopy, I turn up my collar to the cold night. Breaking routine is exciting and scary. *I thought I was dead, but I'm alive! Fuck you, job!* A car pulls up; out jump a bevy of frisky, bug-eyed men with strike signs. I head home to the Wellington Hotel. Screw the Sullivan theatre, and the *Brotherhood*.

Whether the impasse was based on genuine contractual disagreements or personality conflict remains moot. Maybe it was an even mix. Striking without pay struck me as dumb. Dumber yet was walking up and down like a monkey on a leash while the organ grinder (s) sat bull crapping and knit picking in a warm office drawing salaries. So there I was, Mr. Recluse, in broad daylight on Broadway, wearing a picket sign that felt bigger than the Sullivan marquee and twice as embarrassing. A public announcement that I'd compromised my life.

My biggest gripe against the union resulted from what I learned on the line. Better to be forced out and collect unemployment insurance, then walk out and have to wait 49 days before qualifying for money. *We had no choice. The company made untenable demands.* What's tenable about striking with no pay that you never make up? We did get free coffee and a Thanksgiving turkey, compliments of ABC technicians.

While walking I decided to write. I could do it and keep my job, which I figured would resume sooner or later. Little did I know writing meant a deeper escape from reality, darker yet than the nightshift. Deejaying was alive and vital; writing was solitary, and a hiding place of self-indulgence. But the tougher truth is at day's end you have to put it out there.

Scene 2: Under the Sullivan Marquee.

Tech. What's the latest?

Jalanzo. Grab a necktie.

Tech. Colder than yesterday. Must be the wind-chill factor.

Jalanzo. Now you're *the* fuckin' weatherman? (*reads stocks*)

Tipsy Passerby. On TV you see BS. On radio ya hear it. (*exits*)

Commander. Put this paper in your coat, Bunky, flat against your chest. Keeps the wind out and body heat in. An old navy trick.

Tech. Were you in Korea?

Commander. The big one, Bunky.

Tech. A friend took me sailing once off Larchmont. In the boat was Bull Halsey's son. He got seasick. What'd you do in the navy?

Jalanzo. A fuckin' fly-boy inna fuckin' Pacific.

Tech. Oh. See any action?

Jalanzo. A kamikaze shot him in the ass. Tell 'im *The Reader's Digest* version in case he's gotta be somewhere tomorrow.

Commander. Belay that bilge!

Tech. Why did kamikaze pilots wear helmets?

Commander. They wore bandanas painted with a rising sun and a Shinto prayer. Brave sons-of-bitches! Come outta the clouds, or in low under the radar, and suddenly boom.

Tech. You see combat up there?

Commander. Couplah dogfights. I nailed one, another got me. I went down off Kwajalein. Some guys never made it out of the cockpit.

Tech. Where's that?

Commander. Micronesia.

Jalanzo. Below is Melanesia, and off left is the Milk of Magnesia.

Commander. That's where you were, shittin' in your pants. I swam ashore, and slept under a palm tree. Boom! What the hell. Boom! A coconut missed my head by inches. Imagine. Surviving a dogfight, and gettin' killed by a coconut. Next morning I hear noise in the thicket.

Tech. Jap?

Commander. A native in a loincloth wearin' a palm leaf hat and breakin' coconuts. I go over, he looks up, and I see a rising sun bandana.

Tech. No shit?

Commander. We go for our guns, he says, "I no shoot. You no shoot." Do I trust a kamikaze? I sat down and we split coconuts. His plane stalled and he went down before reaching his target. He shows me a family picture. I show him one of mine. Then a boat shows up in the bay. We run onto the beach. It was an American PT. "Come with me," I go. But he runs. I yell out. "American! Don't shoot!" Bullets whiz by me. I get hit, spin around, and the Jap's face down dead in the sand. I got hit in my shoulder. (*opens his collar*) See? (*Tech looks; Commander grabs his knee.*) Y'never learn, do ya, Bunky?

Jalanzo. Ha, ha. Be glad he ain't grabbin' ya pork. The jungle does queer things. (*reading*) Leave it to them to do the opposite. The market's down but the company's up. Go figure. Want a great stock, kid? Central Park, in at 59, out at 110. I was inna Pacific on an island where women walked around naked from the waist up. The chaplain gave 'em all T-shirts. Next day they had 'em on with two holes and their tits stickin' out. Like to see that new female tech we got in one of them T-shirts.

Commander. And what'll you do, pet her?

Jalanzo. Some of them new wave creeps're dressin' in Navy clothes we threw away. Midi blouses and bell bottoms at the crotch. They call 'em hip-huggers. It's the new fashion.

Commander. It's old stuff comin' back. Nehrus and love beads. No class. You want class look at the movies of the '30's and '40's. William Powell and Carol Lombard in *My Man Godfrey*; Robert Montgomery and Adolph Manjou in tuxes, double breasted suits, color coordinated shirts, ties, and chest pocket handkerchief; women in flowing silk gowns and feather boas. We used to dress up for radio.

Jalanzo. Today they dress down for TV.

Commander. What the hell're you wearin', Bunky?

Jalanzo. Fuckin' baggies.

Commander. In a high wind you could turn into a zeppelin. We used to dress up for radio, in suits and tuxes; right up on stage with the actors. That was old radio. Died out after Bob and Ray.

Jalanzo. They were more laughs than a barrel of monkeys.

Commander. Now it's electronic news, vacuous jawboning with an occasional yawn- the glorification of insignificance! The bonehead who dreamt up the Wheeldex of Anniversaries must be worth his weight in gold: July 4th, fireworks; Labor Day, *The* Meany Monologue-

Jalanzo. Ground Hog Day, did the little fucker see his shadow?

Commander. Veteran's Day, it's the oldest vet.

Jalanzo. Some poor bastard in an iron lung with *the* breathin' machine in the background. Boom! Haah! Boom! Haah!

Commander. If and when we go back, I'm packin' it in. It's not my world anymore. Radio's dead. Networks're dishin' it from satellites. Mail and Western Union's slowly disappearin' like the Pony Express. Satellites n' facsimiles, the electronic cottage, Bunky. That's your future. Press a button, you're in China. Press again, it's the rings of Saturn. See these chubby fingers? I can work all ten of 'em playin' piano. Now I'm down to a thumb and index finger holdin' a razor blade cuttin' tape. Soon it'll be one finger pushin' buttons. The wife and I played twin pianos: Debussy, Beethoven, Gershwin. I can still stretch an octave. Look. Put out your hand. See? A full octave. (*grabs nerve in Tech's elbow*) Bunky, you're a soft touch. (*fakes a one-two punch*) I don't play now the wife's gone. One day you turn around, you're 35 years with the company and never been kissed. An old horse at 55. If I had it to do over I'd play piano anywhere. Do it for me. Look, my I.D., 1938. I used to see the boss go through the front door. Gimme a wave, too. Life was simpler then. You filled out a one-page job application; name, address, phone number, experience and a reference. Now they give you an employee handbook. (*takes out book*) A Policy Statement on Employment and the Company's Mission.

Jalanzo. Where'd you get that?

Commander. Our Love of Life contact on the inside. Lawyer jargon. Non-competition; Disclaimers; Non-disclosure agreements.

Jalanzo. What's that in English?

Commander. Bull-ya-baze! "Employee promises and covenants for three years following termination not to compete with the company within 100 miles." One part covers the overnight and never mentions night. It's Guidelines for New Shift Workers. That's you, Bunky. A new shift worker.

Jalanzo. He wasn't workin' on the old one.

Commander. "To better serve listeners requires a 24-hour operation." How to adapt effectively to "new shift" work. "Establish regular sleep habits and meals." Ya doin' that, Bunky? "Avoid caffeine late in the day when it impedes sleep. Arrange for a dark place to sleep."

Tech. Under the bed.

Commander. "Put heavy curtains on the windows. Hardware stores sell blackout shades to block sunlight." Bunchah bull-ya-baze. How about this. "It can be *stressful* working and sleeping different hours from your family and friends."

Tech. What friends?

Commander. "If *problems occur* talk to *an employee assistance program counselor* who can offer *helpful suggestions.*"

Tech. Quit.

Commander. Here's a mission statement, "Diversity and Recognition"- meaning minorities; "Communications, and Empowerment; Patents and Trade Secrets. Employee covenants-"

Jalanzo. What's that?

Commander. A blood promise not to betray secrets to the competition.

Tech. What secrets?

Jalanzo. De-gauzing tapes, pushing buttons, which hand, which finger, middle, index or elbow? Our q-tips have cotton at both ends. Ooh. Shh.

Commander. "Disclose secrets, and the Company's entitled to Injunctive Relief in the event of a breach." (All: Oooh!) Everybody's paranoid, even machines ask, you sure you want to do that? Right now some pimple-face genius who never heard of Ernie Pyle, or the Burrow Boys, is shapin' our future on his *Wang.* This book is shades of the House Un-American Activities Committee. They don't want another free thinkin' Winston Purdett with commie overtones and have to banish him to Rome.

Tech. Lucky him.

Jalanzo. Alexandre Kandrick, alias, Karansky, disappeared, too.

Commander. Burrow was cut loose because he placed integrity above money. I laughed when news went 24/7. Cut the histrionics, it's cheap drama. People's misfortunes live, direct and FREE! The glorification of insignificance! In the old days we were part of something.

Jalanzo. Backbone of radio.

Jalanzo and Commander. TV didn't kill radio. Money did. Destroys everything. Between shows I'd kill time for a nickel in a fleabag movie house on 47th. Once I fell asleep and ran like hell up Broadway to this joint when it was Playhouse Four. Then they went dark, renovated for TV, and went dark again. In the old days we earned less, but then corned beef, potatoes, pie, and a beer cost 75¢. We were on stage with the actors wearing tuxedos in front of the audience. Creatin' sound effects. With live repeats later for the west coast.

Tech. How'd you figure out the effects?

Commander and Jalanzo. Imagination, Bunky. We tested the range of a mic listening off a speaker. Remember, radio was geared for the ear. For thunder we'd shake a metal sheet. Or use a thunder drum made of cowhide. Remember the rain machine? You could get soaked with that. Toilet paper on mic sounds like walking through undergrowth. We had a rolling platform with a jail gate and wooden door on frames. For footsteps in snow I used a box of cornstarch wrapped in tape. I moved with the actor, squeezing the box in tempo with his walk and speech. Timing was crucial. Somebody's going through a door, you can't just open and close it while they're still knocking on it. Remember Orson Welles' Foreign Legion show? He brought in a ton of sand. We walked on it. Sounded like a platoon. There was pride. We were creative, part of the show. Ain't a sound we can't reproduce. Want an effect? Close your eyes. (*does wind; foghorn; pops a cork, bubbling champagne; hoof beats; Indians; escaping steam; love-sick moose; barroom fight; climbing upstairs and downstairs; TB; terminal TB. Ends up dizzy.*) Those were the good old days.

Jalanzo. Wonder how Kahn's doin? Great sound man. Cracked up in '64, poor guy. They carried him out of the old Madison Avenue studios thumpin' and wheezin'. Took the secrets with him.

Commander. I saw him up in Seneca Falls a few years back. Still wearin' his tux and doin' foghorns. Now it's business, the age of the technocrat. We'll be free of it soon, but you're startin' out. Between politicians and corporations suckin' you dry, union dues, and inflation, if ya see fifty cents on a dollar you can cross yourself lucky. Uncle Sam'll beat your brains out. A job's just a few fancy steps between the cradle and the grave. Instead of bein' a labor of love, it's a labor of self-annihilation, and we're inna street defending it. To make matters worse, if, and when, we go back we gotta contend with broads in the work place.

Jalanzo. Give the cunts a toehold, they'll eat us alive.

Commander. They're biologically stronger than us. Their eggs outlive our sperm, according to Ashley Montague. How he knows, I don't know.

Jalanzo. He went up *the* fuckin' shute with a magnifying glass.

Commander. Nature gave women something else, too. Exclusivity for perpetuating man. Now they want to share labor pains.

Jalanzo. Look at this. A job opening for a Pipe Nipple Threader. No experience necessary. On-the-nipple training. Here's one. Gal Friday to balance Tuesday's and Wednesday's books at Thursday's on Saturdays. Call Mondays, ask for Mr. Sunday.

Tech. Who exactly is negotiating for us?

Commander. Guys from the ranks. And they're up against a battery of company managers and labor lawyers like McFitch, the union buster. He broke the *Herald Tribune* and the *Daily Mirror*.

Jalanzo. Qualified Surgeon seeks position with General Hospital. Just in from Cuba. Contact bellhop, Fontainebleau, Miami. Here's one for you, Commander.

Receptionist. Must be attractive. Willing to dict-a-phone.

Commander. Belay that crap. He gets a bonus for everything he knocks down. He smiles, shakes your hand while shovin' a knife in ya back. The man argues contracts 365 days. Our guys do it every three years.

Tech. That's bad.

Jalanzo. He wears Saint Laurent clothes, which ain't for fat guys, unless y'got no balls and a tight ass. Well, so much for the executive areas.

Commander. All y'gotta know is what y'want and what you'll settle for. A guy goes to a lawyer, says, What's your cheapest rate? The lawyer says, $75 for 3 questions. The guy says, Isn't that a lot for 3 questions? The lawyer says, Yes. Now what is your 3rd question?

(*Blackout.*)

Scene 3: Voices in the dark.

The talks are off! The talks are on! They're off again! On again! Off! On! On! Off! Gimme a Dramamine! (*shuffling feet*) I got a sweet side job, projectionist on 42nd Street. A porno house? That's sinkin' low. It's 50 bananas a day. Is it union with benefits? The job's the benefits with early retirement. Got any passes? What's playin'? Him with himself. What's projecting, Bunky, besides you? 'Eight Chinese Waiters'. Three from column A, five from column B. That's after the 'Business Man's Lunch'. They must print those movies on asbestos. (*shuffling*) You get your free turkey from the ABC techs? Yeah. I sent it to the union and said stuff it. (shuffling.) Any progress? They're still at loggerheads. Is that a beer garden? (*shuffling*) Are the talks getting' anywhere? Difficult to assess. Why? Primarily 'cause negotiations, while substantive, have been minimal, therefore, it would be prema-tour, if not imprudent, to voice an opinion at this juncture of time; considering the extreme vulnerability of each party's position in this unfortunate circumstance which, as you know, is tenuous and quite vulnerable to say the least, and don't ask me for a playback. (*shuffling*) Turn to the centerfold. Look at the lungs on that one! If she drowns it'll be face up. Why's she sticking out her tongue? Look at the size of it. She must have trouble keeping it in her mouth. Turn the page. Skip the commercial. Turn the page. Two dames with two guys. What're they eatin'? It ain't apple pie! What'd you pay for the magazine? I found it on the train. Right. The cover says $3. Even the price of masturbation's gone up. Not if you have a good memory.

Scene 4: Judy Job-Job. Place, same as Sc 1.

Tech. (*silence*) Gonna be a cold winter. (*pause*) You can tell by the clouds. They're low n' tight. See? Down Broadway, above the Winter Garden, across from the Awful Falafel.

Judy. That's it! The hook. It was there all the time. (*jots down idea*)

Tech. What're you writing?

Judy. I never peep my action.

Tech. That's a good title. Never Peep My Action.

Judy. Hold off, Ace. Okay? (*pause*) How come I've never seen you before?

Tech. I work nights.

Judy. All night? Horrendous.

Tech. It's okay.

Judy. You kidding? It's the pits! Can't you switch to days?

Tech. Yeah. It's just that, I don't know, you get locked in. Overnight's not bad. None of your daytime politics, nobody bothers you, and it's quiet. That's important. I get time for myself, time to relax and think.

Judy. About what?

Tech. Suicide, murder, the usual stuff.

Judy. You must be a masochist.

Tech. Probably. What's your thing?

Judy. Royalties while I sleep.

Tech. Where you from?

Judy. Virginia.

Tech. I like southern accents. Bye now, heah? See yawl.

Judy. I like Noo Yawkahs myself. My first day here I heard someone say, "Toidy-turd and Toid." Is that a stitch? One of my roommates goes, "You see huh?" I go, "What?" She goes, "Huh, huh. Ovah deh wit da fu-coat." I go, "What's a fu-coat?" She laughs, says, "You tawk funny." Me. Not huh.

(*Enter Preacher constantly looking over his shoulder*)

Preacher. I'm being followed. Don't look. I say, don't look. You look.

Judy. I'm not looking.

Preacher. You looked.

Judy. Not now.

Paranoid Preacher. Before.

Judy. Yes. But I'm not looking now.

Preacher. Swear? Good.

Judy. What am I looking for anyway?

Preacher. I don't know. But if they catch me I'm not talking. And don't you. Shh. Don't talk. Just listen. Use selective speech. Watch your thoughts, for they become words. Choose your words, for they become actions. Shh. Understand your actions, for they become habits. Study your habits, for they become your character. Shh. Develop your character, for it becomes your destiny. Courage. Bon appetite. Vote with your feet. (*Hurrying off*)

Judy. There's a stitch and a half. He was here yesterday doing the same routine. Think this mess will drag on? (*He shrugs*) I got a singing gig.

Tech. Great. Where?

Judy. Shh. Don't look. Near D.C.

Tech. How near?

Judy. Compared to New York, close. Do you have a side gig? (*He shrugs 'no.'*) You married? (*shrugs 'no.'*) Then what's your problem, Ace?

Tech. I'm locked in.

Judy. Translate that?

Tech. Security.

Judy. Like now. You sound like an old man with one foot in the grave.

Tech. It's easy for you to talk. You're a woman.

Judy. Back up, Ace. What's that mean?

Tech. Eventually you'll get married. The guy'll support you. If I go chasing rainbows, who am I gonna support?

Judy. Where is it ordained in heaven that you have to pay for the woman? I intend on supporting myself. I don't intend to prostitute myself or my talent for a man or a job. No way! My dream's going to live! My light's going to shine. I'm shooting for broke. As far as I'm concerned, working for C.B.S is a job-job. Work you do while you're waiting for work you like to do. I'm a singer, actress, and dancer, play guitar and write music. I don't actually write it. I can't read notes. I hum to a friend who goes to Julliard. I'd go myself, but my biz/manager says I'd lose what I have naturally if I over-intellectualize. Just today I was on a go-see.

Tech. A what-see?

Judy. Go-see. Audition. A look-see for producers.

Tech. I see. How was the go-see?

Judy. Lousy. A cattle call. Eight hundred people waiting all day on three possibles in a hot hall. I got a turn down. What a turn off! I told my biz manager no more go-sees or look-sees. One-zies or none-zies. Waste my time! They throw in ringers, you know. Thirty blondes. One brunette shows and gets the job.

Tech. I used to DJ.

Judy. What kind of music did you play?

Tech. Pop and country.

Judy. I sing country. Actually I'm a now singer, MOR contemporary, but my biz manager tells me to sing country-pop because the New York scene is heavy into black pop-rock which is not me. I'm not totally country-country, but more country-pop. There are three different sounds in my voice. I can get raunchy like Joplin. I can sing country-pop or country- rock even pop-rock-country with no problem because I'm told my voice is deeper and wider than Olivia Newton-John, and she's from down under.

Tech. What's her style?

Judy. Now-country, contemporary pop rock-

Tech. So she-

Judy. Crossing over into contemporary rock-folk-pop country. You see. There's country-western, country-folk-rock. Ronstadt's country-pop-rock. Black soul like Brown, yeow! Gutsy gospel Knight and the Pips; hard rock, the Frampton stuff, Rolling Stones, and the New Wave: punk, funk and all that junk. The Ramones; Blondie; R and B; Earth, Wind and Fire; the Cars, the Windows, the Doors, Trunk and the Glove Compartment.

Tech. My father sings Neapolitan. Never the same lyrics twice. I guess you'd called that Off-the-top-contemporary Napoli Pop. I like Perry Como.

Judy. Who?

Tech. Sinatra, Bennet, Peggy Lee.

Judy. And you were a disc jockey?

Tech. Still am, actually. Part time.

Judy. Maybe you could play my demo. Where are you on the dial?

Tech. The what?

Judy. The dial. Maybe I've heard you.

Tech. You got short wave? Actually we're on the tip of Long Island.

Judy. The company allows a second job that conflicts?

Tech. I use a different identity. In fact, I don't use a name at all. I'm known as the phantom... even the station personnel don't know me.

Judy. Don't they see you going in and out?

Tech. I wear a mask.

Judy. How about when they pay you?

Tech. When they what?

Judy. Pay you?

Tech. I have a drop off arrangement.

Judy. Now that's a stitch!

Tech. I don't jock for money. I do it for love. When I'm on the air spinning sides, taking phone calls, doing crazy shticks, I feel complete, alive, and in tune with the universe.

Judy. I get that way singing, like I've flown out of my body, the earth falls away, and all that remains is my voice singing in space. Doing what you love is the best high in the world. Oops. Gotta run to an audition. Later, Ace. Oh, you're right about daytime politics. Nothing worse than a 60 year-old technician wearing penny loafers with taps. (*Blackout*)

Scene 5: Voices in the dark.

Coffee! One black, one regular, Taster's for you. Got it right this time. I'll be the judge of that. Milk. Ycch! This is black. That's mine. This must be yours. The one with the tail's tea. Ycch! This isn't Taster's. It's Sanka. How can you tell with all that milk and sugar? I told the guy to mark 'em. What's the diff? I got the equalizer. Straight Scotch. Well, Bunkies, here's to less work, more people to do it, n' lotsa feather beds! Merry Christmas! If we're not back before New Year's, here's mud in your eye!

> Scene 6; same as Sc. 1. Enter Barrymore look-alike; black cape, long scarf, Tyrolean hat, a walking stick. He plays to the balcony.

Vesuvio. I see you are a member of the entertainment fraternity, so to speak. A question that teases my curiosity. Do you recognize me?

Tech. No.

Vesuvio. Zounds! Possibly from another angle like this, or this, or this. Think, man, think! I was Lorenzo Jones for a day. What is my name?

Tech. Lorenzo Jones For-a-day?

Vesuvio. I was hoping you could point me homeward, particularly in light of the inclement weather. I seem always to end up at Jimmy's Corner, where libation flows continuously, but not as freely as welfare. Where beer is a bower of liquid gold full of bright, promising stars, rising to a crowning white cloud where sits my guardian angel, playing harp for minimum. Perchance- Oh, but my voice is rather deep today. Have you noticed? Non-committal. Zounds! It was a trick question anyway. A yes would have required a previous encounter from which to judge my tonal placement, and since you said we had not met, I'd have caught you in an indefensible deception. I loathe indefensible deception, particularly my own. Perchance you know a Miss Binny Barnesworth, assistant casting director for Stella Dallas, Nora Bayes, and Front Page Farrell?

Tech. I work nights.

Vesuvio. A fellow actor! That explains your diffidence. Perhaps you've seen me on the *Late Show* in *The Curse of the Mummy*? I played the mummy. (*mimes mummy*) I was also in *Curse of the Daddy*.

Tech. You played the daddy.

Vesuvio. Scoundrel! You know me! I appeared in *The Undead* and *Attack of the Crab Monsters* starring Pamela Duncan. Well, so be it. I am entrusting in your care a picture with resume. Voilá! (*snaps cane; picture of himself unfurls*)

Tech. Very nice. Look. I work nights, and right now I'm unemployed.

Vesuvio. Ah, a fellow thespian. What an unmitigated displeasure to make your acquaintance. The name, sir, is Vesuvio I. Styles.

Tech. What's the "I" stand for?

Vesuvio. Me! I've studied voce, meema, sense memory objectivity, body movement, both motivational and arbitrary; nudes; par golf; L'Hommie Deux improvisation: bumping into strangers for quick studied reaction, hence the deviated septum. I've studied television: on-camera, off-camera, bi-cameral, your camera, any camera; dew-ping, dubbing, guaranteed no flubbing. Lip-sync, body-sync, kitchen-sink, always in the pink; also, nouveau surrealistic pop-art tele psychedeli-vision or humanization of inanimate objects: a talking sink, dancing vacuum cleaner, flying box of operatic laundry detergent. In sum, I draw on a versatile background in a duplicity of variegated occupations, some double-gated and some constipated. To wit: I've been a skydiver, a tractor driver, a fork lifter, and a sand sifter; a longshoreman, a hospital corpsman, an agricultural foreman and a Fifth Avenue doorman; a tree tuner, a piano pruner, a nightclub schooner on an ocean crooner; a singing bard quick with a card, a lifeguard for Scotland Yard; a short order cook in a hall of corrections, a hard-nosed sergeant on a ROTC inspection, motivational and arbitrary marching, five years in laundry and starching. A champion on the trampoline, sold Vaseline in Abilene, not keen on Listerine, occasionally take histamine. In short, perform any sport, and never been to court.

Tech. You doing anything now?

Vesuvio. What are you insinuating?

Tech. Nothing. Just asking if you've got anything going. That's all.

Vesuvio. That's all! Why the implication is absolutely fellatio!

Tech. I'm only asking if you're working?

Vesuvio. I am? Where?

Tech. That's what I'm asking you.

Vesuvio. Don't be impertinent!

Tech. Okay. I'll rephrase it. Have you got a J-O-B?

Vesuvio. What the hell is a JAY-OH-BEE? Is that Puerto Rican?

Tech. No. Pig Latin for 'work'.

Vesuvio. Again. That word. Cre-tino! I am presently writing on speculation a twenty second musical version of *The Metamorphosis* in which I play a basso profundo cocka—rrroach! In media res, the refrigerator bursts open, and I fly out of the cottage cheese singing (*deep voice*) "Ohhh, give me a roach who's a stout heart roach and I'll soon give you ten thousand more." (*aside*) Disgusting little buggers! For the denouement, a can of Sure-Shot pesticide leaps from the cupboard and piss-pisses all over my silver wings and into my golden throat. I tailspin into a choking, agonizing death, Oh. Ah! Ach!! The fridge does a rock dance with the sink, and while the mop duels the broom for my remains, the washing machine smiles, says, (*Brooklyn accent*) Sure-Shot's what y'got! Kills 'em dead every time, fah Sure-Shot.

Tech. Very good. I think I've got a job, I mean a performance for you.

Vesuvio. (*leaning in*) What, where?

Tech. Acting normal.

Vesuvio. Cretino! I'll have you know I just concluded 26 weeks at the unemployment office. During my stint I was fortunate enough to be seen by very important people from workmen's compensation with whom I am currently negotiating for another 26 weeks with x-rays. Prior to that I was more at liberty than Patrick Henry! (*Blackout*)

Scene 7: Voices in the dark.

Just got hold of a bulletin from our Love of Life contact inside. What's it say? They're still talking. Terrific. It's a healthy sign. They're talkin' n' we're walkin'. That's healthy, too. The wife's been tellin' me 'take a walk' for years. She meant in a straight line. People only understand violence. I'm cuttin' the power lines. Learn to cut tape first. Why're we picketing? The company wants "departmental seniority". They don't like you, they transfer so you end up at the bottom of the seniority list. Comes a lay-off, you're first to go. They want freelancers, per diem hiring with no benefits. Does it say what we want? The opposite. They want control of Electronic News Gathering, cameras using tape. The mini camera's revolutionizing news. Put it on your shoulder, y'can go anywhere and feedback straight to air. Films dead. History! So are we. Violence is the answer. Before I left I cut pinholes in the coffee machine cups. That's violent. Creative engineering. Only they postponed the strike and I messed up my pants. A guy can get stale on the job. They've got people workin' double shifts. They gotta be hurtin' soon. Big companies don't hurt, Bunky. Right now they're making cost comparisons. What's it cost having us out, against having us in? Is it cheaper to job out to independents, or keep the work in-house? No, Bunky. We're hurtin'. They're just inconvenienced. The wage and scale committee's circulating fliers on the inside, undermining morale, telling secretaries, accountants, "You're working an engineer's job. Why aren't you getting engineer's pay?" NBC's fifteen bucks ahead of us! Here's a letter from the business manager's wife to the company on how they are taking food out of the mouth of innocent children; a poem from a tech's eight-year-old on how unemployment effects ecology. Hippo! Say again? The African hippo cooling off in the river moves his feet around in the silt, drudges up food from the bottom, it floats to the surface, and birds using the hippo's back for a platform fly down, skim the water, and eat. C.B.S is the hippo and we're the skimmers.

Scene 8: Business Report at the Algonquin Hotel. Time, 7PM.

Business Manager. Quiet everybody. Quiet! Let's keep it down to a dull roar, huh? Com'on, Mac. Hold it in abeyance. Put a lid on it, Figgy! Quiet! We been out walkin' a long time- (*Cat calls, jeering; a voice from the back: Tell us something we don't know?*) Nobody has to tell us we're up against an insensitive, hostile management out to destroy our jobs. Nobody has to tell us we been walking amidst an equally unsympathetic public, which thinks technicians already make too much dough. (*Cat calls, jeers*) So I tell 'em, "It ain't the dough." "It ain't the dough?" they say, givin' me the fisheye. "Then what is it?" So I clarify for them and for you who don't know either. It's job jurisdiction. That's what this strike is all about. They say, "Juris-what? Can y'spend it?" *I can't even spell it!* There have been countless rumors runnin' rampant concerning the progress of negotiations. Disregard them. I got the latest poop from our inside contact whose brother just got engaged to the sister-in-law of an accountant who had lunch two, maybe three, but definitely no more than four, days ago with the relative of a lawyer on the management team. He told her, she told him, he called our contact who told me what I'm tellin' you- (*Shrugs Who knows!*) And that's straight from the horse's mouth. Coffee n' donuts inna back. Meetin' a-joined. (*Blackout*)

Scene 9: The Russian. Place, same as Sc 1.

Russian. (*dancing*) I choose happiness, con-tentment, to die enjoying the good fight; to discount completely misery, human suffering, and the self-deprecation that envelops us without let-up. I choose fun, good tidings, dancing, and a healthy appetite. What do you choose?

Tech. All the above.

Russian. Love, comrade. Love! When the bear is coming, embrace him. He will embrace you. All he wants is a hug and a kiss, da, and drinking when hugging is problem. Ha! What is sign? Strike C.B.S. Nyet! Kiss my valenki! In Russia we don't strike, we revolt! Phony bastards! I walk with you, a little. My feet are tired. I walk all the way from my beloved steppes of Russia to America. Here no steppes, only curb with dog shit. America land of free vere nothing free. Crazy.

Tech. Tell me, what's archy-choneya mean? There was an actor, Mischa Auer, who sang Archichoneya in a movie.

Russian. Ochi chernye is beautiful woman. I like to you, a woman. Ochi chernye. Black eyes. Ochi cguchie y prekraznye y mo-guchie! (*very hot, strong; takes out bottle*) Woman and vodka make a *ridiculous* life less *ridiculous.* Just enough to take away, what you Americans call, the edge. Dark you never see like Russia. Day is night. Night is day. Snow white with blood. Blood on hands! Blood on valenki. Is blood everywhere except in heart where it is Siberia. Hoy! Mother Russia. Not like Germany, the Fatherland. Ach-dundt, mein feurher! In Russia it is mother. She weeps ochi chernye for all her children. Ochi mo-guchie! Understand this not acting. In America everything acting. Who is real? Who is actor? Who knows? The milk in the breasts of Mother Russia is dry. Once her breasts were full of milk, overflowing the steppes of Russia into the peasant mouths. Look at 42nd Street? Decadence and pimps.

(*Enter Preacher running; alternates hiding behind each man.*)

Preacher. I'm being followed. Don't look. I say, don't look. You look.

Russian. I not look.

Preacher. You looked.

Russian. Nyet! Maybe him. Not me.

Preacher. If you're caught use selective speech. Watch your thoughts. They become your words. Choose your words, they become actions. Understand your actions, they become habits. Habits become your character. Your character becomes your destiny.   (*Exits*)

Russian. Crazy idiot! Very Russian. By the holy mother! Look up the street what's coming down. She went in doorway. Always she carries black bag. "What is in bag?" "Pleasures of the heart." I ask, "What means that?" She opens bag. Inside is whips, chains, spurs, dog collar, cleats. She says, "Cleats for runnin' up the back." Crazy! That woman belongs to the Silver Fox of 42nd Street, a Spanish pimp with a stable of midgets and freaks. In the amusement arr-cade, ask for Snow White and Seven Dwarfs. Degenerates selling eight-year-old children. Where they get eight-year-olds? Who knows? Where they get dwarfs? Who knows? Father in jail. Mother on dope.

Orphans, run-aways, stolen children. In arr-cade you want a kid you order *Chicken-to-go,* over 18, ask for *Rooster, Boiled* is white, *With Skin* Chinese, grilled is Puerto Rican, *Fried* is black. Crazy! A Russian girl is blinky. Crazy.

Tech. Where're the police?

Russian. On the take. Now, city is broke, and they want more money. Crazy. In Russia we don't strike. We revolt! In Russia we have one rake, one broom, one screw. America, you have hundreds. Crazy. Everybody in business. People with no job want raise. Crazy. If I mayor, I put chicken in every pot. Get votes from freaks and perverts. To read a parking sign takes college degree. Park. Don't park. Today, no. Tomorrow, yes. No standing here to corner. What corner? There are four! No parking 7 to 9, 4 to 6, Tuesday, Thursday, Saturday. Alternate side 11 to 2, Monday, Wednesday and Friday except holidays. Whose? Jew, Christian, Muslim? What is circle with broom? They should put in circle skull and bones. Comrade Lenin was right. Constant revolution! (*drinks*) Tonight ochi chernye. Tomorrow revolution! On 42nd *Barbecue Chicken* is a Jamaican. Ochi cguchie y pre-kraznye y mo-guchie! (*Blackout*)

ACT THREE

TEACHERS IN MY LIFE

1   Venezia

"...O you! whoever you are, that journey toward this exhausted city for the first time, let me tell you how happy I count you! There lies before you, for your pleasure, the spectacle of such singular beauty as no picture can ever show you or book tell you, - beauty which you shall feel perfectly once, and regret forever."
Life In Venice, William D. Howells

I'll go back someday, says a lady out of nowhere, looking down over my shoulder at a two page scene of the Grand Canal. *Someday before I'm too old, I'll go back to that pensione next to the ristorante Gigio where all day waiters are callin out, Risi e bisi! Fegato alla Venneziano! Café e tiramisu!*

I'd been slumbering until Italy, my first vacation. I ended up crying in the Piazza San Marco, the cumulative effect of a compromised career- once bitten, twice shy. I'd been traveling like a leaf in the wind- Dolce far niente, the sweetness of doing nothing- quietly taking in the romance of Italian life, art, and architecture. Suddenly it all came to a head like lava building up in Vesuvius while unsuspecting Pompeii slept. Without warning, I blew apart as I stepped from the train, out of the crush of people in the station, and onto the Fondamenta di Santa Luci. Before me was an outrageous, panorama of the Grand Canal- Swift and the brothers Grimm come alive- a fairy tale kingdom of gondolas, vaporetti, motoscafi plying the canal, sparkling blue and silver, tuti in frétta; and in the distance, buildings floated on water. I was transported along the Fondamente San Simeon Piccolo in a living painting at once abstract and realistic, a child smelling shapes and sounds in a splash of voices eliding with images of excited tourists, gondoliers, and facchini carrying luggage twice their size. Here to behold and touch was the love and art I'd been running away from all my life. After Venice all things are possible. *Nothing's either right or wrong, but thinking makes it so.* I'd come home through the rabbit hole into Alice's Wonderland and Gulliver's Travels, only I was Lilliputian. How did I fit into this gigantic absurdity spread out before me? My heart sank and rose, flew and wept in a million directions. With my heart on my sleeve Venice unabashedly attacked all my senses, even the stones underfoot reached up through my feet to jolt my heart. I'd just been born and Venice was my first breath. Venezia, courtesan of the Adriatic, home to something that had been missing all my life. In a word, art. I succumbed to Venezia and she rewarded me at every twist, turn, bridge, and back alley, filling me with the innocence of youth, the wonder of desire, and fear of falling in love again.

Analysis and criticism I leave to experts. The city forced me to look inward. What I saw I didn't like. I was tired of being someone else, of hiding out on the nightshift, tired of prattling news. It was wearing thin. Something in me kept fighting for light, kept gnawing at me, saying, *you're more than a glorified button pusher.* You've come out of the night into the light of Italy and discovered art and love for which there are no substitutes. I had unwittingly left them behind in middle school and at the feet of my quixotic father. Art and love's greatest expression comes in doses of wonder and amazement. My heart swelled in the intoxicating blue-gray light of a dying duchess decked out in black and white lace.

I thought it was over, but it just began. In Italy in April and May life reawakens from winter sleep, and everywhere in Rome, Florence, and Venice people and flowers abound. In Venice I wandered about alleys and sides streets, along canals, stopped at bacari, *small bars,* for cicheti, or *snacks,* and cappuccini, looked in stores, watched tourists, took in the sights, and felt reborn. I came across a trattoria in the eastern district, off the last stop on the vaporetto before it goes on to the Lido.

A bacaro with several tables, hanging cheeses, a glass counter offering vedura, prosciuto, salami, cold pasta, vongoli, and bacalà mantecato- a tribute to the diet of seafaring people. I got gnocchi and swordfish smothered in olio-algio and cipolle. O you, who go to Venezia for the first time, I envy you for the joy you will feel in that initial reaction.

I came on Piazza San Marco like a babe wallowing in self-pity who returns to mama's breast after a long war. I'd been traversing narrow sunless salizzade paved with flagstones lit by light from shops, corner lanterns, and votive candles in wall shrines dedicated to departed loved ones. Venice. Dangerous to the heart. Strange faces and voices. Even stranger their dialect and joyful faces. Shops in alleys with apartments above. Folks, some old, staring out from behind a flower box, or knitting on a small balcony. I crossed dozens of rii (canals) on low bridges of white stone, under which gondoliers ducked their heads to pass; entered many courts and campi or campielli (smaller open spaces), some deserted and all plain stone with a center well surrounded by brick buildings offering an exit at the other end. Squares, often self-contained little cities within the big city, offering merchant stores: grocers, fruit vendors, shoemakers, old clothing, questionable objects d'art, a bakery, and a café. Crossing them in a dozen giant steps I'd be right back in the warren of narrow streets and lost down a strada senza uscita- dead ending on a canal. They say even locals get lost at times. Retracing my steps I soon learn everything leads into everything else in the direction of Piazza San Marco.

Coming along one alley I heard distant strains of a haunting soprano, a plea to God from Tosca asking why He had abandoned her in her hour of need. Was it a radio, or diva in chamise singing to a mirror? Oh, how lofty that nightingale! Cascading all around, she followed me, or I her, and came out into the noon light of a campo, a church at one end, a tree, a well in the center with a water trough, two chiarchiarone dressed in black sat knitting and whispering. Then the voice singing again from above- *I brought you flowers everyday-* coming from a corner building. Sixty-four stone steps disappearing into a dark terrazzo enclosed by wisteria, green ivy vines, and colorful hanging plants. Vissi d'amore, the voice lamented, reverberating from window to rooftop. A door slammed. Somewhere bread was baking in a pasticiaria and a baby cried.

In several campi I found fruit vendors and restaurants with canopies and umbrella tables that beckoned like a mother's embrace. *Vieni. Mangia con noi al fresco sotto la tendina. Baccala, scampi, calamaretti (squid), calves liver a la Veneziàna, risi e bisi (rice and peas).* Oh, Venèzia! Italia! Where every day's Sunday in Mama's cucina. I treated myself to a guidebook and sat down for a Venitian history lesson.

Venice was founded in 811 A.D. by people from Malamocco on the Lido (beach) in combination with Indo-Europeans, new settlers hailing from Illyria. Of the several possible derivations of the name Venetian I like the more romantic one that refers to them as *newcomers or Venetians from the verb venire, to come. To avoid invaders like Attila and the Franks, people escaped into the lagoons and swamps to small islands inhabited by sailors, swamp hunters, and salt workers. They hung out in tree houses and huts built on stilts until the coast was clear. In 826 the bones of St. Mark, the Evangelist, were taken or stolen from Alexandria where he had been martyred and brought back to Venice, removing them from "Moslem profanation". He became the city's patron saint and his winged lion symbol its coat-of-arms.*

Venice is comprised of islands and lagoons separated from the sea by a coastal strip known as the Lido (beach). The islands were strengthened by countless tightly packed tree trunks sunk into the ground and plastered with earth.

There are about 118 islands connected by over 400 bridges spanning 150 canals. Today the Lido has several luxury beach hotels, pensione, and restaurants; the streets are paved and the travel is by bike, car, and bus. It's the only place in Italy where gambling is allowed.

Venice became a great maritime trading hub, developed a unique culture joining east and west in trade, art, architecture, and intrigue. In the piazzetta il Broglio, (square of plotters) only the gentrified were allowed between 10 and 12 noon when they planned schemes, and hatched plots.

Venice declined due to continual struggle with the Turks, and new world discoveries around the 15th century. The Portuguese rounding the Cape of Good Hope redefined commercial trade with the Indies. Goods and raw material had to pass through the Red Sea and Egypt, then via Venetian ships on to Europe. The new route undercut Venetian supremacy in trade.

I came to Piazza San Marco by way of il Ponte di Rialto, Campo San Luca and along the Calle Dei Fabbri. I was in and out of the sunlight, walking through narrow alleys and small courts, mixing dull looks of natives in silver eyes and shadows and came into a noisy galleria of summer dresses and linen suits in sunglasses. The calle walls, archway, and galleria floor framed the piazza and it was like stepping into a Renaissance painting. I stood back a moment in the Calle before entering the galleria itself, savoring the moment. I could feel the electricity and vibrations from people and objects. What in God's name was going on here? A view from a side street into Byzantium; a Romanesque spring day with the dramatis personae in modern dress. I stepped from night into day and a rush of people, birds, foreign tongues, music, galleries running the length of two sides of a magnificent piazza. Winding my way between the tables of café Quadri, a drum, a violin and a piano playing some nameless but memorable waltz, I took a ringside seat to rest and view the scenery. Birds flew up and swung down, up and down again swarming over excited tourists who squealed with stunned delight at being so close to nature. The more peanuts and corn they tossed out the more the birds enveloped them. A group led by a guide stops to watch and laughs. A cameriere comes up between crowded tables, I order a drink, look around, and see the unexpected, the amazing, and breath-taking San Marco basilica- a dream in a dream- a rectangular shaped Brobdingnagian wedding cake replete with friezes, bas-reliefs, prancing bronze horses, and golden domes. I look away, then back, and it is still there. No wonder Napoleon called Piazza San Marco Europe's *drawing room.* The basilica spans one end of the piazza, has five large archway entrances with lunettes, all repeated on the second floor with a balcony and balustrade and Four Horses of gilded copper and bronze. I find myself drawn to the basilica, eyes upward, and my knees bumping chairs. I sit back down. *Bong!* A bell rings out, startling me and my heart flies up with the birds and settles down. *Bong!* Where's it coming from?

"Sinistra," says a man nearby. "Torre dell'Orologio, the Clock Tower. A gauche. Link. American?" I nod. "Above the zodiac. Zvi Mori announce every day the time for 5 hundred years. They must have some headache."

"Oh, Fritzy!" says his lady companion, giving him a loving shove.

"What about that strange obelisk," I ask, pointing across the piazza.

"Dat," she says, looking in her guide book, "is glockenturn; Bell Tower, 324 feet into sky."

"Nein, libeling."

"Is in the book, liebchen."

"Then must be true. If book say Wednesday is Tuesday. Must be true."

"Stop such joking, liebling."

"It's out of place," I go.

"Yah. Out of place," he says. "Like undt bleistift. How you say, pencil."

"Is sanctuary when flood is coming," says the lady. "From top Venezia you are seeing all around."

"Yah, mein eichhornchen," he says. "Is for ships and sailors. Yah. Up there you feel like a bird. Then you think maybe you have wings, too."

"I never had such thoughts, Fritz."

"Gut. I vouldn't like home to take mein ganse mit a sponge. Undt that Leaning Tower of Pisa. Oof! You valk up, round and round. Oof-ah! Is like krumm, eh, liebchen?"

"Nein, libeling. That means dishonest."

"It does not meet the eye, that is for sure. Betru'gerish, unehrlich. A better word is Korkenzieher. A corkscrew you are climbing. A mother was down coming holding a boy crying, *Jamais, Mama! Jamais.* Tourists eating panini and drinking. A ledge with no rails. Mein Godt! One slip, auf wiedersehen."

"You were whiter than the Pisa marble. Ha, ha, ha!"

"Not funny, liebling. I am thinking, 'Heilige geist, mother of Godt. Get me down I swear to be a good boy forever.' Mein wife grabs me."

"You me was grabbing."

"I say, 'Mama, what in Godts name we doing up here? Verrükt', crazy in our old age. Let's get down, undt no short cuts.' Und then comes this fat Swede eating a panini. Right, liebchen? A Duseldorf beer barrel in kulats. I am struggling for the inside, holding mein wife, mit the city down below. Undt Dusseldorf is eating a panini."

"Undt drinking Cumpari. Ha, ha."

"Mein wifes says, 'Andiamo.' I say, 'If her vee are passing, you are dreaming. One hiccup, I am dead duck."

"Two dead ducks, Fritzie."

"Yah, two, liebchen. Ha, ha. But we are not then laughing. Nein. I tell mein wife, 'Liebchen, if vee fall, grab the fat Swede undt keep her between us undt the ground undt make a soft landing."

"Fritzy, you made me laugh undt I almost fall. Yah. There is a time and a place for jokes. That was not the place."

"I climb down like the little boy. Jamais. Mai, mai!"

"Amazing nobody falls," I go.

"Who knows?" he says. "Eyes and ears you don't have everywhere. But you would know if that fat Swede falls. Half the city she would crush."

"Oh, Fritzie! You are terrible."

"If I was nice you wouldn't marry me. This is our 40th anniversary."

"Congratulations."

"Dunkah. The guidebook says the horses from Constantinople were stolen in the 12th century. They are a gift from the Doge Dandelion."

"Doge Dandolo," she corrects him.

"Yah. Dandelion. Vell, liebling, it is pomer-ridge-oh. Lunch undt siesta. Auf wiedershen."

Off they go, pointing to flood marks on a pillar, one about knee high.

Store windows display black and gold Venetian furniture, jewelry, and ebony-wood; Negroes bearing torches, lace, and blown glass from Burano and Murano; black velvet masks suggesting ancient intrigues; colorful shapes and designs intended for festivals and Arlechino (Harlequin), a black and white patchwork comic figure of the Commèdia dell'Arte.

Flocks of people flutter and move about. The basilica San Marco, a mix of European and Byzantine architecture, dazzles my eyes; stage left is the odd Spartan sentinel. In contrast, a man stands like a scarecrow, hands full of corn, shrouded in birds, his eyes full of joyous wonder.

Romantic music wafts about from both sides of the piazza from six quartets, three on each side. Sweet, heart-wrenching melodies float one into the other, ranging from

Viennese waltzes to *Summertime In Venice* and *Autumn Leaves.* By imperceptible increments the combination of people, birds, architecture, sun, and music begins to stir my soul. I sit down at an open-air café. *Cameriere, un cappuccino.* I watch the strollers: tour groups, couples, lovers, no one was alone except me. Even the birds have each other. My heart caves in. The scene goes blurry; a tear wells up, and I think, never come to Venice without a woman.

Between the doorway arches of the basilica are six curious bas-reliefs in primitive Christian style, depicting St. George, St. Demetrius, and Virgin Mary. The cameriere brings my cappuccino. *There are two famous cafés in the piazza,* he tells me in broken English, *the Florian and Quadri. This is the Caffè Florian, signore. Il Caffè Quadri é di la.* Grazie. *Prego. The Florian has been here since 1720. Many celebrities sit here to take in the rose colors in the sun of the Doges' Palace: Byron, Goethe, Sand, Wagner.* Which Wagner, Richard or Robert? *Both.* Laughter, violins, a sea of happy faces thrill to Venice. A young couple stands statue-like, eyes closed, arms out-stretched, hands full of seed. Birds settle on their heads, shoulders, wrists, to eat off their palms, some drop down to eat what has fallen to the ground, then all rise up in a windy flurry to delightful squeals and resettle on the next handout.

Stage right of the basilica is the Torre del'Orologio, erected 1496, with Moors striking the hour, and the inscription: *Horas non numero nisi serenas- Only happy hours;* left, behind the Bell Tower, is the piazzetta and the Doges' Palace, a smaller square opening onto the Grand Canal. At the waterfront or bacino di marea, (*tidal dock*) two enormous columns frame San Giorgio floating in the distance. One column is topped by a griffin, symbol of Venice; the other a statue of St. Theodore, first patron saint of Venice, and his dragon. This was the grand entrance to Venice. Water laps the bows of gondolas moored to palli - *posts*. Gondoliers mill about the bacino with their paddles like birds waiting for peanuts. A glance inward and up from the nearby Paglia Bridge one sees the Bridge of Sighs that connects the back of Doge's Palace to the execution house. Its name comes from lamentations heard from prisoners as they crossed over to their fate. Casanova had been a prisoner there locked in a low ceiling cell for over a year. He finally escaped by digging his way out. One day while exercising he found a spike and with a lot of spittle he dug his way to freedom through the floor and fell directly on top of a dining room table. History is everywhere in Venezia and all of Italy. The streets, alleys, and backyards are an outdoor museum of ancient ruins. In Firenze at The Academia Del'Arte there is Michelangelo's *David*, and *The Slaves*. The Ufizi Gallery overwhelms with room after room of paintings and statues rivaled only by the Vatican. I laugh to myself. Dead smack in the middle of rococo-ville, my glass is half empty. I started out tighter than a drum to find in the blue-gray, pellucid Venetian light, a voice in me crying for love. *Look,* it said. *Open your eyes.* The David. The Pieta. Two Moors in a Bell Tower. Above San Marco four beautiful brass horses stolen seven lifetimes ago.

The young couple is now at the next table. I envy them. I read. *The piazza is 175 meters long and 82 meters wide.* The lovers touch knees under the table. *The church side is 52 meters.* What's that in feet? *Venice was made for Renaissance lovers of architecture. Romanesque-Byzantine kisses, rococo hands warm with blood, baroque hearts bursting with amore. Under the table their feet touch.* How many knees to a meter? A quartet plays Velar. Across the way, music fades in and out, led by a plaintive violin crying *Summertime in Venice.* The music goes under the table between the knees of the lovers, and right up my back. In the shade of the gallery people mosey along carrying shopping bags, giggling and examining hands with new rings and bracelets. The lovers nibble pasta croce, sip espresso. *The rich décor earned the basilica the name of Chiesa d'Oro or Golden Church.* The lovers dash out into the piazza, splashing through the birds that fly up into multi-colored clouds and peel off settling in a hail of feathers at my feet. *God blesses innocence and young lovers.* I sit motionless like the Bell Tower, feeding bits of my heart to the only takers, the birds of San Marco. Check that. There were takers only I wasn't giving, and the nightshift wasn't helping. Zorba, the Greek, was right. *Daytime's a man. Night's a woman. Never mix them up.*

The air is pungent with sweet cakes, fragrant flowers, and plaintive violins. The lovers pose for a quick draw artist to freeze them for all time in pastels and charcoal. On the wing again, they flit across the piazza, circle the Bell Tower, disappearing into the colonnades of the Ducal Palace. It was then that I returned from the dead, yearned for a woman, and it scared me. But I knew I must come back, and take my lumps like a man. *Never go to Venice alone. It will break your heart.*

☺

2.   Christine

The New School. I enrolled in a writing course with Russell Friedman, and joined a writer's group that met outside of class. I learned that good writing comes from re-writing, talking kills creativity, and Arthur Miller was right, *writing is not democratic.* Like giving birth, you have to bring baby to term yourself. Groups are okay for "B" material experiment, but opening up too much too fast to wrong people can undercut germinal impulses. Save the "A" stuff for a select few. If they yawn or their eyes wander, it's back to the drawing board.

The one and only time I ever went to Fire Island- a bunch of shopping coves connected by wooden walkways and small bridges- was with an older woman, a New School classmate, who owned a charming home nestled among the dunes. I recall the long boat ride to the island, the wind and salty sea spume in my face, her delightful European accent and cheerful personality, and something more, something very important that I needed, but couldn't name it then. She gave me acceptance and encouragement on a silver platter. Her calm, simple manner was elusive, but came back to haunt me years later. She was a nurturing drop of female friendship that cut two ways, but I was too insular to understand. I remember her saying what I misconstrued as a geriatric definition of life. *It's a good day when I wake up in the morning with no pain.* To grasp it's significance requires sensitivity and maturity, which is not given to youth. Like they say, too young dumb, too late smart. My last contact with her came as a gift in mail from Greece, which I cherish to this day: brass renderings three inches in size of the masks comedy and tragedy. God only knows what they meant in her own life as a Jewess.

In all my years I have never known a Jew to put a gun to my head. The only thing they ever put to my head was a book, and that book was the Torah. As a kid, I may have resented some Jews because they made me think. A lost name comes to mind. Ethel Hauptman, my homeroom teacher at James Madison High School in Brooklyn. Ethel gave me *Tea and Sympathy* at her apartment, and the wisdom of her years. I knew she was trying to talk sense into me, but the process was slow. First, I had to rise like a phoenix out of the ashes and destruction created by my father. It would take years. So, to the Lady of Fire Island, and especially Ethel Hauptman, I owe the light in my head that has given me understanding and the real meaning of humanity.

My first theatre instructor was Dr. Earl Ernst at the University of Hawaii. To a 21-year-old he looked ancient, roughly in his late fifties. It was the good doctor who set my theatre foundation, but it took 40 years for the building to go up. Dr. Ernst was a tough bird, centered in art, and not influenced by trends. He was a forceful, salty, no-nonsense teacher who specialized in classical Japanese Kabuki and Noh Theatre. He did not think or dress like his faculty colleagues. He was out of the '30's in cuffed pants and sport coats of herringbone and tweed with wide lapels, while his peers wore the '60's wash and wear, narrow lapel suits, short-sleeved shirts, cuff-less chinos, and go-aheads, or shower shoes.

When engaging Ernst, one always had to be relevant and succinct. He did not suffer fools lightly. He'd often answer questions with sarcastic deliberation. *You were present for the lecture? Check your text.*

Dr. Ernst was a good teacher/director, if somewhat dictatorial. In May of 1960 I wrote a piece for the school paper, Ka Leo O Hawaii, about how he directed a faculty production of *Hamlet*. It was written under the pseudonym Kapulu (meaning sloppy) and titled The Myriad Faces of Ernst. Instead of allowing the actor to find his own way, Ernst would give line readings, which good actors abhor. In his defense, his directing style was probably the result of brief rehearsal time and bad actors. At any rate, in my article I had Ernst playing all the parts. Luckily for me, the article went to print after the grades were in.

Looking back I see that over time the initial excitement of teaching, which is a form of stand-up performing, can harden into dull routine. Students are mostly uninspiring and that takes the wonder out of teaching. Professor Ernst wasn't nasty by nature, I don't think, just impatient and bored. Years of repeating himself to callow youths made him abrupt, sarcastic, at times snide, even supercilious. Intentional or not, it was his way of shaming students into cracking the book and thinking.

Teaching's a thankless job. You bring students up to speed and they're gone often forever like children who leave home and never write their parents. All the years and changing faces get lumped into a family that never grows up. Once Dr. Ernst fixed me with twinkling eyes and offered his wry opinion of proverbs as guideposts. *My two favorites are, 'Look before you leap,' and 'He who hesitates is lost.'*

☺

Diary: Mizzie just showed up one night in Newsfeed. A good soul with a hearty laugh. She sings, tap dances, and used to do an interview show in Buffalo. She has an inner ear problem, which affects her balance. I have an equilibrium problem with reality. When her gyro was off and I was out of it, we'd hold hands to keep from falling down.

Mizzie was first to read my writing and to give me her time. When I said my writing lacked imagination, her guffaw was heard clear across the newsroom. "That's the last thing you need, honey. You have to work on technique and narrative: who, what, when, where." She suggested a writing class at the New School, and her pal, Chris, an editor. "Here's Chris' address. Write her. Introduce yourself in a note and include some samples. She'll give you the time free. She has lots of it. She's on leave from a big publishing house and just walking the family dog." "What's that mean?" "On sabbatical."

Then I got a note from Laurel Lockhart, friend and actress, who was performing in a musical, *The Buck Stops Here*, about Harry S. Truman.

Hi, Saw the enclosed ad in Backstage. Bill Talbot's play writing class. He's Senior Editor at French, and runs an annual play festival for new writers. Classes are at Double Image Theatre, an off Broadway group at John Jay College. Love, Laurel

For moment I put the note on a back burner and focused on Christine Macintyre. I'd mail her pieces and she'd critique them. I think the reason we never met was fear on my part that my personality might color her objectivity. It must've taken lots of focus and will power to deal with my writing. As I later learned, Chris had a full and heavy plate. Once she forgot to mail back a critique and apologized. *Sorry. Thought I'd mailed it out, but found I'd mislaid it in my desk.* While giving me her precious time Christine was fighting for her life. It breaks my heart that *walking the dog* was really a euphemism for cancer.

Strange we never met. Was it fear of ruining a working relationship? Dear, Christine. Your guidance gave me hope, and lifted me out of the C.B.S Chateau d'If. Here's lookin' at you, kiddo.

☺

3.   *The Yellow Bird of India*

Laurel was a member of Jack La Lanne's Health Club in the Biltmore Hotel on 43rd Street, above Grand Central Station. After going to the club as her guest I joined up. Soon her fitness friends became mine and a routine started. After a swim and a steam bath we'd *meet under the clock,* go to a nearby restaurant for a late snack.

One evening I'm under the clock when along comes an Indian; walnut complexion, head in a navy cap, yellow robes flashing under a black, oversized winter coat with a long wrap-around scarf. You'd never miss him in a crowd. You might even duck to avoid him. *How are you?* he says just like that. *Come to yoga class. What hell else you are doing, standing around with your finger up your ass? See where that gets you.* Like Bogey told Claude Rains in Casablanca this was the start of a *beautiful friendship* that changed my life.

"What is your problem, Miss?" *Headaches.* "Stop the sugar. Drink two tablespoons apple cider vinegar in a glass of water with honey." *Swami, I get cramps in my foot.* "Before or after you are having sex?" *Before. No. I mean yes. How did you know?* "Take apple cider vinegar with honey twice a day." *I have trouble breathing?* "You are breathing okay now." *It's at night. My right nostril clogs up with mucous.* "Then breathe through the left one." *Sometimes both are clogged.* "The clog is in the brain. Your nose is speaking to you through the mucous in your body. It is saying, help I cannot breathe. I am full of impurities. And I am saying you're full of cow piss. Stop all dairy. Cut out the cheese and white flour. For one week, when you are getting up in the morning, if the right nostril is clogged, step out of bed with the left foot first. Do not sleep in the fetal. To clean the body your are taking four times every day two spoons apple cider vinegar in water with honey. Apple cider pressed from the whole apple not peelings. If I don't see you next week I will know both nostrils are clogged and you are dead from not listening." *Hey, Swami.* "Oh, my new friend from under the cock. What hell am I saying new? You cannot meet someone without knowing him. So, what is your problem, the hard dick?" *I hate apple cider vinegar.* "I hate it, too. Drink it five times a day to purge aimlessness wise cracks. What else is bothering you?" *It's a long story.* "Americans are full of long stories. I find the longest story is really the shortest. To cure the long story take apple cider vinegar with honey twice a day until you learn to love what you hate. Let's get out from here and go for coffee before somebody else sits on my head with questions the answers to which they are not hearing."

Full membership at La Lanne's Health Club included yoga classes. I went every night and drank apple cider vinegar. After class Swami joined our group for a chat. We were simpatico like he said because you can't meet someone without knowing them. Swami was a Jackson Pollack painting and a talking Calder mobile. I grew to love my new mentor. *My good time swami.* He understood the loneliness of man; he was after all a man himself, and not without his own misgivings. He saw the lost soul in me, took me under his wing, and we went to various suppers and parties where he was always respectfully Swami Gee.

A student once pointed to a health book, saying, "Look, Swami. It talks about apple cider vinegar." He shot back, "What hell. Your head needs writing on a piece of paper before you believe me, or what your body is telling you? When you are fucking your woman, do you read a book to tell you if you are enjoying it or not? Don't lose that book or you are going to die." Then, winking at me, he says, "I give out the type written page of what to do everyday and nobody reads it. Some foolishness is written in a book and everybody reads it. That is the American dilemma. I told someone I witnessed a car accident. He says, 'Really, Swami?' Yes, I say, a big accident. The next day in class he says, 'Hey, Swami. You were right. Last night I saw the accident on TV.' "Oh," says Swami. "I'm right today not yesterday because some idiot on the tube tells you what my eyes told you. You are not an independent thinker. If you're knocked down and robbed, you won't believe it until somebody on the tube tells you. You're life is a comic book. The *Boob Tube* is your religion and all you see is your own face. To you I'm not a Swami, but a TV interview." Later, Swami says, "People like to go inside my head with questions and leave me empty. I don't want always to answer questions. I'm not a TV interview. They only believe the printed book or the fucking *Boob Tube.*"

Swami was separated from his wife and daughter, Shanti, whom he dearly missed. When we met he was living with another Jewess, who told me his wife and daughter had moved to Canada. After that I called him the Shvami. To me he was an American Indian, an unceremonious guru, and a funny character who loved good jokes, and could be, according to his girlfriend, a real stinker sometimes. On being vegetarian, he told me, *the smell of grilled meat is like burning flesh.*

Swami often meditated in the wee hours by the river at West 79th Street. "One night around 3 I thought I saw my old teacher standing in front of me like he was when alive and so strong my heart starts to cry. Then I feel something in my kidney, and I'm thinking what herbs to take to cleanse it when a voice says, 'Give me your money!' What? My kidney is talking? 'Your fucking wallet, asshole!' I open my eyes and see this crazy guy with a gun. I say, 'What for you are sticking that stupid thing in my kidney?' He says, 'Shut up!' I say, 'I'm going to stick it up your ass?' Now he is looking at me like I am crazy and he says, 'Your wallet or I'll fucking kill you!' I go, 'Killing me will not solve your problem, only make it worse when you find I have no money and all you will have is a dead body on your conscience. So throw that stupid gun in the river, sit down, and let's discuss what is really bothering you. He sits, apologizes, and starts crying. That's it. People act, and cry when it's too late. 'It's too late for me,' he says. 'Now I can't stop.' I go, 'Are you on drugs? I have herbs.' He says, 'It's years of doing bad things, very bad things.' He robbed, broke people's legs and arms, worked for some crazy family in Brooklyn called the Casanostras. The more he talks, the more I am thinking this could go badly, he will end up shooting me because I know too much. So I take him home like a stray dog. Give him some tea and herbs to calm his nerves. Now he comes to me every week for herbs, and he tells me mafia stories I don't want to hear and he cries. He calls on the phone for advice. 'Should I kill this guy or that guy? I'm tired of seeing broken heads and fingers cut off.' So I say, 'If you want to hurt someone you can always find a reason. A moron can do that. You are not a moron. You are bothered because in that body you have the good soul. When you hurt someone, even yourself, the soul cries. Why does it cry? The tears are begging you to do only good because otherwise after you die it doesn't want to come back a bigger jackass."

One night after class I stretch out on the floor, relax, and wait for Swami who is pigeonholed by students. "You are asking the right question," he says to an obese lady, "but what you are doing about the answer? You know the answer without asking me. You see it every day when you brush your teeth. Why you are asking me what you already know? Stop the foolishness." The lady tries to get a word in, but Swami cuts her short. "You have a friend in phony dreams. Food is taking the place of something bigger. The supermarket is a social event with a quick fix. Put a zipper on the mouth, stop eating meat, and cut out the junk food. That's it." Someone else says, "Swami, I can't touch my toes." He replies, "Do what is comfortable for you. How far you can go and that's it." The same voice says, "I can do it in bed, but not on the floor." "Then bring the bed to class. Or stay in bed. That's it! People who ask too many questions like to sleep. Sleep and don't worry. But don't expect that when you wake up you'll be skinny or can touch the toes. You are tired from working all day. I am sorry. Lay there with a candy bar. Whatever is comfortable for you- shooting chocolate and donuts and watching the tube." The fat lady tries to talk again. "Listen," says Swami, bringing the mirror closer to her. "You have been asking the same question for two months, but you don't hear the answer. I understand your problem. But I cannot get inside your head and fix it for you. That is your job. Okay. Time to go. I have an appointment."

Later, over tea, I learn he really has an appointment with someone at midnight." *Midnight?* "Yes. What the hell you are thinking, pain is a 9-to-5 problem? Psychiatrists like to make it so. Soon they'll be giving advice on the fucking telephone like the drive-in confession. If I am right, you can kiss Swami's ass in Macy's window. Where is Macy's? That must be some window. People are crazy. Like the fat one in class always sitting on my head about nutrition. Fooling herself, asking the same stupid question in a different way. She has no self-control. That's it! What is good, what is bad, Swami? Should I eat this or that, Swami? Then she read things. Oh, Swami, is it true that chocolate is addictive but not vanilla? Stupid. Yes. Chocolate has the caffeine. She is a chock-head. The sweets are in the head. She thinks good nutrition is a soap opera on the boob tube that you can turn on and off, skip a week, come back and miss nothing. You, my friend, are like the fat one." *How?* "You have to control yourself. Discipline desire. Stop jerking off. Grab the bull by the horns. Talking is a cover up for not taking control." *Avoidance.* "That's it! Giving up the junk food, the candy, and ice cream is giving up a pimp lover. That inner voice that says, 'don't eat three slices of pizza,' that voice is your real friend. I know her problem, but I can only lead that fat horse to water. I can't make her drink. Last month I gave her a food guide, what to eat, what to avoid, and she gains 10 pounds. She goes to the scale, weighs herself, takes off the shoes and socks, spits to reduce water, and then says, 'I'm not fat, Swami. It's my clothes. I lost half a pound last week.' Come on, lady! Who you are kidding? Not me." *Themselves.* "That's it! Once I fell in love with the chocolate donut, the one with sprinkles. Donuts and hot chocolate. I was helping a man who was killing himself shooting heroin. When you help someone you can't just tell them, don't do this or don't do that. You have to hold the hand. His close friend died shooting drugs. I tried to help him. I'd meet him at Dunkin' Donuts. He'd eat donuts and drink hot chocolate. I started to fall in love with the smell of donuts and chocolate. I got such a craving for them it was killing me. I asked myself, Swami, from where is this craving coming? My head, not my mouth; maybe both. I could not control this craving for the donut. In the middle of yoga class I start to get the craving. I put them into meditation, go out to the Dunkin' Donuts, and I'm standing looking at the chocolate donuts. The students are going 'Om' and I'm going 'Mm.' My mouth starts to water from the smell. I tell myself, 'Swami, this is no good. Donuts are bad. They are ringworms and the sugar will harden your arteries and you will either die from a heart attack, or get a stroke.' I convinced myself to stop. The mind is funny. You can't stop a craving, or a habit, because a voice says stop. The thinking has to change. You have to give yourself a good reason, convince yourself that the donut and hot chocolate are poison. You have to make the mind pay attention. Otherwise you are fooling yourself. A parent comes to me with a fat 9-year-old boy who couldn't focus. His attention span was impossible, jittery, always jumping about. 'Lady,' I go, he needs proper diet and love. 'Tell him you love him. Don't tell him when he is crazy. He doesn't need pills to calm him down. He needs love and proper diet. Lay off the junk food, soda, and chocolate. That is what makes him crazy.' She came back months later and the boy was another person. I'm telling you this because all the chemicals in food; red dye, DDT, MSG, are killers. Sweeteners in place of sugar just pander the taste bud for sweets. The real reason they are not removing. Even the light bulb is killing us, TV, telephones all electrical waves giving us tumors and destroying the body's immune system."

☺

4. The Sugar Daddy

Something was missing. Another student agreed. It's the spiritual part of yoga, which Swami neglects. *That's it. Simple. I kick them all out. Go. Get out. Find another goo-roo to cry on. Eat his food, kiss his ass, and all your life remain a child. A baby in the womb.* Swami had his own plate full of devils, and those of others became burdensome, especially the insincere and weak-minded. In the end he may have lost the battle with himself, but he fought the good fight. To do it he had rid himself of everything and everybody that cluttered up his mind. He had offers to open a school, but chose to remain simple and live in New York. It's hard to be simple in New York. It's like living in a Christmas tree and denying the lights. He tried to be one man doing only what his hands could grasp. *I kick their asses into the street. Always falling into the same trap. Crying like babies over spilt milk. Go! I told them. You want to suck mama's tit. What the hell! Children talking the same nonsense everyday. You know, a dog is a wonderful companion, but it never grows up. All they know is the hand that feeds them. They never ask where does the food come from. The hand that feeds is the binding in the cheese. I did not want to be that binding. Some yogis like adoration. They have too much ego. The dog is what it is from another life. So are we. Here we have a chance to change, to work toward a higher good, but it's work. It takes discipline to restrain the appetite, cut out the chocolate devils, and achieve simplicity. One day I decided to kick them out. They just wanted to play all day playing with blocks like in the kindergarten, building fantasies, knocking them down, rebuilding them, and never going to the next stage. Every day they were eating my food and talking in circles, sitting on my head with the same nonsense. Today it's blocks, tomorrow finger painting, or kick ball. Anything but facing their own reality.* Which is what, Swams? *That is the big question in life. What the hell is reality? Sometimes I think it is being 21 years old, having a good fuck, and a dinner. What hell is reality? It's different for everybody, but impossible to understand using logic. It starts with taking control of your life, being strong, not afraid, disciplined, and not looking outside of the self for the sugar daddy. What the hell. I am not the sugar daddy. I would like a sugar daddy myself. Layback in the bed, somebody feeding me, kissing my genitals, telling me how wonderful I am, and never grow up. I kick them out. Kicked them out on their asses. All of them. Sleeping on my floor, eating my food, throwing themselves at my feet. Go kiss somebody else's feet. Find somebody else to replace your mother's tit. Stay children, dependant, never independent. To be independent is lonely. Who wants to be lonely? Nobody. Not even a swami. That's one reason people get married, have children, and friends, to keep from being lonely. What is loneliness? That is reality. Loneliness. Yes. The answer to loneliness is pure love and not some sugar daddy dream.*

To pursue spirituality at a fitness club is like a baseball coach looking to win a World Series ring in the minors. Reality is a knuckler. The only way to hit it is close your eyes and pray.

After about a year, Swami quit La Lanne's over policy changes under new management. Yoga class was taken over by Cathy, a Caucasian in her late 20's. In class she was into ritual, recorded sitar in the background, incense, and an Indian guru named Baba. He was her North Star, her loadstone, a *saint with powers to awaken joy and strength in all who receive him.* For me, Baba sounded too close to Bubba. Then she said, *Baba flows with shakt, energy.* So did her body, which was shocking my joint. But she was in the stages of re-newing her marriage. *Baba is shakti, which he can pass on to others.* She put him in an exclusive group of masters with super powers. I'd heard of ninjas walking on water; Shao Lin experts who felt no pain when stepped on, who could kill by striking pressure points; an Indian guru who could manifest things out of the air. Then someone says, *How come Baba's fat?* Cathy says, *He is big in the middle from air retention in the practice of levitation. Baba will conduct an Ashram at De Ville Hotel in South Fallsburg. This weekend is Baba's Day. Please take a flier for directions and information.* Later, Swami Das says, What *the hell nonsense she is feeding you? Baba is fat because he loves too much to eat the cherry chocolate. That's it!*

Diary. So. Fallsburg, 5p. Driving up to the De Ville Ashram, a Borscht Circuit hotel in its previous incarnation, I'm greeted in big letters over the entrance "JAI RAM", which adds up to God and love. The lobby teems with motley "da-votees" milling about wearing sack dresses, dungarees, sandals, and backpacks. All of them have red dots on their forehead, even a wooly dog wandering about freely. Baba's dog, I'm told. K-nine karma. The dog is friendly and rolls over immediately. *Good doggie,* I say. *Be nice or you'll come back as a fire hydrant.* I wonder, *Does Baba roll over too? No. The people roll over.*

The De Ville turned retreat looks like a honeymoon hotel of virginal hearts pulsing in anticipation of Baba's coming. The air hums like high voltage wires. There are lots of women, some attractive. Eyes glow *ram, om na vah she vaya,* eager for spiritual awakening. Here and there I hear phrases and mantras designed to put one in touch with self. *Om. Ram.* Baba's face is pictured everywhere; in posters, 8" by 10" glossies, fliers, on books and audiocassettes. He's even in the bathrooms. Ram that!

6:15a. Indian chanting and a sitar float down from wall speakers in the dining room, a bare bones cafeteria. What'd I expect at $15 a day, a maitre d', candles and tablecloths? Two huge picture posters of old gurus, probably deceased, and much venerated, lean against a wall. A chalkboard lists activities. A bearded Caucasian in a rainbow colored beanie moves around the room in a spiritual fog, lighting votive candles and incense set before full length pictures of gurus in various states of undress, including one of Baba in a loin cloth on a beach and another of his naked feet. Bearing his souls, I guess.

The food is vegetarian. Today's Specials: Wheat Grass and Energy Soup with choice of Lemon Grass, or a Green Juice. Some would call it rabbit food. *Would you like a tossed salad?* Yes. Toss it in the pail.

9:30A. *Today I have the strength of ten men. Hari ohm. Ram! Ram! Tomorrow I'll be withered like an old tree. Ram, Ram, Ram! Shaktipat, shanti, Om na-mah shi-vaya.* New words save shanti from T.S. Eliot, meaning peace. Oh, to bottle youth for a rainy day. Four months shy of 40, but just turning 20. Distant chanting. *Hari ohm! Ram, Ram, Ram!* Songs of nectar rattle the windows and my heart; creaking metal pipes heat my bones. I reach up begging for guidance. *Let the heart blossom like fingers of hands in prayer. Ram! Ram! Ram! Hark back. Witches at the stake, crucified bodies on the Apian Way. Jesus in nails, broken flesh and blood rising to God. Hari Ohm! Ram, Ram, Ram!*

Baba talks through a translator. People prostrate themselves in tears. "Oh, Baba!" cries a da-votee, "I have a need to be near you."

The nearer you are to someone else, the farther you are from yourself. I used to sit way in the back when my guru spoke because I was afraid, full of many doubts and fears of rejection. I would sit far from him for a long time because I was afraid. Only by keeping my distance could I remain his disciple. Clever, yes? But I also retained my fears, doubts, and my ego. I was afraid if I went near him he would tell me to go away, and I always wanted to be near him. By never giving him a chance to send me away I struck a perfect balance between meditation, my guru, and my ego. A very clever arrangement, yes? Then, when I did go to him it was simple. Yet I lived in fear that he would leave; or tell me suddenly, go to that mountain. Remember, the guru dwells within us all, guides the way, if we are faithful to our intuition. No matter how far you stray, the guru is always there in the mantra and in the seed of your shaktipat, in the kundalini of the seeds sown in your subconscious without your awareness. Shades of Swami Das. *Oh, my friend, my other self, my love. One can not truly know what darkness they are living in until they have first seen the light. Our own particular darkness is not like night or day. It is imperceptible, subtle, made of ghosts and fabrications, of ego and worldly desires.* Swami Das: The lost familial connection. Confused children in search of the severed umbilical; yearning to hear once again the words of their lost parents mollycoddling them before the first word ever formed, saying through voice and touch, hugs and kisses, 'Yes, my little one. Yes, my little tike. Mommy and Daddy love you very much. You are the most beautiful baby in the whole wide world.' *Oh, my friend! What moves in me moves in you. Love, bliss, warmth, and compassion dwell in everyone, for we all drink from the same well.* "But Baba, to give is to open up, to risk everything." *Yes, little shaktipat. Some of us are in deeper sleep than others. It is for each of us to awaken ourselves fully and to help others awaken. The greatest sin in the world is to die not knowing who it was that inhabited your body. The pain, anguish, heartbreak that you feel is your soul karma.*

I watch silently from a distance like at C.B.S. I never reach out and let no one in, not even me. Yet I didn't want to leave the ashram with its atmosphere of good intentions. The question is not Baba's authenticity, or whether he is the one, but rather as Swami Das says, *What the hell you are doing with your own life?*

A flower child kneels at Baba's feet unable to talk. *It is good that you are speechless before me. Silence is the first step to understanding the self, and cutting away tape loops of regret. Before you were but a child.*

Now you are a beautiful woman. Go to him, I tell myself. Cut away the ego, the self, the I, me, my, mine! *People who speak much know little. Do not take them seriously. Truth will weed them out.* Who is it that dwells within me? The I, the me, the self, the grasping, covetous "who", which is only the outer self. Yesterday I was a child. Today I am a man who loves unconditionally, without thought of I, me, my, mine. He gives not to receive. He fears not death, but embraces him, for then the spirit is free to rejoin nature, which is amoral, and forever building and destroying. *Oh, my children of the porcelain horse. Jai Ram! Jai Ram! My buttons, books and pictures- Buy 2 get 1 free! - are only guides, like following the drinking gord.*

☺

5.　The Real *Shakti*

Wednesday, 5:30a. I ran into Irv, a tech who'd also joined C.B.S in '67. "You look calm," I go, "and peaceful. Unusal for this place, especially in TV where it's always sturm undt drang."

"Been doing yoga and meditation, my friend. Just finished a retreat. Touched by the light of inner peace and love."

"Good for you. How do you keep it going on the job?"

"By modifying the self. The ocean may toss and turn but underneath the water is tranquil."

To this day, the serenity in Irv's voice and on his face comes back like warm bread. Jesus came to us with love and open arms. What more do we need to know?

I told Swami Harihar Das about Baba. *You are on your journey.* So was Swami only I didn't know it. *Baba,* says Swams, *claims to heal, but he is sick himself. He comes to me for herbs. The thing is to live to do good, to take care of your mind and body; kill the greed, avarice and ego trips. I was offered 30,000 dollars to teach in California. I said no. Swami Gi, somebody said, you are going crazy to refuse that offer. I said, Hey, listen! What you are saying? Money isn't ruling my life. I like what I am doing not because of money but because it is my life and I believe in it. To help the people and not to give a kick about the money. To stay free of worldly nonsense. A swami said to me, you are crazy. You've been in this country longer than me and I already have a chauffeur. I said, Hey, listen. What I'm going to do with a chauffeur? You have one chauffeur, but for a dollar I have my pick of hundreds of chauffeurs going up and down the street in yellow cars. That kind of swami is too ego-oriented, too much organized publicity surrounds him. Jesus Christ did not advertise. That swami likes danger. Speeding cars excite him. In India he had an American chauffeur who was high on meditation, eight and twelve hours a day at the ashram. Baba told him it's time for you to leave for America. He thought he would go live in the mountains somewhere. Baba said, Go to New York City and drive a taxi. Get to know the city. I will be coming and you will be my chauffeur. The chauffeur told me every day is like driving in traffic with a crystal chandelier in the back seat. Anything can happen anytime. Suddenly Baba will start singing and chanting tripping out on this and that, or shouting it is all Shakti! Use it! Enjoy it! If you question him, he says, do you think the God in you is so niggardly that he'll deny you good things, clean sheets, and fine clothes? It's all Shakti! Energy! Drink in everything. I don't like his way of doing things, but I am not living his life. He will answer for that. He has too much ego. What bullshit he is feeding the people. Baba comes to me for herbs. He had two strokes, is diabetic, and fat from levitating chocolate. Crazy for the chocolate with the cherry inside. I give him herbs to flush out the sugar. Ha! He doesn't even speak English. The translator twists what he says. He has come this far because people are jackasses looking for mommy and daddy to tell them what to do, when to wipe the ass. I had followers. I kick their asses in the street. Hey, what the hell you are doing here everyday sitting, doing nothing, eating my food, and talking nonsense. I am not the silver spoon. Get out. Get out! They are looking for someone to replace Jesus Christ. I never bowed to my teacher. I don't believe in that stuff. I show respect, that's it. To reach the level of guru you must kill the ego and five evils: avarice, greed, lust, desire, and power. One day my teacher said, I am dying. He sat cross-legged and three hours later he died. Before he died I asked him what would you like me to do? He said, Don't worship me, and don't raise my picture.* Baba has many followers. Some work for nothing and some pay him. I paid $30 for two nights' lodging with meals. *But did you get laid?* During guru-gita Q and A an alarm clock rang. The translator says time is up. *Listen what I am saying. Give away everything but not your time.* Then Baba says, we are talking too much. Let us practice silence. In that silence I heard coins dropping in a basket. *With no receipts. That is the real shakti! Listen. Give away everything, but not your time.*

☺

6.   Do Not Raise My Picture

Monday, 4.5.76. Called in sick. Caught something in the drafty De Ville halls. Stuffy nose; raw throat. Sicking out again tonight. Over time the nightshift is debilitating, anti-circadian, and goes against the rhythmic biological cycles that happen every 24 hours, i.e., a confused body clock weakens the immune system. I'm a New York ghost living on Hong Kong time. **Saturday.** Swami's Health Day Celebration. Big crowd including the La Lanne gang. His Indian friends call him Swami Gi- master teacher. There was entertainment, health talk, and a vegetarian buffet. Ritchie Havens gets up, sings, 40 rings on one hand, playing a guitar with a missing string. In a mandarin-collared jacket, buttonless, wrapped at the waist, he's a cross between lumberjack and coolie. Scruffy with a sparce beard, dental floss hanging from a brown balloon. He talks about Swami. *Health is wealth. Attitude's number one.* He sings original songs, *I Am An Animal*, and one untitled he calls, *No Name Yet-* passive, social comment songs. His preambles and lyrics are soulful, compassionate thoughts. The party gets lively. *A confused body clock weakens the immune system.* Swami dances; brown face in striking yellow robes, arms akimbo, and two left feet. Swami plays a sitar. "It's easy to play for Americans. You can't tell when I am out of tune. I'm 51 years old and still strong." Applause and boos. "Okay. I am really 12 going on 61. But who is counting? I can hold my breath, you know, 30 minutes. If you expect me to do it now, don't hold your breath." *Swami Gi. Why do you always wear orange?* "Because I hate orange. My teacher saw that and said wear it every day to learn tolerance. You see, I am still learning."

Diary, undated. Working on the second act of my play *Chiaroscuro*. The Old Man sums up women libbers. "They don't-ah produce-ah, trancarlo. Cut them like a dead tree." I'd like him to say something about life, but in Italian, one word only. What? Sparisci - *disappears.*

Bag woman, old lady, pokes a free hand in garbage in the gutter, her other hand clinging to her life's belongings in a shopping cart. She sleeps in one of the knobless C.B.S doorways on 11th Avenue. Is she as old as she looks? Life in warm doorways under cardboard, a bust out dead to the world with no past, present, or future. She's bedding down while I'm going to work. Even she knows the difference between night and day...

This morning I hand carried my short story, *The Cucchiaio (Spoon)*, to *Weight Watchers Magazine* on Madison Avenue. Suddenly, I thought of my Hawaiian friend "Cubby" Chun, something he said, when he'd grown weary of the rat race. I'd love to *stumble drunk from bar to bar swinging my arms with no responsibilities.*

Tuesday Evening, Yoga class. Crossed Legs and Eyes
Cathy asks if I read the article on Baba in the New York Times. I hadn't. It was all babaganoush to me. But things were starting to penetrate. Bit by bit, I rejoined society.

Baba was no saint, I go. Too much veneration. A person who has understanding of self and others is beyond ego and has great humility. Baba is a Madison Avenue advertising campaign full of posters, buttons, and brochures. Cathy says softly, *There's nothing wrong with that. It's all shakti and transference. Something should always pass between giver and receiver, a show of appreciation.* I wanted something to pass between us. But she was spoken for. Funny. She was more Indian than Swami with her burning incense, mantras, and long class meditation. Swami spent more time doing exercises and counting to 24 each position, because, as he says, *that is how long it takes blood to circulate in the body. Exercise disciplines the will. Meditation is the way to the soul. It does not mean sleep. For that, go home and fall asleep in front of the TV.*

Cathy had been through some down time and yoga provided a new lease on life. I wanted to renew that lease as over-tenant and her as under-tenant. *Money,* she says, *is a good means of transference, a show of appreciation, as good as anything else. There is no shame in it. You should read more.* No. I should read less and get laid more. No shame in that either. *I know an elderly woman,* I go, *a former ballerina and teacher, who helped establish the Royal Ballet. She was living at Carnegie Hall, got around on a cane. She had a guru seven years in India and didn't pay a penny.* Nothing could shake her devotion to Baba Muktananda. She had been one of those lost souls who renewed herself when she found Baba and price didn't matter. Swami Das used to say, *When the student is ready the teacher appears.* I was ready but didn't know I'd found my guru; like everything in my life, through the back door in an atypical, anti-mystical, debunker of nonsense, orange marmalade in a coconut.

Cathy. *I've been into yoga nine years. I used to keep to myself a lot. I had different feelings, then mostly about various schools of yoga. I was leary, rarely participated. I felt unreal within. I hadn't found myself. When I met Baba, my life came together. There was no resistance. I knew he was my guru. I believed in him wholly and I haven't been disappointed. My entire life has changed. Through him I've touched my own reality. I've become more full, creative, even my marriage has improved. Thoughts come out of me now, expressions, which I'd never before been able to articulate. I have no need to read. I know how to answer all questions. I've tapped my inner understanding, my intuition, that inner well-spring of life's energy, which is the source of joy, expression, truth, wholeness and love, my true center, my true soul, and it's wonderful.*

I was beginning to see that finding the true self is recognition of a long lost friend; a sensation like when the body comes to rest after a weary day; a rediscovering of a lost homeostasis or contentment. It is the self for whom questions are irrelevant because it is all loving.

The best thing about De Ville was that everybody spoke the same language. Talk was about love, grace, and shaktipat. They were reaching out, striving to be human and civilized, and not society's robots. They understood the importance of breaking from the work-a-day world which doesn't exist for an individual's happiness. Shucking the ennui that goes with effete endeavors, the alienation engendered when there is no love or pride in one's work. When at the end of the day all one has is barrenness of heart resulting from disconnection from purposeful work and the joy, or satisfaction that comes from contributing to a job well done. If we're not satisfied humans first, then we're animals.

Many devotees were earnestly *soul searching,* had been in one group or another. Those I met weren't naïve hearts chasing rainbows arcing from some guru's ass. They talked of harmony, love, and tape loops, i.e., how to break habits, preconceived notions, subconscious fears that stifle each new and potentially gratifying experience.

Yin was a divorcee who left her husband with two kids in search of herself. "I'm 60 years old, and still lookin'. I tried lotsa things: Reiki; est, Erhard Seminar Training,-est is Latin for 'it is'-, founded by Werner Erhard, born John Rosenberg, a Christianized Jew. The goal was to 'Get it' by 'rewiring' and 'reprogramming' the mind. Think positive, even if you have to lie to yourself. But nobody defined 'it'. I mean, at first I felt good. Like when ya start a vacation. But I was also scared. Like maybe I won't like what I find. I defined scared as fear of failing. Then I had a reversal. The tide comes in and it goes out. I got bored. Know what I'm saying? The last weekend of the retreat, I wasn't going back. People breaking down, crying all over the place. My gut said get away from these weirdos! But it was an excuse for avoiding myself. So I stayed on. What I got, who knows? Est was supposed to blow my mind but I couldn't even blow wind. Know what I'm sayin'? They make ya sit in this room all day with no breaks. They force you to confront yourself, to get passed the lie, the superfluous self, and bring out your problem. I was forcin' myself to hold myself. Nothing superfluous about that. Know what I'm sayin'? No breaks. Hours sitting in a cold hotel ballroom my bladder busting like I'm in a concentration camp. The doors were guarded. Nobody could leave. I felt like yellin' fire. I said, I get your point. Do you get mine? My bladder's bustin'. So I went in a corner and peed on the rug. If I'd been a man I would've whipped it out peed on his shoes. Ha. What a riot. I mean, if you can't relieve yourself you can't listen, or think straight. Know what I'm sayin'? Ya sit meditating and a whiff comes floatin' across the room, and ya know some poor bastard's in trouble. In truth, what can you do on a weekend with no toilet? Wallow in your own urine, that's what. Est was a fad, one of those kitchens that dies when the cook leaves. It was a smorgasbord philosophy, a little existential, some motivational research, a smidgen psycho-cybernetics, Freud, Hinduism, Dale Carnegie, Norman Vincent Peale, and Mrs. Goldberg's 'take a piece of fruit'. Then, I followed Allan Watts with his Zen shtick. Frankly, I never met anyone whoever got 'it', unless 'it' was a bill for the seminar."

I tell Yin I'd studied Tai Chi with Master Cheng. She brightens up, and says, "Canal Street, Chinatown. He had a daughter. Good people."

"Except for one character," I go, "an aide-de-camp."

She jumps in, says, "Tam!" I nod. She smiles. "I never liked him. A rather offensive, oily person with bad vibrations. The last thing you want in Tai Chi is someone giving off bad vibes."

I go, "I saw his type in Hollywood when I taught Karate for Ed Parker. Covetous characters out of a Chinese fairytale. Consummate 'da-votees'."

"Oh, my," she says. "Touched a nerve here. Good. Work it out."

"I took a mandarin class with Miss Cheng and there was Tam like a jealous lover. Again, I let a creep get in my way."

"What was the problem?"

"Maybe he thought I was out to steal secrets and commercialize Tai Chi in Hollywood. Parker ran a successful Martial Arts business."

"How did he connect the two?"

"I was obviously no beginner and forthright. I said, I'd worked for Ed Parker. Tam had a redheaded buddy, a Californian, heavyset, bearded, and slightly friendlier. They'd watch me, ask my intentions. I should've said, to kick your ass if you don't back off. Cheng's daughter put me in an advanced class and they pushed me back. So I quit."

"Let it go," she says. "You didn't continue because you didn't want to, deep down. It wasn't for you. After all, it's a fight game. Send it down the drain like bath water. The toughest thing is to know when to come in out of the rain. Most of us don't. You're Italian? It takes un grand viaggio- a great trip; lots of love gets mutilated along the way. In the end, it is ourselves we mutilate."

At first I scoffed at Baba's devotees for their careless life-style. I was mistaken. They were the Berkeley, Kent State, anti-war kids, dreaming of love, a just life, and mutual respect. We need that spirit today. *Do not raise my picture,* Swami Gi said. *Drink apple cider vinegar with honey.*

☺

7.   Grand Central God

"That's it!" says Swami Das. "If it stops them from killing each other and keeps them off the psychiatrist's couch, that is good. Popping the pill, crying the blues on somebody's shoulder who can't fix himself a cup of tea, is ridiculous. What can a psychiatrist do? Charge money. That's it! You talk, he listens. You cry. He sympathizes, sleeps, and wakes up an hour later. Writes a prescription, says, take two pills a day. You will feel wonderful. $100. Thank you. People are looking in the wrong places for answers. Americans like to cry about their problems with someone who'll listen, but they don't face themselves. That's why we have so many psychiatrists. Complain to a friend about this and that and see how long you have a friend. Hey. Listen, what I'm saying. Look inside yourself, in your own body and mind. Nobody is doing that for you. We have greater healing self-power than we realize. We don't know it because we are running around too much, listening to teachers who are giving the wrong information. You have to feel yourself, your nervous system. Take time each day looking inward in meditation. Don't expect miracles in 15 minutes. A man came to me, 'Swami, show me God. Where is God? I said, 'Go to Grand Central Station. Maybe you will find Him there in the garbage pail.' What the hell you are talking about? If you help yourself, God isn't going to give you a miracle. You'll wait a long time at Grand Central Station for that miracle. People want it all to come to them sitting down, drinking, popping pills while watching TV, waiting for a knock on the door. It's me God. I'm here with your Chinese dreams. Come on. Give a break to reality. It's time to be responsible for your own life, to start to discipline yourself. Here what I am saying, Mr. C.B.S, under-the-cock? Discipline yourself by asking the right questions and looking for the answers inside you, not on a psychiatrist couch or between a woman's legs. Although that is a good place to start. Only be careful. Those legs are a nutcracker. Ha, ha! What hell you think yoga is all about?" *Sex.* "Shut up with your sex." *You started it.* "I was testing you." *Bullshit.* "Listen. Give to your brain a rest. It is not some mystery out there. It is developing your inner self, your own awareness, self-reliance, and will power. You have to discipline the mind and body through will power. It is the will, which separates the foolish from the wise, not miracles. Make up your mind and eventually you will do whatever you want to do. Find a nice girl, somebody who'll be there when you come home. Somebody you can depend on 90% of the time. You will get 40 but shoot for 90."

Cross-legged thoughts like monkeys in trees. A doubting Thomas asks about Baba. Are doubts cynicism, lack of trust? LBJ 'good ole boy womanizer' said Humphrey trusts his enemies too much. We trusted LBJ too much. Let your thoughts come and go like monkeys swinging in trees. Who am I, this self-thing, passion fruit cake, loop tapes of invisible garbage? When hunger and thirst cease the true self emerges. Watch your breath come and go. Drink apple cider vinegar with honey. Feel your nervous system. Hari om. Beware 5 evils: Lust, greed, avarice, ego, and desire. 'Hey, Italiano! What you are doing? Still under the clock thumb up your ass? Don't raise my picture. Don't worship me with words. Don't look to miracles in front of the TV. Get hold of your will power. kick the bullshit to the moon! Now I am free of the yellow robes.' Where are you? Under the clock? 'Venice in a gondola drinking espresso waiting on you.'

☺

8.   Morton's Minute

Diary. Terry Mortin, an extremely bright and conscientious editor/writer, took a minute between hourlies to look at my writing. Terry is tough and demanding. He curls his hair in that habit of his, in those days he had hair, some anyway, and says, "Okay. But you changed voices." *What do you mean?* "Second graph you switch from one-liners to narrative with no transition. Two different styles." Later, I saw it clearly and took a big leap forward in understanding writing. When I landed *it was no picnic.* I had to rebuild from scratch. Jokes and character are two different things. Morton's minute was epiphanal.

9. Rock and Roll News

Devious Septum: Coming up the O'Fey Café, the Chink and Cholly Show, but first this.

Diary: One C.B.S producer/editor couldn't recall a rule of usage. *I go by the sound. If it sounds right.* At first his answer didn't *sound right.* Pros work from habit and feel not by conscious definitions. A sentence is right when it sounds right regardless of grammer. Is it 'none are' or 'none is'? Who cares about who, whom, to whom, whomever, or whatever! Only pencil freaks. Well, some of it matters. Language defines who we are, so I read. **Objective-Subjective:** An icicle breaks from an eave, glistens in the sun like a silver knife. I'm trapped by the velvet glove. Marriage, family, mortgage tie you to the stake, but steady pay steadies nerves and builds a life. Whose life, if you end up colorblind to your self? I check out Strunk's bible about tight and loose writing. KISS! Keep It Simple Stupid!

Then, news went 24/7 turning night into day. More phoners and tape. "Roundy" turns on the lights. *This is a radio studio not a nightclub.* Learn to work in the dark. *Why? I can't get you to work in the light.* What if y'go blind? *I am listening to you. Take the top off.* Let's do news in Braille. *I'll keep it in mind.*

☺

10. *The Stray,* An Evening News Producer

We met accidentally coming off the job and shared a cab uptown. She was brunette, had dark, brooding eyes reminiscent of Monroe's lost lamb look, and tits like a clarion call. As we drove uptown, I sensed something feline about her, desireable yet remote, and in silent moments I swear she purred. It would not have surprised me had she jumped to the shelf and curled up under the back window. Her general reticence, and the softness in her voice when she spoke reminded me of a homeless cat. Later, I would go on to discover that this Stray had more baggage than the storage room at Grand Central. To win her affection all one had to do was lend a sympathetic ear, act tender, and wash every five minutes.

"Who is it?"

"Me. (beat) The tech, we shared a cab uptown."

"One sec."

After half a dozen locks're unlatched, the door opens a tad and a dark brown eye stares at me over a chain lock. I go, "Happy New Year!" She goes, "What's happy about it? What do you want?" I go, "We have a dinner date." She goes, "I already ate." Holding up a bottle of champagne, I go, "Then let's drink to the New Year." She goes, "Alcohol makes my urine burn." I go, "We'll drink seltzer. But if you're not up to it-"

"No. Wait." She opens up, sprays me with anti-bacteria deodorant, and says, "Take off your shoes, leave them outside, and come in. Shoes are dirty. God knows what's on them from the street. I live here. I mean you wouldn't want someone walking in your mouth with their shoes on?"

"No," I go, gagging from the spray. "Your phone was busy. I, ach-"

"It's off the hook," she says, her eyes darkening. "Should I hang it up? You think I should, I know. Don't move." She goes to a white couch room center, takes a white phone receiver from the drawer of a white end table, replaces it on a white cradle, and sprays it. "Invisible things come in from the hall, you know. I never use the elevator- well, sometimes. It's a germ incubator. I hate touching those icky buttons. Is that good champagne?"

"Piper Hiedzick."

"Oh, expensive!"

"You like it?"

"No. Yes. I mean, I like it but it doesn't like me. Know what I mean? Upsets my stomach. Gives me gas. Frankly, the idea is better than the taste. I'm not supposed to drink alcohol. I have a urine problem and it burns me. I'll get two glasses."

"We'll burn in the new together."

"I just got back from a family dinner in a Brooklyn restaurant. Promise you won't walk around." *Ok.* "Some people make promises but don't keep them." *Not me.* "Breaking a promise is sacrilegious and dirty. What are we if we don't keep our promises? Just dirty beasts."

"How was dinner?"

"Dirty," she says, becoming agitated. "Good thing I brought my own salad. They served conventional veggies, gunky white bread, and goopy cheese with casein which binds cheese. Imagine what it does in your intestines. The food was cooked and micro waved to incineration. Everything deep-fried; full of free radicals. The floor smelled of bleach and Clorox. I could taste the poisonous chlorine in the water. I wanted to run out, but it would've been rude."

"There should be a culinary food school that teaches how to cook without over-cooking."

"Yes. Uncooking 101. Food heated over 110 degrees kills the enzymes critical to digestion. Since I stopped eating sugar and white flour I don't get headaches or stomach pains anymore. My nutritionist says I need to drink two gallons of water a day, distilled, or reverse osmosis. Distilled is harder and tastes better than reverse, which is flat because the minerals are taken out. You drink water with your meals? It dilutes the enzymes, which break down food and causes constipation."

"You vegetarian?"

"I'm a foodist. I eat sprouted food. It's live and more nutritious. An hour after food is out of the ground it's dead."

She lived in a studio with no electricity or gas.

"I refuse to pander to big business.

"That's fair enough. How do you cook?"

"I don't. I eat raw. I wash everything with reverse osmosis water and biodegradable, non-chemical soap. I don't usually have people come up. Most people are slobs. They don't know to leave their shoes in the hall. You did it automatically. Do you flush the toilet with the seat down?"

"Absolutely."

"Cause if you don't, germs fly up and settle on everything. I have to clean the knobs and handles all the time. I use a homemade vinagrette of apple cider, balsamic vinegar, and ammonia. Tap water's filthy sewage. Drink it; you might as well poison yourself. You know, 'there's a world of germs under your fingernails'? People touch their mouths, stick fingers in their nose. Disgusting. That's how you get sick. I never touch myself directly. I use medical gloves. I haven't been sick in years. I haven't dated in years. People are always shaking hands. Men want to kiss your cheek. It's awful. Breathing can make you sick."

"So can not breathing."

"I mean in public places."

"You've got a high rise log cabin. How do you run the refrigerator?"

"The what?"

"Refrigerator."

"I use a cooler."

"How do you get around at night?"

"A flashlight."

"Instead of champagne I should've brought a six-pack of batteries."

The conversation went along fine until we got into an argument over what defines tragedy. But I checked it in time. Gabbing kills romance.

"*Salesman*'s not a tragedy," I go. "Loman was a plain man, not a king."

"His death is no less important. He represents everyman."

"In the Aristotelian sense. He doesn't fall from a great height."

"His death is the dilemma of modern man."

"True. But it doesn't affect the course of a nation."

"In time, it will. Big business, dissolution of loyalty."

"Willy Loman means, low man. Get it. Look. How about that drink?"

Stray takes hold of the bottle with a napkin, starts for the refrigerator, but I'm in the way. She steps back, goes left, right, smiles nervously, takes a circuitous route to the kitchen, cleans off the table top, puts the bottle on a coaster, and then dusts.

"Sometimes I'm restless. You get restless? Sometimes I'm depressed. You ever get depressed? Sometimes I'm restless and depressed." She takes a sanitary toilet seat napkin from a box, spreads it on the couch, sits, and says, "What's happening to me? I can't get hold of myself. I was never like this. Well, yes, and no. But never this bad."

"You look fine."

"It's inside. I feel I'm losing myself." As I turn to the kitchen for glasses, she screams. "Stop! You promised. No walking around." I go to sit she screams. "Stop!" Now I'm squatting in mid-air, arms up like a prisoner. "Too late," she goes, clutching her mouth and pointing to something back of me.

"What?" I go, like it's charades. "The wall? The ceiling? Something I ate? The couch?" I try smoothing out the seat. "Stop! You're making it worse." With that she starts cleaning the couch and a white album resting on it. "Would you do something? Promise not to laugh? Wash your hands." *No problem.* She indicates the sink, gives me specific directions like I'm walking through a minefield. Afterward she says, "You didn't wash them, did you? I'll bet you didn't. Some people would lie and take it like a joke."

"Not me. Touch my hands. They're cool."

"No. That's okay. Use these baby wipes. You never know what comes out of the tap. I know it must sound paranoid. I have a thing about dirt."

"Really?"

"It never bothered me. Now if something falls on the floor I have to throw it out. It's dirty."

"What if it's valuable?"

"Doesn't matter. I get rid of it. Although lately I've been able to keep a few things, but only after I've thoroughly washed them."

Looking around, I go, "You've got a real cozy studio."

"Alcove."

The place was hospital white, spotless, and spartanly furnished. An easel stood in one corner covered with a white sheet, wastebaskets everywhere filled with tissues, and everything rested on coasters and sanitary napkins even her.

"Furnish it yourself?"

"No. A friend helped me."

"Who? A surgeon? Mind if I sit? You say where."

A dumb question. There was nowhere to sit except on the couch.

"Sit over there. The windowsill. No. Oh, dear."

"How about the couch?"

"No. Yes."

"You sure?" She nods yes. So I spread a sanit wipe and sit, which pleases her. "Comfortable," I go, putting my elbow on the armrest.

"Look out!" she screams. "You touched the album." She grabs it, dusts it with a tissue, and says, "Am I making you uncomfortable."

I go, "No. I'm fine."

"I get nervous if people touch things. You understand?" *Definitely.* "I didn't let you in right away because I was afraid you'd walk around. Sometimes I can't stand for anyone to walk on the floor. Am I depressing you?" *No.* "I wish I were a bird and never have to touch down."

"Ever consider suspension ropes?"

"Yes. But I'd still have to touch them. I considered hospital gloves. But they give me a rash. Changes have to be OKed by the co-op board. I don't want them knowing my business."

"Hey, we're forgetting the champagne, or do you want to wait for midnight?"

"Let's wait. I didn't always feel this way, just since I broke up with my boyfriend nine years ago Wednesday. Maybe I will get the champagne."

Stray pours the champagne into disposable cups, using napkins to shield her hands from directly touching anything. She turns with a beckoning look, extends a cup of champagne, but as I reach for it she puts it on a coaster on the table and walks away. "I love champagne, to look at not to drink. Bubbles, like so many lives rising up and exploding. They remind me of forgotten things."

"Like what?" I ask, picking up my drink.

"Don't know. I've forgotten them. Mostly, inexpressible things."

"A toast to the inexpressible." As I move to clink cups, she pulls back suddenly annoyed.

"He made me feel dirty, ashamed of my body."

"Dirty from dirt or dirty-"

"Dirty dirty and dirty sexy. Oh, I don't know anymore. I think my body's clean. He wanted me to play down my body, as if showing it were shameful. I'd buy bikini underwear and he'd hide them. He was the dirty one. Why do I feel dirty?" I shrug. "He made me feel dirty."

"You bathe, use clean soap, right?"

"Castile. No animal fats. It's the feeling I can't wash away. Sometimes I take several baths a day because stepping from the tub I'll accidentally touch something."

"So just wash your hands."

"No. I'd feel icky."

"How many baths have you taken in a day?"

"Sixty-nine. Why should I feel dirty?"

"Right. Waterlogged, not dirty."

"Shouldn't I be clean after all those baths? He made me feel dirty. If we'd stayed happy, like at first. He made me feel dirty. Him!"

She became more distraught with each word, her eyes deepening into black tools. "It never bothered me before," she says. "Only lately. I can't get hold of myself. It was *his* fault. The bastard! He never cared for me for myself. Always showing me off like jewelry. If I didn't dress his way, he'd yell so that after awhile I got so nervous. While cooking I accidentally cut myself. See? Both wrists. The snake! He messed with my mind!"

"Why'd you let him?"

"I loved him. I kept hoping he'd change. I wanted him to love me. He used to love me. Here. Look." She puts a napkin on the end table, her drink on it, covers the top with a tissue, and then shows me an album. "See the pictures? He even wrote me poems. 'Naked, naked. To be naked is not nearly naked enough.' One summer we swam nude in Central Park and ran in the Sheep Meadow in the moonlight, and the sky was full of stars. In the city you forget the sky is full of stars. We even took classes together at the Art Student's League."

"Naked?"

"No. Silly. Well, yes. We'd arrive early and take turns sketching each other. That's my painting on the wall to the left- latex, acrylic crayon on coco leaves with potato skins. His is on the right. It's called *Nieve.* That's French for snow. Covered on the easel is something he was working on when he left."

"The Snow painting blends in with the wall."

"That's because nothing is in it. The genius was his decision to have an empty frame lends structure to the space within. The one on the easel is called Triptych because he tripped and fell on it. Now, close your eyes. (*draws cover*) Open them. At first it looks gaudy, a monstrous montage, which it is, predominantly orange and yellow depicting the obvious life and earth cycle, birth, death, post-nuclear war, volcanic turmoil, and snake-like humans on a caducean resembling a phallus. It's one of his happier works. There were others, but in a drunken fit he did a Jackson Pollack and threw them in the East River."

"What do you mean Pollack?"

"Pollock threw his early works in the river."

"How do you know?"

"He worked for my father at the time. Daddy was an expert silk screen artist. This was before Pollack became famous. My dad helped carry the stuff to the river. He kept Pollock from jumping off the pier. My father said he should've let him jump and kept the paintings, but in those early days, who knew? You like this painting?"

"He likes orange."

"No. Hates it. But it's his karma, which is learning to live with what you hate. Then he started painting me naked. Not on canvas. On my body. That's when I knew he hated me. He said the paint was non-toxic, even ate a tube of vermilion to prove it and threw up all over the canvas. That's why it looks vomity. Then he said bad things about my body that made me ashamed. Nasty, inappropriate things. I hate you, hate you! I'm sorry. Maybe it's the holidays. I feel more lonely on holidays."

When I suggest we sit down, she spreads two new sanit wipes on the couch and close together. I go, "I don't think you mean to talk about your boyfriend. So let's talk about something else."

"My father's dead. I hate my mother! I haven't seen her in years, and don't care if I ever see her. She's a dirty woman!"

"Let's go back to your boyfriend."

"Do your folks get along?" I nod no. "Mine did at first. But not around me. Do your folks still have sex?"

"My father does."

"My mother hated sex. I felt sorry for my father. She did it for children. That's all. For herself, she didn't care. I think my father used to get turned on by me. You know, a Jewish version of Arthur Miller's *A View From the Bridge*. I'd walk around the house, and sometimes sit on my father's lap and we'd play submarine. Once he got mad because he saw me walking by the corner candy store and he said, You wiggle too much."

"Did you like your father?" I ask, gently touching her shoulder. "What do you remember most about him?"

"Not much. One thing. It's in my mind to this day. I never saw his penis hard. You'd just think in all that time living in the same house and all, there was no lock on the bathroom door, you'd think that I'd have seen it hard once, but I never did. It was always soft."

"You sound disappointed."

"I was. For him. Because I knew he wasn't having sex with my mother. I guess it made him appear less strong to me. I don't know."

"You feel bad about your folks not making it?" I go, moving closer.

"Someone had to fill in. Know what I mean? I wanted him to be happy. I hate my mother!" Rising suddenly, her shoulder hits me under the jaw, knocking my head backward. "I don't ever want to see her. She's a bad woman. Kept a dirty house. I was always embarrassed to bring anyone home. She never admitted the house was dirty. She denied it. But I could see. I could see. It was dirty! I had to sleep in a dirty bed. She insisted it was clean. But it was dirty. Full of bugs, and she made me sleep in it. I hated her for that. She said there weren't any bugs in the bed. But one night I couldn't sleep, there were so many bugs. She stayed up all night picking bugs off my body." With that she starts picking bugs off me. "In the morning I went to school with red welts all over me. That's how I know she lied. There were bugs. She lied."

"Maybe your dirt thing started there," I go, scratching myself. "Put it behind you." I had to laugh. The blind leading the blind.

"Don't you see?" she says, stepping close to me, and I find myself backing up. "I want to, but I can't. That's what scares me. Lately I can't even stand on my legs too long. They hurt. I haven't done anything today except that dinner, and somebody picked me up. I was going to do my laundry, wash my hair. I took fourteen baths but I still feel icky. I'm going to die in ugliness, in filth and garbage and dirty clothes. If only I had somebody to love. I wouldn't feel so bad. Someone to hold my hand, to take care of me."

"You have to take care of yourself first. A man's got his own problems."

"Then he couldn't love me."

"What's love to you? Full time administering to someone else?"

"I don't know. I used to think I knew, but I don't, not anymore. I don't think that one should take another too personally. People can be cruel."

"They'll hurt you."

"And desert you."

"Break your heart if you let them, but don't you let 'em."

"Even if they're inconsiderate and die on you."

"What could be more selfish?"

"I mean die before their time. You know, giving up on you. Real love never gives up." Yes, I think, we're on the same page. "I wouldn't make love with someone unless I really felt something for them."

"Then," I go, "You have to learn to separate the heart from sex, have the erection without affection. So to speak."

"Yes," she says, eyes widening. "The erection without affection. You know, there's something about you, a naturalness, which makes me feel comfortable and draws me to you. Being comfy with someone is very important. It's really the first step to feeling good and warm. I'm feeling warm. Are you? I was never warm with my boyfriend. I guess I loved him too much."

"It's no good lovin' too much."

"The pits. Can I tell you a secret? Promise you won't laugh. I used to go with an analyst named Cuckoomani. You're laughing. He had degrees in physical therapy, and transcendental meditation. He believed physical and mental problems were related. His theory combined transcendental meditation, yoga, and needlepoint. I paid 300 dollars for a mantra. My designer mantra. A special incantation expressing my essence. It's worked out astrologically according to my age, birth, cycles of the moon, my menses, and Master Charge. I'm not supposed to tell anyone my mantra. It loses spiritual potency if you tell anyone. Mine's OM."

"Oh."

"No. OM."

"OM?"

"Mm. Actually, he only gave me half my mantra."

"Should've given him half the money. What's it mean?"

"It's ancient Sanskrit, chanted by monasties in monasteries for years, hundreds, imbuing it with spirituality, healing powers, and very holy. Om is the hum of the universe. Energy rises from the solar plexis, here, touch." She puts my hand on her chest. "Feel it rising up to the crown of your head? Ha-ri, Hari om. Feel it rising up?" *Yes.* "Relax your body. (lost *in a trance*) Watch your breath come and go. Keep closed the eyes. Feel the belly rise. Direct your attention toward releasing all of the tension and toxins, the dirt and poisons that in the chalice of the body gather. Breath in the good, exhale the bad. In with good and out with bad. Omm." *Mm.* "Tighten every muscle in your body. Tight, tighter, and release. Let the anxiety in your breasts dissolve. First the right breast. Wiggle it, tighten it, relax, and forget it. Now the left breast. Wiggle it, tighten it, relax, and forget it. Now both breasts, wiggle them, tighten them, tighter, relax, and forget them. Om. Gently begin to spread your legs. Om. You no longer feel 'em as you relax your perineum. All tension dissolving, melting, flowing out, out of the body. Slowly, ever so slowly, begin deep breathing through your vagina. Let the inhalation be longer than the exhalation. Feel the prana enter your vulva, filling you with life. First, through the labia majora, then through the labia minora. Forget what you learned in the Torah. Hoy. Ha-ri Om. Do you recognize your inner self? I recognize you're in myself. Hoy. Om. My boyfriend was a thinker. Spoke nine languages. He killed himself."

"In which language?"

"You get one thing with one, something else with another. I need a supermarket man who has it all. No more shopping around. My men are always going out of business. One jumped from a five story building." *That's bad.* "And lived." *That's good.* "But he's paralyzed." *That's bad.* "Yes. Cause now if he wanted to finish the job, he can't even lift a finger." (wiggles a limp finger) "He must think about what he did, which is the worst part of all, because maybe now he would like to live and can't. Am I talking too much?" *No.* "When I'm comfortable with someone I talk and can't always control the outcome. I'd go back to analysis, but it cost 18,000 dollars to find out what I already knew. I'm depressed. I need answers not questions. I used to have a cat. But he ran away like my boyfriend. Sometimes I miss the excitement of my boyfriend. Once we made love in a Greek church."

"Orthodox?"

"No, standing up."

"Where could you go from there?"

"Bergdorf Goodman's, the dressing room. Then he started saying the life had gone out of me. It was a lie. Oh, sometimes I'd feel life was futile and what's the use of picking up a fork. At first he cooked for me, did my laundry, even bathed me. Then he got angry, did less and less, and after nine years he stopped altogether. That's when I got depressed, felt like I had no more to give. I was all given out. Nothing touched me here." She presses my hand against her breast. "You know? It's all out there. Nothing here."

"I wouldn't say that."

"Why?"

"You're beautiful."

"I am?"

"The city's not for you. It's too harsh, too brutal. You need a family."

"I'd like to rent one and try it. Walk in and have everything there. I'd like a baby and we'd live in the country with flowers and pine trees. I love the smell of pine, and winters so quiet you can hear the needles falling. Ping! Ping! Ping! In summer a stream where I could bathe nude with my baby with no one for miles around."

"You have somber, wistful eyes."

"In the city you forget there are stars in the sky."

"Full of longing, expressing dark feelings of trouble and sadness." With that, I kiss her cheeks and breasts.

"People who like me for myself like my eyes. Am I all you want in a woman? Is my body nice?" I drop to my knees, kiss her belly, and she screams. "Stop! Your knees touched the floor! You're dirty, dirty, dirty!"

☺

11. Along Came Ayn

Diary, 1978. Swami was always having birthday parties, or *moments of enlightenment.* Every new day was a rebirth, an awakening. On one of those celebratory occasions I was in an east side apartment, smoky with pot, drinking, dancing with different women, when up comes a goose in balloon pants and waving her arms with two fingers in a splint. Talk about enlightenment! She was a good friend with Swami's woman. They'd met in Dance Therapy, or what Swami derisively called the *Talking Class,* run by an Argentinean *she-nomenon* with pipes deeper than Darth Vader. In Dance Therapy you dance out your woes. Apparently, the night before Ayn was dancing out hers in a navel picking, cathartic tear-jerker, hit a wall, and broke a finger. After that, whenever she went to class I'd toss her the finger, and go, save the next wall-tz for somebody else.

Ayn was born in Silk City, which is my preferred name for Paterson. Though I'd never been there, I imagined it was the ass end of the world.

In 1978 downtown Paterson reminded me of De Kalb Avenue, Brooklyn. A once prosperous business area shot to hell.

"Nylon killed the silk business," Ayn said. "Subsequently, Paterson collapsed, relying as it did on one industry."

Grand department stores were deserted, windows busted, buildings boarded up. The rise of malls dealt the final blow. But the scary thing about Paterson is the

Great Falls, or Passaic River. Right in the middle of the city a tremendous falls that looked bottomless.

"I walked across it," Ayn says. "I did it when the river was low."

High or low, it was crazy! The falls gave me the creeps. A big hole in the middle of town made me uneasy. I looked over the edge once, and never again out of fear I'd be sucked down into Dante's bottomless pit. Just thinking on it gives me the willies.

"And you really walked across it?"

"I was a teenager then. I wouldn't do it now. Somebody once went over the top in a barrel and lived."

I couldn't wait to get back to Manhattan, built on good solid rock. In the city you don't know from bottomless pits, unless you hit a pot hole and then it's over the dashboard and through the windshield to Lenox Hill Hospital you go. In truth I was fooling myself. Manhattan's built on stilts. Just under the pavement in some places there are drops of a hundred feet or more. Miles of tunnels for trains and water ducts, phone and electric lines, gas and steam pipes. Better not to think of it.

Before Ayn and I married, we tooled around New York in her mini Mazda truck with my dog Scuffles wedged between my actor friends. God only knows what would've happened had we hit one of thiose deep pot holes. Ayn and I married in Our Lady of Peace Church on East 62rd, precided over by Monsignor Holland. Afterward everybody walked to the reception at Wine and Apples, a Greek restaurant on West 57th. On the way people greeted us with the usual NY encomiums. *Ya ruined a good thing! Need help, call me!* Sidewalk diners at the Park Restaurant cheered us on. As we turned down Avenue of the Americas, I circled a hand in the air and shouted, *Another round, Cameriere! Drinks on us!* It would be at Wine and Apples following Ayn's amniocentises that we named our son Christopher Ion. Today he questions that decision. *Where'd you get Ion? It's not even spelled with an A.* Came to me in a dream, son. Your lucky. Your mom wanted to name you Amniocenteses. Has a Latin-Greco ring!

☺

12. Swami Goes Balmy

Diary. Weekend in Pocono Mountains, my sister's house. When we first arrived at Indian Hill Swami and his woman looked around to take in the place and then I showed them their room. As they were pulling the beds together something triggered a fight that lasted a long time. She came flying out of the room fuming, throwing a book, and her eyeglasses on the floor. Swami grabbed her shoving her down onto the couch, his palm on top of her head. "Okay, sweetheart. When we go back everything is going to be okay. You'll see. You pack your fucking bag and I'm going to put you in the street. Then you'll find out what life is all about. One year I didn't send you to work. A whole year. I'm too good to you. Well, now we shall see who is important, that fucking Tuli or me! You like to talk? Okay, sweetheart. Pack your bags and move in with her. Then you can talk all the time and do nothing."

"Swami," I go, "take deep breaths; count to 25; drink apple cider vinegar." He didn't think me funny. After things calmed down there was silence. Now she was sweet and apologetic. Swami is dead set against the Talking Class. He believes in self-therapy and action.

How do I escape death? How do I merge with the good that knows only life? I looked into the Swami's eyes.They were open but his mnd was closed. He's dying, I thought, dying on me just like his teacher died on him, and now he's leaving me in a world without orange and yellow robes, and a brown face laughing, mocking false idols. He's on his deathbed. I look down at him, not believing he's going to die. How could a man with so much life die? He looks up at me, but does he see me? I am a helpless fool with no magic gift to save him. Give me one wish in this world and I'd ask for the secret to life and death. Don't give a kick for any bullshit and die gracefully. I told the nurse, "Reach under the covers and grab his balls. If he doesn't react he's dead."Sad to say, Swami was in another place. Wherever he was, I knew he was happy, and glad that I was doing positive things and not pissing away my life talking.

A man could travel the universe on a beam of light and return to earth years later as young as the day he left. Ah, to return younger than my son. I don't think I'd like that. A thing perceived by the human eye has already moved to the future by a tiny fraction of a second and what we see really is the past. I'm already slightly older than the way you see me. You see me now, but I am in the future, so are we all in the future by that fraction of a second. The world as we perceive it now is actually the past. "You see me now, but I am already in the future." How to grapple with past and future, bind all time in a nutshell hermitically sealed and cast into space and the distant stars might burn it up completely. We would then become free and always youthful on this earth. My friend Swami is dying. He is in the hospital with tubes up his nose and IV's in both arms. His breathing is shallow. His eyes are narrow slits, his body thin; it's old age evident, the grays of his stubble beard and head more prominent than ever. He has sunk into a state of lethargy, a coma. I kissed his chin. I stick my head under a tube and kiss the stubble on his chin. I missed you, Swami, I said. I hadn't seen him in some time. You must not go. Get well. How do you feel? I love you. He recognized me, I'm sure. A tear came down the side of his eye. "You see, I am helpless. We are all helpless." Yes, and I curse my kind for not attending to the problems of the helpless first...for spending millions on bullshit wars and vanities rather than on curing disease and helplessness. I get angry and short tempered, and I run from sickness out of fear and disgust because we are liars and cheaters and deny the real miracle that comes with each breath and every time we see each other.

☺

13. The Music of Two Hearts

Diary, 4a. "Swami's blood pressure was up," said the nurse on the floor at Roosevelt Hospital. "Earlier, he was talking, even complaining."

"He'll be okay now?"

"We're monitoring him closely."

"Get those tubes out of him. He's not unconscious, just meditating."

Then he had a relapse. What happened? God knows.

Who was the Swami? What was the truth beneath the words and orange robes? He preached love, but needed love himself. He was a jumble of paradoxical truths, and rules to live by. "Where there is no love," he'd say, "put love, and love will appear... errors flow like straws on the surface of the ocean, one must dive below for truth...you can't meet someone without knowing them." Did he live what he preached? Not wholly. But he was closer to truth than most men.

How'd Swami reconcile his Indian philosophy with that of free-styling America, a nation that is all things to all people? He was the priest and America was Thais, carnal knowledge. We often laughed together and he'd say things like, "The fall from a woman's bed is greater than the drop from any throne. Love is a silent killer. Heartaches are the devil's footsteps. Only the purest heart can walk among the sick and not be touched. America is a great big sprawling land of plenty; full of crazy people with more twists and turns than Shiva has arms. Compared to India she is just a baby." Swami saw youth and vigor in America, and hope, a place to live and be human, a temperate place, where he could be both man and swami. "Americans can be appreciative, loving, cruel, and monstrous. They are looking to replace the father image, Jesus Christ, and decadent leaders, but underneath there is a longing for death."

Where are you now, Swami Gi, with all your mantras? I saw you one summer day, an orange butterfly flitting about my head. Where are your jibes, your rigid maxims now, Swami? You never sanctified your role as yoga teacher and herbalist. You played it all down and spoke angrily at times about your peers who took advantage of weak-minded people, pulled them by the nose with lies, taking their money and devotion and laughing up their kimonos.

Where to begin my final account? How do I express love for a strange brown-skinned man who wore orange, preached love, yearned for it, and died of booze? Should I start by being angry with myself for being narcissistic, for not reading the signs in him? After all, he needed friends, too. Why had I abandoned him seven months before his death? Was he my friend, or a freak show? In his presence I became once again my unconventional self. People would ask, some in earnest others sarcastically, *Is he your Swami?* I'd smile, my often all too quick smile that belies what I feel. *Is he your Goo-roo? Where'd ya find him? He brought him home one day from Jack La Lanne.*

Figgy was a C.B.S messenger-courier who, come rain or shine, made pick-ups and deliveries of tapes and film at airports and railroad stations. Figgy knew the road like the back of his hand. In traffic jams he'd ride on sidewalks, or cling to the back of an ambulance or fire truck to get the goods through. He was Fed Ex, the US Post Office, UPS and the Pony Express on a Harley

Davidson. Neither rain nor sleet nor snow, yada-yada, could stay him in his course. Sometimes he went out in a raging storm to pick up hot stuff slated for air immediately. Thanksgiving morning Figgy zoomed up to the C.B.S entrance, climbed off his hog, and dropped dead of a massive heart attack. It was so quick and sudden he had no time to think, *How can I drive around this son-of-a-bitch?* He just hit the pavement like a tree struck by lightning. I knew more about his death than the Swami's, which came in contradictory bits and pieces: pneumonia, herbs in tandem with vodka, but they don't explain the man.

Swami looks at me without seeing me. His eyes have no depth. Where are you, I wonder? I make a silly-ass remark, but he just stares straight ahead unblinking and serene like a dead man with eyes opened. Can you hear me, Swami? He gives no sign. The skin on his face is smooth. I touch his forehead. He continues staring, dumb faced, saint or sinner, seeing but not seeing. All that vitality, love and concern for life, layed low. What is the story here, the mystery? We squander time in pursuit of vanity, taking each other for granted only to discover too late, however briefly, something fundamental and elusive. It's life that matters; breath in the lungs, tensile in the muscle, blood in the heart, and love.

Swami's diagnosis flew in the face of what he preached; love, patience, self-discovery, and discipline. Not that his philosophy must be deemed bullshit because he couldn't live it himself. No. It becomes questionable as to the merit of its pursuit when you realize that the greatest minds of all time could not in the end beat the odds.

Swami pined for his Shanti, daughter by his first wife. He loved Shanti very much. That I know. When he spoke of Shanti tears would well up in his eyes. *What could I do? Her mother loves her. The man cares for her very much. So I made the decision to let her stay with her mother. It breaks my heart, but I do it for the child. I don't want her to grow up and say I took her from her mother. This way she visits and knows both of us. But sometimes I wish I... I had taken my Shanti back to India. They would never find us.* His eyes were distant and watery.

I think of his shaven head, the brown texture of his smooth skin, olive brown eyes which could be serene as if waking from deep sleep, or flashing with quick emotion like a brief rain on a sunny day. I think:

> Lies killed my Swami. Lies we tell ourselves. Lies we tell others and lies they tell us. Swami, you bastard, I did love your lying ass. Now you are gone. Off to dance la rumba with Malcolm and Lamumba. We were going to India. Remember? But you left without me. I could've loved you more, kissed you more. Asked about your feelings? You were tough, you know. 'A stinker,' said your girlfriend. Even now I hear you saying, *'Stop with the pity, you are giving me.'* And you didn't always have answers. Maybe that's why I hung back in the end, playing judge and jury. I wanted answers. I wanted you to have the answers where I had none. You saw the foolishness everywhere and laughed. So many lost souls searching for mommy and daddy. *Stop kissing your own ass,* you'd say, *and get on with life.* Here's looking at you, Swami-la; American guru, lover of wine, women and song.

Swami died Sunday, November 16, 1980. My friend Figgy, the courier, died Thanksgiving morning; John Lennon was shot at the Dakota, December 8th. Each died a peculiar death. All death is peculiar. One man preached goodness and health, the other had a gold heart, and the third talked of love, peace, and strawberry fields.

God is that you in me, in every blessed thing? Death hooks us on a lure of our own fantacies. Swim with joy little fish. Swallow life with joy. Forget lurking dangers, or you die every day a thousand deaths. In being eaten you live again.

Nurse Deborah, a doctor's physician. *"Swami checked into Roosevelt Hospital with a case of diarrhea, but the real trouble was a case of booze. He was a secret drinker of vodka and chewed cloves to mask his breath. Diarrhea was the first symptom of a larger problem of alcohol plus herbs, which taken in combination can be extremely toxic. In the hospital he contracted pneumonia.*

Swami told me read the signs in people's actions. Do not get carried away with their words. I was carried away by my own words and forgot to study my actions. Swami, I asked, "How can you listen to people's crap when they don't follow your advice and repeat themselves?"

"I listen with my eyes. Look with my heart."

Om shanti om.

☺

14.   Substance Abuse

In the '60's reporters and correspondents were still penetrating writers in the Burrow tradition. They were huge figures, solid blocks of cement, exuding integrity, and objectivity in their work. My first impression of Dulles Townsand was of a man who was scholarly, precise, erudite, and unpretentious. When I first focused on Dulles anchoring the News Roundup (NR), I thought, he's writing history. When I called him a talking historian, he humbly replied, *Oh, Poppycock.* Then, in the '70's and '80's, the powers-that-be, completed the murder of what was left of Burrow Boys. There's a saying, those who go along get along. The go-alongs know that you can knock at the gate just so many times before "they" cut your head off.

1967-68 was the start of *produced* news, turning an anecdote into a yarn with fanfare to grab attention. It is corruption of straightforward news reporting that misleads listeners into thinking there is simultaneity of events. It is flat out *bastardization of news.* There ought to be a media nightclub called Catch A Falling Reporter emceed by Dan Rather, who'd rather be somebody else these days. Ninety percent of the average news day is the Perils of Pauline without a cliffhanger scene. It's mostly fill-swill to generate money. Give me five minutes daily of Mal and Dulles on the NR, and you can pull the plug on the rest.

News ought to never be bias, censored, or *produced.* It should present the naked truth and never pander to prurient interests. *Paramount in a free society is an independent press.* You can't very well keep a man's feet close to the fire if he's paying your mortgage.

At night I was completely underground, hiding from the day timers and myself. I figured *out of sight out of mind.* I went to several schools during days and somewhere in between all my classes, I met Ayn through the Swams, and eventually got the hell off the nightshift.

There is absolutely no upside to working nights unless you're a bat, and if you're not, you'll end up batty, and sleeping upside down. In one revealing night scene in *Red River,* the men are bedded down by the campfire after a day driving cattle. Night with its fear of the unknown presses in, a coyote howls, and everyone is jittery including the cows. Walter Brennan says to Montgomery Clift, *It's funny what the night does to a man. You're all right during the day,* and Clift says, *During the day they can see.* My eyes were closed day and night.

15.   E & E

Yee Olde Tech Lament
Oh, give me a razor, some cotton swabs,
A jar of alcohol and I'm set for the day   (Anon)

Diary: No amount of "night differential" – extra pay, can compensate for the harm done to mind and body. Often knocked out and disoriented, living between the nether world and reality, I was a forgotten man, but expected to perform equally well at midnight and 8a. I'm told that the Mohawk's ability to walk steel girders hundreds of feet in the sky is not a natural talent, but inbred, which is what it might take to work nights. Build a newsroom on steel girders and hire Mohawks. News is a balancing act anyway.

Three years on the Dracula shift. Negatives outweigh positives. Hourly news now goes all night. I teched them at first then they brought in another body. Sleepless nights-mother of irritability and crankiness. Is it my moods, or the Martian nights? People wanting to work overnight should send up a red flag to employers that something's wrong with them. But the business of business is business. Empathy with workers subtracts from that end. The job's 9 to 5. Personal problems are 5 to 9. You want loving kindness, sympathy and understanding, get a dog. I did. It was a start. To save myself I perfected an old army tactic called E & E, Escape and Evasion. It's my disappearing act. Hide out. Get lost. Go for coffee and take forever to get back.

My dream of returning to DJ work was dying, but then something else was being born, something deeper and more meaningful. I was learning to express myself through art and education. Still, the dream flickered like a whore's wink. The real war was not the jobs I kissed off like a possible DJ gig in Okinawa, or reporting from Vietnam, but the inner battle between me and myself, the 'I' and the 'who', between what men say and what they do, between Joseph Conrad's 'horror' and the innate joy that was me as a newborn child. The battle was grabbing the high ground from my demons and how to reconcile contradictions: blood plasma and guns, Florence Nightingale and Stalin, a kiss and a knife, pets and vivisection, a poet dying of starvation and prattling millionaire news people. Out of a clash between the need to succeed and the repugnant notion of compromise would come a new self that has taken a lifetime of understanding. When I decided to think, I chose a lonely, close to the bone-solitary life, darker than any nightshift- an inward hegira in search of immortality, dissolution of pain, nirvana, and a living wage in a state of homeostasis. One day I would cringe looking back at an earlier incarnation of a sometime fool and wastrel.

For now I wear what co-workers call the velvet glove: good money, benefits, and a pension plan. But the price of comfort, the antithesis of art, is death. I am content dead. Man is born from struggle, out of which he becomes a man. I had to come to grips with periodic depression, feelings of malaise, a tendency to run from trouble, and withdraw when things weren't right? What's right? Purity and love. I want what Stray wants, only I want to be her baby hanging from her big tits. *A life in the country with flowers, the smell of pine, and winters so quiet you can hear the needles falling. Ping! Ping! Nude bathing in a stream, pooping, and swimming away, and no one for miles around.* But I wake up in this chuckleheaded dream, knees on the floor, before a radio console, and I'm *dirty, dirty, dirty!* I need challenge! *You want challenge, booby?* I hear my friend Heshie say. *Join the marines!*

Around 1970 *the powers-that-be* disrupted my nightly routine of chats with the film developers, the Nigerian cashier and Oscar in the cafeteria, writing in my diary, reading, and sleeping, all the things that made those ungodly hours tolerable. The hourly news was extended 24/7, which strained both sides of the window, and forced nosies to get inventive. In 25 years nothing ever happened on the overnight that couldn't wait. It's one thing to glorify insignificance in the daytime but at night it's gilding the lily. Sometimes I couldn't tell if what I heard really happened or I dreamt it.

Newsfeed expanded to three closed circuit, pre-digested offerings to affiliates of secondary pickings, and pieces phoned in by nosies around the world playing Dick Tracy through a keyhole. The feed provided affiliates and low-budget stations with a window on world news. With newsfeed came fruitcakes, nervous Nellie, over-producer-types out for fame and fortune. So I ratcheted up my E & E shtick and became the *Houdini tech, famous for Disappearing.* One writer looked up and said, *Who are you? How'd you get by security?* I walked a fine line between strained compatibility and indifference.

Occasionally I wonder what might've been had I gone to Vietnam. How about dead, face down in a rice paddy? I'm not the sort to hang back. I'd want both sides of a story. I'd ask hard questions like I did in Anaheim. *What the hell are we dying for anyway?* Instead of intrepid reporter, I'm Mr. All-nighter playing safe in the bosom of Manhattan heading for a rocking chair of dull memories. Ironically, I was my own Vietnam, playing guerrilla warfare with my job and the poet in me, and one day I ended up face down in a rice cooker.

Back in the '60's ad-libbing news or drifting from a station format, was like messing with a papal bull. Formatted stations dominated the air with Rock & Roll. One rock jock had index cards on which were written phrases he had to repeat in between records to plug the station. WANV, Your Country Music Station. KEZY, The Sunspot On Your Radio Dial; K-POOP, In The Air Everywhere! One PD said, "Nobody wants to hear what color pants the sax player was wearing in Glenn Miller's band in 1939." When I told Ayn, "As a jock I was fighting for airtime," she says, "As your wife, so am I."

Through the opened studio door of Newsfeed clucking voices, clacking typewriters. Dulles, a Lautrec in profile, two fingers flashing across a Remington; Roundy Terkel, a frontal view, short sleeves, bowtie askew, looks down his peanut nose proofing copy for the NR. Cholly calls for a pronouncer on a singer's name. Is it Neil Sa-dock-ah or Sadaka? I tell him *the latter. Neil was a year or two behind his brother Martin, a schoolmate of mine.* I knew them from Avenue U and Homecrest Avenue, Brooklyn. *Ring!* Mal picks up. Calls out, *Dulles, line one.* Three additional cuts are dropped off for 7:15 feed to affiliates. Dulles to Mal: *My daughter gave birth to a boy.* Mal says, *Congratulations, grandpa! We'll lead the Roundup with "Dulles will not be heard this morning. His daughter just gave birth to a boy making him a five-time grandfather. He's out gettin' smashed."* Cholly leads the 7AM hourly with "commie soldiers seeking asylum in America." *If they want an asylum,* says Mal, *come to C.B.S.*

Though I lay low, I still earned a rep. I blame loneliness, sleepless nights, my old man's DNA, and the artist in me, who refused to go gently into the good night. My quarrel was with over-producers, Ivy League Notre Dumb, freeze-dried farts. Pour airtime on them, they dissolve into *heavenly chuckleheads, the best radio-bembas money can buy.*

The "Dracula Shift" brought simple problems like, *where am I? What day is it?* I'd wake up at noon thinking it was midnight. Daylight Savings meant I lost or gained an hour's pay. Occasionally, temp workers would pass through full of themselves. They'd come in midnights; bright-eyed, bushy-tailed, aggressive, thinking time flies by working- For me it was sleep. - and burn themselves out by sunrise. I'd toy with them, turn up the thermostat, or put it on freezing, or I'd lower the lights with soft music in the background to lull them to sleep. At the first sign of a yawn, I'd go into the newsroom, call them on the phone, and hang up. Ring! *Hi. I'm in the cafeteria. Want anything? Sleep? Coffee? Pep pills?* I found one guy cross-eyed, flat on his ass, crying, "Kill me! Tell me I'm dreaming!" Another one drank so much coke and coffee he was bouncing off the walls. By 4AM he was up on the ceiling calling for landing rights. Mal Terkel was the only one I knew who took nights in stride. He paced himself. I paced myself, too, to anything that would hold me up.

An Over-producer. Here's the tape for the upcoming.
Mal. That was fast. What happened in the studio?
O-P. Nothing.
Mal. Really? How'd you get his nibs to move?
O-P. I edited the tape myself.
Mal. That's a union violation.
O-P. That's what he said. I go, 'So's sleeping on the job.' He goes, 'Well, in that case two negatives make a positive.' Is that right?
Mal. Never listen to him. Give me the damn tape.

Being difficult was my defense against humps who'd find fault even if you crucified yourself. I took the offensive to ward off workaholics and to protect my free time. Hell! News was mostly *make-work nonsense.* So I'd act churlish and dumb, which came natural, and eat lots of garlic. When a new creep barged in hot to trot, switching on the lights, thinking he had history by the short hairs, I'd chuckle because what he really had was, *the* Gagootz, *wild man of the overnight.* Take that tape n' shove it!

16. The O'Fey Café

End piece: Here's Lookin' At You, Kid, Through a Germ Mask

Drew. Over the weekend two of our colleagues tied the nuptial knots.
Sue. At an ante-bellum inn in Wildebeest, Connecticut.
Drew. It was an outdoor Renaissance affair.
Sue. Which is cheaper than one indoors.
Drew. There were fairies and sylphs, lutes and lyres-
Sue. Played by liars and looters.

Drew. Dancing satyrs-

Sue. Bill collectors.

Drew. Wood nymphs in diaphanous muumuus, waving envelopes and crying.

Sue. They hadn't figured in gas and tolls from NYC.

Drew. The couple exchanged "I do's" and "I don'ts" in a pre-nuptial agreement.

Sue. In case the show crashes and burns.

Drew. During the ceremony they sat on mopeds with saddlebags containing water filters, quinoa seeds, and a six month supply of non-dairy Cheez-Its.

Sue. They wore germ masks and radiation suits by Deva of Miami.

Drew. Deva's in North Dakota.

Sue. Not this Diva, honey.

Drew. Oh, I see, Sue.

Sue. No. You seesaw Marjorie Daw, Johnny shall have a new master.

Drew. He shall make a penny a day.

Sue. 'Cause he can't work any faster. Ha, ha. Gosh. I'm silly today.

Drew. Today?

Sue. Bite me.

Drew. Hold that thought, helmet hair. They wore the latest Sierra Club's *"Just-in-Case Backpacks"* stocked with iodine tablets, vitamin C with rose hip, and suicide capsules of concentrated Oreo cookies.

Sue. The bride's gun boats were Mexican huaraches and Tibetan anklet bells of Hershey kisses. The groom's light-up boots flashed *Bonnie Scotland!*

Drew. The ceremony took place inside a circle of poi, garlic, and wolf bane to ward off Kahunas and the hotel bill collector. For a wedding ring, the groom gave his bride a gold wrapper from a Panatela, their wedding gift from Chairman Chuckler. Instead of kiss, the health conscious twosome touched elbows, winked, and then greeted guests by bumping hips. Back to you, Drew.

Sue. No. I'm Sue. You're Drew.

Drew. Bang. Gotcha. Let's switch one night. You be me. I'll be-

Sue. Hold that thought. Moving along. Dinner was birdie cut cheese-

Drew. Birdie cut?

Sue. Finger food. Tuna wedgies. Back to you, uh...

Drew. Drew, Sue. Drew, like in the past tense of draw.

Sue. Draw Drew! Bang! Gotcha. Ha, ha.

Drew. Ha, ha. Moving along. During the encomiums someone tried to toast the newly weds with a torch. Another said he was starving and telephoned for pizza to go. That was me, Sue.

Sue. Misu's Japanese soup.

Drew. No, Sue. That's mee-so.

Sue. Ah, so! Ha, ha.

Drew. Meanwhile bride and groom ate Philly steak n' cheese sandwiches in the kitchen. For my part, I thought the table water was brackish.

Sue. That's the iron in the well water, Drew.

Drew. Iron, Sue?

Sue. Leached from farm tools. Farmers throw busted tools down the well.

Drew. I thought iron came from capsules. Well, what d'ya know? Say, what're their names? Oh, well, that's showbiz.

Sue. This just handed me.

Drew. Don't hand me that.

Sue. From BOD to the staff. D___ is retiring after a long distinguished career. He says, "He's glad to be retiring."

Drew. P.S. We're all glad too! Creep. That's it. I'm Sue.

Sue. And I'm Drew. Nightie-night. Don't let the bed bugs bite.

Drew & Sue. Hey, my turn to close. No. Mine. Bite me! Haven't had my rabbi shots. I remember the names. Phil and Bill. Both spelled with a Y. Put a zip on it. Kiss my membrane. What brain?

<u>Music In</u> Gene Autry and **Sons** of the Pioneers: Hear them chucklin'along, Hear them singin' a song, Out on the air where they belong, Chucklin' along with the chucklin' chuckleheads.

☺

17.   The Double Image

According to "Papa" Hemingway, journalism is a good starting place for a writer to develop fundamental writing skills. It's barebones, concise, precise, and objective. What I learned at Chuckler I got through osmosis. Anyway, from there, while one is still young, and close to their soul, they must get out to develop their inner voice, and individual style. To that end, there have been many Santas, and a few devils, in my life. He also said it's critical to get that first publication behind you. It settles the nerves and affirms you're not whistling in the dark.

While at the New School under Russell Friedman, I learned that my strongest writing point was dialogue. So I would lead my pieces that way, and do minimum narrative. I made a point of never handing in a first draft. It takes me at least four to get rolling. So every week for a year after class I'd start writing on the bus uptown to my pad. I wrote about a dozen pieces, 90% of which Russell read to the class.

Actress and friend Laurel Lockhart steered me to Bill Talbot at Double Image Theatre (DIT), an off-Broadway group run by Helen Mayer. Bill conducted a writer's workshop at DIT. In real life he was senior editor at Samuel French. Additionally, he put on the Annual Original One Act Play Festival, which DIT produced. I studied under Bill shy of four years. My first year, I was runner-up, and the second year I won first prize, which was publication by French.

His class was a hands-on seminar without texts or strictures of deadly academia. Once on request, Bill provided a reading list and brief summation of playwriting in a nutshell from Aristotle to Arthur Miller, i.e., the end is prefigured in the beginning.

He ran the workshop like a laid-back ship's Captain, rarely interfering with the work process. We swabbies wrote, read our stuff in class, and then listened to a round robin critique from fellow writers, even from those who had fallen asleep. One guy woke up, said, "All the voices are the same." Sure. One person read all the parts, asshole. In time I found myself nodding off, too, particularly while reading my own stuff.

Bill said, *Listen to comments, but you're not obligated to respond.* I once asked, "How do you decide at French what to publish?"

"We flip a two-headed coin," he says, blue eyes twinkling. "Actually, I go to see a play on its feet. This Saturday I'll be in Chicago." *What if the acting's lousy?* "I never let acting get in the way of the writing. I might add, and this applies to critics as well, we rarely go to plays without having read a copy of the work beforehand. Publishing is generally by committee. A play script by itself is like an architect's plan; just lines and directions, 20% of the finished product. To judge a play properly it must be on its feet, to use a venal allusion, in the flesh and blood."

And I thought critics were geniuses. They'd say, *last night such-and-such opened,* then draw parallels with the Greeks and mythology. How'd they do it between 11PM and the morning edition? *Simple,* said Bill. *They read advanced scripts and see previews.* That night I note with "conceit" in the bulldog edition of my journal, *Walking out on my career was a dramatic mistake in the Freudian sense of putting ego before libido, which is Aristotelian tragedy.* How turgid, yet it has the ring of erudition.

Bill could see good in a story poorly executed, and bad in one told well. Periodically he'd send me flying to a dictionary with funny sounding words and phrases like *lazzi, mise en scene,* and *denouement.* Then I hit back with a character direction, *sotto voce-* I got it reading Pirandello. Bill's blue eyes said *fancy.* Under his wing I began to grow as writer and thinker. I found those who knew grammer and Latin had a leg up. It had nothing to do with actual talent, but helped the way materials and tools aid a carpenter. Bill was always encouraging, never condescending or pedantic. He'd go, *The writing process of how you get there is subordinate to the results.* He had a coy sense of humor, too. Announcing a class break he goes, *The smoking lamp is lit. I'm stepping out to cough.* In editing Chiaroscuro for publication, he says, *You could trim the opening. It's up to you whether you wish to get down to business or do a cake-walk.*

Swami Das said, *when the student is ready the teacher appears.* I had studied theatre at the University of Hawaii, LA City College and Desilu, - I had even started to study Italian privately.- but when Bill came along I was ready. The quintessential playwright teacher, Bill crystallized the business of theatre for me. Later, I used his hands-on method in my own teaching of theatre to young people. If a child wanted to act or write, I'd get them on their feet and working. I left definitions and grammar for theoreticians and pencil freaks. I never used a blackboard or text. In my class, we're all carpenters and everybody gets a hammer.

Over the years, I had several students around five and six years old who couldn't wait to grow up. They were born for the arts. With them, and all the children who came to me, I tried never to step on their creative impulses. Each of them had doting mothers. Amy, the writer, was from Leonia. She was winsome, alert, clever, and liked to poke holes in my spiel. Like when I said 'everybody gets a hammer,' she said, 'Can I just have a comb and a blow dryer.' David was from Paramus, a circumspect dynamo, writer, musician, and self-starter. Brad came from Tenafly. His mother walked into my

Bede School theatre group and signed him up. His mind was a fertile playground. He brought me a story that needed trains, soldiers, planes, parachutes, and the deus ex-machina. *What's that?* Something out of nowhere that saves the hero. It's not organic. *What's organic?* You reap what you sow. Plant apple seeds you get apple trees, not orange trees. *Oh. Then let's go to a farm.* You have to think of ways to do your ideas visually, using sound and light in a box called a stage with the fourth wall being the audience. Right now we need Newark Airport, Merlin the magician, and the Gods. *Okay,* he says. *Let's get them!*

Whatever I did in my productions it wasn't by the book. Toward the end of my time, Bede merged with a private school. The administrator, a preppy snood, fearful of parents and law-suits, had his own agenda. Before we left he said to me, *I hear you have children standing on tables. That's not safe.* His source was Ms. Frankenstein who wanted to get control of the lucrative after school program. *They could fall,* he added, *and hurt themselves.* I said, *In my class chairs are bridges, tables are mountains, and water sprinklers are stars.* Sadly, credentialed people are murderers of young souls, passing on what the sytem did to them. Most schools are death camps that burn out of children their natural sense of joy and creativity. Moving on. Because children're easily bored I'd always give them a task right off or lose them. Eventually I lost them all. They grew up. Me, too.

Bill Talbot wrote the following letter when I applied for life credits at Fairleigh Dickinson University. The Dean said, cherish and frame it.

LONDON   HOLLYWOOD   TORONTO

SAMUEL FRENCH, Inc.
PLAY PUBLISHERS AND AUTHORS' REPRESENTATIVES
45 West 25th Street
New York, N.Y. 10010
15 January 1988

The Assessment Officer
Fairleigh Dickinson University

Dear Sir,

I have been asked by Louis Coppola to affirm his having studied under me at the Off-Broadway Double Image Theatre, and I am happy to comply.

Louis took both my Fundamentals of Playwriting and Advanced Playwriting courses – the latter for about three years – and in that period covered the same materials that I have taught in academic sessions at Iona, Columbia, C.C.N.Y. and, at the graduate school level, at both City University of New York and Hunter College.

He learned with alacrity, and I am pleased that one of his works under my tutelage was a winner in the Annual Off-Off-Broadway Short Play Festival.

Sincerely yours,
William Talbot
Editor-in-Chief

☺

18. The Italian Lesson: Non Vale La Pena

Voicer: Santayana. Runs: 19 sec. Time: 1945
*"Modern life is not made for friendship: common interests
are not strong enough, private interests too absorbing.
Even in politics, colleagues are seldom or never friends.
Their ambition, being private and not patriotic, divides
instead of uniting them."*

Maestra. Our goals condition our manners, which
determine genetic development. More than ever we are
profit-minded in love, business, church, art. It is our new
religion. We kneel to the most profit. You see, his dreams
got lost, tangled up with daily necessities. In revolving
door competition, it was too much for him. He worked
for a big oil company ma era troppo insensibile. Capisci?
They were very insensitive. He could have cared less for
success. He would've been happy in a little store selling
trifles, objets d'art, antiques. That's what he really wanted
to do. I never understood until it was too late. He hated
the revolving door of big business. Era un'uomo troppo
gentile, sensibile (*He was a very gentle man, sensitive*).
He had gone against his nature, and little by little it
made him sick inside. It ate him, his soul. Capisci? Like a
cancer, it ate him up, and he died at 42. He gave himself
the heart attack. Yes. I was too young and naïve to see it
then, what he was doing to himself, what I was doing to
him by not encouraging him to break away, to open that
little store of trifles, but I couldn't read between the lines,
or I didn't want to. America, New York, the suburbs,
Montclair. It was all too much. Even with a bad heart
people will shout and enter into imbrolgios. For what?
Why? Habits can kill you. He gave himself the heart
attack to escape. Si. Very intelligent of the subconscious.
The soul inhabits a body, and when that body goes in the
wrong direction, that soul says the house is on fire. Time

to get out. It yearns for a new body, one that can take it where it wants to go. It, the soul, encourages death, by any means, so it can be freed. Capisci, carino? He came to me in a dream. I am much happier where I am. Don't worry. I am happier than I've ever been. Three killers: lo stress (*stress*), insicurezza affettiva (*job insecurity*), and insicurezza monetaria (*money insecurity*). Non c'è comprensione, rispeto, niente. Hai capito? In English, there is no understanding, no respect, nothing.

Tech. Why is work often detestable?

Maestra. We're not free.

Tech. To do what? You like teaching and yet-

Maestra. I love teaching Italian, my culture, especially in this country where they seem only to know about pizza. Well, it's the movies. So I love my work. But work when it becomes indispensibile, *a necessity,* then you are trapped, and that love can kill you. When one has to work to support oneself, a must, cannot otherwise survive, then, as in my case, I no longer teach freely. I cannot pick and choose pupils. At the school where I am the directress, petty organizational problems, people and their machinations become intolerable, but I accept them to survive, and this goes against the grain. Call it compromise, acceptance of a bad situation, learning tolerance, whatever. It eats your insides and kills you. Let's begin. Pagina trenta. My husband used to say he could understand, had simpatia for derelicts. He envied their freedom. It's that desire to be free. His feeling was correct. Lo stress, worry over denaro, push-ah, push-ah like the devil was chasing you. Non vale la pena. Mi capisci? It's not worth it. The ways of society, civilization they call it, but it's not civil. Oh, perhaps for the big picture, but not for individuals. It eats up the sensitive, the intelligent ones. Breaks their back for the good of society. 'Orribile! How we accept one another, what we do to each other, the misplaced emphasis on materialism, the idea of survival, is still a primitive force beyond our control. Hai capisci, Signor Technico- *Understand, Mr. Technician?* We reach a point of non-rational, non-caring struggle to keep alive and we no longer play by the rules. Some people maybe, very few, live in a forthright manner, but I have not seen this kind of person in my life. They exist only in books. In realita (*reality*), in business, I see people, my poor husband, all locked in a death struggle, instilling fear of God, loss of position, whatever, in one another when things are not up to snuff. So, insicurezza affetiva, e monetaria, being unsure of affection, of money to survive, and stress squeeze us into a vice from which very few escape. My poor husband died from it. I wish now that I had understood all this when he was alive, had had the strength to advise him, but I was too young and ignorant with my own foolishness, my own callous upbringing. At night I could hear him next to me breathing heavily. I could feel his body growing older from the aggravation and his silence, the gradual hardening of his gentle side. Now I see it all, now when it's too late. He was sick of big corporations, of trading favors, which is the way big corporations do business. The life of a corporation is separate from that of each member. It's a life of it's own, has it's own mores, and those who don't bend don't last. They hang out the bait; pension, benefits, encourage competition, rat race thinking, and boobs that we are, we go along. We have no choice. Society has fallen into line. If we step out of that line, act as individuals, we're looked on as failures. To survive we must eat. Providers are looked on as good, family and children all good. Single people bad, non-providers are outsiders who don't contribute. It is simple and primitivo. We disrespect innocence, destroy our sensibilities. Addesso. Comminciamo. Pagina Trenta? *Si.* Corporate gigantism, social or societal requirements are killers, Signor Technico, killers of freedom and sensibility. The top people in any social structure are its best killers. È vero (*true*). They are cold to feelings, affection, sensitivity, and love. They foster the evil code of intellectual capitalism. The cold reality is that we are no better than the worst that we condemn. We are like worker ants and bees, the good of the elite at the expense of the many. The way to escape is walk away. The way to survive is to do only what the heart tells you. Otherwise, boo, boo, you're dead. Non vale la pena.

Ayn and I studied privately with la maestra. After our son was born we'd bring him to class at her Manhattan apartment. As Ayn holds Ion in her arms swaddled in silk, cotton and wool he sighs contentedly, ehh, ehh. La maestro smiles, says, he speaks Italian already. Then, chucking him gently under the chin, she sings him an old Tuscan lullaby.

Maestra. *Una volta c'era un rei, caro e bello come te; Che guardavo nel bel cello, luna, sole, e le stelle; C'è la camera tanto buio, no, no piangio, no aveva paura;C'è la mama qui da canto, che ti velgia col suo canto.* I heard it as a child in Lucca. Once there was a king, dear and beautiful like you, who looked up at the sky, moon, sun, and stars; the room is dark. Mama says, don't cry, have no fear, Mama's near singing, watching you with her song. Tuscans don't speak in dialect but they have an accent, always sh, shh. Velgia is from survelgiare, to take care of someone. The modern verb is velgiare, to look after a person.

☺

19.   The Cafeteria

Studio B, 6:20 AM. Nigel was overnight cashier in the cafeteria. He was in his twenties, had an opened, brown face with tribal marks on cheeks that got puffy when he laughed. He laughed a lot. Nigerians are like that. In conversation his brown eyes would often gleam like a child discovering new things, or cloud up from the odd ways of people. But more often than not he had a welcoming smile even at 4 in the morning. We'd talk now and again about one thing or another. He was really over qualified as a cashier. In fact he had a full plate of work and ambition, which was to finish college and become a jet pilot in Nigeria. Toward those ends he worked several jobs. He had already attained certification as a private pilot and had begun lessons flying jets. I was amazed to learn that a one-hour lesson in flying a jet cost over 5,000 dollars. *How often do you go,* I asked, *once a year?* He laughed. *I take half an hour lesson about once a month.* It must've taken every spare nickel he earned to do that. When I learned he also had expertise in electronics, I suggested he consolidate his time for maximum salary and apply for a position as a technician. *It's twice the money in half the time. I'll show you how to work the board.* But something in his eyes said he didn't trust the situation and he'd stick with what was safe.

I remember clearly something the Nigerian taught me in an off-handed moment around 3 in the morning. A woman came up to the cash register, smiled, expressed some pleasantries, paid, and left. Nigel leans toward me, dark tribal marks dancing on puffy brown cheeks, and says, "Now there is a woman to make a good partner. No matter when she comes here, she is always cheerful, and polite. That is important in a woman, a good disposition. The kind of woman to wake up with in the morning, always smiling. Disposition is very important."

Disposition became important in my perception of women and in my decision to marry Ayn, who always smiles even after looking at me.

One morning I'm in Studio B twiddling my thumbs and the Nigerian walks in. I almost didn't recognize him without the cash register.

Nigerian. Good morning, my friend.
Tech. Oh! Come in, come in. Have a seat.

Nigerian. Thank you, my friend. I have the information together for the resume. I just have to type it up. What I want to show you something I had in my wallet, but I forgot about it, a copy of my college diploma.

Tech. Good. It's better then what some people have around here.

Nigerian. I have two other diplomas in electrical engineering. One certificate in servicing, another in wiring.

Tech. Can you stay until 8 or 9? The boss comes in then-

Nigerian. No. I can't stay. I have too many things to do today. I just wanted to show you my diploma. So how are you, my friend?

Tech. Okay. And you?

Nigerian. Things have happened. You won't believe where I just come from. You won't believe it. I'm back from a week suspension. Yes. That is why we have not seen each other lately. This is my first day back and the supervisor put me on washing garbage pails. I'm telling you.

Tech. Who is he?

Nigerian. Jack, Reilly. You know him, the supervisor in the cafeteria.

Tech. Yes. Never thought he'd go out of his way to be mean.

Nigerian. Oh. A very jealous man. If he knows you've got something more than him, he doesn't like it. He knows I've got a diploma and it bothers him. Why? I can't understand these kinds of people. He knows I've got a car and it bothers him. Why? He's got a car and a house. I don't have a new car just a car to come to work. I don't show off. Nothing. Yet the man hates me. Yes. He is too stupid to understand what I know. So he hates me because I have what he lacks. It will be the same wherever I go. I will always have more than somebody and he will hate me for it.

Tech. That's not a healthy outlook.

Nigerian. They give me no choice. It happens over and over again. People are afraid. That's it. Ignorance. That's it. They are too ignorant to know anything. I worked one year for an electronic corporation. I didn't want to quit, but the supervisor hated me. Why? He's got two cars, a big boat, and a house. Why hate me? I've got nothing. Once he said "I hope when you fly you crash and die." I just got my solo permit and he tells me to crash and die. Isn't that something? What can I do? I don't want to die over some worthless job. Back home in Nigeria things would be different. I could have somebody to back me up. Here I have nobody. Besides, back home they would be afraid to try anything because of what I know, what I am. But here, I'm alone. Who will believe me? If I were Caucasian it would be different, but I'm not. I'm not even a black American. I'm African. Some people think, oh, he's going to take the money, bleed this country, and go back to Africa. I'll tell you my main resentment. It's that I work hard to get my diploma. I didn't steal it, or muscle in to get my job. There are 24 hours in the day. We all have the same 24 hours, not 36 for you and 20 for me. If I make better use of my time, that is my business. I work two, three jobs to pay for my school. I studied night and day. If somebody else decides to go fishing with his time, okay, but don't hate me. They refuse to consider all the work I put in day and night. The sweat, the years- it means nothing to them. The man says go crash and die. I said to him, "What's the matter with you, to say something like that?" He apologized, telling me he was only joking. This is my life and he's joking about it. Some people are jealous. They don't want to see anybody get ahead. At the phone company they used to come to my desk and move things. One time I left a note for the clean up person not to touch my desk. I don't smoke, I don't drink. I don't eat at my desk. The next day when I came to work an important microfilm was missing, a schematic of electric wiring. Somebody took it from my desk. I almost lost my job. It made me look incompetent. It was the only copy. They had to send for a duplicate. Lots of things were classified. Every time I'd go in and out they would let the others go but take me over to the side and search my bag. I can't live that way. So I quit. I'm not going to die over a job. There are plenty of other jobs I could get, not them. I've got what it takes. They don't. So they hate me, but no one is going to take from me what is mine- my diploma. What I know I can do. They can't take that. Well, I'd better go. Will you be here Saturday?

Tech. No. Friday. Come around 8 or 9, when the bosses are in. I'll take you around.

Nigerian. Okay. I'll try. I have a new second job. That's where I have to go now. But I'll try. Thank you. Those people will pay for their attitude. One day I'll pass them by and they'll be in a wheelchair. I'll say, here, take this penny and help yourself. Okay. See you, my friend.

☺

The Bacteria Cafeteria had a funny cook. Oscar was a man of "misty ethnic origins"- anachronistic; a sharp-nosed, happy-eyed Creole, an ex-pirate out of Port au Prince; a patois spieling Mississippi River card shark who might've been cabin boy to Long John Silver and sous chef aboard a New Orleans paddle boat. He spoke with a murky Caribbean accent that made me wonder where truth ended and fiction started. He was in his 60's, had a sunny disposition, and was once a cook on a schooner that plied the China seas. He'd gambled in Hong Kong, dealt from the bottom of the deck, and escaped to Macau on a sand pan. His off-the-cuff stories were as colorful as his face, coming as they did from an old salt in a white apron standing behind the counter of the C.B.S cafeteria, the last place you'd expect stories of adventure and daring-do. The best thing about Oscar was his "patat frit avec con-con", hash browns with scrapings from the bottom of the pan. There's nothing like a free radical to liberate your taste buds and kill you simultaneously.

Looking back now I see time and place has lots to do with believability. In my own case who would believe that I was next to Ed Parker when he introduced Martial Arts to America? But Oscar was sharp! He'd laugh and say things like, "Je vien Amerique verse 1936", a stow away sur la ill d'Estomach.

One night Oscar got mad at me. I couldn't find him so I went behind the counter to whip up some fried eggs. I started to clean a frying pan with soap and water. Suddenly Oscar's shouting, *Mon Dieu! Fermez! Fermez!* He grabbed the pan. *This Oscar's pan. Privot. Oscar's personal pan. My babee. Ecoutez. No one touch babee but Oscar. Compriz? And never clean with soap. J'mais!* I apologize and go out front. *When Oscar leave work the pan goes under the stove. Nobody touches it. Everybody know this Oscar's pan. Compriz? Regardez-vous,* he says, breaking eggs with one hand and dropping them in the skillet while re-heating potatoes on the grill. He flipped the eggs in the pan and then onto a plate with the fries. *Voila! he exclaims looking in the pan like a hand mirror. Nothing stick. Ne plus pas! Only Oscar's face.* He smiles. *Pan is only for eggs and omelet's. No fish, no meat. Compriz, mes ami? To clean wipe with a towel, then use kosher salt. Rub it all around, com'sa, to take up the grease. The salt turns brown. Eats up the grease. Keeps the pan new. Après rub in olive oil e fine.* Since then, I clean my home frying pan that way.

Oscar could whip up mean pigeon peas and rice with curry chicken. When I ask for the recipe, he laughs, and says in patois, *Le recipe, mes ami, is in my fingers. The fingers change from day to day. Compriz?* At the bottom of his pot, the oils and food crusted into a great tasting, burnt residue. *Qui, qui, mes ami. The mouth tells the fingers, fingers tell the food, a pinch of this, a pinch of that. E voila! Compriz, mes amis? In South Amerique, con-con. Puerto Rico, pegado, or paga'o. Better than pork rine!* That sticky, burnt bottom was dee-licious. I liked the part above the bottom. Announcer Hale Syms liked the bottom of the bottom. "Bun-bun," he says, racing me to the cafeteria. "No," I go, "It's con-con! Pega'o!"

As we pull up to the counter neck and neck, there was no pot, and no Oscar. He was gone suddenly, like the grand piano in Studio F. Those wonderful fingers and the pega'o disappeared forever. Oscar had been a staple on the overnight like Mal and Dulles on the NR. Swoop, the newsfeed producer, refused any food handled by the new, fey counter man. "Y'never know where his hands've been." *To everything there is a time, there is place, a time to live and a time to pega'o.*

☺

20.   Grand Piano

It was around 3a, a dead news night. They're all dead to me. So I left word with Roundy Mal, overnight editor/ producer, that I'd be in Studio F. He used the studio himself when he wanted an uninterrupted break. It was removed from the main newsroom and out of commission between midnight and 7a. The most accessible place to chill was the tech lounge, off the newsroom and air studios, but it was a joke, especially 9-to-5; people always coming and going, turning lights on and off, banging lockers, the fridge, checking themselves in the mirror to see if they were alive, or yacking into the wall phone.

Anyway, I'm in "F" stretched out in partial light coming through the control room window. The last thing I saw before drifting off was the old classic grand Steinway that predated the Golden Age of Radio. It had to be nine feet long. Now, this magnificent invention, and work of art, stood   neglected, silent, off to the side like a ghostly sunken ship at the bottom of the ocean. Who will raise it from the dead? What voices are hidden deep in its wood? Whose magical fingers pressed those ivory keys?

"Now Beethoven's Moonlight Sonata... I'm Jack Sterling. I'm Gary Moore. I'm Ted Husing. It's Arthur Godfrey time. This is Robert Q. Lewis. We're Bob and Rei. He's Bob. He's Rei."

Merlin, Associate Director, radio. *Back in the 1950's I was just starting out as an assistant director on the Robert Q. Lewis Show. Really, just a gopher traffic cop. I was eager and glad to be at C.B.S. Lewis was popular; a bright and funny talk show host. But I discovered it wasn't peaches and cream. Lewis was extremely temperamental. I never knew what to expect from him. He had strange mood swings. Very unpredictable. My job was to keep an eye on him. Get him ready for each show. We did two a day live for different audiences. I'd see that he had everything he needed. Not easy, believe me. I never knew how he'd react to anything, especially when I said "five minutes to air". Once coming up to air I couldn't find him. He wasn't in his dressing room. I look in the men's room, the lady's room. No Robert Q. Lewis. Nobody can find him. I check behind the seats in the auditorium. Maybe he fell down. In my distraction I thought this is the end of me, and I neglected to draw the curtain. I'm on stage in a panic, the audience is filing in and no Robert. It was raining outside and the ushers let them in early. Then, I hear a growl, 'What's that goddamn noise?' A head pokes out fom under the grand piano. Robert had been napping under it and the piano cover. He looks out on all fours, sees the audience, screams, 'Get out! It's too early. Out! Out!' and pulls the cover over his head. I close the curtain, move everybody to the lobby, come back, and he's under the piano in a fetal position. When things didn't go his way he'd pout under the piano, and refuse to come out. He'd enter a state of mental dejection and you couldn't reach him. We started running late because he'd be catatonic under the grand. I'd go, 'Come on, Robert. We're all waiting. The audience is waiting. The second crowd is lining up. Please, come* *out. We love you. The audience loves you.' Sometimes he'd look out at the drawn curtain and say, 'I'm ready. Where's the damn audience? Get the bastards in here! ' I'd open the curtain, he'd scramble out, switch on a smile and we'd have a show. But to that point it was anybody's guess. That's when I started seeing a psychiatrist to figure out how to stay calm and handle him. My best day was when he left for California.*

I crawled under the piano and it felt transcendental like a womb. I hummed 'OM', and the strings answered in sympathetic vibration. The grand was part of the roaring twenties and radio's Golden Age. On my watch came Luigi Barzini, Rosemary Clooney, and June Alison, even Tommy Tune stuck in his long-booted, gangly legs. My fondest memory is of weatherman Dr. No Trans-fats jamming on the grand between weather reports. Sitting in occasionally was trumpeter Pete Carlisi, night editor for local TV. I drummed along with number 2 pencils.

One morning around 3a I went to sit under the grand and it was gone. I went looking for it and found it by the freight elevator marked, "Sold. Hold for pick up." I was destroyed. It was an heirloom, the heart of old C.B.S. How could they? It belongs in the Broadcast Museum.

From that day I'd only go into Studio F when assigned. Do the job at hand while avoiding my reflection in the control room window on a shabby, ratty hovel background with jaundiced acoustic tile. Then, I heard the good news. The piano was in good hands. The new owner was Robert Q. Lewis' former basket case associate director, Merlin, an accomplished pianist. He refurbished it and sleeps under it. I hope he wills it to the Broadcast Museum. Chances are old man Chuckler never knew about the sale of the piano. Regardless, it's indicative of his unsentimental business approach and the degeneration of the company.

☺

21.   Heshie of Kelly Park

A writer hands me a wire release about the Benson show. I'm looking to sell Witt-Thomas a second story called ABSCAM, a reverse sting on the FBI. It's better than my Checkmate story, about an 11-year-old Russian chess genius who defects in the governor's mansion. Guillaume, SAG, and AFTRA are arguing over a bigger share of Home Box Office. Jessel was right. *Show biz, kid. Y'can stick it in your hat.*

> Los Angeles – AP – The company producing ABC-TV's 'Benson' series is suing its star for $1 million for alleged breach of contract, according to Superior Court records. Witt-Thomas-Harris Productions said in it's damage audit Wednesday that Robert Guillaume violated a 1979 contract when he failed to appear last Monday for filming of next season's shows. Guillaume portrays a butler named Benson with a rapier-like wit in the show of the same name. The lawsuit alleged Guillaume has indicated he would not return for tapings. The suit also alleged that his representatives induced Guillaume not to appear in order to win a more lucrative contract. Representatives of Witt-Thomas-Harris refused comment and efforts to reach Guillaume were unsuccessful. The strike is in its ninth week.

Feeling glum, I wandered into Studio F, the wire release in my hand, and I started crying. The studio and I had something in common. We were both empty. I broke up on the damn floor; absolutely wretched and disconsolate. I'd had the Chinese tiger by the tail and let go. Now I was tethered to a whorehouse. I dozed off, woke, and drifted off again.

(*Heshie seated on piano; our weatherman Dr. No Trans-fat at the keys*)
Heshie. Hey, kiddo.
Tech. Heshie? God, I miss you, man. The jokes, the fun-
Heshie. On the boardwalk-

Tech. Coney Island.

Heshie. On the bench, feet up on the railing. Bay 7.

Tech. Near your house.

Heshie. That Benson show you wrote was pretty good.

Tech. Oh, I don't know, Heshie. With you, it could've been better. After you died it went down hill.

Heshie. But you came back with the show. I told you it would come in time. When we worked the Borscht circuit. You were hot kiddo.

Tech. Then I froze, Heshie.

Heshie. Remember in the park, the basketball players who kept at it went furthest. How do like workin' with big shot news people?

Tech. I'd rather be in Philadelphia.

Heshie. That's funny. News people make big money, don't they? It's stealin'. All they do is take a story off the news wire and read it.

Tech. Mostly.

Heshie. They get big money for mostly. How much?

Me. You'll laugh.

Heshie. Make me laugh.

Tech. Five million, maybe more.

Heshie. That's a lotta gelt, kiddo! We should've gone into news instead comedy writing. Maybe do weather on the piano. 'Today it will be,' and you hit low keys for thunder. The piano feels like rain tonight.

Tech. And now the grand 5 day forecast. Is that corny?

Heshie. Better then the crap I hear. By the time they catch up with you you'll be a millionaire. When things go wrong blame the piano. It's out of tune. So, you're machen a laben, eh, kiddo? Good money? That's it. In the Parks Department I was lucky to make 30,000 for the year. Those news people get paid for, what do you call it?

Tech. Rippin' and readin'.

Heshie. A million bucks for rippin' and readin'. We were in the wrong end of the business.

Tech. Sometimes they go out to cover stories.

Heshie. But it's right in front of 'em, somebody's tellin' 'em the story.

Tech. They re-write-

Heshie. Who, what, when. It's a formula. You don't have to rack your brain from scratch. They do the obvious. We had to put a twist on it for a laugh. The wrong end of business, kidoo. We should've gone into news.

Tech. Produced funny specials. Most reporting is straightforward.

Heshie. We could've added that twist.

Tech. That creative kick. Most news is copycat, but when you can add a twist you can make a couple of hundred thousand a year.

Heshie. Being a copycat is easier than fishin' off the boardwalk for ideas. Blank paper's a scary thing.

Tech. In news they always fall back on copy.

Heshie. Where's the money come from to pay those salaries?

Tech. Advertising.

Heshie. Rip and read, eh? It's stealin'. Remember that Halloween in the park? I came out from the clubhouse to play half court and coach the girl team. I go for a lay-up and you pop out up from behind the backboard wearing that crazy mask and white gloves. Scared the hell out of me. I just thought you were a crazy goy.

Tech. I was lookin' to get laid.

Heshie. That's why you went into show biz where nine out of ten times you get screwed. By the way, the pretty one everybody liked with the big chest and great legs? A dyke. What a waste. Remember those comedy schticks at the Vet's hospital in Fort Hamilton? They paid us in T-shirts. After one washing they made good handkerchiefs.

Tech. The Borscht Circuit. Mrs. Goldberg's Bungalow Colony. They had great comedians up there.

Heshie. We weren't exactly chopped liver.

Tech. One guy came out in a tux, cleared his throat, started to sing a high note and fell straight backwards on his ass. Broke everybody up. Under his cut-away he had on a white shirt with a bowtie, but it was just cuffs and a bib. Heshie, if only we could go back the year I jumped out of that backboard. The fun we would've had. Better than doin' *The Lucy Show*. I went back to Goldberg's Colony the summer after you died. In the middle of my routine I went blank. I look at them, they look at me, and I had no words, nothin' came. I don't know what happened, Heshie. Suddenly I drew a blank. I said thanks, walked out, and quit.

Heshie. You fight through it, kiddo. You have to develop the balls.

Tech. Heshie. Jesus Christ. I froze. Lost it. Maybe if you'd been there-

Heshie. I could've given you that T-shirt for a hanky to cry in.

Tech. That's what I mean. All I needed was a few words like that. I don't know why. I just collapsed. I couldn't go on. I needed you more than I realized, Heshie. I had nobody. Nobody. Anaheim, Hawaii, Eve, Parker, Karate. You were the one happy light in all of it. Who told you to go get a stroke?

Heshie. My swimming instructor. You think I asked for it? Afterward, I'd think funny, but the words wouldn't come out. Like when we were writin' silly want ads. I couldn't comeback fast enough. Eh, eh, ah. It's timing, rhythm. If only we'd talked back then in the park. But who knew? Today I'd say, Booby, let's go into the news business. Toss in a joke and be millionaires, millionaires, kid.

The Transplant Specialist

Q. Dr. Bernice, Time magazine calls you "the world's foremost transplant specialist..." where did you get your knowledge?

A. *I was a gardener for years.*

Q. You use advanced surgical techniques way ahead of your contemporaries. In a recent day's work you removed 98 kidneys. What method did you use?

A. *Dynamite. One stick goes a long way.*

Q. They say you perform miracles with the human heart.

A. *True. Very true. In the last operation what I had I took from the body the heart, massaged it, put it back, took it out again, played a little pool with it, shot a game of basketball with it, made a very nice lay-up.*

Q. Doctor, you believe in heart massage?

A. *Oh yes. Heart massage is a wonderful thing. Once I kept massaging a heart 14 days. I hugged it, kissed it, gave it a nice caress.*

Q. What was the outcome?

A. *I got 30 days.*

Q. Famous people come to you from all over, Doctor, seeking answers to coronary diseases and transplants. Who was the biggest person you ever worked on?

A. *Only yesterday I had a woman 6 foot 8, 485 pounds. In your whole life you never saw such a klutz!*

Q. Many doctors give up their practice and go into medical research. What is your opinion of MR?

A. *I.M. for M.R. R.U.? Only yesterday, that's two days before tomorrow, I discovered a cure for which there is no disease. This morning somebody took mine cure and dropped dead.*

Q. Dr. Bernice, would you describe your last operation?

A. *Well, I'll tell you, I used a very big knife, a sword my grandfather used for dueling 250 years ago. In the operating room we had standing there three nurses. One, a real beauty. She had nothing wrong, but I gave her a shtick with the sword anyway 'cause I like to keep in shape. I made an incision was a real beauty. A masterpiece! I cut that boy, three legs from the table and two nurses in the next room. We played 18 games of Tic Tac Toe, I lost. I cut.*

I made an incision, I ripped opened the arteries, yanked out the capillaries, jerked around with the veins, then put in one leg, I bend the kidney, I even stepped on the kidney. Well, it was no good anyway.

Q. Then what did you have?

A. Big hole! You could drive in there a truck.

Q. What condition was the patient in?

A. Terrible! White like three ghosts. Blue, purple. Then he started to moan and groan.

Q. What did you do?

A. Vomited. I can't stand blood.

Q. That was some operation. How did you feel at the time?

A. Miserable. I got sick. We almost had to call a doctor and take me to the hospital. But then I went outside took a couple aspirin. Meanwhile the patient died, but I felt much better.

Q. You don't use anesthesia on your patients. How do you relax them?

A. Very simple. I take a warm sweat sock, put it on the patient's face. He takes couple breaths and 1,2,3 he sleeps like a log. Nobody yet count to 4.

Q. You certainly have your work cut out for you. What do you do to relax after leaving the operating room?

A. I visit.

Q. Who?

A. Next of kin.

Q. You must be under enormous tension in your work: consultations, studying new techniques. How do you find the time? Do you sleep much?

A. No. But I faint a lot!

Q. What was extraordinary about your last operation?

A. The patient died three times. It was a poor person. Stubborn. Couldn't afford a burial, so the fourth time he died we worked out a very cheap funeral. 75 cents.

Q. 75 cents?

A. *That's right. We wet the ground and he slips under himself.*

Q. I still don't see what was extraordinary.

A. *Well, the operation took 14 hours! Afterward, he got up on the operating table, gave a look and 30 seconds later he was as good as dead!*

Q. He died? Then what was unique?

A. *Usually they don't waste my time. They die right away. There's no wait.*

☺

22. Nelson of Fairleigh Dickinson

And then came Big Ben. I took a year of graduate study in Modern Literature at FDU under Professor Ben Nelson. Ben leaned on plays, themes, and playwrights. He brought the Greek Gods down to earth. What was Olympus? A picnic on a mountain. Who were the Furies? An *avenging posse!* The Orestaia Trilogy was the sins of the fathers revisted by O'Neil in Morning Becomes Electra.

Ben helped me focus my thinking by studying the methods behind great writers and the milieu in which they placed characters. It was all behavioral, how the self is perceived, how it acts in circumstances and in relationship to others based on strengths and weaknesses, personal fate, and why honesty is accepted or denied.

Great! But how did it apply to me and C.B.S?

Cholly is a radio bard who rhymes news. But real poets are seers on the edge of society with their finger on its pulse. Nosies are poets of the inconsequential. They fear the story they hunt because it reminds them of the lie they live, the bent truth, the compromise for a buck. At C.B.S there were several kinds of truth: commercial truth, or what is said on the air, and personal truth, or what each person believed in their heart, which was generally left at the doorstep. The unspoken, dangerous poet's truth, we all know it from birth, comes at a price. If one can't make a living telling the truth one can get rich by dissimulation and rhyming mainstream nonsense. Here the poet as prophet is the poet as profit.

Here are excerpts from a term paper written for Prof. Nelson's Modern Literature class on Eugene O'Neill and John Steinbeck's use of illusion and reality. The essay was a turning point in my thinking.

Truth, reality, and the value of illusion... in self-defense... one's pipe dream born of *suppressed desire, memories...* We all have something we want to forget, *disappointment, thwarted aspirations.* There's danger in seeking truth. Self-deception is so *tortuous* it defies *consciousness.*

Illusion: daydreams for better times, or a self-induced ploy that hides some forgotten, distasteful truth, a buried mistake, a semi-conscious recognition of personal or ancestral guilt? The psychological suicide of clinging to half-cocked pipe dreams. Illusion is rouge covering guilt, primitiveness and hidden desire beyond our control. O'Neill, Eliot, Gorky, and Conrad were poets in search of truth and salvation. Perhaps it came in the quiessence of death. "Droll thing life is- (*Heart of Darkness*) that mysterious arrangement of merciless logic for a futile purpose. The most you can hope from it is some knowledge of yourself that comes too late- a crop of inextinguishable regrets." Art is an unrequited love song.

☺

23.   For Ayn On Her 60th - Tibi Dabo

Once Was What

"It attacks the muscles first."
I woke up feeling achy all over.
"Then the nervous system. You have all the symptoms."
Am I going to die?
"Yes."
Of what?
"When you have all the symptoms the disease doesn't matter.
Muscles then nerves. That's the classic pattern."
The symptoms? Yes. Then where to go for the finale?
To the Dowager Queen, the Duchess, die in her dying arms.
Shall I be careless and superficial?
"Your life attests to that. Try something else."
The moment of birth and death are one and the same
And in between flows a river, and the naked lady of the lilacs stoops
To catch a glimpse of herself, of something fantastic shimmering in the river
A vision of self in the river, naked, and innocent passing on.
I shall go to Venice to the arms of the dying Duchess.
Listen to ariettas on violins, watch people,
Drink cappuccino, dreaming and wondering,
Where did it all begin, my mother's breast, my father's knee-
Lovers stroll by resilient, unsuspecting.
Shall I visit the Accademia or the museo in Firenze,
There's a rare showing of what's-his-face.
I could wander the corridors of the Uffizi-

Or look for Rozano Brazzi's Antichita shop
At the foot of Ponte S. Barnaba and the canal off the
campo
Where Hepburn fell in when it was Summertime in
Venice.
Caught an ear infection and fell again, but in love.
I'll jump in too n' people will say-
It attacks the muscles first, then the nerves-
And wisely leave me to sink down among the rotting
pilings and silt-
Drawn and pulled by the current as gondolas glide
overhead
And gondoliers duck heads beneath low bridges
trimmed in white stone,
Calling *"Ooh, way!"* as they turn an elbow of the dying
Duchess.
Birds sing no more, forever silent
Above the shuttered eyes of the dying Duchess.
What can be said for certain? They make glass in
Murano, lace in Burano,
A south-east sirocco gale force in winter equinox
When the moon pulls hardest in the Adriatic.
A double tide Aqua Alta rose to the Florian viola da
gambi,
The Quadri viola da braccio- above the bodice under
the chin
To lap the cleavage of the dying Duchess.
Breasts, lips, eyes shuttered, framed in lace of black
Gothic glass.
Muscles first, then nerves and feeling.
All the symptoms of classic symptoms and death on
a rose-colored evening.
Gondoliers glide out of the bacini of the Grand Canal
onto the mole,
Between St. Theodore and the Winged Lion,
The Ducal Palace and old library

Slipping along La Piazetta to the loggia circling the Campanile.

i Mori strike the anticipated hour,*"Lu-way! Lu-way!"*

I float up out of mawkish silt into the arms of the morning star.

ACT FOUR

1   What I Saw At the *Evolution*

Diary: Regrets are the Reaper. At home, dozing and rocking, I look into my fish tank lit by Christmas lights, wondering whether I should quit teching, and go back to deejaying. Goldfish glide silent as silk, speckled with silver, circling up and down, bottom nibbling, then sailing upward only to swoop down again. Death appears. I didn't know it until I woke up. A shadow came from behind the piano, tried to take my hand, a voice said, not yet. My Italian teacher; black eyes and hair in a bun.

A memo came down from Chuckler President A.T. extending seasonal greetings with a bonus of a day off with pay. It was so unprecedented a holiday gift that everybody read it at least twice to be sure they weren't crazy. Then, this wonderful show of respect for workers turned from an *appreciate the grunt holiday* into that Jack Nicholson outing with inmates in *Cuckoo's Nest* before they gave him a lobotomy. Rumor called it an error in dictation, others said it was a premeditated payback by A.T. who felt betrayed by Chuckler who reneged on promises made when he was hired.

C.B.S Memorandum

From: B. S. Chuckler   To: The Organization   Date: March 25, 1976

The Board of Directors adopted a plan today for the future development of the corporation's top management organization... In line with that decision, the directors have elected J.B. President to succeed A.T., who resigned.

The change is keyed to the long-term requirements of our diversified company. It will assure an orderly progression in management and continuation of business success.

You are all familiar with J.B.'s fine record as President of C.B.S/Publishing Group, which he will continue to head until a replacement is selected...

A.T. brought high ability and dedication to his post. We appreciate his decision to make other plans for his future.

Easter's coming. He might give us another holiday!

313

Grunts in the trenches can read between the lines, are well aware of salary imbalances, of who's getting what on their sweat, and resent it.

☺

2.   G'Nigh n' G'Luck

"Good evening from London. This is Edword R. Burrow. Question: What is news doing in prime time? Somebody, light me up a fag." *Here you go, sir.* "Ah! Satisfies the nerves, even of this old soul. Thank you. I've always had the highest regard for technicians. Of course, in my day they dressed better. Judging by your outer accouterments, you don't take yourself seriously." *It's defiance.* "Against society or yourself?" *Both.* "How clever. You've got yourself coming and going- a sado-masochist's dream. I've been looking over your shoulder, young man. Rather than seek truth and trust your own opinion, you opt for baseless humor. Which is rather shallow, don't you think?" *Helps me accept what I've become.* "Get above it, son. Life without dignity and self-respect is no life at all. Smirking is okay backed by understanding. Get my meaning? A certain amount of humor and cynicism about life is warranted, but don't let it rule you." *Being serious is painful.* "Welcome to the club. Now, educate yourself. Knowledge will raise you above self pity." *How's it feel being exploited as the founder of Chuckler News when they-* "Forced me out? Some good came of it. Not as much as I would've liked." *You're the media's guilty conscience.* "Assuming 'they' have a conscience." *The Hamlet of news.* "There is more than meets the eye in that. Sometimes in my Jacob Marly wanderings below along the railroad tracks, I yearn to get back in the mix, but my time has come and gone. It's up to you to carry on my fight." *Me?* "And your co-workers on both sides of the window. You'll find a way; maybe through that journal you're keeping. Dig, follow through, and be fearless. Bare bones and honesty. Bailey was an oligarch. Cut it how you will, the buck was his religion. Philanthropy and displays of the aesthete had no substance. Undeniably, he built a communications empire. But an organization is only the extended shadow of the man who heads it." *That's why he trades on your name.* "He bought the station with $400,000 of his father's millions earned in the cigar business. He was a pioneer who kept an ear to the ground, and knew when to circle the wagons. He never mixed business with pleasure, and was unsentimental, a requisite for success in business. Bailey had a long-time friend, Kalin, a lawyer, whose firm represented the company. He and Bailey were chums, saw each other at various social functions. Very prominent in New York society. Both men were on the board of directors of the Museum of Modern Art (1969). Bailey was its president. One day he circumvented board protocol, fired a director without due process. Kalin questioned his bending of the rules. Bailey responded by ending their relationship and dismissing Kalin's law firm. It troubled Kalin because they continued to meet at social functions, concerts, and important groundbreaking ceremonies. Kalin said, 'Can't we keep at least part of our friendship?' Bailey said, 'We were never friends. You were my lawyer.' Business is an animal in itself with specific requirements, which if not met, lead to disintegration." *The company went from Seville Row woolens to Orchard Street polyester. You were right about the argyles.* "Colinwud was an exception." *Would you hire me?* "Want the ten cent answer?" *I used to wear twills, black watch, wool pants, had corduroy Irish walking suit.* "I had a Calvinist kneeling suit; rather severe values in many things, puritanical, if you will. I doubted Collinwud's work habits because I thought for a serious reporter argyles were like a priest wearing red socks. During our first talk everything went well until he crossed his legs and I saw those argyles shining beacon-like, suggesting inconsistency and flamboyance, an ego that might interfere with objective news reporting. But I hired him and never regretted it." *I designed the baggies I'm wearing. My wife sewed 'em. Swoope, the newsfeeder, calls 'em "curtains because they're so wide. Very comfortable with lots of ballroom.* "I always had my crotches let out, slightly long. Swoope, you say? Related to publisher Bayard, is he?" *Yes. For the archives I want you to know my pants're midnight blue, quality wool with high waist, wide leg, no outside pockets, one inside, and a drawstring belt. I wear argyles and black wingtips that go for $175. I'm making another pair of pants from shantung.* "As in Shantung, China, where the cloth originates." *Yes. It's a dyed pongee silk with a rough surface.* "Well, there you have it. You in a nutshell. Shantung; a rough silk character. If I sent you on assignment, there is no telling what you'd bring back, if you came back." *Long enough to cash my paycheck.* "You might do well unseen on radio, but then your clotheshorse mind would require restraint. Your voice is a cross between Bill Shire and Aldo Ray. I had a devil of a time convincing the powers-that-be to hire Bill. Finally, I cabled my boss, 'You want a slick voice or great journalism?' At any rate, a reporter's personality must never rise above a story. News reporting requires consistency and levelheaded thinking. You're better suited to the arts, which is subjective journalism." *Let me give you an audition. This just in. Several years ago, agreement was reached between Chuckler and the writers' and technicians' unions on the question of compensatory pay for overnight work, known variously as the lobster shift, graveyard tour, Dracula shift, and zombie freak time. Quote: "Overnight workers shall receive extra pay in the form of a differential amounting to .045 % of base salary; the money is to be distributed in cash during the night, but you must be awake to receive it." No one yet has qualified. The Connecticut Lab is developing a robot to work nights,* *but so far it hasn't come up with one dumb enough to do it. Soon as a robot's programmed for overnight, it self-destructs.* "That it?" *No. Yes. Life on the job is too damn serious; nerves fray easily, tempers and grudges abound, and people are always appearing and disappearing like death squad victims. Even you disappeared.* "I was Bailey's conscience, which he feared. He let a public trust degenerate into a soap opera. I refused to get in bed for a buck. In 1958 in Chicago I told members of the Radio and TV news Directors Association, 'If radio news is to be regarded as a commodity, only acceptable when salable, then I don't care what you call it, I say it isn't news.' I honored free speech and battled corporate suits to keep news free of commercialism." *You're colleagues should've backed you up.* "You're an optimist." *They were incapable of seeing that your end was their doom.* "What you do to the least you do to all. Subsequently, I became director of the United States Information Agency." *C.B.S is a busted toilet that keeps backing up. Flush and the shit keeps comin'. They have a pipeline to a cesspool-* "We're all victims of a paycheck. Usury greases the wheel. But the Fourth Estate cannot be independent and act as a watchdog when constrained by politics and corporate greed. Authority and accountability for truth in news must rest on the shoulders of a free press guaranteed by law as an inalienable right. Fundamental to a free society is a free press. Reporters must be accorded time for objective, in-depth analysis of events. Speaking of time, this is Edword R. Off-the-top of a Tech's Head." *Could I get my baggies made on Seville Row?* "Good night and good luck."

☺

3.   *Mudge and Grudge*

Englewood, 4:55AM. Our new house, a lovely Tudor, talks. It wants to go back to England or southern France.

It talks more at night when time is fearfully quiet and everything gets magnified. The house creaks and groans, steam rising in the pipes meets cold air with a bang, like an old man slapping himself to warm up his bones. At night I'm more human; lying quietly in bed, but not really in bed, or even in my body. I'm floating above the roof, looking down on the trees and lawn, watching the cats subdue a terrified mouse. In the earth Mother Nature does violence to herself. Sometimes downstairs after midnight little boy fears come back. Only light from the breezeway and lampposts save me screaming.

Nighttime brings you down to basics: bed, house, family, and self- inventory. You go to bed putting two and two together, and in your sleep it adds up to five. If the positive outweighs the negative, you sleep the good sleep. Wake up refreshed and give life another shot.

Twelve years on the Dracula shift ruined me. Even after I switched to days, I sleep in fits and starts. I should have two beds. One for fits and one for starts. Ayn sleeps like a baby curled up with a doll and lavender sprigs. One evening as we're retiring I go, "G'night, Mudge." The name came out of the blue. "If you're Mudge, who am I?" She says, "Grudge."

Working overnight is debilitating, discombobulating, disconcerting, and an act of self-annihilation. Your best pals're caffeine, booze, drugs, and the ghosts of Christmas passed. Our body clock is diurnal, based on sleep cycles of the moon. Sleep deprivation confuses the diurnal cycle and weakens the immune system. If you're awake when you should be asleep, the body and mind get out of balance. My adrenal glands think it's day, while my hypothalamus sends sleep signals to a body that's AWOL. The other day I found myself driving to work on my day off. It wasn't my fault. The car was confused.

Recommendation from Human Resources Department: 10% discount on cemetery of choice. Advise cremation since employee is halfway there.

Teching was supposed to be temp. A way to build a nest egg. *What happened?* The velvet glove happened, money, the settled life, and then fear of returning to the gypsy life. Jessel was right. *Show business is so big you can stick it in your hat.*

A distant bird chirps. What's the time? A few more minutes. Houses and people are affected differently by the sun and moon. How's that? I don't know. The body clock, gravity, and electro-magnetism. To-weet! To-weet! Birds sing at my window and go silent. I stretch my back- a bear rubbing himself against a tree trunk. Thunder rolls in the distance. A burst of light rain rushes through the trees.

> *i'm 48 and it's raining, will i ever be 48 again*
> *old friend wrinkled and gray with family, big house, 2 cars, a dog*
> *48 outside something else inside*
> *time is a rainy day coxcomb popinjay*
> *pious pinafored full of solemn poppycock*

The birds resume chirping. They know the sun's coming out. Being high up they see the horizon. My pal's back again this year, singing, 'Tippy-Toe! Tippy-Toe!'

Some fool down the street guns a motorcycle, peels out in first, shifts to second, va-room! He's headed for the moon, or ER at a Hospital. The motor recedes into falling rain, fades into birds singing more radiantly, and clearly among them, my morning pal, Tippy-Toe.

What day is it? It's not Friday. That's my Saturday. I reach across the bed, no Ayn. Where the hell is she? The house is silent. Still in New York in dance class. I roll out of bed.

"Oh! Jesus!" I just miss stepping on Ayn who's on the floor flat on her back. "Sorry. What're you doing down there?"

"Looking for my space, my comfort zone," she says. "We all occupy a physical space, but a personal space is outside the self; full of resonating cosmic vibration."

"You sure it's not full of something else? In New York if they find out you occupy two spaces they double the rent."

"They said in class, when you find your space your body and soul will feel in tune with the joy of creation." She's my gullible Ayn; Mudge, a babe in the woods.

Driving to work, I think, there's no joy in that circus of radio-bembas busting at the gills with death counts and negative news. I haul ass, as they say, for the GW. Should I take George or Martha, upper or lower level? Since the man is usually on top, the lower level means Martha. What's the diff? Day or night, the road's a fucked up crapshoot. Some asshole blows a tire; George's jock's in an uproar; Mary's having her monthlies; a trucker jack-knifes, and there's a humongous road spill of organic cranberries, goat milk, and third party certified watermelons.

What's that up ahead, Martha's bush? I swerve left narrowly hit an evergreen. What the hell's a tree doing in the middle of the goddamn bridge? Maybe it's Arbor Day! I swing onto a deserted West Side Highway, play the idiot, gun the motor, zoom past the only other car on the road and the driver tosses me a finger. At West 86th Street cars are backed up. Now what? I come along side of a driver dusting his dashboard, another is shaking his head, another one's chewing his steering wheel, and a blonde lady is putting on makeup. I cut off the highway by backing up the West 79th Street entrance; tool down West End Avenue; park my ass on West 56th Street off 12th Avenue, under the archway that connects the NY Sanitation complex, and prepare my car for parking in the city: lights off, interior-exterior; leave nothing on the seats; any characters lurking about; no glass near the tires; put a sign on the dashboard, "NO RADIO. NO

320

SPARE. DOORS NOT LOCKED. BATTERY DEAD. WENT FOR TOW TRUCK." A fellow tech laughed when I told him about the signs, saying, "What makes you think they can read?"

I drive an unimpressive car. I figured it was of no value to chop shop crooks. Then, I find out spare parts for old cars are hot. What I have lost in the last year are incidentals like the battery, a spare, a car jack, a wool blanket, a poncho, and my wife's umbrella. One tech says, "I come off the overnight, bleary-eyed, looking to go home. I get in my car out front on 57th, turn on the ignition, step on the accelerator, and the car doesn't move. I hear the wheels spinning, but the car's doesn't move. I get out, look, and the car's up on blocks, all four tires are gone. Right in front of the building. Where the hell's security?" In a year he gave up four tires on his Dotson, hubs, and rims, twice. Now he carries a baseball bat.

Up the street, where 56th crosses 11th Avenue, part of the company two-story brick building is illuminated by roof floods and security lights. A windowless prison. All that's missing is a watchtower and roof guards. Knob less fire doors and delivery exits smell of urine, and the unwashed homeless zonked under newspapers and cardboard. The joint takes up 75% of a city block with entrances from the front or the rear by loading docks. I go in the canopied entrance-on an exterior wall a gold plaque etching of the late Burrow smoking a cigarette. Every time I pass it, I think, cancer, and what a self-serving travesty of his legacy. I ID'ed my way in, and I'm a willing, bricked up prisoner 40 hours a week. Welcome to Alcatraz, and the day hasn't started.

Lately, I'm cynical and impatient. My doctor says, I haven't found my equilibrium yet. I vacillate between appreciation of steady money and a need to express myself. Odd, to be laying low at night, and still earn the reputation of *the wild man of the over night.* Am I wild?

The wild man's a defense against a world that can't be trusted. I closed my heart to save myself. Study piano 10 hours a week, you're a pianist. Play *wild man* 40 hours a week; what's that make you? Buddha is as Buddha does.

☺

Phones are quiet. I take a book from my locker, Strindberg's *Son of a Servant,* a "third person" autobiography. Strange, like doing an autopsy on yourself. He was a self-torturer who purposely alienated himself from society. Killed the joy in life, as if he had penance to do without clarifying the sin. His family wasn't open or objective. Contrary to belief, the family isn't always a family in the true sense of the word. It's often a cesspool of clashing egos and tyranny- a deadly environment for innocence and curiosity. Strindberg said, everything hinges on parents who create the quality of the soil from which the mind draws daily nourishment and sustenance. Little time is devoted to spiritual matters, propriety, and honoring others as one would one's self. No wonder each generation grows into mad dogs.

☺

4.   The Warm-up Monologue

Then, out of nowhere, announcer Bill G. asks me to write him an audience warm-up for a pilot TV news show. I thought, you kidding? When he offered money, I knew he was serious. It meant getting my ass out of mothballs and putting it on the line. Could I do it? Did I want to do it? Maybe he heard I'd worked the Borscht Circuit, hung around with Danny Davis, comic-writer, and we'd go to joints like the comedy Improv Club where I met an early Rodney Dangerfield. But that was back burner news. Now Bill was asking me to come forward. My fear was could I do it to his satisfaction. Was it a test, a real show, or a tax write-off? In the end, I told myself, shit or get off the pot. He didn't mind a few chestnuts, so I tailored the monologue to fit his easy southern manner.

Welcome to radio with pictures. Strange meeting like this without a priest (referee). I'm__ the show's announcer. Usually, I'm the voice in the BG. A little bit ago the producer says, "Flash, warm-up the audience." So I turned up the thermostat. If it gets tawdry, just tell ole B, the thermal man. In TV everything's pre-recorded. Right now my voice is live but my body's pre-recorded. That's what my wife said last night. So I said, (*cup hand to ear*) "Please be patient. We're experiencing technical difficulties. Stay tuned. Our program will resume momentarily." She says, "You'll never be lonely. You've got you and your voice." Our first child was born with his hand on his ear. The second came out with his hand on his hip. He lives in San Francisco.

I'm the face you never see but the voice you hear off-camera. One fella said I had a handsome voice but my face sounded like hell. I do the pronouncing from a studio backstage. It's a small room; not a room actually, but a converted broom closet called the Announce Booth. It's so small when I breathe the walls go in and out. If I hold my breath you can't open the door. If I die in it, they'll put handles on it and bury me in it. My pappy can't believe I earn money-doing pronouncements. He says he never heard me yet. But he has. It's just that on mic the announcer in me takes over. Heck, even I don't recognize myself. (*Announce voice*) This is the C.B.S Television Network in New York. Now I'll do it so Pappy'll know it's me. (*Repeat in Southern voice.*)

You're a great audience. We're just shirt-tailing along. In the south we're more poetic. There are poets up here. A guy came up to me with a gun and says

'Stick 'em down.' I go, "Don't you mean 'Stick 'em up?" He says, "it's my first job. Don't confuse me."

Tucked away in a telephone booth with a microphone waiting on a red cue light, a fella gets lonesome. So it's nice to get out and see the inside of a microphone. Live critters! Whoopee! Maybe I'm dreamin'. Somebody pinch me. It's okay. My wife's married, not me. Actually we're separated. She's in the next building. Pinch me. Use TWO fingers. It's easier. OW! Sadist! What're you doing later? If anyone's still wondering who I am, close your eyes you'll recognize my voice, while an usher comes around and picks your wallet. I'm the guy who says, (*Cup ear*) Back after this. And Stay tuned! Makes me feel like God talking to a piano. Stay tuned!

Now, since we're doing a new show, a lot of producers are in the audience. Every time I read a script at an audition they close their eyes. Wouldn't you like to see my face, too? No? Thanks Mom. When my face is on TV people gain weight. They go right to the refrigerator. (*Point to face*) These aren't wrinkles. They're character lines. The face that launched a thousand TV sets out the window. Whenever there are problems in fraudcasting we blame it on technical difficulties, or equipment failure. They failed to equip me with a script. The tech union's strong here. If you think lightening is quick watch a technician going home. His relief looks like rigor mortis setting in. You can't get a tech off a break with dynamite. One day I'm ready to go on, but no one's in the control room. Then two techs come in carrying a third one on a stretcher, just in time for him to turn on my mic. Afterward, I go, "What's wrong? You sick?" He says, "No. We just signed a new contract. Now I don't have to walk."

When announcing gets boring, I find I say one thing but think another. (*Cup ear; Italicized words are your thoughts*) You'd be surprised how many people use it. *Nobody!* Kids under 12 are admitted free. *They should be committed free!* After 2 years of using Toothy Toothpaste, junior has only 1 cavity. *Where his brain should be!* Do more women have arthritis than men? *I hope so.* Indigestion? Do as thousands do. *Belch.*

News terminology is confusing. There's hard news and soft news, which I don't get. So I asked NR editor/producer Mal Terkel and anchor Dulles Townsand to explain. I go, "If I die, is that hard news or soft news?" Mal says, "That'd be good news." I go, "I know hard news is a big story and soft news is a small one. What constitutes a big story?" Dulles says, "Four thousand words or more." I go, "What's an end piece?" Mal says, "That's the heel of the bread." Dulles says, "Or a pretty girl at the end of the bar."

In the end Bill said, "Isn't it good to know you can do it?"

☺

5.   A BOD Post-it

SAVE WATER *Drink Your Booze straight!*
REPORT LEAKS & WATER WASTE
Peed on my break.

☺

6.   C.B.S Memorandum

From: B.B.A.   To: ALL TECHNICIANS
Date: July 17, 1973   9/1/76 A Reminder

There have been several recent instances of false starts in actuality in the hourly news. It appears necessary to review recording and editing procedures.

1. Recording – if the correspondent stops and indicates he will start again, the tape must be rewound to the top to RECORD OVER the false start.
2. If the correspondent fluffs a word – it's still preferable to rewind and start over. Some correspondents may object to this procedure; nevertheless, time will be saved by doing it this way as against editing out the fluff.
3. In the final analysis, the technician recording the spot is responsible for the final product, which means ALL Material that may end up on the air, must be monitored, and the content must be listened to carefully, so that any necessary editing may be done intelligently. It must be stressed that lack of time in which to check the final product can never be an excuse for getting a false start or similar disaster on the air. It is better not to use the piece if it cannot be checked properly.

☺

7. Tech Lounge Post-it

ANTI- STRESS KIT
BANG HEAD HERE
→ O
<u>DIRECTIONS</u>

1. Place sign on firm surface
2. Follow Directions in sign
3. Repeat until stress is gone, or you're unconscious

☺

8.   The Usurers

Dr. Stinton had been largely responsible for establishing the company image of integrity and taste. He was Bailey's enforcer, like Pope Benedict was to John Paul, II. In 1966 Stinton was in line to take over when Bailey stepped down at the mandatory retirement age of 65. He was surprised and shocked when Bailey changed his mind suddenly while they were walking down the hall to a board meeting. Stinton made a graceful exit when he turned 65 in 1973.

Dr. Stinton's departure left a hole at Chuckler. He embodied the company more than its founder. In the succeeding decade four company presidents were dismissed. There was no time to fire the fifth. He beat them to it by dying unexpectedly, probably from anxiety. There were a lot of lower level dismissal, too, as well as policy changes. It affected morale in the trenches. There was a sense that the great ship had sprung some leaks and was floundering. Old timers covered their real feelings with jokes like "man overboard", and "executive musical chairs". Soon even the old man himself would become Chairman Emeritus.

"In me own head," I once heard Slappsie Maxie Rosenbloom say at the Palace, "I thunk it in me own head." He was referring to a corny joke he'd made up on the spot. Well, there was nothing corny about what people were thinking in their own heads starting with Stinton's departure. Up to then, Chuckler had maintained a steady button-down, gray pinstriped operation that was solid except for the Burrow fiasco, which I attribute to the old man's decision. It was an insipid lowering of standards amid a rising 'get them into the tent' mentality. The power at the top did not insist on integrity in news when the alternative was money. In fact, it declared itself the day Burrow left. Madison Avenue was God. Paying the bills was more important than who really killed JFK.

Money created a newsroom caste system, and made it difficult to work beside a colleague who was a millionaire, but couldn't write as well as the next guy. Imagine? Stars of news reporting! Kings of the public trust. Absolutely ludicrous. But there it is, nonetheless. And not one of them ever wrote anything of lasting value or found a cure for cancer, or unlocked the secrets to DNA and stem cell research. Just awful!

In 1983 Wiman, the Dillsbury Dough honcho, was selected by the old man to be president of Chuckler. The executive board was *levened* by the choice. Maybe the "Over-the-Hill Flourheads" thought they could get a rise out of the Dough Boy, that he'd be the yeast in a flat marketplace. Wiman was handsome, big, and capable. Chuckler and Dillsbury had only one thing in common; they liked dough. Since Wiman had been a vice chairman of Dillsbury, it was assumed he could make dough, but he couldn't rise to the occasion because Chuckler, true to form, refused to turn over authority as promised, and kept punching him down. Wiman tried to force the old man's hand by threatening to resign. Fearing yet another change at the top would damage the company, the board voted the old man out, and he became chairman emeritus. With only a few board members in his pocket, Wiman tried to sell the company to Coca-Cola in a secret deal, which upset the board. They voted it down, which signaled no confidence in Wiman, and a subsequent resignation. What was his golden parachute, I don't know.

In 1985 Ted Turner, the phantom corporate raider allegedly out to buy C.B.S, but never did, was already into cable TV. According to industry pundits, cable was economically unfeasible. C.B.S, under Wiman, went into debt buying back its own stock to head off a potential takeover from corporate raiders like Turner. Now the company was in "play", and in need of a savior. But the way you make your bed is how you sleep in it. The old man had set the tone when he sacrificed Burrow for bread. It came back to bite him in the ass when Dante's prototype money gags Lorenzo di Pesce (*Fish*) glommed up more company stock than the old man had, and got himself elected to the board. Between them, they held a majority of stock and controlled the company. What followed had to be something the old man concocted in a backroom pipe dream with Pesce. They had three things in common, ethnicity, cigars, and moneybags for a coat of arms. Pesce worked a deal that reinstated Chuckler as chairman with himself as CEO. Then, Fish went about dismantling the company and working deals to supposedly to increase cash equity. Fisch couldn't handle Yetnicove, president of Columbine Records, so he sold it under market value. He justified it by promising that the money would go to building the company's core business. His ulterior motive was to build up the company's stock market shares and then sell out, which he eventually did. There is no beneficent one, no heaven or hell; only alive and dead, and in between strange notions of loyalty, integrity, and an everlasting deception that men are other than what history tells us.

Lorenzo di Pesce had zero broadcast experience. He got rich in the insurance, tobacco, and hotel business. He was Geryon, *a beast with an outward face innocent of guile, benign and gracious, but underneath a double duplicitous brute, ugly, vile, and reptilian. Loe,* says Dante, *the sharp-tailed beast, he breaks through walls, and weapons. Loe, the usurer, the beast that infects, that makes the whole world stink.* Usury and deception, especially in a family, no less in business, is a sure way to lose one's soul for eternity. Because man is the only one capable of fraud, it is all the more offensive to God. This Geryon deceiver spoke of a vision for the company's future direction. In fact, he had two visions, the inner, truer one was liquidate and run. His bible was Barons, his pillow the Wall Street Journal. In God's eyes, says Dante, only man is capable of fraud. So it offends Him more. Amid the screams of agony and pain in *The Inferno*, a voice cries out, *Who is that walks the halls of corporate America lining his pockets with other people's lives? One such is Lorenzo di Pesce, soon to be among us. He uses his mind not to benefit others but as a weapon to defraud. Poor, lost soul! With such coin all will pay who have been presumptuous on earth. Chuckler, too, grown fat on the labors of others. Now, old and sickly, it is too late for penance, for pandering to the prurient interest to line his pockets. So, too, self-seeking flour-headed board members of corporations. A place in hell awaits you.*

☺

9.   *Rabble Zingers and Stingers*

Personnel is impersonal! Down with up! *Human Resources* is inhuman! The company nurse is sick! Management's managemental! The house psychiatrist's psychotic! Construction's losing its grip! Maintenance can't be maintained! Accounting's unaccountable! Fisch is a real fish story!

Tech. Operator, this is an emergency. Gimme the nurse's office.
Operator. That service's no longer in service. You must dial out to dial in.
   Ring!
Tech. Give me Columbia Records?
Operator. Sorry. We sold off our drug division.

CC's outta control! The anchor just sunk! Television should be heard not seen. Radio should be seen, not heard. The Foreign Bureau's full of foreigners! Our chief correspondent's despondent. Aristotle hit the bottle! What color're your eyes? Which one?

Tongue Twister. The inferior cafeteria has interior bacteria Now in the anterior affecting our posterior.

Jalanzo. *The cunts* wanna change Memorandum to ***Mamorandum.***

☺

10.   Meanwhile back at the The O'Fey Cafe

Napkin notes: 1973

Femme-Tech. Used in the non-pejorative sense, "girl" is acceptable. However, most men use it condescendingly.

Tech. "Girl" is not negative to me. It means woman, maybe youthful.

Femme-Tech. The use of "girl" is part of the American fantasy that woman shouldn't grow old, which is bullshit. We're expected to remain forever like some tight-skinned teenager and about as dumb. Until men learn to accept us as equals, i.e., until a mediocre woman rises to a top position as many men have, and is accepted just like the mediocre man, without reference to her being a woman because a mediocre woman on the job immediately receives nasty epithets, etc., concerning her sex and not her mediocrity as in the case of a similarly bad male. Until this straightens out, the problem of equality of sexes will continue.

Tech. "Broad" is descriptive, often appropriate. What's the quarrel?

Femme-Tech. That it is used interchangeably by men with the term "girl" or "woman", and it's wrong thinking.

Tech. You called someone a real cunt. Isn't that a word libbers frown on?

Femme-Tech. Yes. It's wrong, according to them. But I live with a man who curses. Maybe that's where I get it. Profanity does cut to the quick. When it comes to insults, I'm an equal opportunity user. That broad's a real bitch! I'd say prick, but that somehow seems complimentary. She's a cunt! What can I say?

☺

11. March Madness Becomes April Fool

Dead Air Mamoranda
Date: March 5, 1977

WORLD TONIGHT: 7-7:14:55 PM, Thursday, to Central & Mountain

Dead air occurred within the broadcast at about 7:02 and running for <u>nine</u> minutes. The program was reinstated when the problem was narrowed down and an alternate loop was used to feed Telco from CC. It was later determined that a possible cause of the problem may have been a <u>Dirty Jack</u> in CC.   tc

☺

Date: March 11,1977

This newscast opened with the sound signature followed by eight seconds of dead air before the Newscaster started the broadcast. After air (*end of show*) the editor reported that he was discussing the script with the Correspondent and was aware of the time. The Associate Director reported that he ran into the newsroom 10 seconds before air to alert the Correspondent. By the time they returned to the studio the dead air colapsed.

☺

Date: March 19, 1977

Hourly News 4:00-4:06:55 PM, Tuesday – To Pacific only

At conclusion of this newscast, 5 seconds of dead air was heard before the scheduled 60 second Adventure Theatre promo started upcut. The CC tech reported that as soon as the adjacency cartridge started, it immediately dropped air. He manually preset the cartridge and sent it to air. It was determined that the cartridge was not <u>seated correctly</u> in cartridge machine. As a result, a new cartridge was made.   TM

☺

Date: March 29, 1977

<u>THE WORLD TONIGHT, 6:00-6:14:55 PM, Tuesday to the East.</u>

Twenty-eight seconds into the show, the correspondent introduced a Mike Papoose insert. Stations heard three seconds of <u>dead air</u>, followed by the Papoose tape coming in three seconds upcut. The TECH reported his selectors were "improperly selected".   hm

☺

Date: April 1, 1977

<u>WASHINGTON WEEK, 5:30 – 5:38 PM, SATURDAY, TO FULL NETWORK</u>

This program originating in Wash did not start on time, and there was <u>dead air</u> until 5:31:45 PM, late by 1:45. The mistake was not corrected until the New York CC tech was able to raise the Wash tech, and he put the taped program on the machine. The Wash tech said, "I forgot Wash Week," after performing prior assignment. A re-feed of program was sent to the full network via tape from New York, 5:45-5:53 PM.   df

The fuck was in the sack!

☺

Devious Septum: Recent Technical Trouble Reports sighted blame for goofs on the following culprits: Mal Function, Miss Labeled, and Aired Uncut. When CC's computer crashed the day was saved by Manual Preset. Stay tuned for a new network radio program called, *Dead Air.* Starring: Anchor Missing, Jump-back Switches, N.D. Sack, Noah Tapes, Dirty Jack, and introducing Non-functional Entity.

Trouble Report or Irregularity   *(Some old timers are irregular!)*

Date: 11-23-77. <u>Reported By:</u> CC tech. Equipment: cart transport. <u>Nature of trouble:</u> STOP/READY BUTTON ILLUMINATOR OPERATING AS A <u>NON-FUNCTIONAL ENTITY</u>.

☺

12. Anniversay *Mamo*randum

C.B.S RADIO   A Division of Chuckler, Inc.   New York, New York 10019
From: JDB, President

Dear Fellow Employees: September 18, 1977

Fifty years ago, the first C.B.S broadcast went on the air and the long journey was begun which finally led to the company we know today.

What an extraordinary journey it's been, marked by the style, and creative energy of Baliley S. Chuckler. Any salute to C.B.S is is salute to B.S. as well.

Blah, blah, blah. And the firing of Burrow which scared all future news wannabees into submission. Thank you kindly.

13.   The O'Fey Café

Napkin Noodling from the Greasy Spoon
Our flamboyant, resident blow-dried Chucklehead Chronic Chronicler salutes a half century of blowing smoke up people's you-know-where.

Cholly: This year marks the 50th Anniversary of the Chuckler Fraudcasting System, founded in 1928 by Bailey S. Chuckler, a Jewish cigar store Indian with seed money earned selling cigars.

MUSIC: Sons of Pioneers. Hear them chuckling along, On the air where they belong, chucklin' along with the chuck-a-lin' chuckleheads (under).

Cholly: Early on our CEO earned the soubriquet "B.S." when he was found cheating in bed with a Su named Briquet. His wife, Sue, sued, leaving him without a sou.

He married the Su who was far from true blue,
Every night it was toodle-lu and nuts to you!
One night in bed he decided to tell her
Blowing smoke signals with a panatela.
One ring meant you fat head, two rings a liar.
A steady flow he fell aslee n' the bed was on fire!

Radio redefined cigar advertising. (Actuality)
"How radio not smoke but span many mountains."
"It's powered by watts."
"What's watts?"
"You don't know watts from what. Look at that tower."
"Plenty big panatela, fella, but no smoke."
"It's an electronic panatela- a radio transmitter. Talk into this microphone and that tower sends your voice miles away."
"Electric smoke blanket talk on wind?" *Never tires.* "Span many rivers, many mountains?" *Rain or shine.* "Invisible smoke signal show personality?" *Yes.* "Mm. Burn many blankets trying to do forked tongue. Me take two boxes."

Cholly: Today, the Chuckler logo, a peace pipe, which is a piece of pipe, is known worldwide. This is Cholly Chuckles, on your Many Rivers, Many Mountains Network.

MUSIC UP. Hear them chucklin' along, On the air where they belong,Chucklin' along with the chuck-a-lin' chuckleheads.

☺

Devious Septum: Stay tuned for the Chink and Cholly. But first this.

14.   The O'Fey Café

Our Lady of the Tolls

Ma Rainey owns a GW toll booth. *I can dig it.* People drive up, she says, I am the toll taker. Gimme the money, Sonny, and don't get funny. You pay extra cause you been a motherfucker on the job and at home. Don't play dumb. You want to go, gimme the dough. You ain't leavin' no tip so don't gimme lip. The money, Sonny and don't get funny. No backin' up. Messin' with my treadle. Pull your ass over, mistah, park it (*sings*) Don't get funny. I wants the ma-honey, Sonny. I'm the co-lector of green nec-tar. What's that? Harlem? Straight on. Can't miss it. It'll find you. Say, what yawl burning in that motor, elephant piss? Get on outta here. (*sings*) You heard of the undertaker, the caretaker, the landscaper, the odds maker? Now you met the toll taker. Co-lector of green nec-tar. Soon, me and my treadle'll be on your doorstep. Every time you cross the threshold, ya gots to pay mama. For Whom the Booth Tolls? It tolleth for thee, Sonny. Six bucks a pop. Ma's righteous reparation.

☺

15.   Signs of Trouble

Devious Septum: This is the Evening Snooze with God's Vicars. From His lips to C.B.S! We reviseth upward and downward! Now, from Mount Porto Potty, *it's your number one Electronic Asshole, the compulsive labialiser, the trusted one, revealer of light, and the People's right*

336

to know even if paralyzed to act. It's Oral Anus with the Evening Turds!

Lately I'm getting these chest pains.
Company Nurse. You've got high blood pressure. How tall are you?
Tech. On a good day 5'8".
Company Nurse. What causes high blood pressure is still a mystery. Buzz words, genetics, emotional stress, lack of self-esteem. Ask your doctor about Tenormin.
Tech. I hear it makes you impotent.
Eve should've shot me in Benedict Canyon.

☺

16.   A Chink & Cholly Prelude

Diary. I'm in CC in Jalanzo's lingo to show my fuckin' face and to check for fuckin' curve balls.

Jalanzo. You inna fuckin' barrel? Lucky you. Ya checked out? Very good. The fuckin' twins're runnin' around like chickens with their heads cut off. Everyday it's the end of the fuckin' world. I told 'em, the fuckin' world ain't ending today 'cause it's already tomorrow in Australia. Ever see a bigger bunchah fuck-your-buddy assholes? *(Ring!)* CC. Speakin'. Keep y'drawers on, pal. He's here. Everything's checked out. *(to Tech)* Ya rollin' on TV? Yeah. He's rollin'. Goodbye. *(hangs up)* It's always somethin'.
Tech. When he phones me in the studio, I don't pick up. He comes running in. "Where were you?" I go, "Right here. What's up?" He goes, "You didn't answer the phone?" I go, "It didn't ring." He goes, "Well, I called." I go, "Well, I would've heard. Maybe you dialed wrong. I'm here. You see me." Sometimes I pick it up, hang up, and when he

runs in, I go, "Was that you? We got disconnected." But it doesn't beat your line.

Jalanzo. Gimme the minutes. I fah-get.

Tech. They were feeding from the San Francisco convention. You yelled out to the Chink, "You're halfway home. Keep goin'!"

Jalanzo. When he got back, he come in here wantin' to know who said it. I go, "Me. I read it in a fortune cookie." Who gives a rat's ass. People like him, ya can't insult.

Tech. Cholly told me, *Good producers are hard to find and harder to keep.*

Jalanzo. The Chink's kept awright. He's a bitch with a cunt's sensibility. "How's ya fuckin' pork, boss?"

Tech. Who started that pork line?

Jalanzo. The wife. I don't know. Years ago I'm waiting on the platform for the train and I hear this cocksucker calling me from across the tracks. I didn't recognize the asshole. Then I see it's an old army buddy goin' back 30 years. He yells, "How's ya pork?" I go, "Great. How's yours?" He yells, "Not good, pal. Going for a fuckin' check-up. Prostrate trouble." He yelled it, too. What do I care? It ain't my fuckin' pork.

Studio D, 5:40AM. Chink runs in kicking the door open to do a phoner. Roll tape! He hums while dialing an outside number.

Skoshi. Hope we haven't woken you up, sir. This is C.B.S-
Voice. Fuck you! (*hangs up*)

Diary: Cholly's hot to rehash a TV piece he'd done for Evening Snooze. The Chink suggests a possible on a C.B.S executive who's linked to some impropriety. NG, says Cholly. He knows better than to tackle someone who down the pike can bight you in the ass. I pray, essay. They do a piece on a kid who was electrocuted climbing around Con Rail live power lines. The kid was partly fried. Great for the breakfast crowd. The Bruise Brothers split and return with a videocassette. Here we go. It's close to airtime and they're still fine-tuning. "We're in deep shit!" says Cholly. "I still have to write the show." I make a dub. Cholly's got great retention. We don't listen twice. One, two, three, we're done. When he goes out to write, the Chinoise wants an internal. Link two words into one. I get it right off, but he says cut it finer. He's got me working the cut to death. Cholly comes back. "Why aren't we done?" The Chinoise says, "You wouldn't've liked the edit."

17. Calder

From the 60's to '80's there were so many management changes you needed a scorecard to keep track. Firings and cut backs were politely called revision, consolidation, and repositioning. First to go was Jim *Smiling Cobra* Aubree. The nickname speaks for itself. The following men had a cup of coffee with Chuckler: R. Tailor, President; T. Wiman, CEO; J. Schnider, executive vice-president then President; B. Woods, President of TV Network; Bill Lenardo, VP in charge of Special Projects like moon shots; Bill Smaul, DC bureau chief...

The corporation had become so big, and consolidations so frequent, it was necessary to draw a weekly block schematic updating department changes and who morphed into what. Lines from the CEO's box dropped like umbilicals connecting boxes in order of importance. Several boxes were merged one week and disappeared the next, as the company "repositioned" itself in a "volatile market." A few boxes had VP names only, and dangled in space like they'd been hung out to dry. It meant "out of favor, but still enjoying cafeteria and exec toilet privileges." The schematic was a Calder mobile of an iconic multi hangman's scaffold.

☺

18.   Nightshift In Maryland

Dateline: Baltimore. Federalies on the job. Two postal workers get 1-year suspended JAIL sentences...and are ordered to do 100 hours community service. On the night of September 18th, postal inspectors watching behind TRICK MIRRORS monitoring activities on the nightshift at the Baltimore post office, caught the men eating cookies and candy out of a damaged package. A video tape had them cold. No good being TOO human or they'll get you on a chocolate chip COOKIE rap.

☺

19.   A Snowball in Hell

There were two rectangular windows in Studio E. One looked into the air studio, and the other had an end view of the newsroom, some 60 feet by 125 feet, with everybody in profile, and news Teletype machines at the far end. TV's courier scheduler was on the left, and on the opposite wall was a window onto the TV Flash studio. A common hall encompassed the whole shebang, which made for several entrances. While the sun never set in the newsroom, I kept my lights off. They couldn't see me, but I could see them coming, when awake, and I'd duck out through CC. Mal "Roundy" Terkel was nobody's fool. He'd start for me, go the other way, and catch me at the Studio A door. "How're you?" "Good. You?" "Peachy. Back in your cage, booby."

With the passage of The Equal Opportunity Act, the powers-that-be got a wake-up call, soon followed by a dose of affirmative action by the FCC: *Hire women and blacks!* So they hired women in black. "No! That's 'Women *and* Blacks!'" Circa 1972, the Washington bureau hired China Ching, age 25; Barnard Shawe, token African-American, age 31; and a blonde, age 30, who was soon dubbed "Helmet Hair" for using Weld-On hair spray. While doing an on-camera stand-up in a blustery rainstorm her umbrella turned inside out but her hair never budged.

Like repertory theatre, every company has its ingénues, soubrettes, leading men, wiseacres, clowns, goats, and village idiots. In 1973, a mix of "the kind" hired an inexperienced, blue-eyed, blonde female, to be the first full-blown lady anchor with the ulterior motive of toppling NBC's iron grip on morning television.

To make a short story long, let's back up in time to my vision of how, and where, it all started, the Chuckler executive boardroom with old man Chuckler at the helm of a flour head Ship of Fools. *Gentlemen, the ghost of J. Fred Mugs, the chimp, still haunts us. Sir, that's Fred J. Mugs. Good Lord! They had a chimp. I've got a chump, several chumps. The point is we need to turn a profit in morning TV. Let the word go forth that a new generation is on the move. Send word down the chump ladder "X" dollars available to revamp morning TV. Leave the details to the news division. That's what they're paid to do. We're out to trump the Chimp! Here, here! We need a ballpark number on the budget. Let them tell us! Then cut it by half! Now let's seal it with a Philly cigar. Crankcase, light me up. Yes, sir. By the by, sir, must I retire at age 65? How old are you now, Crankcase? Fifty-four, I mean forty-five, sir. I had a dyslexic flash. You should only get one at contract time. Now smoke my cigar and tell me I'm enjoying it.*

Dick Salient, ex-lawyer, and President of the News Division, passed the buck to G.M., VP of news, who gathered his staff to run it up the flagpole. *How about a female chimp, J. Frieda Jugs? Hey! Baba Waba interviewed a Washington Post style reporter. What're her credentials? She don't need no stinkin' credentials. She's blue-eyed and blonde. Who ha! We need a swingin' dick for counter balance. Our resident curmudgeon, Hue Cud! Good writer, but a testy bird. His dick's too old to swing. Any back up suggestions? In DC we got Helmet Hair, and China Ching. She Chinese? No. Lithuanian. She does shirts on the side. America's not ready for an electronic chink in the living room. What about Bess Myerson? Inked elsewhere. We need Shirley Temple with tits! We don't want Einstein in the morning. That's a great title. Bacon and eggs equals coffee and toast squared! Arrange dinner, up here. Hate those assholes in DC.*

At dinner the talk went like this. *How about 40,000? I hear more like 75. Maybe later. What time do I get up? We'll throw in 3,000-dollars for clothes with bennies, a private limo to and from the station.* She signed, met her co-host for lunch, and had several wet runs in place of dry ones.

One morning the Flash Studio comes on like the sun. Cameras pan the busy newsroom for background shots to start the *Morning TV Show.* Everyone in radio had to look involved: sport coats hid shirttails, ties tightened; no breakfast in sight; no feet up on the desk; ramrod backs; copy in hand; no chewing the end of pencils because on-camera it looks like the pencil's up your nose. NG on butt pinching, which crimped Reed's style. Once I crossed a camera holding an industrial razor with cotton swabs in my ears. Understated humor. Under what state, I don't know. The state of confusion. The show never got out of the toilet. I taped a sign on their window: "The Mourning TV Show".

Clueless may have had several reasons for doing the show without experience, but in the end, there's notoriety even in adversity. One of my mentors was Milton Steifle, founder of the Iverton Theatre. I asked Milton the 24-dollar question. What makes a successful show? He smiled and said, "One that entertains the audience. If you knew that you'd be a genius. In theatre you know you've got a hit from the box office. How do you judge a TV show, or know who's buying a product, and why? It's smoke and mirrors, surmise and projection. The trick is to look like you're reasoning things out when it's only educated guessing."

"Who hired her?" the press inquired. "No me, senior."

"It was a *group effort,*" replied a company spokes.

Deek Salient interjected. *I'll take credit if the show succeeds, and we'll find a fall guy if it bombs.* His adroit and facile answer garnered chuckles as it slid from first person to third in a single sentence, but it summed up corporate thinking. Like the government, Chuckler Fraudcasting takes from Peter to pay Paul, and passes on the red ink, i.e., 60 Shminutens was in the red seven years. Since one in a hundred shows succeed, what's experience got to do with it? It's a crap shoot. In the end, the fall guys are always the hands-on people who end up disappearing into the media woodwork.

In the '60's, Chuckler News moved from public affairs into quasi news and entertainment programs. They bought the Shakespearian line, *All the world's a stage and we're all players.* In all my years at Chuckler no one succeeded in morning TV. To succeed, a hostess would have to be beautiful, naked and make house calls.

In her post-mortem *he said, she said* auto-bio-confessional, *We're Going to Make You,* Clueless talks about what it was like being the first woman to anchor a news program. Up front someone in the know said, *You got as much of a chance to make it on TV as a snowball in hell.* Doing TV is like stepping in the ring with Mohammed Ali. You'll dance around for a time thinking you might sneak in a knockout punch, but the hard news is that when you wake up you'll wonder what really possessed you.

She further says, "They" were asking her to "piss all over" Barbara Walters, co-hostess of NBC's *The Today Show,* a daunting job in light of an abysmal track record of failed attempts, including a try by 'Sticky Face' Aces of the short memory, and big ego, who scoffed at Clueless. In news talk, everybody's on general assignment from the great Editor in the sky, and nobody's got exclusivity on anything. As I recall, Sticky's early television years were lackluster. He was a pop-up character who kept re-surfacing in failing venues. He had no personality except a pock-marked face and an abrasive voice. In the '50's he did a TV gab show with Stuffy, his first wife. The Sticky and Stuffy Show, and their marriage tanked together. Then came Night Scowl with him in chiaroscuro veiled in cigarette smoke, a la Burrow, but he lacked that man's integrity and scholarship. In '63 Sticky was unimpressive doing morning TV. He and producer Hugh-it are radio-bemba Gilas. I'll illustrate with an old army joke I heard in the '50's. *The Gila monster's a mean critter. Every day the Gila monster wakes up mean, looks around, and everything makes it meaner and meaner. Look at the Gila monster; it'll bite your head off. Why's the Gila monster mean? 'Cause it can't shit!*

My choice for host of the *Morning Show* would've been Mohammed Ali. He'd go live from outside NBC rope-a-doping Baba Waba as she steps from her limo at 4a plying her with dumb questions, then stick his fist in her face, *Lemme hit yawl once. Guaranteed you'll never lisp again. Com'on woman. Lean in.* Then I'd bring in the powers-that-be and he'd knock 'em all out! His co-host, Jake La Motta. *Time to Parooze da Nooze: Speakah a da house says one ting, but he's tinkin' anuddah like screw youse n' da horse y'rode in on! Now, da weather with Slappsy Maxie Rosenbloom. Tanks, Jocko, I mean, ya worshipness. It's beastly outside, ladies and germs. Rainin' cats and dawgs. I know. I just stepped onna poodle. Y'like dat? Made it up outta me own head.* I met La Motta several times. He always seemed preoccupied. Wonder why?

☺

20.   *Get Me Off This Horse!*

Scene 1: TV "Flash" studio in radio newsroom. Time: 7 AM, July, 1973.

VIDEO	*AUDIO*
	<u>DEVIOUS SEPTUM:</u> From The Chuckler Newsroom, New York, it's The Morning Show.
1. OPEN LIVE: BUSY NEWSROOM. VOICE OVER THEN TWO-SHOT:	

CLUELESS

If you're 10 times better than they say you are, if you can adjust from print to TV, spend a million bucks to make the show work, get a great script, the best production and direction money can buy, your chance of success is 1 in a 1,000. On that note, good morning, you old curmudgeon. Our debut and already I'm going blind from the hours. I feel like I been run over by a steamroller.

HUELESS

I should be run over by that steamroller. Up first, Iacocca and Ford- Oh, not ready. May I sip your coffee?

CLUELESS

I've got a soar throat.

HUELESS

Your voice looks great to me. Iacocca has a black book. In it he rates executives. They have to be cost effective.

CLUELESS

My clothes are cost effective, from Goodwill.

HUELESS

That's cost defective. What's the difference between a lavaliere n' a boutonnière?

CLUELESS

A boot in the ear hurts. Keeps a black book?

HUELESS

Like a baseball manager. Who produces, who's good in the clutch.

CLUELESS

I'm good in the clutch. In baseball it takes four balls to get on. In the corporate world, it only takes two. My dream is to pitch for the Yankees. I even have a name. Fanny Fingers, feared for my curves and breaking balls. I want a Hawaiin catcher named Kini Popo, and a manager named J. Akuhead Pupuli In Hawaiian you pronounce every letter like Ka-a-ava. I saw a sign in Waikiki, Peepee lin nay. The guide says, No. That says pipe line.

☺

A joke attributed to Hugh-it circled C.B.S. After Clueless debuted on the *Mourning Show* with a sore throat, he says, "We were promised *deep throat* and got sore throat." Sticky Face chuckled loudest, forgetting his own failures and mediocre writing skills.

Tennessee Williams wrote, men don't *recognize women* unless *they're in bed*. He should know. From my vantage point, a skip and a hop from the TV "Flash" studio, I sensed it applied to Clueless who would've been an instant hit had she anchored from a 4-poster. Fame, said Barbara Streisand, is an accumulation of *misunderstandings* that build up around *somebody new*. There's no room for honesty. We kill what we love, despise what we create, hate success and long to destroy it. Rise up and you're shoved down again. We like the notion of an underdog, but despise the success. We love the process but are jealous of the results.

Hundreds of thousands have been spent on TV sets most of which are ridiculous like the shows themselves. Renovation to the Flash Studio cost over $250,000 in 1973. The show was budgeted in the tens of thousands per week. Where'd the money come from? Advertisers. They pay for everything, which means they are the real bosses. What can be expected when the life style of top CEO's is a testimony to greed and usury? Bertrand Russell: Man will be unhappy even in heaven. Where other animals eat to survive, man eats to think. Other creatures sleep at night. Man sleeps with one eye open and schemes.

To give life to the *Morning Show* TV cameras took shots of the radio newsroom through the flash studio window. It gave authenticity to the program to see news people on the job, presumably on behalf of the TV show, but, in fact, it was the network radio staff. So it was slight fabrication, but then they were already into "producing" news.

A pan around the newsroom showed a happy clan of benign radio herbivores foraging for news, who are really hunter-gatherers competing with each other, and television for the hard stuff, and the blood-boiling scoop. Everybody drinks from the same well in a love-hate relationship guided by the law of diminishing returns. A slow news day is equivalent to a severe drought when it's everybody for himself.

My idea for an opening shot was to super-impose the newsroom on a parched Serengeti with everybody fighting over first dibs to a story. The TV lion scoffs up the best bites and the pickings go to the radio hyenas. Then, the "flash" studio implodes. The newsroom gets sucked into the camera lenses and explodes into every home with a TV. Funny, in all my years at C.B.S I was like Edmond Dantes returning to the chateau d'If looking for the treasure map I forgot to sew into my body bag.

In the summer of '73 Clueless entered a news profession dominated by men. Baba Waba had made inroads, but was neatly titled co-hostess, not anchor. Scuttlebutt in the halls painted Clueless in *over her head*. In the army they had an accelerated officer training program dubbed '90-Day Wonder'. Clueless was our '90-Second Wonder', sent into the battle for ratings without a weapon. *Nobody explained the red light to me. I didn't know it meant a live, or hot camera. To me, a hot camera fell off a truck.*

Thinking you can do something and doing it are two different things. C.B.S tried to create a modern, female Icarus, said she could fly, stood her on a mountaintop, and for a second before she leaped even she thought she just might make it to the sun. In the end she melted under the lights and the whole fiasco turned into a 'Hail Mary', or the all-American long shot, that left lots of finger pointing.

Clueless' motivation to succeed was based on a distorted self-image, and the Fifth Amendment guaranteeing every idiot's right to roll the dice in any game. Mixed in somewhere is the puritanical, protestant work ethic of not refusing an opportunity. Clueless characterized her decision as frivolous curiosity. *Like taking an assignment from a big magazine to be the first lady astronaut, only to realize at countdown time, oh, shit, I actually have to fly in space.* In his book *Bring On the Empty Horses,* David Niven speculates on why Garbo quit Hollywood. Some people who climb mountains and rest on a summit sometimes look down and to their horror they suffer vertigo. Jelly-kneed with thumping heart, they inch back down and never climb mountains again.

To Clueless, G. Mann, Hugh-it and Wally Aces were contemptible, asshole buddies, who appear to suffer the agony of their art, and will cut off your ear to prove it. In '73 Hugh-it worked out of New York and his wife lived in DC. A sweet deal when you're a casting couch Don.

Back then people on both sides of the window were learning that entering people's living rooms is tricky business, and success amounts to catching lightening in a bottle. In part, that's why there are so many re-runs, copycat shows, and anyone with a long career is called a survivor.

By the mid-70's *the* skirts were everywhere, which ratcheted up the *glorification of insignificance* because they were out to prove themselves. It was laughable because 90% of the time you can write a day's worth of news on a piece of confetti. What wasn't funny was the Eva Braun's, who'd zip a guy's fly with his dick in it faster than he could say ouch!

In 1980 Reefer anchored the Mourning Show for 21 months, i.e., until Cactus Stan Blather got the Evening News gig. Reefer had embraced the ungodly early hours, and estrangement from family in D.C, in the hope that TV facetime might get him the anchor job. When it didn't, he went back to reporting news in the beltway. Neither he nor his predecessors on that show ever made a dent in the NBC ratings.

Around that time, anchor Rajah Mud believed himself heir apparent to Crankcase, got pissed when he lost out, and packed up for NBC. It was the year of presidential conventions, and lots of TV face-time, but Rajah had signed a contract with a clause *barring him from on-air work in the metro area for six months after leaving Chuckler.* Rajah posted an adios note to colleagues in the newsroom. It was my army lesson all over again.

Promises mean nothing. Always dot the 'i's' and cross the 't's'. Why do people sign unfair contracts? The company's the boss. You want to work, you sign. Later, when you're a proven asset, it's payback time. Rajah closed out his news career with PBS.

One guy did beat the company at their game, but time caught up with him on another matter. Dr. "No Trans-fat" was our network weatherman. He was sharp, talented on the piano, and a super guy. He had the same face on mic and off. He and his wife invited me to dinner at their home in Riverdale, NY. Afterward Dr. "T" played the organ with the preface, *this is always my after dinner swan song.* That night he told me he'd let his contract lapse beyond the six-month period. They didn't ask. He didn't tell. Meanwhile, he found work as a weatherman elsewhere in the metro area. I was sorry to see him go. Years later I was surprised to learn he didn't have a real doctorate. He claimed the competition was so great that he had to fib in order to get the edge on the next guy. Well, he was encouraging to me, good medicine, and will always be my Doctor.

Anyway, back on track as we head for the finishing gate, actor Warren Beatitude allegedly told Clueless, *you're making a mistake by allowing C.B.S to promote you without TV experience.* Gardner McKay flopped on his debut in *Adventures In Paradise.* A victim of over-promotion, he couldn't live up to his advanced publicity as the next Clark Gable.

Clueless may have been a good socialite reporter, but stardom is an X-factor given to few people. She had nothing solid beyond the bathroom mirror. Failure and bruised egos are mollified by money. Later, you say, *I'm an innocent babe of exploitation.*

Had Chuckler offered her a break-in period, she says, I'd've rejected it. The allure, and exposure to millions of people, was hard to deny. Flop, and at the very least, you're a household name. From such moments come memoirs and notoriety.

In August 1965 the Colander Show moved to 7a, morphed into the *Mourning News*, a two hour yawn full of chuckleheaded dry goods, vain sports scores, and presumptive weather forecasts. By '67 AM radio was talk-news and deejays were history. Then, money went to FM, which everyone thought was short-wave. TV did to radio what cable and the dish are now doing to TV. In the 21st Century the new, replacement killers are digital, wireless, satellites, and indifference.

When the powers-that-be allowed sponsors in news they violated a public trust. Sponsors bring demands and censorship. Today, news is totally driven by demographics, and home mortgages. The fourth estate is our petite bourgeoisie, an entrenched bureaucracy- an immoveable, self-indulgent, self-aggrandizing army of noxious gadflies and paper pushers whose real talent is impeding truth and protecting their asses.

The term "news colleague" is laudable in concept, but a misnomer in reality. It doesn't include jealousy and envy. Freud and Eugene O'Neill agreed: man has a latent desire to crush *the thing he loves.* Murder has many faces: indifference, ridicule, ostracizing, you're fired. People can smell weakness and will exploit it, even if it's only through insults to puff up there own failures. "Clueless couldn't find her 'mark' without a seeing-eye dog." *Chuckler, that old fly-infested milk barn, painted gray, looks and smells depressingly like the inside of an Army hospital.*

In the corporate world like the army, it's pass the buck, never stick out your neck, and cover your ass. *Everybody loves your pilot, kiddo!* Who? *Everybody. They thought it was great!* Who's they? *Everybody!* When *everybody* and *they* are not defined, then nobody is to blame for anything. One day you look in the mirror and you see the dregs of what you've become. So you snow yourself to keep going as a dehumanized soul. The only way you can face the lie is to bury it with bigger lies, which make you calloused and turn the corners of your lips down.

After the debacle called the "64 Thousand Dollar Question", executive-producer types went underground, but resurfaced in news in variations of the old con game, scratch my back I scratch yours. They know the public has a short memory. If you say, "bend over," they say, "how far and how wide?" They are long distance flukes who outlive their betters, and wind up in the catbird seat by default. Most jobs are easy. It's the long distance whore's politics that kill you. Hugh-it's half century at Chuckler was the longest blowjob in media history.

In the '50's Lenny Bruce was just another jittery stand-up comic. Later, he said he learned his craft over a four-year period of steadily working gigs and standing in for no-shows who fell out because of booze, drugs, or whatever. In that time Bruce developed an intuitive feel for the rhythm and technique of humor, the ability to sense contradiction in commonplace situations, which allowed him to read from his own court transcripts and be funny. After four years I could tech blindfolded. Some thought I worked that way. After ten years you become a parrot and only the young are fooled. Two old bulls Hugh-it and Aces are standing on the C.B.S roof looking down at a crowd of aspirant females. Wally says, "Let's run down and get one." Hugh-it says, "Let's walk down and get 'em all."

Fifty years after the fact, the *Today Show's* old host Dave Garroway (1952) and J. Fred Muggs, a chimpanzee, are still more vivid than any shows since. And by the way, the news magazine concept originated with Pat Weaver of NBC.

Princess Anne's wedding date was announced in England. Clueless was to report it. Hugh-it-Man was to direct TV coverage. The stage was set for a royal indiscretion with the damsel in distress, Clueless of the bad, bad ratings.

Hugh-it is a pragmatist who made a fortune. *Art's for dreamers, TV's for schemers. Everything else is jerking off!* He planned to play both Fox and Rescuer to Clueless. *Don't worry, darling. I'll make you a star. We'll dine out with my C.B.S charge card. Roses, wine, and tutoring. Nothing sweeter than tutoring on company time. Gather yee the rosebuds while yee may.* All business and no play make Smilin' Jack a dull boy.

Clueless had a decision to make. Lots of people use their positions for social ends, - She knew it well. She met with GM, news director, for clarification.

Scene 2: The Nibbler

GM. Just watch the floor manager.

Clueless. I do, but he's a sexist. Keeps giving me the finger. I feel like Cinderella's sister trying to squeeze my foot into the glass slipper. Will Hugh-it help me? He seems a bit of a lech.

GM. No. He's playful. Flirts a little. But he won't eat you. Oh, he'll try to nibble here and there, but he's harmless.

Clueless. Nibble?

GM. Nibble.

Clueless. What's that mean?

GM. Nibble is nibble.

Clueless. Does he take 'no' for an answer? Is he vindictive?

GM. It'll never get that far. He's a married guy.

Clueless. She's in Washington.

GM. Sweetie, listen. Can you blame a man for nibbling? I nibble myself. I call it noshing. This is conjecture anyway. How far he goes is up to you. Sure he's on the make. Who isn't? I'm not. But I'm not everybody. Let's do lunch before you go England, to tie up a few details.

Clueless. Okay. Great. I just hope his helping me is not conditioned on-

GM. Don't worry, Sweetie. You can handle it. Believe me. It's the least of your worries. Just stay on track, prep yourself, get to know England, the Royal Family- you know, background information, color stuff, and you'll be great. Remember, Hugh-it is the best. The best! Do what he says, hit all your marks, and he'll make you a star. He's the best, the absolute best. I've seen him operate for ten years. He's a genius.

Behind the cameras pointed at England's royal wedding was the plebian story of whore mongering, expenses paid by C.B.S. When Clueless refused to Erica Jong him on the flight over, or in the hotel room, Hugh-it screwed her on-camera by reducing her to voice overs. *They should get <u>him</u> into a tent and collapse it. His naïve, sexual advances reminded me of a high school boyfriend who said if I didn't let him, he'd get warts on his thing. But to this lech, I'm a conquest to laugh about with the boys in the back room.*

☺

21.   The Best

Mizzie was Sticky Face's radio writer/producer. She'd do phone and studio interviews, research and write his radio show *Aces Wild*, dubbed by insiders, *Asses wild*. She and I were in Studio F waiting on Him. He pops in like he'd rather be elsewhere, and rips apart her script.

Wally. This is baby shit! She broke her leg dancing. Right?
Miz. It's in the last graph-
Wally. Y'buried it, for crissake! Lead with it. Call me when the son-of-bitch's right. (*exits*)
Tech. Why do you let him talk to you that way?

Miz. Because he's the best.

Tech. You want me to say something-

Miz. Don't you dare.

Tech. I'll be nice. I'll remind him of the Haiti story.

Miz. No you won't. Don't bring that up.

Tech. Intrepid reporter kills story-

Miz. I'll kill you.

Tech. Fears reprisals against family clothing store in Port Au Prince.

Miz. Shh. He's liable to come back.

Tech. Somebody on the wife's side married a Haitian. People who live in glass houses-

Miz. Enough. Okay? It goes with the territory. Besides, he's right. I buried the lead. He's just making me sweat.

Tech. Goes with the territory.

Miz. Something you should think about very carefully.

Tech. Oh, turning it around. What's that mean?

Miz. No pain, no gain. Now, will you shut up, gagoots. I'm trying to fix this script. I'm learning from the best. The best in the business.

Tech. I'll show him best. One phone call, he'll be walking bowlegged.

Miz. Don't you dare. He just got upset. He's been busy lately. Let it go.

Mizzie had in mind moving from radio to TV. A kick in the ass from Sticky'd go far. It remained to be seen if taking his guff earned any points. Even the Chink remarked "he treats her like shit". She and the Chink were alike, except she wrote, put herself out there. Maybe that's what she was telling me. No pain, no gain. She wasn't letting pride get ahead of common sense. In my imagination, I socked it to him.

"Level check, please."

"What?"

"Say something, Sticky Face. Anything."

"Roll the tape. I'm reading straight through. Any errors you can work on later. I gotta catch a plane for the Vin-yahd."

"NG. Back off. Angle the mic to minimize popping. For those who're the best, it goes in front of the mouth. For those who're the best and have planes to catch, it's goes down your throat." *Ach!* "Mr. Port au Prince, long distance runner with a short memory. Failed anchoring *Mourning TV:* Crankcase, '54; Jack Paar; Dyke Van Dick; Will Rodgers, Jr., '56 (Until his horse crapped on camera). You've been crapping on camera since the '50's. Breezener, '61; Venti; Alacarti; Shoyu and Cureall, replaced by Kurtiz. All you're good at is running in between the rain drops, pushing lies that're so fantastic and abundant we don't know who to believe anymore. Who killed JFK? Shot Malcolm X? Was back of Allende's supposed suicide? American taxes called "dirty money" backed Pinochet, trained soldiers, bought weapons, toppled regimes. What about John Negroponte, Mr. Intrepid Port au Prince? Neil Tush and the Lincoln Savings Bank? Where're the hard questions with the follow through?"

Everybody kicks back his chair as Sticky Face closes an interview with LBJ's biographer. Sticky's a *yenta*, say his colleagues. Yiddish for gossip. I prefer the Italian *chiachiarone*. It's onomatopoeic, like buzz, hiss, and gurgling brook. Sticky is noted for interviewing skills, which never uncovered a major truth, or enlightened the world with new information. He looks up, says, *Stop rolling,* and goes into an anecdote that speaks to LBJ's character, and to the integrity of his producer.

In the spring of 1971 we went to Texas to cover the opening of the Lyndon Baines Johnson Library at the University of Texas Campus in Austin. LBJ had been living a reclusive life at his ranch in Texas in the hill country since he'd been chased from office two years earlier over his Vietnam policies. While the library was an important event, the bigger story was Cambodia, and what led to his decision to not run for re-election as president. That was the deal. The library and Cambodia. Otherwise, why schlep an expensive camera crew to Texas when our affiliate can cover it cheaper? Now Johnson was a cagey man. He liked to let you know who was boss. He took us on a tour of his ranch in one of those canopied jeeps. Johnson's driving slowly along the perdanales, a park setting with benches and trash cans; I'm in the passenger seat; Hugh-it's in the back with a cameraman. Now I know the president knows Hugh-it's our producer. Johnson stops, points to a candy wrapper by a bench, says to Hugh-it, "Get that, would you, and toss it in the trash can." Well, I look at Hugh-it, he looks at me and we wanted the Cambodia story. So Hugh-it gets out, picks up the wrapper, and tosses it the trashcan. As he's coming back, Johnson accelerates slowly and Hugh-it has to quickstep to catch up. Johnson accelerates a little faster. Next thing Hugh-it's running to catch us and he has to jump to get into the jeep. That was Johnson. He liked to let you know who was boss. Then the son-of-bitch reneges on the deal. Flat out refuses to talk about Cambodia, disappears on us, and then sends word that he'll talk about his presidential library, but nothing else. So there we are, running up a bill with an expensive crew and nothing to show for it. We start packing up when I decide to give it a last try. I couldn't find Johnson anywhere. I go to his library. I call out from the lobby, "Mr. President!" Nothing. As I'm leaving I hear this voice coming from the lobby balcony at the head a stairway. It's Johnson. I go, "Mr. President. We came out here to talk about Cambodia." He says, "No." I go, "Mr. President, with all due respect, the library is important, but Cambodia's the story." He turns to go, I yell out, Mr. President! JFK had Helen Thomas. You had Cambodia. Let's be fair. You fucked the country and the country fucked you." He stops, turns, grins, and says, "I admire you, son. Ya got balls. Okay. And you will give time to my library." That was LBJ. He liked to see if you had the guts of your convictions.

☺

When you're out of the loop you know who your friends are. Long after I retired, I phoned Mizzie. Our conversation was short and like we'd never been intimate friends. *I'm expecting a phone call about a special delivery package.* She rang off asking for my e address. I sent her an autographed copy of *Homecrest Avenue* with a note of thanks for helping me. I'd been thinking of Christine Macintyre; that they both would be proud to know the time given me had not been lost. I never heard from Mizzie again.

One day the wife and I were walking along 79th Street on our way to our son's softball game in Central Park. "Isn't that Mizzie's building?" asks Ayn. *Yes.* "I always loved that rococo red brick." Yes, I thought, glancing at the sand-colored Italian stone entrance with coach lights and a coat of arms; inside the marble and granite lobby lit by sconces. "The oak side table is still in the lobby." Then, I told her about the phone call. "Maybe she's out of business and was embarrassed to talk about it."

"I'm not surprised," says Ayn, as we scoot across Amsterdam Avenue. "Based on what I've seen of her, and the things you've said, she prefers riding the coattails of successful people. She was at our wedding. Broke bread at our house. What changed?"

☺

22.   Double Think, Double Speak

"Men are peculiar," remarked artist Julius Kramer, nearing 96. "I've always gotten on better with women. They're sensitive and considerate. Men are pigs always on a horse. Y'have to knock 'em off to get respect."

A psychologist once suggested I write about C.B.S, not the Russian revolution, because the media's identifiable pop culture. Protracted and undivided attention watching talking heads affects subconscious family myths and deep-seated loneliness. He was right. Some people look good in person but bad on camera and vice-versa. Complicated people who look over-worked are hazy on camera. Simpletons can come across as honest and intelligent. Everyone on TV is an actor. Newscasters are practitioners in the art of how to deliver audiences and ratings while being bland and non-committal. Few people offer opinions on TV and survive. After a half-century, people and shows still come and go, and nobody knows why. A terrific looker may give bad vibes on camera, and a clod might win sympathy. As a result, few people make original decisions and everyone is motivated by fear.

While teching Wally Aces I met retired General Haig, former Secretary of State under Ronald Reagan. He had a discursive way of answering press questions, which reporters called Haigspeak, i.e., "I non-concur on that." It's not a lie. "It's a terminological inexactitude" (first spoken by Churchill). The age of double speak and double think crested with Donald "Rumplestiltskin" Crumbsfeld whose speeches were like a demented Gettysburg Address. "Reports that say something hasn't happened are interesting to me, because as we know there are known knowns; there are things we know we know. We also know there are known unknowns; that is to say we know there are some things we do not know. But there are also unknown unknowns- the ones we don't know we don't know." On Iraq's WMD's: "The absence of evidence is not evidence of absence... simply because you do not have evidence that something does exist does not mean that you have evidence that it doesn't exist." Or, "Death has a tendency to encourage a depressing view of war." "I would not say that the future is necessarily less predictable than the past. I think the past was not predictable when it started." The screwball talk put me in mind of Scrooge bouncing around his flat after a visit by the three spirits. *Ho, ho. I don't know anything. I never did know anything, but now I <u>know</u> that I don't know anything. I don't know anything. I never did know anything. (sings) But now I know that I don't know all on a Christmas morning.* Scrooge came to his senses. America should have been so lucky after 9/11.

In his book, *Inner Circles,* Haig echoed Marshall McLuhan's ideas on the effectiveness of TV, which was unkind to Nixon. According to Haig, the impression of Nixon's face overwhelmed everything. Dark jowls, guarded eyes, and "sweat glistening on the upper lip". In *Understanding Media* Marshal McLuhan nailed the results of the Nixon-Kennedy TV debates. Nixon came off suspicious looking while Kennedy was fuzzy, awkward in appearance, even hesitant, and conveyed the image of a football coach, which let the audience fill in the picture. One can speak truthfully into the camera, but come off a liar and the reverse is true. Something in the face of the projected person has to be acceptable to the viewer, a folksiness, and vulnerability along with non-intimidating looks.

On substance, Haig was convinced that Nixon beat Kennedy in the 1960 debate, but lost it on negative looks, whereas JFK appeared "urbane, handsome, and cosmopolitan." Looks and voice projection are poor indicators of character. Nixon, says Haig, was a superior politician who rose above inherent physical disadvantages and voice timber that instilled uneasiness. On foreign affairs, says Haig, Nixon was an original thinker. He had a lucid, uncluttered writing style equal to Ben Franklin.

One morning Mort Sahl popped up on a studio monitor that was tuned to the Morning Show. He said, Japanese Prime Minister Nakasone visited President Reagan. He asked him to rescind the auto import restrictions, saying, we've had a rougher time of it; consider Hiroshima. The president replied, What's Hiroshima got to do with it? Nakasone said, Well, we've never destroyed one of your cities. Haig interjected, What about Detroit?

I sensed early on that TV was made for low-key chitchat, perfect for teachers who could talk for hours. But there was more. People are fussy about who they let into their homes. Nixon was never able to cross that TV threshold for several reasons: his part in the House Un-American Activities Committee and his physical appearance, the dark blue beard which was evident even after a close shave, a low hairline, and heavy eyebrows, shifty eyes, the sharp-eyed look of criminal intent that was not there when he laughed. Someone said in the '50's that Nixon reminds us of three arch villains of the day: Max Schmelling, German heavyweight who fought Louis; Rudolph Hess, the Nazi; and Wisconsin Senator Joe McCarthy, the red-baiting witch hunter. All had low hairlines and dark beards. The key to success has always been elusive and mysterious. Blonde bombshells, I've read, are types less apt to succeed in TV over the long haul than non-threatening neighborly-types with middling looks.

President Johnson hated TV. Just couldn't get the hang of broadcast techniques. He came off homely and uncouth. He hated TelePrompTers. Allegedy, during a tech rehearsal, the president missed cues, looked at the wrong screens, goofed lines, and lost his place, all while conveying emotions to rival a Shakespearian actor. Finally, Johnson bellowed at the TelePrompTer, *Get this fucking thing out of here!*

To Haig, the *beltway* press corps was a guild of *moody misanthropes,* the brightest of whom are often *the most dangerous.* They can eat their benefactors alive. Haig to Kissenger: *keep away from reporters, except for news conferences and open encounters. Best of all, stay away from the press altogether.* I non-non-concur.

Sidebar: The media is passing entertainment, but subliminally more is going on. Over-exposure to media blurs the lines between real and unreal. Noted actor Nick Adams told me he changed his phone number several times during his *Rebel* series. *One guy says, Get your gun. I'm coming down your street at High Noon.* On radio in 1945 Bing Crosby called out to America: *Let's sing out in the family key. Com'on gang. Join in. Tap your feet. Gee whiz! Do something.* JFK's Televised funeral pulled a nation into one family by getting Americans involved in a *ritual process.*

Marshal McLuhan wrote that TV teachers seem endowed by viewers with *mystic* or *charismatic qualities* beyond feelings developed in class. A TV teacher has a dimension, of sacredness that speaks to TV's character, which is less visual and more of a "tactual-auditory medium" involving all our senses. For people used to visual experiences of the typographic and photographic kind, it seems to be the *synesthesia, or factual depth* of TV that removes viewers from *passivity or detachment;* focuses perception into a telescopic perspective, cutting off peripheral vision, and affecting the subconscious like a gospel experience. In life we never focus on anything to the degree that we do when watching the screen.

Today the danger to Americans is media take-over by mega groups like Clear Channel Communication (CCC), a San Antonio based organization, with a self-serving agenda. In Minot, North Dakota in 2002 a train cargo of Anhydron (used by farmers in fertilization) derailed and the chemical spilled into the countryside. Anhydron sucks oxygen out of the air, can shut down a car engine in half a minute, and destroy the respiratory system about as fast. The Minot incident illustrates that a warning can't get to the public in a timely way because conglomerates like CCC own broadcast stations miles away, and have replaced local news, music and talk shows with prepackaged programs fashioned in remote studios and fed out via digital voice and tracking systems.

The FCC caved into business and allowed monopolization of broadcast stations, a turn-around of its initial purpose established in 1934: to monitor the air waves in the public interest. President Truman started Conelrad, now called the Emergency Alert System (EAS), to alert America in case of national emergency. Now, that warning system is in the hands of conglomerates. After 9/11, Tush didn't use EAS, but tucked tail for middle America. When he spoke at the WTC, he was dull as dish water. He's prepackaged like those Minot stations; the outward face of the new digitized Frankenstein oligarchy we have yet to fully see. The monster showed itself when the Supreme Court ruled against American voters in the face of electoral fraud in Florida, a state governed by brother Jeb Tush. Frankenstein reappeared as Paul Bremer and John Negroponte in the administration's premeditated destruction of Iraq's infrastructure. When General MacArthur entered Japan he did not fire everybody. Albert Spier didn't listen to Hitler and blowup the bridges, mines and factories when the war was lost. They understood destroying everything meant no work, starvation and chaos. The Tush junta talks of democracy, but it's secret agenda is sectarian division to mask its ulterior motive, which is lining the pockets of special interest groups, and, *Get the OIL, baby!* America has gone from Water Gate to White Water to Black Water. Soon it'll be no water, privatization of air in bubble cities, Monsanto single germ seeds, and Mad Milk disease from Prosilac- a biosynthetic beauvine growth hormone- a poisonous chemical that forces cows to piss more milk from ulcerated, cancerous udders.

☺

23.   That'z the Way It Iz

The arrival of women in the '70's added an exciting, if sometime acerbic twist to the good ole newsboy's club- a mix of women's rights and button-downed sex. Some were new to broadcast news, others slightly wet behind the ears from print, or an affiliate. For all of them, the "on-air" studio was a holy tabernacle, news writing was biblical, and anchors God's vicars giving sermons on the mount.

One time several ladies chatting in Studio E suddenly stopped and stared into Studio A through the control room window as a handsome TV anchor with black hair and mustache entered to record an audio track. As they giggled, gushed, and ogled the Gilbert Roland of News, I smiled knowing he was a stolid, non-committal, dime store dummy that I had dubbed Sir Rollin Dead-pot. But from a woman's pov, I admit, what's substance got to do with it?

In time *the* women settled in, made fun of themselves, and equaled the men in use of profanity. *Ring!* Ztudio E. Mizz Z zpeaking. Mizz who? One zecond. For you, Zarah. It'z the azzignment dezk. (*Sarah into phone*) Yezz. One female was reading copy, her back to the door. Two techs sneak up behind her, yell, BOO; she jumps in fright, and goes, "You cocksuckers!" and everybody laughs. In one incident, a tape-ops woman reported two maintenance techs for using profanity. The news director demanded an explanation. *"Well, sir,"* says Dilido, *"me and the chief here are workin' in Studio A. He's standing up on top of the console soldering a wire on an overhead speaker, and I'm standin' under him holding the flux. By sheer coincidence a drop of hot solder falls, lands inside my shirt, and I look up and go, 'Really, Alfred. You <u>must</u> try to be more careful.'"*

I became friendly with a woman-anchor who dreamed of becoming a female Crankcase. She was hard to get, until I teched her hourly wearing an Uncle Woolly

Crankcase mustache. After I go, *That's the way it is,* it was straight sailing to her bed, where she tunes in the hourly while I'm about to give her the hard news, and says, I want to wear the mustache. I go, no. She goes, *That's the way it is.* So I light a cig, say, *Good night n' good luck.* Zhe zcreamz, jumpz my bonez, n' *that'z the way it waz.*

☺

24.   Nobody's Perfect

Diary. Rain on the roof and into the tall surrounding trees. Felt vital yesterday walking in the city with Christo, a delightful, cheery boy. Absorbs everything like a poet. Maybe it's the result of many walks through Englewood with Scuffles, our dog. I'd stop, take time to see, to smell, to hear and touch life around us. I'd put his small hand on the wide trunk of our silver maple, and say, feel its rough texture. Not like ivory piano keys, hey, Christo? *Look at that, Daddy bear, the flower, and the funny bird talking.* Yes. I'm that odd bird. Ayn takes him to Flat Rock Nature Center and points out things. *Mommy's mother earth; daddy's father sky.* Ayn gets him skiing. I get him playing piano. Each of us in our way shows the other the music of life.

☺

25.   The Chink and Cholly Show

Scene 1, Studio E

Tech. You read Coonan's new book? A copy's floatin' around. She's got her nose in her navel.

Dilido. I'd like to have my nose in that navel.

Tech. You and da boyz of Pointe du Hoc. She says Cholly's sweet.

366

Dilido. Sweet like a pit bull.

Tech. She didn't mention Reed.

Dilido. Selective memory.

Tech. I stopped at page 38. After that she's in DC. If she says this place was a fun house, how can I trust what she says about speech-writin' for Reagan? You have to mention Reed to get the history right.

Dilido. Yeah. Great pipes. One of the best anchor-writers.

Tech. Wait. She does, indirectly. She took an audition and was told her voice wasn't *ballsy*. She says, most ballsy-voiced men are short and have large heads. That's Reed.

Dilido. Which head was she referring to?

Tech. They get that way, she says, from listening to their own voice roll around in their head. Who can blame her? She was young and that old batam cock's been married several times. He waltzes in at 5a, smokes, shmoozes, gets coffee, pinches butts. It's like her time here was an elegiac experience.

Dilido. Wonderful! (*clapping han*ds)

Tech. Is that possible? The tech who Chinked and Chollyed before me said one's a prick, the other's a super prick. I go, "Which is which?" He goes, "Take your pick."

Dilido. Beautiful!

Tech. I'll tell you what's elegiac. A film clip of the Chink gettin' booted in the ass. I'd make a loop and play it all day. That's elegiac.

Dilido. Beautiful! I'm comin' in my pants. Who's techin' after you?

Tech. Probably bust seniority with that new kid. I heard them yell, get in here! and he goes, I'm runnin' as fast as I can.

Dilido. No place else will you see a bigger conglomeration of suck-up and fuck-your-buddy assholes.

Tech. Well, she's not burning her bridges.

Dilido. She'll burn yours first.

Tech. Maybe I should be nice, too.

Dilido. Nice's boring. I love it when you hate. More venom. Com'on. Tell me about the bitches, George. Love you tell me 'bout the bitches.

Tech. To put it politely-

Dilido. Don't.

Tech. Our esteemed female colleagues, the Miz-fits: Ms. Carriages, Ms. Anthropes, and Ms. Sojany, i.e., *The Cunt Collective!* Well, the clit parade started arriving around 1972, headed by Gestapo Frau Richter!

Dilido. Beautiful! *The* Frau. I'm pissin' my pants.

Tech. You vill piss your pants, undt love it. I luf it you piss in my pants. Put up ziss tape. Up where, Frau Richter? Up your ass, dumkoff! Ya-vul, Frau Ritcher. Then comes the A-1 ball breaker. The alabaster anchorette; started in tape-ops chasing ambulances on the phone. Shoved her ass in on the coattails of Equal Rights doing female features. Ask Jalanzo. *The* cunt's a fuckin' pain inna the fuckin' ass from the fuckin' word go. Her repulsiveness is exceeded only by the vacuity of her show's cunt-tent.

Dilido. Ooh. Vacuity? Brilliant!

Tech. Jalanzo held *the* door for her, and she says, *You're usurping my rights of independent choice. Don't you feel put upon to open doors for a woman capable of doing it herself?* He says, "I'm fuckin polite and the cunt's bustin' balls. I do it for everybody." When she was on at night, if a cut came in a second late, she'd copy the show, give it to management, and blame us. During cutbacks she was nervous, chatting like we were pals. She goes, *After Conan left, Marlene took over in Reed's bed. When you come in at 3ayem and go home at 11 you take what you can get.*

Dilido. She married? Any children?

Tech. No. Says they'd detract from her career. Babies should come from breeder farms.

Dilido. Beautiful! Like in Plato.

Tech. She says, my husband works days, I work nights, and the bed's never made. Coonan was different. Blue eyes, willowy legs-

Dilido. Stop. I'm getting' hard. How'd she get to Washington?

Tech. Buckley, Irish. She can write. Once I gave her a lift up the West Side-

Dilido. I'd like to give her one up her backside.

Tech. She says another tech gave her a ride and then came on. He was nervy. I only agreed to let him drive me home.

Dilido. He was lookin' to drive somethin' else home. She was chummin' the waters for you, pal. Hell, they just write news. You write plays. If you had a name, they'd jump your bones.

Tech. They all want a pinch from Reed. Some got jealous, like Aldo Ray in *Pat and Mike*. *Why don't he pinch me. Don't I count? I'm somebody.* Miss Equal Rights bought a male dog and had it fixed.

Dilido. Figures. Mics make her nervous. Phallic symbols.

Tech. When puppeteer Henson died the Third Reich bitch had his last interview. The women fought over first dibs. *It's my tape! It's C.B.S's!* If we all won the lotto the joint'd be a desert.

Dilido. Except the newsoom. They'd make a sharper turn left.

Skoshi. (*kicking door open*) Roll on radio, TV, and the bird.

Tech. The herd, the turd, and the absurd.

Dilido. Ciao. I'm outta here. (*exits*)

Skoshi. The white line, the red line, the clothes line. Let 'em eat tape! Love it! (*Ring!*) Hello.

Nurse. (*in BG*) Pressure pills are for life.

Skoshi. No tape?! The man loves tape. Actuary! Vox pop!

Nurse. You need a major change.

Skoshi. Moaners and groaners, screamers and weepers.

Nurse. In lifestyle and attitude.

Skoshi. Get on the horn, re-act, people's fears, irate citizens! *(hangs up; dials)* This is C.B.S, operator, press emergency. I need a clean line. *(dials; hangs up. Ring!)* Hi. Milk, eggs and bread. OK, honey. *(hangs up; dials)* Pickup, sucker. *(slams phone down; exits, bumps into SING's entering.)*

Sing. 'Scuse me. Any actuali-tay, vox poop? *(Tech nods no)* Commercials, bro. One sixty, first position; one thirty in the second. Run 'em down later. I've got to set up NR next door. I might be transferring to TV.

Tech. As what, a prop? *(rolls up sleeve; Nurse checks his pressure.)*

Sing. Prop this, paisano. Mr. Aw-dee-o. When I got the call somethin' weird happened, like I'd been reprieved from death row. All I need's the old man's stamp. He told me he'd give it. But that was a month ago.

Tech. Why should he change his mind?

Sing. You're asking why a schizo, self-centered, manic-depressive should change his mind? I deal with him like I do the women around here.

Nurse. You have some misconceptions.

Sing. I throw 'em raw meat and if they go for it I split. *(exits)*

Nurse. To determine high blood pressure, we measure the pressure of the blood on the artery walls when the heart muscle is pumping and when it's relaxed. The top number, or systole, is the actual pumping measurement. The bottom number, or diastole is pressure against the blood vessel walls when the heart is relaxed. For adults under 50 an acceptable level is 130 apostalic over 80 bialy-stolic. While your diastolic at the moment is lower than your last reading, it's still too high. So, you're a technician? Television?

Tech. Radio

Nurse. Local?

Tech. Network.

Nurse. What exactly do you do?

Tech. Put on news shows.

Nurse. Is there lots of pressure? You like your work?

Tech. Sometimes. *(aside) I hate it with a passion! My balls're in hock, I'm mortgaged up the ass, trapped with anal retentive news junky electronic assholes, and she wants to know if I like it.*

Nurse. Would you care to participate in a job satisfaction survey?

Tech. That's an oxymoron. Who's it for, the company? *(mimes jerking off)*

Nurse. No. Someone is doing a doctorate on the working place. Think about it. Are the cutbacks affecting technicians?

Tech. No. Mostly news and management. *Somebody should turn up the thermostat in the board room and toss in oven cleaner. Then hit the producer's unit with De-Con bombs and roach motels. Now some asshole with diaper rash is asking about JOB SATISFACTION?* I'll look it over.

Nurse. *(hands him survey)* Everything'll be confidential. Don't sign it, just indicate your department. No rush. Have you talked to your doctor?

Tech. He gave me two weeks to lower my pressure, or it's pills. I've cut out salt, been dieting, and walking more. I lost weight. It's my clothes. I'm down, but I leveled off. A bad weekend. Stress and spaghetti. Frankly, I do my best dieting between meals.

Nurse. You're at a critical crossroad. Don't take it lightly. You need a proper regimen: diet, exercise, and right thinking.

Tech. I've been taking garlic pills.

Nurse. We can't say it works for everyone. High blood pressure is an individual problem, a 90% mystery. Try the garlic. First priority should always be non-pharmacological intervention. Do people bother you? (*HE shrugs*) Are you sensitive? (*HE shrugs.*) Would you say hypersensitive? (*HE nods, yes*) Do you dwell on things? Are you self-critical? (*HE nods, yes*) well, I'm not the final authority, but a man in your situation can't afford dwelling and brooding and giving into hypersensitivity. You've got to exert control through self-awareness. You know when things crop up. It starts with an uneasy sensation, graduating to a warmth flush feeling of being woolly-headed. At the first inkling, step back in yourself, take a deep breath, and relax. Breathe in the air; inhaling the good, exhaling the bad. In with the good, out with the bad. Always loose, always relaxed. And don't fight the doctor's recommendations. He knows best. Blood pressure is a subtle killer. It can't be treated like a common cold. Also, changes occur, as one gets older. Small muscular blood vessels at the end of arteries appear to contract more in some people than in others. It could be psychological, physiological, combination of both, or the by-product of an unconscious human process, the primordial daemon, the lingua franca of instinctual processes, striving for identity, a need to belong, and denial of intuitive self. Then, veins constrict, plaque builds up inside the veins from bad diet and gook under the gums from not brushing and flossing. It gets into blood like bilge and builds up on the walls of arteries. The heart struggles to pump blood through the system, bah-bump, bah-bump. Combine that with bagels n' cream cheese, job pressure, family life, bacon burgers and trans fats, social responsibilities, hash browns, buttered free radicals, and you're a walking time bomb. (*Nurse fades away as*)

Ayn. (*dances in*) Fifty million dollars! Imagine if we won fifty million dollars. I'd probably die of a heart attack before I could spend it. We could buy a brownstone in Manhattan, an apartment in Trastevere, weekends in Venice with violins everywhere. (*pulls him to her*) When I die bury me in a gondola in Venice, the gondolier singing as we go, the echo of his voice guiding my soul as it floats under the bridges, turning corners. Oo-way! Slide me over the side wrapped in manicotti, a gnocchi in each eye, ziti for leg warmers, a basil leaf in my mouth-

Together. Oo-way!

Ayn. I'm off to Dance Therapy. Smirk, but it's making me a better wife, mother, and companion. It's cheaper than pressure pills. Remember, when you flush keep the toilet seat down. Water churning in the bowl releases germ particulates that rise up and settle everywhere even under your fingernails. You can get sick picking your nose.

Tech. Let's wear face masks and talk in sign language. How'd you pay for Dance Therapy?

Ayn. The checking account. I'll make it up.

Tech. How? You quit you're job.

Ayn. I'll find a way. The money will appear.

Tech. Tell that to your dance therapist guru. Money? Don't worry. It'll appear. You don't, cause she'd disappear. I'm bustin' ass on a shit job, and you quit yours, and take dance lessons. Maybe I'll quit, too. Screw the mortgage and medical bills. The money'll appear. We'll dance into the golden sunset. What do you do in class? Float and touch? Touch what? The neurotic sex muscles? Touch mine and I'll touch yours.

Ayn. I'm not listening.

Tech. I'm going with you. I'll dance naked with vine leaves in my hair.

Ayn. No. You're intentionally disruptive.

Tech. I want to go through that disruptive me, get to the buried me, the me I quit on. I wanna know my Bohemian middle-aged wife.

Ayn. I resent that. What I do in that group is important to my growth as a human being, a wife, and a mother. Laugh. That's your answer to everything. Well, keep up your cynicism, go on living in the suburbs of your real self, stewing in your own juices, your job, this crap house. Your American dream. You weren't happy in the city, too many phonies, and you're not happy out here, too many lawnmowers. When you come home I don't even want to see you, let alone touch you. You've always got a face on. Never a kind word for anyone or anything.

Tech. What're you talking about?

Ayn. My life with you in this house. It's stifling. We don't go out, or read the Sunday paper. When you talk it's always, "people are deceitful, and everybody's a self-aggrandizing asshole."

Tech. I never said "everybody".

Ayn. Then let's talk about somebody who isn't.

Tech. I don't know any.

Ayn. Did it ever occur to you that to someone you're an asshole?

Skoshi. (*on phone*) Good morning this is Radio-bemba in New York. I produce *The Chuckler Files*. Not piles, *Files*. We saw a wire release on your story. You don't have a story? Is this Professor Putts? Oh. Sorry. (*hangs up*) Doo de do-do, dum dee dum dum.

Ayn. How you do it, deal with these people, is a feather in your cap. At Cholly's cookout, they all had saccharine voices like they swallowed a zucchini. Do they talk like that at home? *Good morning. This... is... your husband reporting for breakfast. Give me eggs, toast n' but-ter, and, this just in, coffee with milk. Stay tuned. I'll be back in a minute.*

Tech. That's blasphemy. They're the watchdogs of society.

Ayn. You mean, movie stars delivering dime store news.

Skoshi. (*re-dials*) Com'on, sucker. Doo-do dee dum.

Ayn. I hope you're not holding your job for us, and the house. *No job is worth getting sick over.* That's why I left mine. We don't have to live in the suburbs, a manicured cemetery with invisible neighbors. Who are they? The

Hedge-cutters, the Lawnmowers, the Blowers and Weedwackers. We were alive in the city. Remember the Alternative Museum? Let's go back to the city and establish priorities before it's too late. For me it's not a house. It's finding out who lives in this body, who laughs and cries, who yearns to dance. It's got nothing to do with my feelings for you. The two are mutually inclusive. But they don't include the life of a dull minded house frau shackled to a feather duster and a sink of dirty dishes. Let's take the joy, the good before it's too late.

Tech. Should we spend our lives picking our navels?

Ayn. Anything's better than life dictated by Corporate America. I've got to go. Frankly, our house is depressing and I hate it. But I hate myself more for leaving the city. I hate our house, and what you've become.

Skoshi. Good morning, Professor Putts?

Ayn. You're like a stranger to me-

Skoshi. Sorry to disturb you at this ungodly hour.

Ayn. Who comes and goes and smells like a bear.

Skoshi. I produce for C.B.S. Your story ran this morning, Sir. On all the news wires. We'd like to interview you. We're heard all over the country. It would be an opportunity for you to get your story heard. (*to Tech*) Roll. We got the sucker. Yes. Coast to coast. (*on intercom*) He's on the line.

Tech. Let's check quality.

Skoshi. It's clean on the phone. Sir, would you like to take a minute to compose your thoughts before we start? You're sure? We go to air soon, so keep your answers brief and to the point. (*CHOLLY enters, sits*) Give 'im the red light.

Cholly. Morning Professor Putts. (*silence*) Good morning to you, sir.

Ayn. You eat too much because you're unhappy.

Cholly. (*Tech mimes put on headphones*) Can you hear me, sir?

Ayn. At first I felt guilty-

Skoshi. You patched in right?

Tech. Yeah. Are you?

Ayn. I thought maybe I lacked womanly qualities.

Cholly. You there, Doctor?

Ayn. That whole juvenile myth of multiple orgasms with fireworks, but it was you, your martyr's attitude.

Professor. (*fading in and out*) Hello...I... very lo-low.

Ayn. Two cars, a big house, the American dream, a mindless wife in the kitchen, who comes running to greet you after a long day; yours, not mine. Take off your shoes, honey. I'll massage your tired feet. How was work, darling? Guess what? I made cutlets like your mother makes. My needs, my wants, my aspirations, forget them like a good self-effacing house frau. Well, to borrow from your vernacular: Screw that noise.

Skoshi. (*leaning back*) I hear him on my phone. What's wrong?

Ayn. An opinionless frau, barefoot, pregnant without temperament, safe, and secure in big daddy's cucina with lollypops on my face.

Cholly. Christ! When are we going to get these things right the first time?

Skoshi. (*into phone*) One second, Professor.

Cholly. If we've done it once we've done it a million times. (*whirls angrily wraps headset cord around neck and chokes. As tech extricates him, one side slips, hits Cholly's eye.*) Ouch! Better get out of here. Damn! (*tosses headset*) All I need's to go on TV with a black eye. I still have to write this monster. Has that occurred to you? Have we got the man, or not?

Tech. Tell the man count backwards.

Skoshi. He's clear on the phone. Call another tech.

Tech. (*takes phone, speaks into it*) I didn't marry a teacher. I married a dancer. Gimme a level, professor. Anything.

Ayn. No one is one thing. You're other things besides a technician, some of which are more important.

Tech. Some? All! The mind can lose elasticity, like muscles on a dancer.

Ayn. More rationalization. I'll never be Martha Graham, or dance in the White House, but I can still put dance in my life.

Professor. (*fading in*) -Umpty D-d-d-umpty sat on a w-wall-

Ayn. We're Nomads. Nothing belongs to us but ourselves. We don't own our house. It's on hold for somebody else. My mother never knew how important dancing was to me. Maybe I never knew. I got side-tracked. It happens, but you don't give up. It's time to nurture that inner voice even if it means being a child again. Right now my voice says dance, dance.

Cholly. Can you hear me, sir?

Professor. You're f-f-far away.

Cholly. So are you, in Minnesota.

Professor. I am? I thought I was in T-T-T-Texas.

Cholly. So you are. Land of the big horn. You prefer Doctor or Professor?

Professor. P-P-P-Peter will do f-f-fine.

(*the stutter gets Cholly nervous; he picks it up subconsciously*)

Cholly. First, let me start, Professor P-Putts, by asking-

Professor. That's Pewts, spelled P-P-Putts, but pronounced P-P-Pewts. (*Cholly points to his mouth, mimes NG*) If I m-might. I'd like t-to say that I've l-l-l-long b-been an admirer of ya-ya-yours.

Skoshi. (*phone: Ring!*) Skoshi here. Call us when you know. (*hangs up*)

Cholly. (*flashing thumb down*) Sir, I'm do on TV in minutes. My producer will arrange another convenient time. (*comes into control room*)

Skoshi. (*Into phone*) Professor, I'll get back. He clutched under pressure.

Cholly. Tell him I'm on assignment. The show's three minutes editorial. He takes two to say his name. What's working?

Skoshi. A no-nuke sit-in; *Hitler Diaries;* a vet in an iron lung- not bad if you like heavy breathing and thumping in the BG from a respirator.

Cholly. The Diaries could be fraudulent. Who's that on TV?

Skoshi. We're not endorsing them. That's Dr. Cosmo Lovepants. He's not on the run down sheet.

Cholly. Rack it back. Let's hear a little.

Tech. The tape ran out when you were talking to the professor.

Cholly. Good, Christ! (*kick chair*) One machine stops, you start another. What could be simpler? It's not higher mathematics!

Skoshi. You're supposed to roll dead pot on TV always.

Cholly. Forget it. Get him before he leaves. Meanwhile, I'll work up a thumbsucker. Christ! Look at the time. We're in deep shit. I don't have a word written. You realize that? (*exits*)

Skoshi. You're supposed to keep a roll on TV. Cholly wants something, I do it. When I want something, you do it. When you want something, we talk about it.

Cholly. (looks in) For crissake. Get the man. Before he gets away. (*Chink runs out*) He can be damn difficult at times.

Tech. (*to Ayn*) He's a banana; yellow outside white inside. The last time he ate Chinese food was at his mother's tit.

Ayn. Forget him. Remember our wedding? We walked from the church along Central Park South, you blew kisses at people in the sidewalk café of St. Moritz and you shouted- Drinks on me! Everybody laughed and applauded. (*together*) Cent'anni! (*THEY dance*)

Scene 2   *(Same as 1)*

(Cameo in limbo. Cholly rings a church bell; All knee! Cholly and Skoshi as priest and altar boy prepare communion. Skoshi hands him audio tape which he cuts, drops into a coffee cup, blesses, and then administering communion. Skoshi kneels, opens his mouth wide and swallows joyfully. They give communion to mics, Ayn, and Tech who turn and spit it out. YCH! Blackout.)

Scene 3   *(Same as 1)*

Doctor. Bet your children love it.

Cholly. Indeed. They could ride that pony all day. But I'm the one who cleans up. We've got a domestic who's been taking off on Saturdays. So there I am in the garage turned into a corral in my brand new wingtips, shoveling horseshit on my day off. It's unfair.

Tech. You shovel enough around here all week.

Doctor. Absolutely dee-vine!

Cholly. It's odd, but I have the feeling we've always known each other.

Doctor. We can't meet someone without knowing them.

Cholly. We rolling? Good. We'll chat and then I'll cut you up-

Doctor. Oh, heavens!

Cholly. In sound bites and weave a script around them.

Doctor. What's that? *(Tech motions Doctor to get on mic.)* Move away? Closer? How do I sound? My voice okay? How's my breathing and my articulation? Am I nasal? Wonderful! Your technician is sensitive, slightly on the physical side, which marks temperament- I must tell you I've been an admirer of yours for many years. To poeticize news as you do in verse and doggerel, reducing it all to the lowest denominator for the highest consumption, is a wonder. Yesterday, you juxtaposed "cranium" with "uranium" and said "We cannot abide hexafloride-" God knows what you might've done at the Kennedy murder

379

the "grassy knoll." Does it pay well? (*Cholly nods*) It must be extremely gratifying work?

Cholly. Which I'm likely to be doing for years to come. I've got nine children. Three in college.

Doctor. Busy man, night and day. Stopping at nine, or is your wife too numb to talk about it?

Cholly. She loves a family.

Doctor. Family? You've got a baseball team.

Cholly. I'll be working years before the last one finishes school.

Doctor. People should never retire. Work to the end. When one of my appointments cancel, I go insane. I hate to be idle. Right away I find something to do. I write, call a friend. Work is everything.

Cholly. We'd better start. I can fumfah, but your answers should be smooth. Feel free to restart an idea if you word it improperly. There must be lots how-to books on the shelves. Why's yours special?

Doctor. I offer ways to change. Change is scary. People lock into habits for comfort. But change can be joyful and positive.

Cholly. Do people need change to succeed?

Doctor. On buses and subways, yes. First, break a dollar then work up to fives and tens. Faccia una scherzo. The world's full of unhappiness. People spend too much time locked in negative thinking, which makes for depression, and limits success. If you say, I can't, you won't. Negative self-criticism sets the table for failure. (*looks at tech*) So get straight.

Cholly. How?

Doctor. If double jointed, unwind clockwise facing north. Kiss yourself, your hands, elbows. If you can kiss your elbow, change doesn't matter. Your neck's broken. Move your right foot in a clockwise circle and draw a number 6 with your right hand. You can't do it. See? Faccia un scherzo. People are full of self-hate and self-destruction. The problem is in their attitude toward their bodies. If you doubt your body, you doubt the world. Hate is a manifestation of inner conflict toward the self. When you do work you hate, if at that moment you can be kind to yourself, then change is possible. Change, Le Boyer said, does not occur suddenly, but in a tub of warm water with supportive parents cuddling, caressing you.

Cholly. But you've-

Doctor. Peer pressure and societal admonitions, create inhibitions, a twisted self. People lose the keys to themselves. If we can be our own parent, our own Mr. Rogers. (*sings*) It's a wondrous day in the neighborhood. A wonderful day if I only could, and you can, will you be mine. Accentuate the positive. Don't mess with in-between. Most people appear positive; at parties they joke, laugh and sing amiably; slap each other on the back, but in truth things are contrary. Often people come to me in tears confessing worthlessness, and suicidal tendencies. But in public they're jovial, ebullient good-timers, and life's terrific. It's a lie! There's too much hate, self-defeatism, and lies in the world. I say, no more lies! Finita la cucchiaio!

Cholly. It's unfair to ask this, but can you sum up your book briefly?

Doctor. Nineteen dollars soft back, 25 hard back. You can get a hernia lifting it. Faccia un scherzo. There's a formula to success. It's being positive. Nothing's either right or wrong, but thinking makes it so. For many people failure is their lover, but failure should be their guru. They count failures; bask in them over cocktails and dinner. Start counting wins like each breath. Breathing's a win. Think of all the dead people who can't breath. People have notions of what they want, but are afraid to go for it; afraid they won't Make It, and give up. Successful people fail 75% of the time. Their secret? They don't count the failures. Failures do nothing, so one failure c'est tout. It wipes them out. Ya can't hit a homah, homer, unless ya swing da bat.

Cholly. The year DiMaggio hit the most homeruns, he struck out the most. Babe Ruth, too. All great home run hitters were strike out artists.

Doctor. They're not compromised. They swing for the bleachers with great will power, but will alone is not enough. It must have desire to make it so. At my retreats I have a pitching machine that throws 200 miles per hour. My patients strike out, but with grace and dignity, and get A for effort. One place you don't fail is the cemetery. There is no good and evil. It's all evil, but will and desire make evil less evil.

Cholly. Do successful people have a plan?

Doctor. The majority of people I have spoken with- I've met thousands, believe me, read countless depositions- What was the question? Oh, yes. Work is equated with jail, putting in time until they get sprung, sliding along with minimum effort. The trick is to will things, want them, desire them. Think it, picture it, and you'll get it. Successful people work with the passion of jealous lovers. If they're do in at 9, they show up at 6. To them work is sex with a beautiful partner. Wouldn't you show up early?

Cholly. I suppose-

Doctor. Live in the country close to nature. It helps the subconscious tap the universal mind that embraces all things. Enter the great silence. Edison said, ideas come from space. Thought and its radiations are an electrical aura connecting the whole pattern of the universe. Thoughts have creative force in the exact ratio of their consistency, intensity and power, but it takes a dig through the rubble of self-destruction, denial, and years of embracing failure to get plugged in. The eyes are poor reflectors of reality. Parental admonitions, peer groups, social pressures condition how we see with those eyes, and that vision often has nothing to do with our inner truth. We need to be reborn to trust our bodies, to see with our ears, and listen with our eyes. When we make our bodies second-class citizens through neglect and feelings of inferiority, we limit our potential for success. In every stiff muscle lies a story of forgotten hope. So talk to your body. Say hi to your biceps, kiss your pectorals, and pat your behind. Hello, you cheeky fellows. Introduce them to each other. Right cheek meet left cheek. Lips, say hello to toes. Have a kinesthetic soiree of self-adulation, kissing and touching this and that. This way, one evolves higher feel-good standards. I call it cranio-sacro-illiac unwinding of the bodygenesis through sexercises. I hate the word exercise. So debilitating. In the toilet, look at your feces. Blow your bowels a kiss. Bye, bye, my darlings, flush, and new joys will appear.

Cholly. Why do successful people go to you?

Doctor. I don't make house calls. Successful people are driven. I have a chauffeur myself. With success comes great insecurity, fear of failure; that compulsive, psychopathic- What was the question? Oh. People're like batteries and need recharging. Success often neglects the human side. I help people become epicureans of living, savoring every moment. Consequently, home life becomes richer, and sex improves.

Cholly. Well, that's it. I'm do in TV. Feel free to come back any time.

Doctor. Tomorrow? Friday's good. (*Chink shows him out*)

Cholly. (*in control room*) God, look at the time. We're in deep shit. Play the tape. We'll take a hunk with my questions.

Doctor. (*poking head in*) Saturday's good. I'll cancel sexercises. (*Skoshi shuts door in his face*)

Cholly. We're in deep shit. Play the tape.

Tech. You want "horseshit on your wingtips"?

Cholly. Back up. Back, go back. Too far. Forward. Wo. Play it.

Doctor. My voice. How delicious!

Skoshi. Take the question?

Doctor. Play it again.

Cholly. Go back 10 seconds. Play it down. Cut there. My question through his answer. Jesus, we're in deep shit! Out cue: "change is easy". You don't seem to appreciate time is critical here. In cue from the question. "There must be an ungodly..."

Tech. You want the "Well"?

Doctor. Would you autograph my book?

Cholly. Jesus! Just cut the thing.

Doctor. I'll sign it for you.

Cholly. Take the "Well". Let the man breathe. Don't you think?

Doctor. Just touch the book. Thank you. Goodbye. (*goes*)

Skoshi. You're the boss. Gimme the "Well". Runs a minute. Another chunk and we're home free. I've got notes. It'll save time-

(*NURSE enters, sprays disinfectant; grabs Tech's crotch, reads pressure.*)

Nurse. Your systolic's absolutely bucolic! (*sprays Cholly's ass*)

Cholly. (*looking up*) Who's that on TV? Turn him up.

Skoshi. It's dated.

Cholly. We rolling? The doctor's fluff. We can always go to him. Com'on. Spit out the question. We don't have all day. God, he's long-winded. We want the Secretary, you idiot! Let him talk!

Skoshi. I think she's-

Cholly. Shh. Let me hear him. Shit. He stepped on the answer. Damn! (*kicks chair*) He's doing it again. Jesus, Joseph and- how the hell can I use that? A four-part question. Great! Brevity's the soul of wit!

Skoshi. He's trying to advance the story.

Cholly. It was never established.

Doctor. (*looking in*) How do I get out of the building?

Skoshi. Take a left, then a right; at the elevators turn left, but keep right. You'll see an emergency exit. Don't enter. It's a sub-level stairwell. Turn right, left, right again, and you'll be in the lobby. Goodbye. (*close door*)

Cholly. Thumbs down. He posits questions with answers. All the man can say is, 'yes' or 'no'. Some reporters are afraid to ask dumb questions, afraid someone'll say they don't know the story. A lot of good reporters do their homework, read up, check sources, Reuters, AP, and then make the cardinal error, break the first rule of journalism-

Skoshi. Which is?

Cholly. Come here.

Skoshi. I am here.

Cholly. So you are. When you lead into a story- (*Skoshi repeats key words.*) All the homework goes out the window, if that knowledge interferes. The key to reporting is arithmetical. Lozenge, please. Thank you. When I was a child on my grandfather's farm in the Grand Titons of Baltimore- I'll never forget what's-his-face that rainy night. In other words, to lead into an interview, to presume. I was maybe four at the time. Tell the fucking story! Those best qualified to tell a story- I am absolutely convinced. Come closer. The one best qualified is someone who...knows the story but plays dumb. A guy's sitting on a flagpole. You know it, he knows it, but the audience doesn't. He's been up there six days. You don't say, "Sir, you've been sitting on the flagpole for six days protesting short pants in public." Right? Wrong! You must be tired and hungry. Right? Wrong! Never summarize. We want the target's words. Reporters who ask long questions are ego tripping. Afraid of looking dumb, they ask questions that say, look what I know. A dumb question's not dumb if elicits honest react. That's the meaning of actuality- Actual! Real! There's 20 feet of snow in Idaho. A stringer's on the line. Do we give him a weather report? NG. How high's the snow? Over the roof, still falling. The only way out's up the chimney! Boom! Out cue: Up the chimney.

Christ! Look at the time. We're in deep shit. Play the tape.

Tech. I erased it.

Cholly and Skoshi. What? *(throw pencils down)*

Tech. If you hadn't rushed me-

Cholly. Rushed? That's your job, damnit! It's not higher mathematics. I'll go to air. News and commentary. My tech erased the show. Thank you. Goodbye. We're in deep shit.

Tech. Sometimes, moving quickly, mechanically, to do something you've done a million times. It's not like I did it on purpose...or did I?

Skoshi. Let's go with an evergreen.

Cholly. We used it and never replaced it.

Skoshi. What're we-

Cholly. Shh. I'm thinking.

Sing. *(entering)* Any tape?

Skoshi. Shh. Cholly's thinking.

Cholly. We're in deep shit! *(stomps out to studio; Skoshi follows)*

Tech. I have a thing about washing dishes lately.

Sing. Say again.

Tech. I scrub 'em to get rid of the dirt and grime and I feel good. I get my hands on dirty things and get 'em clean. Maybe when I erased the show, I was just doin' dirty dishes.

Cholly. Put up the doctor cut. Hello. The doctor tape. Thank you. Set up a roll. Where's my watch? Jesus, Joseph, and Mary. We're in deep shit.

Skoshi. Give him your watch.

Sing. I need it for the show.

Skoshi. No sweat, Cholly. Watch me.

Tech. Why? He's already in deep shit.

Sing. One cut? Commercials ready? Thirty seconds.

Cholly. My notes? Where are my notes?

Tech. Mic check, please?

Cholly. Now? What've you been doing all morning, besides erasing tape?

Sing. (*on TB*) Fifteen seconds.

Cholly. I just wish we could take care of all these problems once and for all, and do it so we could just do it, ya know.

Sing. Coming up in five. Standby. Ready... open mic.

Cholly. Good morning. This is-

Sing. (*on TB*) Hold it. My watch misfired. (*SKOSHI enters control room*)

Cholly. We're in deep shit.

Sing. You mean you are, Red Ryder.

Skoshi. Can we start? Anytime today would be fine.

Sing. Look. My watch is moving backwards.

Tech. Like this show.

Skoshi. Use your backup watch.

Sing. Cholly borrowed it and never returned it.

Skoshi. Let's do the sucker!

Sing. Ok. On the wall clock. (*on TB*) We're set.

Skoshi. Safety tape racked back?

Tech. Flagged.

Skoshi. No false starts when we whip this sucker around. You ready?

Sing. Your buddy's not ready. Wanna start without him?

Skoshi. (*on TB*) We're ready.

Sing. On my watch. Three, two- too late.

Cholly. What's the hold up?

Sing. You can't stick five minutes into-

Skoshi. Keep rolling. Let's do her for time. No commercials.

(*CHOLLY times script using the wall clock*)

Sing. May I finish a thought? I'd like to be given that courtesy. It would be something of a miracle if one of us *lackeys* were allowed to complete a thought. Maybe just once we might work ensemble-

Skoshi. On what? Let's get something straight. I'm the producer.

Sing. Sorry I-

Skoshi. May I finish my thought? As producer I have final say. If I say roll, we roll, even if there's doubt. I'm the producer. (*rolls two steel balls in his hand*) I assume full responsibility. Take the incident of the missing tapes. A classic example. I put out a total of thirty sound bites, thirty. No more, no less. Yeoman's service above and beyond the call of duty. Sure. One could quibble here and there over quality; a garbled word, an unintelligible phrase. But in a God-fearing court of inquiry, any sensible juror'd conclude that it was hairsplitting, that these sort of things are strictly matters of individual taste, and, mind you, more often than not, rooted in errors of a *technical* nature, having nothing to do with editorial judgment. My accusers say I wandered off in a "producer frenzy"; misplaced my reel of sound bites, thirty, mind you, thirty perfectly good bites. Yes, I went to the bathroom, but on company business. I did not "wander off" in a peak of "producer frenzy" as my accusers suggest, and "inadvertently" lose thirty sound bites. Absolutely not.

Sing. Sixty seconds to air.

Skoshi. It was a case of will, malicious, spiteful sabotage pure and simple. Naturally, as producer I assume full responsibility. But I contend that lassitude, sadistic pranks, personal vendettas have no place on the job. Work by definition is labor not a happy hunting ground.

Cholly. How long was I?

Sing. Didn't get a time.

Skoshi. So, without undo polemics, I was innocent, completely.

Cholly. Nobody ran a watch? You people sit around like bumps on a log.

Skoshi. It would never-

Cholly. All right, by God!

Skoshi. Never occur to me to-

Cholly. Two can play the game. Batten the hatches. We're going live!

(*Silence. THEY ALL look stunned. SKOSHI comes out of his delusion*)

Skoshi. Dive, dive, dive! We go live, live, live! Ha, ha, ha.

Sing. Standby. (*raising arm*) We're going live!

Cholly. Live you want, live you'll get. Heads up! If I goof it's accidental. If you goof it's because you don't know any better.

Sing. In ten. They get away with murder around here cause nobody challenges them. When the old man denied my transfer, saying a job freeze is on, I almost- Three, two, one, open mic.

Cholly. This is *The Chucklehead Show* and I'm Cholly Chucklehead on the Chuckler Radio Network. More in a minute.

Sing. Close mic. Hit commercial.   (*Cholly waves, "cut mic."*)

Skoshi. Kill his mic. (*Tech kills mic.*)

Cholly. (*on TB*) Wake up in there!

Skoshi. I don't hear the commercial.

Tech. It's on. Watch the needle.

Sing. Stay loose people.   (*From here out show done in BG.*)

Tech. (*to Ayn*) They break your spirit here like in Gunga Din. Turn you into good soldiers so you march along, boom, boom! Like Freeman, the director, a real southern gentleman. Never raised his voice. Took all the crap for 35 years. The year he was to retire and go back, they found him alone, dead on the floor, the TV going. There must've been a time when he wanted a career, but he gave it up and started coasting. Never had Christmas off in 35 years. He asked off the year he died and they said no.

Sing. Fifteen seconds.

Tech. Nobody asks about him. It's like he was never here. The same with family. Your father dies and a year later you don't even call his name.

Sing. Ready to open mic. (*cues Cholly*)

Skoshi. If you can't handle the board-

Tech. Oh, shut up!

Sing. Stay calm people.

Tech. Tell the asshole.

Skoshi. The door swings two ways.

Sing. Standby.

Cholly. (*on TB*) What's the time coming out?

Sing. Open mic.

Cholly. Of late, I've heard the proposition 'less is more'.

Sing. Gentlemen, we've got a live show.

Cholly. According to the less is more proponents, you achieve more by doing less. Sound backwards?

Sing. I can't concentrate with you actin' like a banshee-

Cholly. The presumption is that MORE is garbage and less is quality. The less you know, the more ignorant you are, but the more you know, the less you believe.

Skoshi. Directors're supposed to have two watches? Why don't you?

Tech. This is the pits.

Cholly. No one would say, ten lousy things're better than one good one.

Sing. Your buddy took it and lost it.

Skoshi. Replace it.

Sing. Tell him. He lost it.

Skoshi. I want a discrepancy report. Erased tape, slow mics.

Tech. You pain in the ass!

Skoshi. Yes. But you erased the tapes.

Tech. I'll erase you.

Cholly. Less is only more when less is obviously less.

Tech. That gorilla mask you wore Halloween was an improvement. You're ugly outside and inside.

(*SING signals Cholly for commercial with one finger touching palm.*)

Cholly. That brings us to the end. Back in a moment.

Sing. Hit commercial.

Skoshi. You're off the show now!

Sing. Hit it!

Skoshi. Get another tech.

(*Sing leaps across control board and hits button.Tech kills mic.*)

Sing. (*on TB*) No date. Short close. Standby. Ready mic. Open.

Cholly. I'm Cholly Chuckles.

Sing. Close mic, punch off. (*CHOLLY enters.*)

Cholly. Is it a buy?

Sing. I'm back timing. (*beat*) We're over by six.

Skoshi. We'll shave the commercials. Let's cut the sucker. Rack back.

Tech. I envy their resolve and tenacity. THIS JUST IN! YOU'RE ASSHOLES! (*each time all freeze; smile, say: Hello. Hi ya doin'? and resume working.*) Insults roll off them like water off a duck's back. They knife you and the next minute it's (*All: Hello. Hi ya doin'?*) like nothing happened. Hit 'em in the head with a baseball bat, they smile, (All: *Hello. Hi ya doin'?*) Pull their pants down in public n' it's, (All: *Hello. Hi ya doin'?*) Complain, and you're immature. If you're forthright, you dig your own grave. Know when they listen? THIS JUST IN! (*All freeze; look up*) KISS MY ASS! (All: *Hello. Hi ya doin'?; resume work*) They come in every day whistling, humming, glad to be trading on people's misfortunes; coroners of human suffering, gadfly ghouls hopping from one death to another. It's revolting. Be like the rest of us. Come to work disgusted, fed up, angry, miserable. Normal! Every year, new people show up, carbon copy HUMPS AND ASSHOLES! (All: *Hello. Hi ya doin'?*)

Sing. Five minutes for the turn around.

Tech. But I'm brittle, too civilized- (*Ring!*)

Sing. Eight minutes.

Skoshi. You said five.

Cholly. You have to take risks.

Nurse. (*dancing in with pencil and pad*) I'll debrief you if you'll de-bra me.

Cholly. Any cub reporter knows that.

Skoshi. Trust me. I'm your producer. Ha, ha, ha. (*Ring!*)

Sing. When TV called it was like a reprieve from death row.

Nurse. Arterioles contract more in some people.

Tech. First priority should always be non-pharmacological intervention.

Nurse. Look for the child in you. Lost in the recesses of your Scooby-do.

Tech. I'm not growing old gracefully.

Nurse. So take up ballet. (*Ring!*)

Skoshi. Back up.

Nurse. Your bialystolic is bucolic (*Ring!*)

Skoshi. Go forward. Back.

Cholly. Forward. I take risks.

Nurse. Your diastolic-systolic is absolutely apostolic. (*Ring!*)

Sing. In 20 years you get a watch, then a tray, and a silver goodbye bowl!

(*SING dances around with a bowl on his head.*)

Nurse. It's primordial, the lingua franca. Try non-pharmacological intervention. (*Ring!*)

Cholly. You clipped my word. Put it back. It's not brain surgery. I want my "Well". (*Ring!*) Gimme my well.

Skoshi. Let the man breathe.

Cholly. We've got a show to put out.

Tech. Then you do it. It's not brain surgery.

Cholly. Give me the razor.

Skoshi. Don't touch it, Cholly. Contract violation.

Cholly. Next thing I'll need a tech to hold my razor when I shave? I got a product to get out. To hell with unions. We're going live.

Skoshi. Dive, dive. We go live! (*Ring!*) Yes? Send copy. (*on TB*) There's a disaster in India. A net alert in two minutes. Copy on the way. (*in phone*) Talk to me. (*repeats what he hears on TB*) Hundreds dead in Bhopal!

Cholly. Volcanic, man-made? Who's on the scene?

Skoshi. A stringer. He can't get near the place. Where? India. Switch him in. Gimme details. Gas. Alpha naphthol, carbon oxide, phosgene and what? Methyhl iso-cyanate. Deadly pesticide explosion. Thousands dead.

Cholly. Confirmed?

Skoshi. No. Muslims.

Cholly. Let's not get egg on our face.

Skoshi. (*Ring!*) That's him. Live two-way. Ten seconds to air.

Cholly. Gimme a name.

Tech. What line? Eleven, twelve?

Skoshi. Union Carbide, chemicals.

Sing. Flash on my cue. In five. (*Board lights on*) Hit it (*Tech hits pre-recorded Net Alert cartridge.*)

Devious Septum. We interrupt this broadcast with the following news bulletin, bulletin, bulletin.

Sing. Open mic. (*Cues Cholly*)

Cholly. There's been a tragedy, hundreds, maybe thousands, are dead in an explosion at a Union Carbide chemical plant. For details we go to our Stringah. (Tech opens line 11.)

Phone Voice. What tragedy?

Cholly. You tell us. You're in Bhopal.

Phone Voice. No. I'm in the boiler room. Sub level 9. How about Friday? Friday's good for me. Is it good for you? Kiss your body, hands, knees, toes. There's a crypt down here, says, "G'Night and G'Luck".

(The real story: There was a race between chemical corporations to corner the pesticide market. In the rush, people got careless.

Black aphids, for example, were one of 850,000 insects eating our food supply. UC developed Sevin, the *promise of a bright future with pesticides.* Phosgene gas plus monomethylamine produces methyl isocyanate. MI plus alpha naphthol produces Sevin, a deadly insecticide. MIC is the deadliest compound ever conceived. Tests on rats prodcuced results too terrifying to publish. MCI vapors alone kill immediately. Inhaled, it destroys the respiratory system; causes blindness. In 1976 at UC there were warnings of unheeded leakage poisoning water, killing cows. Water tests in the south and southeast revealed high levels of mercury, chromium, copper, nickel, and lead. Well water had traces of chloroform, carbon tetrachloride, and benzene. Allegedly, UC did not stop the pollution. 1976: UC moved from New York to Danbury, Connecticut into an 800 million dollars plant. 1978: about to launch their factory. Trained abot 20 Indians in a West Virgina facility. They had a 400-page book on safety procedure which in the end went unheaded. Leaks in West Virginia didn't get attended; waste product emptied into the ground. They had check seals of circuits. A hundred miles of pipes, a thousand valves, joints, pumps, reactor tanks, and instruments. It was a metal leviathon. Safety checks? Flush pipework with nitrogen. Soapy coating applied to joints, pressure gauges, sluices, and valves. Bubbles indicate a leak. Phosgene and monomethylamine gases were heated and combined to produce MCI. They built a plant in India, put a thousand Indians to work, most with different origins, castes, religions, and languages. Gave them a condensed 40-page manual of use instructions. MCI was to be kept in storage tanks at zero degrees Celsius. Vishva arma, god of work. Workers mostly from surrounding *bustees*, poor districts of shacks by railroad tracks. There was an early warning of one death. 1982: there was a third accident. UC attributed it to worker negligence. Many workers didn't know what they were making. Some called it "medicine for sick plants". There is possibility of collusion between UC and local authorities. A reporter got into UC Bhopal plant and smelled phosgene, which smells like cut grass. Methyl isocyanate smells like boiled cabbage. Hydrocyanide acid smells like bitter almonds. MI and phosgene is two and a half times heavier than air, and tends to move along the ground in small clouds. Sixty breaches of operation and safety regulations found by inspectors. Mistake, an engineer had cleaned out a section of piping without blocking off the two ends of the pipe with discs designed to prevent the rinsing water from seeping into other parts of the installation. The demand for Sevin was not as great due to drought. Cutbacks followed, inferior parts used, maintenance delays resulting in a gaseous apocalypse, a cataclysmic exothermic reaction of methyl isocyonate, a whole tank full. Forensic pathologists found in bodies that blood had turned viscous, like jelly; lungs were ash colored; blue-red lesions with hearts, livers, and spleens tripled in size; clots in wind pipes; brains were covered with gelatinous, opalescent film. Broken down MIC released hydrocyanide acid, which instantly destroys the cells ability to transport oxygen, and that killed the majority of Bhopalis. There was an antidote, a common- place substance, sodium thiosulfate or hyposulfate, which was not given to the people. UC's reaction? They let its Indian subsidiary tackle all the blame. It was culpable homicide, causing death by negligence. Hydrocyanic acid blocks the action of the enzymes carrying oxygen from the blood to the brain, causing immediate death. It instantly destroys the cell's ability to transport oxygen. Eight thousand dead by reliable independent organization, but possibly between 16 and 30 thousand died. Two weeks after the incident, a jaundice epidemic broke out, striking thousands who had lost their immune system defences. People suffered neurological attacks, convulsions, paralysis, coma, and death; ghabrahat, or panic syndrome-uncontrollable anxiety; permanent nightmares- heightened vertigo and other fears like sensation of drowning, depression, impotence, anorexia, desolation, despair, and suicide. UC never revealed the exact composition of the toxic cloud. UC settled the matter with 475 million dollar compensation. Chairman Anderson announced to shareholders that the Bhopal accident only meant a loss of 43 cents a share. The people who died were the poorest of the poor. CEO Anderson retired to Vero Beach, Florida. In 1991, the Bhopal Court summoned Anderson to appear on charge of homicide in a criminal case, which was called the worst industrial disaster in history, but he did not respond. He left Vero Beach and his whereabouts are not publicly known. In 1999, Union Carbide was divided up between Rhone-Poulenc and the Dow Chemical Group. Estimated dead: 20,000; a hundred thousand suffer in the aftermath. Bhopal was India's Hiroshima.)

After the full story was known, the following post-it appeared:
"Who killed more Indians than Custer? Union Carbide."

26.   C.B.S Memorandum

To: Mr. Over-nighter   Date: July 22, 1979

   I received a number of complaints from people in the shop that when you are in Newsfeed you are taking tapes that need cleaning & distributing them to other studios without cleaning them. If this is the case, this is not accepted practice and not fair to the other technicians. Working afternoons & evenings I have first hand knowledge that many other techs, even though the workload is heavy, do their share of tape repair in the newsfeed studio & distribute reels to other studios cleaned and properly repaired. If the above complaints are valid, I would appreciate your cooperation by lending a hand with the tapes repair that has to be done. Also, if you would like to talk to me about any problems there may be in complying, give me a call when I'm on shift.   Thx *RB*

   I called him at home at midnight. Why should I call on my time

☺

27.   Newsfeed, Tape-Ops

Zeecraft. Don't you just love memos? I look at them whenever I can, just to see how they're saying what they are saying, why, and to whom. Look at this nonsense. New lows in generating news.

From: A To Z (Newsfeed editor/producer)

FYI. Friday 9/28/79 is the fifth anniversary of Betty Ford's mastectomy, if you want to try to do something with that. (You should be pretty full Friday, I would think, with the Pope, et al)

Zeecraft. What am I supposed to do call the lady, ask, "How are your tits doing, I mean, tit?" He's like a kid on that computer. Somebody said he wasn't serious. Looks serious to me. He was probably digging around, saw this, and thought it worth passing on.

Powel's tenure as news director was short. One day he got anxious and scooped the competition by prematurely releasing embargoed news. It must've been thrilling, until they bumped him upstairs to a dead end.

☺

28. *Radio Rookies*

Diary, 1980's. When the "other" network started, it introduced a young generation of nosies who brought with them a tight writing style, and lots of vigor, i.e., new jargon, rubber band fights, and dive-bombers made of news copy. Radio Radials. Sounds like a stutter? It was in the brain of whoever dreamt up this second, youth oriented Network. Like we needed the first one. It could've been a glitch in mental wave patterns like hitting a bump in the road and your head knocks against the car's roof. These baby faces were a new generation and they altered both the news and the newsroom complexion. They went on ten minutes to the hour in a two minute rock and roll news format. The old-timers looked on in silent abnegation and Burrow turned in his grave. It was a case of acne meets psoriasis. Tin Pan Alley at the Met. *If I were teaching Fraudcasting 101,* I told one perky face, *and you submitted 'Radio Radial' for a network title, I'd flunk you cold. You don't understand, uncle. It's not arbitrary. It comes from a contemporary pop lyric. That gives it historical weight.* He wasn't kidding. One day I actually heard the song...Young guns, enthusiastic pisspots, quick on the uptake, and cooler than the veterans who had been their heroes. The underlying truth, I sensed, was really a changing of the guard. Time was already knocking off the old timers. Suddenly I'm the old kid on the block- a jaded, back seat driver. *It ain't who you*

*know. It's who you blow. Nobody's all-wrong. Takes two
to tango.*

Still, I envied the Gerber kids, their youth and panache.
When nobody cared to reach out to help them in their
early growing pains, like *where's the air studio?* I'd point
them to the janitor's broom closet. That's for calling
me uncle! I surprised myself, however, and volunteered
to tech their dry runs so they could get oriented. One
of them turned out to be Charlie K. Our paths had
crossed at WTHE, Long Island when I was a DJ. Back
then he made me aware of numbers and dates on wire
copy, which connect to previous stories on the subject.
Years had gone by since we last talked. Seeing him in
a group tour that first week gave me such a sinking
feeling that I almost dived under the console. Teching
was an admission that I'd failed. He made it easy with a
big "hello" and said for all to hear, *he was a good jock,
funny, too.* I'm even funnier as a tech.

Around this time, I started getting more headaches,
less sleep, high blood pressure, and developed angina.
On a subconscious level, the Gerber kids made me feel
old. Calling me "Uncle" didn't help. One day I went over
the top. Why doesn't matter. It could've been the color
red, or the phone ringing. Writer Steve B, a cool Gerber
kid, calmly said, "Look at yourself, man. You're losin' it."
He was right.

When they heard I was published, and had written
for ABC/TV's Benson, they said I was *the only tech who
could split a studio faster than an infinitive.* Aside from
youth, what endeared them to me was the way they'd
switch days off, or relieve each other by phone. *I'm on
my way. Take off. Where're you? Hoboken.* Or, swing in
singing, *Lucy, I'm home!* Their take on the senior staff
tickled me, too. *How'd the phoner go? Bor-ring! Takes
forever to say nothin'. Give it to grandpa, but don't wake
anybody.* And, *Waddya want with the rest of the tape?
Nuke it!* They had élan, an ebullience and prescience,

which I envy even now because it only comes through the door once. *Lucy, I'm home! Yab-ah-daba-do!*

☺

29. *The Prince and the Piper*

Mal and Dulles were thinking journalists who delivered the morning news from the '60's to the '80's with Latin eloquence, anchor Dulles with two flashing fingers, producer-editor Mal with a rapier number 2 pencil. Two opposites, one short and round, and the other tall and regal, yet a perfectly matched news team. They anticipated slants and angles on unfolding events with savvy and intuitive directness. Under them, News was *talk history.* Their desks were catty corner, separated by an aisle and steps from the air studio. Dulles never minced words. Asked, to what do you attribute your longevity in news, he said, I focus on work, don't fraternize, and never write memos. Each man tended to his own knitting and was not above saying "thank you".

C.B.S Memorandum
From: Mal   To: Mr. S.   Date: 3 April 1973

I call your attention to the efforts of several persons who made the NR for March 29th and 30th excellent broadcasts. It started Thursday with Stunning's fine report on the Army stepping down in Vietnam, a report forwarded from Hong Kong by H.D. who was burdened with a television bird feed and still "got the mail through" in time for our use. Friday's contribution from Bob Beerpoint and George Hermann in DC enlightened the roundup audience regarding the President's speech.

Tape work of TM, PS, and BM was an important factor in the programs. And a nod also to technicians EH, SG, PY, AV, and LC. All in all a fine effort by everyone.   *M T.*

Diary: 5:10AM.   (Two war horses lining up NR stories.)

Dulles. Have you read Clueless's new book?
Mal. And I don't intend to.
Dulles. She claims she's been jilted by TV.
Mal. The feeling was mutual.
Dulles. She drops names. Steps on a few toes. I found some oddities, like her spelling of Black Crock with a lower case "c" and making it one word. Then referring to her producer's objections about something, she says, *They were overridden by Blackcrock, which – who? Oh, I never get that pronoun right.*
Mal. Black Crock takes "who". It's people who make decisions.
Dulles. I should think. "Who" modifies people at Black Crock.
Mal. "People" is understood. Say, is that "people is" or "people are"?
Dulles. A person is. People are. People in quotes can take an "is". Using "which" insinuates there're no human characteristics at Black Crock.
Mal. She should've gone with "which".
Dulles. Now, Mal. It's too early for invectives. My wife says, "'Which' sounds a lot like 'witch', as in Halloween; scary; an automaton."
Mal. I'd say "Black Crock made a decision which," Or, "Black Crock- which signs our paycheck- 'ain't' the most hospitable looking building in the world. It has the feel of stone under foot on a winter day." Well, back to work. We've got a five sec cut from the kiddie pond. You like?
Dulles. You're a prince. Let's lead with it.

Mal lays into the Times delivery man who shorts radio ten papers.

Mal. I told you yesterday, twenty-seven. Is history your weak point?

Man. I'll bring 'em tomorrow. I only got fifty. Thirty for TV.

Mal. Give 'em twenty-three.

Man. They'll get mad.

Mal. Radio can get madder. Make up the rest from your truck.

Man. I'm runnin' late and I'm short.

Mal. Short of what, brains? Read my lips, *seven more copies.*

Man. Tomorrow.

Mal. Tonight.

Man. Fuck you. Tell the office.

Mal. I'm telling you, asshole!

Man. And I'm tellin' you.

Mal. You got it backwards. You're the delivery guy. I tell you.

Man. It ain't on my requisition.

Mal. You wanna argue? Step outside. We'll work it out. Com'on. Oh, suddenly you can count. Twenty-seven from now on.

Tech. Mal?

Mal. What're you doin' out of your cage?

Tech. You got an extra paper?

Mal. You trying to be funny? Here. Two tapes for the upcoming. Cut the top off one; two's an internal.

Tech. That radio talk? Upcoming, cut the top, an internal?

Mal. The sheets're marked in red crayon.

Tech. I like blue.

Mal. The only blue here is the desk waiting on you.

Tech. This work comes as a shock. I'll have to notify next of kin.

Mal. You don't have any. You were spawned.

Tech. I'm looking into my contract. Insults and work come under the heading of harassment. I'm still recovering from the last edit.

Mal. I apologize on behalf of C.B.S for the inconvenience.

Tech. I'm going to the cafeteria. You want coffee?

Mal. Wait. I'll go with you.

Tech. You were really mad. That's not you. What's bothering you?

Mal. This business pulls you like an invisible rubber band until one day you snap, and then it starts all over.

(*over coffee Mal opens up*)

Mal. Journalism's hurried writing. Print has the edge, because writers have more "think" time before going public. The downside is that once a paper goes to press the die is cast until the next edition. We can correct an error in the next breath.

Tech. When I was at local, Joyless was news director. He recorded the competition and compared them second-to-second with our own air check. *What're they saying? What're we saying?* One editor always read the Times before deciding his lead.

Mal. We're a copycat business. Nobody wants to get egg on their face. Mistakes are unfortunate, but it's a bigger mistake to lie about it. *Integrity in news, as in life is everything, which is news to some people.*

One guy was a tape cutting machine. He'd turn out cuts from cuts, and make jump cuts linking disparate remarks. To him, *there was no such thing as an outtake.* Once he squirreled a hot item for Newsfeed. I advised against it. When Mal found out, the guy played innocent, and said the tech had mixed up the tapes. Mal looked at me, I shook my head, and a month later the guy was an outtake himself.

One morning Mal asks Dulles about a story he suspects has a parallel years earlier, but he can't recall. Dulles gave him chapter and verse.

Tech. How do you know that?
Mal. He's a walking encyclopedia.
Dulles. A veritable *treasure trove of trivia.*
Mal. A mind like a steel trap.
Dulles. Oh, fiddlesticks!
Mal. A genius.
Dulles. Mal, you're a prince.
Mal. And you're a gentleman and a scholar.
That's the way it was for two decades. No fuss, no bother, no smoke.
Dulles. Have you seen the grammatical error in Sauter's last sentence?
Mal. I haven't had time to check it; so much has been happening.
Dulles. He says, *Neither so and so or such and such are*.
Mal. The either, or trap.
Dulles. Shall we take out the last sentence?
Mal. We could. Can we dub an "is" from another sentence?
Tech. Probably. Where's the piece?
Dulles. Well, let's leave it.
Mal. You could come out saying, *There's very little agreement in the Sahara today even the verbs don't agree with the subject.*
Dulles. Mal, I knew I could count on you. You're a prince.
Mal. Thank you kind sir. And you're a gentleman and a scholar.

☺

30.   *The Razor's Edge*

C.B.S **Mamorandum**

From: MG, DIRECTOR OF ENG. OPS. To: ALL
TECHNICIANS Date: August 15, 1979

Upon inspecting the Studio control rooms, I was virtually shocked at their condition. Reels lying around on top of machines, leader strips tangled within, and **razor blades** lying in vulnerable locations, and apparently a reminder is in order. All of the above cannot be blamed on anyone other than the technical staff, because all of the above are handled by technicians. In addition, the area behind the Consoles is not intended for Newspapers, Magazines, etc. There are lockers provided for personal effects.

There is no reason, regardless of the activity of an assignment, to leave Control Rooms in the condition that I observed. It's unfair to your colleagues who may not be part of this behavior. I hope it won't be necessary to remind you of this again.

Diary. Techs edit audio tape with industrial razors on the Editall block, invented by former C.B.S technician Joe Tall after discovering the hatchet was clumsy. He left no instructions on disposal of editing razor blades that got dull, but were sharp enough to cut skin. After some accidents, yee shoppe stward posted a How To memo. *Dispose of razor blades by taping edges. Do not put them in drawers.* Thank you.

Additional suggestions were posted on the bulletin board.

1. Tape self to blades and toss in garbage.
2. Hire per diem sword swallower to eat blades.
3. Put blades in desk drawers in newsroom and management offices.
4. Stick blades up your nose.
5. Slip blades in pockets of various employees.

6. Grind blades and give to newscasters for gargling.
7. Save blades for Halloween to put in apples for trick-or-treaters.
8. Recycle blades for military use in land mines.
9. Edit wrists when scheduled to work the nightshift.

☺

31. The Newsletter

Been offered union news editorship. Ayn says, "Take it. A couple of issues under your belt will look good on your resume." What resume?

Dateline: Houston. A mayoral race campaign dominated by issues of aids and homosexuality. Seeking a third term, Mayor Kathy Whitmeyer, running against former five-term mayor Louis Welch, was quoted in the media as having said, in response to how to deal with AIDS, "Shoot the queers." ***Item:*** *60 Shminuets* producer Hughe-it was heard singing, *It's my potty and I'll cry if I want to!* He weighs 170 pounds of which 160 is intestinal fecal matter. Bulletin board post it: **WE THE WILLING, LED BY THE UNKNOWING, ARE DOING THE IMPOSSIBLE FOR THE UNGRATEFUL; WE HAVE DONE SO MUCH FOR SO LONG WITH SO LITTLE, WE'RE NOW QUALIFIED TO DO ANYTHING WITH NOTHING.**

☺

32. *Yee Razor's Edge Continued*

One day Yee Olde Nearing Retirement Shoppe Steward, posted a memo on Yee Olde Tacky Tech Lounge Bulletin Board. Techs were putting used razor blades in *vulnerable locations,* and some guys ended up in yee olde nurse's office with yee digital laceration. Therefore:

10-20-79

ALL Hands: It seems some fellow co-workers are becoming very lax in disposing of <u>razor blades</u>. When you are finished with a blade, put it in the "used blades" box. If there is no "used blades" box where you are, wrap it up and then dispose of it. The consoles and drawers are not proper places for used blades under any circumstances... The IBEW constitution and by-laws include rules for protection of fellow workers, and penalties for not observing them. Please do yourself and those who work with you a favor, and dispose of blades properly... Thanks. Shop Steward, JKS

(*Never put used razor blades in your drawers, unless you're into circumcision.*)

☺

33.   The TR

Trouble Report or Irregularity. Date: 5/12/79. **Location:** Studio F. **Reported By:** T.
Equipment:: Phone Selector Switch 12. **Nature of Trouble or Irregularity:** At 11:05p we got a call on PL3-1165 for a live switch. We wanted a level test but we couldn't bring up any phone on Selector 12. Afterward the show, we found that the knob Selector Switch 12 <u>was on backwards</u>. To bring up a phone in the 5:00 position, you must turn the point of the knob to 10:00. Please turn the knob around correctly. THX.

☺

34.   The Keeper That Got Away

On reading confessionals written by news people I've known, I find contradictions between what they say and what I remember. Then I read Louis Nizer's *My Life In Court*: "sympathy or bias" can change what one sees into what one "would like to see." Our eyes are attracted to part of a picture and not the whole. A model sits motionless while the artist's eyes go back and forth to get the picture right. With each look more is perceived. But life doesn't sit still. It's fluid. Though we play quick draw Q and A artists, passing judgment on others, all we actually know of each other, even of ourselves, is an approximation. We spy on each other, watch artificial personas in movies and on TV, but never devote the same concentrated time one-on-one, except on a stage, in a hospital or in court rooms, and it's discovered, we *ain't* what we seem.

Harry Breezener was more than I first perceived him to be. His gray head was distinguished, his commanding voice exuded strength plus credibility, and his writing was the cleverest. Harry always had a coy glint in his eyes, which some translated as a *liquid lunch buzz*. He was too smart for the powers-that-be, and a fast-moving, money-minded society. Harry was collegial, made 'em think, where his peers played Doris Day to an audience of Shirley Temples. They were fear driven and never got ahead of the curve. They saw what happened to Burrow.

One anecdote has Harry Breezener shaking Crankcase's hand, the man who got the position he deserved, and saying, *It's hard to stay mad at somebody who does his job as well as you do.* He had to swallow that bitter pill again in 1983, when Blather took over. Harry stayed because the company's reach in the world was essential to his ego as a reporter. It was also love of the Burrow ideal that went south. Bill Moyer disabused himself of that ideal pretty quick. He had a cup of coffee at Chuckler, decided against being a neutered news pussy, and took his cigars to PBS. Ernie Kovacs once said: *TV is a medium. It's neither rare nor well-done.*

Harry wrote a wonderful piece in the 70's for a picture book about the history of baseball titled, *The Sunshine Game.* With the sun setting on his own game he continued to step up to the mic with his trusty Number 2 lumber adding and subtracting to graphs right up to air time. There was still life in the old Burrow Boy, who in his own right could play on equal footing with guys like Ring Lardner, DiMaggio, and Runyan. News and baseball, stories and games, are forever young and spark the cockles of the heart like nothing else. Makes no difference who you are, as long as you can play. Americans love a player. News and baseball link you to a family stretching from sea to shining sea. Harry's piece went yard, out over the flags in the upper deck, back to Des Moines of the '30's listening to radio telegraphed reports by sportscaster Dutch Reagan who went on to become an actor, governor, and future president. Baseball, wrote Harry *The Horse* Breezener, why it's everybody's game. So's news! To follow it all you need's a scorecard and an understanding of hits, runs, errors, thumb suckers, soft and hard news. There's drama and tension in the pitch of every word. Will the bat meet the ball and find a hole, the word meet the thought, to delight audiences? Baseball and news loosen tongues and make instant friends of strangers. A young mother with a doctorate in classical music once told me, *Given a choice; I'd rather anchor third base for the Mets.*

Harry's piece might've have been knocked out yesterday. Fresh, too, are the days of DiMaggio, Gehrig, and Ruth, who're still swinging the bat in our minds. The Yankees of '96 embodied the Murderer's Row spirit of '27. In the '40's and '50's, C.B.S had its own Murderer's Row, the Burrow Boys, but old man Bailey fixed the game, sold 'em out, and climbed in bed with Madison Avenue. By the '80's scholarly writing meant strike three, and arch was a passé slap bunt.

Toward the end, Harry, in rumpled suit with loose tie, would pull himself up from his desk amid chattering wire services and ringing phones, and drag his heavy feet into the on-air studio. As I tossed him the air lights for another turn as God's vicar, I'd watch him with mixed emotions, a tatterdemalion hung up between the old and new. All along his dogs were saying what his mind would not accept. Hey, Babe! We've carried you far since Edward R., and those carefree, barefoot days under North Dakota skies. Harry wasn't listening. He trudged on into the '80's doing radio and TV assignments, had even joined another network to get his licks in prime-time, only to return years later an object d'art in a new generation of rock and roll news junkies. Still, Harry swung a mean number 2 Louisville, could still go "yard" in perception and insight, and even end with a kicker, faking bunt then going yard over the heads of the on-rushing field of commercials. He was a thinking news writer, the Babe of broadcast journalism; the true Evening News air apparent. In baseball, homers are keepers. Harry, like Burrow, was a keeper that got away.

☺

35. Production Guidelines

Mal. Look at this copy. Three sentences into the piece and already I've found four grammaticals; and I'm not even talking content.

Tech. There's a bear in all men.

Mal. Put up this tape. Please.

Tech. The trick is how to handle him. He's a nasty, hairy old son-of-a-bitch; ornery, difficult, kind and evil, tireless and indomitable. Plead, beg, cajole, and make him sacrificial blood offerings, yet he will not be appeased. Don't ask me what he wants. All I know is that when I see him, the dance is on.

Mal. You're certifiable. The tape, if you please.

Tech. Roundy, crossing the room to put up a tape is a labor-intensive engineering fete.

Mal. Wrong. It's listening to a schmuck.

Tech. I got a question. How do you work a story when VIP's die?

Mal. Dead, deader, deadest. Paul Wyte came to us in the '50's. He used to say, 'radio's not subtle'. Telling a story is transitory, like a Broadway show done in one straight performance. In news, repetition's vital to making a point. *So, set 'em up for what you're about to say, tell 'em, and then tell 'em again what you just told 'em. It's called recapitulation!*

Tech. How do you work a phoner a minute to air from a guy who's got news, but you can't understand him?

Mal. What changed?

Tech. The guy didn't die. The alleged killer tried suicide.

Mal. You could try suicide, too. You just summed it up. The victim didn't die, and the alleged killer tried suicide. K-I-S-S. Keep It Simple Stupid.

Tech. What if the guy's an insider and doesn't want to be named?

Mal. Fix this tape. Then come to my desk and read something.

From: President of News.　　　　To: **NEWS PERSONNEL**
　　　　　　　　　　　　　　　　January 19, 1977

Production Standards... *we must be free to expose- we have a responsibility to expose- criminal activity, wrongdoing, and abuses of public confidence and trust.* Since each investigative effort involves different facts and questions of procedure, policy, and law, it is not feasible to formulate specific standards for investigative reporting which will address all scenarios and questions. But here are some basic standards... *Producers and reporters should provide all the information possible,* without endangering the source. Chuckler News must decide that the material is of sufficient newsworthiness to warrant its use despite the fact that we can't reveal the source, and that the source is trustworthy.

Some information about the nature of the source should be provided, assuming that this information will not lead to disclosure of the source. Where the news story involves advocacy of a particular course of action, then information on the nature of the course should also include the motivation of the source or the position the source favors on the issue.

Occasionally, anonymity of source is vital. Our policy is to protect the source. When threatened by legal action and jail, reporters have the right to reveal the source since their liberty may be at stake. As a rule, Chuckler endorses a journalist's fight to avoid naming sources. Our policy is to provide legal counsel, and pay attorney fees after agreement on the validity of counsel.

Subject: Latest addition to NEWS STANDARDS

June 6, 1977

<u>Investigative Reporting</u> must be done under supervision of the news President, who will insure investigations are consistent with standards of journalistic integrity, accuracy, and fairness.

Whether information on a crime investigation must be available to public authorities depends on the facts of each case, considered in light of the potential crime involved and purpose of the investigation. But information that a potential crime endangers the person or property of an individual (e.g., arson, rape, murder) must be reported promptly to appropriate public officials.

In approaching individuals or organizations for interviews, avoid misrepresentation. In some cases, an important story can't be done without the reporter's or producer's withholding his or her identity. But this should be an exception, acceptable only when an activity could <u>otherwise</u> <u>not</u> <u>be</u> <u>reported</u>. We will not engage in criminal activity in reporting news, nor encourage anyone to commit a crime. But there may be exceptions, on an <u>ad</u> <u>hoc</u> basis. Some investigative reporting may involve commission of acts technically in violation of law, i.e., purchase of guns (where forbidden) or of liquor in a dry state, to establish accessibility.

☺

36.   The Hoy Vey Café

Date: 7-12-77
Reported By: The Wild Man of the Overnight
Nature of Trouble or Irregularity: Death of the Hard Question

Despite the length of the Warren Commission's Report, the small print, big words, and no pictures, it belongs under glass in the Children's Museum.

C.B.S did its own JFK investigation, spending $500,000 to figure out scenarios. They simulated Oswald's view from the Book *Suppository*. An identical gun alleged to have been used by Oswald, *not the original one*, was fired by experts, who concluded, *it could be shot three times with JFK in it's sights*. From the mock-up firing range, it was also established that what Texas Governor John Connelly, wounded as he sat in front of JFK, heard and thought was a shot from the grassy knoll, was just an <u>echo effect</u>.

C.B.S decided on the side of the Warren Commission Report. Crankcase: "By gum. It was a disappointment. The 'story' would've been way better had we been able to disprove the finding. Yes. A bon-a-fide world smasher." As for the alleged Cuban Plot, later revealed, that can only be conjecture. *Some written accounts say Jack and Bobby Kennedy had tried to assassinate Castro, failed, and the favor was returned with stunning success in Dallas.* Conspiracy theories arising from the crime are speculations resting on a foundation of heavily structured imagination, sprinkled with uncorroborated and distended fact. *Crankcase's face with mustache and big mouth should mark the entrance to every funny house.* As to the movie *JFK*- well, it was a mélange of the most sensational theories and produced a concoction of poison whose ingredients were Cubans, mafiosa, homosexuals, Johnson, the CIA, anti-Castro sharpshooters, and oil cartels. Crankcase characterized New Orleans District Attorney Garrison as one who went after innocent people for headlines; he pursued homosexual business man Clay Shaw out of jealousy because Shaw was New Orleans high society. The media monarchs pressured their news departments on implicit threat of unemployment to buy the government line of a lone assassin. Kennedy's death marks the rise of "avuncular" and "pretty boy news", and the death of truthful, in-depth reporting. Crankcase still maintained a lone assassin, even after seeing Abraham Zapruder's film. Kennedy's brains were blown out the back of his head, not the front. Oswald shot from the rear. The "Grassy Knoll" second shooter was dismissed as an echo effect. The government and the self-serving Fourth Estate shoved the "<u>Book Suppository</u>" story up America's keister to protect itself, not America. Attorney Jim Garrison: *We bought a fairy-tale.* And Europeans laughed. <u>JFK's death was a coup d'etat!</u> Gimme a name? Pick one out of a hat. *Beware the military-industrial complex.* The press *must be free... to expose, indeed, we have a mandate to expose criminal activity, wrongdoing, and abuses of public confidence and trust.*

Other examples of shallow reporting: LBJ's Gulf of Ton Kin lie; our CEO's brother Andrew Fisch, head of "Lori Lard", saying <u>under oath</u>, nicotine's not an additive; Neil Tush's bumbling in Denver's Lincoln Savings fiasco; Sticky face killing the Haiti story. Will the people see the JFK evidence in 2038, or will "they" find a reason to extend it? A mock scenario doesn't prove motive. Why has the press failed, and continues to fail America? Simple. Get too far ahead of the curve you could find yourself alone with no job. Artist Julius Kramer: *Not only that. The reason we didn't react angrily to JFK's death is that we didn't see a man die. What we saw was the death of a myth. It's hard to relate to a myth. It was a dream, a myth that died, not a human being. People live on illusions. How we're able to function as a society amazes me. Occasionally reality breaks through you get revolution. People don't want truth or reality. It's too harsh and vile. Man's history is replete with horror. Maxim Gorky says through Bubnov in The Lower Depths: "What makes human beings so fond of lying?" Natasha replies: "Lies must be more pleasant than truth it seems." What is the truth? Is it Kurtz's "Horror" in Heart of Darkness? Is it that inability to face our guilt, our depravity? Another O'Neill character, Satin to the Actor: "Bunk! You'll go nowhere. It's nothing but a pipe dream." Later, the Actor kills himself. About Nastya, a streetwalker, she's "used to painting her face- so she wants to paint her soul, too- put rouge on it. But why do others do it?" The baron says, "All human beings have gray little souls- and they all want to rouge them up." Gorky skims the possibile answers, but not O'Neill, who goes beneath that rouge to the pessimistic conclusion: we're lost souls adrift in a cesspool of human emotions in a world without absolutes.*

After writing Checkmate for ABC's *Benson*, my partner Mark Barkan summed up a conversation he had with Bob Guillaume. *That son-of-bitch says I should grease my ass, bend over, and open wider.* Are Americans doing that? The press has been suborned, and if we listen long enough they'll have us believe even the dead shall rise.

☺

37.   And All The Ships At Sea

Diary. September 9th. Head feels hot. Can't stand being cooped up. Nose bleeds every time the phone rings. An Italian proverb: *Dove entra il sole non entra il dottore- Where the sun enters no doctor enters.* An anchor who is intolerant of other people's mistakes leads hourly with, "Prior to the explosion that killed several people, the

Green Piss was..." ***October 1.*** Somebody screamed, "Can't stand it anymore! Shove the tape up your ass!" It was me. ***Slugged:*** Small Town Water Tower Tells Demography, "If you're listening to me, said a DJ, flush your toilet." The drop in the water tower level indicated the number of people for or against a politician... Change affects the poor and rarely the rich... Fear and anxiety always lurks below the good-fellow veneer and deepens with each rung up the ladder. Techs and writers are protected by contracts, and individual deals with clauses like "no strike". A young reporter: *I signed a two-year agreement with a thirteen-week dropout clause, which means they can legally fire me and don't have to honor the remaining time. I didn't like it. But what was I going to do, say 'no'?...* Editor Mary G goes back to the Burrow days: *I love it when somebody gets something out of this company. Too often it's the other way around...* **Who's on 1ˢᵗ? 1972.** The company owned the Noo Yawk Yanks. One day the hourly anchor announced the wrong score and the company got egg on its face. A memo came down, and was leaked to the press. To wit: *Sometimes inaccuracy in news is unavoidable. But we own the Noo Yawk Yanks! If we don't know the score, who does? ...* Miss America joined the *Mourning Show*, was let go before the end of her ironclad contract, and got a million a year for foing nothing. The contract mistake was linked to Mr. Sorta Van, who soon after bailed from Chuckler with a golden parachute. **This just in.** Newsman Dell Vaughn was killed in a helicopter crash while covering a story. Del was a vibrant, unassuming reporter; part American Indian; smooth skin; Alan Ladd with fine baritone pipes. Del took time to talk with everyone. He had a cup of coffee with us and was gone.

1981. Shortly after I wrote an episode for the *Benson* ABC/TV series, the word went out that it was going to be aired on a certain date in New York. I got a congratulatory note from GW, a sister technician who could speak several languages and belonged to MENSA. She told a sister tech, LT, also extremely bright, about the airdate of the show. So, one day, LT comes up to me. She had watched the wrong *Benson* episode- a week too soon. She says, *I'm sitting there watching this piece of crap because of you- and then when I find out it wasn't you, I really got bugged. I could've crapped away my time with my own crap.* Or some such crap. LT was not one to pull her punches. She straightened my tie once while running CC, and I was nearby at the console in Studio A acting disdainfully about the job. She says, *Nobody's keeping you here. You could walk out and join a thousand other unemployed writers.*

Diary. Reporting news is more important than news itself. On TV the US Open men's tennis championship match runs over, bumps the *Evening News*, Blather storms off the TV set, leaving seven minutes of blank TV. It was two rackets battling for air turf.

☺

38. DISPOSABLE TV BULLSHIT BAG SEALS BS IN

DIRECTIONS
1. **OPEN BAG BEFORE OPENING MOUTH**
2. TUCK OPEN BAG BENEATH CHIN
3. START 'TALKING', LET THE BS FLOW
4. WHEN FULL, SEAL BAG AND DISPOSE

WARNING
Do not attempt to dispose of your BS through a government agency since they produce more bullshit than they can dispose of themselves. Send it to the major networks in return for all they send out each day.

39.   Excuse Slip

We missed the pipe (feed) because:
- A. Tech went for coffee
- B. Tech was asleep
- C. Tech was in lounge
- D. Tech was not scheduled
- E. Tech had seizure

If pipe was missed because of writer error, please indicate and send five copies of report to top executives list, which can be found on the permanent editor's board. If the list is not there, please indicate so on this slip before sending it to the list of executives.

A. No executive list on clip board

(If this box is checked, editor on duty must fill out excuse slip #489.)

Notice: When pipe is received, but fucked up on the way, please check appropriate reason:
- A. Missed the top
- B. Up cut from Washington
- C. Level sucked
- D. Rolled with gate open
- E. Selector on wrong number
- F. No tape on machine

If more than three of these boxes are checked, please indicate whether you wish your final check sent to home address or you will pick it up at cashier.
- A. Send me my check
- B. I'll pick it up
- C. I want to appeal

☺

40.   Memo to All

As you know, Zeecraft died last night after a long illness. Mrs. Zeecraft said they knew the end was near early this week and his father was with him when he died. Z will be buried tomorrow, Friday

May 1, at 3pm, at Fairfax Cemetery, 4401 Burke Station Road, Fairfax, Virginia. His father, who was a minister, will officiate.

Z leaves his wife, and three children.　　　C　　4/30/81

Z had been sicking out periodically. In Newsfeed I asked what was wrong, thinking he'd been cured. He looked up over his reading glasses, and his last words to me were chilling. "I've got a sore that won't heal; starts inside and works its way out." Strange, I thought. Usually it's the other way around. Twenty years later I still see his blues looking at me. *It starts from inside and works its way out.* He meant big casino.

☺

41.　　Mal Becomes An Update

Diary. Fall, 1983, 1:15AM. Back from vacation I find a glum Mal in the lounge looking thinner. *No way to lose weight. They found a cyst. Went up my penis with a tube and quaterized it. I take it one day at a time.* Any pain? *Let them stick a tube up yours and see how it feels. Lucky are those who don't suffer.* Mal thinks and speaks. *We look in the mirror everyday, but we don't see our real selves, and if we do, we deny it like going through the threshold of pain before we faint. It's a godsend like a sense of humor that makes life bearable. Better to have lived a day and understood yourself clearly, than a lifetime of lies.* I hear regrets. *Kid, the number one killer's not cancer. It's entrapment by big business. Lately, I see myself back in France in a tank outfit pushing toward Germany. I'm sitting on the turret moving along a road. Suddenly, a German comes around a bend. I start firing; my hand froze on the trigger. They had to bang my wrists to stop me. The poor bastard didn't have a gun. He was trying to surrender. I turned away and threw up. The man didn't even have a gun. Goddamnit!*

Mal raises his heavy body out of the chair, goes into the newsroom, and begins pulling together his last NR. Mal, the fighting Jew and I love him for that, for his spunk, his intelligence, his manliness, and because he never broke balls. Problems, he resolved immediately with no grudges. And Mal, old pal, maybe that German was unarmed, but what was he doing in somebody else's backyard? The Versailles Treaty wasn't harsh enough. They say, ignorance of the law is no excuse. Well, so's ignorance of human rights. The swastika bit that poor bastard in the ass, not you. Your finger on the trigger was the voice of the slaughtered dead.

Mal and Dulles two princes, who were gentlemen and scholars.

Memo: Mal went into the hospital Thursday, April 30, for some tests and on Friday we learned that he has a tumor hidden in a small pocket of the bladder. It will be removed on Wednesday, May 6, by cystoscope. Mal will remain in the hospital for additional testing after the operation.

He's at Franklin General Hospital, 900 Franklin Avenue, Valley Stream, N.Y 11580, room 150, Ph: 1-516-825-8800, ext. 2453

We talked with him this afternoon and he sounds fine. Phone calls will be welcome.

As you realize, this will involve schedule changes and sixth days for a while. Please read Sue's revised schedule for next week very carefully.   Clare, May 1, 1981

MAL UPDATE: May 3: Talked with Mal this evening. Some change in plans. A biopsy via cystoscope Wednesday to be followed by surgery, not via cystoscope, on Monday. Food & service good and plentiful, he sounds good.

MAL UPDATE: 5/10/81, 9p. Mal in an up mood. Doctor thinks malignancy is confined to tumor and that only a section of the bladder need be removed instead of the whole bladder. Cat Scan tomorrow is expected to confirm this and the decision on a future course of action—the tumor surgery—comes Tuesday when all the test data are in. But Mal sounds optimistic.   C.W.

<u>5/11/81 10p</u>. Mal got his first radiation today. He leaves the hospital tomorrow to continue getting the radiation treatments on an outpatient basis. The radiation, it's hoped, will shrink the tumor and make surgery Tuesday, May 26, easier. Mal sounds even brighter than yesterday.

(Who knows with all the pills they give you.)
To Everyone from Clare 5.11.81
The following log note from M. Glick is the latest on Mal .

NEWS   RADIO EDITORS' LOG/date: Thurs may 11, 1981
10:50p, Mal note. Now the good news; Mal called awhile back and said the situation is much improved. Says he's going back home tomorrow, and he'll call the office when he gets home and is settled. He had his first radiation treatment today (with no apparent ill effects; he was in quite (a) cheery mood)..... He'll continue the treatments as outpatient, driving himself, with Dr's OK; Dr. says he won't feel weak or dizzy ... ultimate goal for operation Tues May 26. Dr. says problem is localized in bladder, has not spread anywhere, thus entire bladder need not be removed. Question is how much surgery can he take ... altho original estimate of operating time now has been cut in half, Mal says. But the Dr. says – get it out. Mal says he is in no pain (and we hope it stays that way). Mal says it would be nice to hear from people when he's home – but reminds he'll be out from about 10:30am to 1:30pm for treatment. This is a long note, but people kept asking.   M. G.

NEWS RADIO EDITORS' LOG/date: May 22,1981

7p, Note... Mal called. Says he's not leaving the hospital. Beginning next week he'll be getting three more days of radiation treatment. Then they're going to operate. He says he doesn't know when or why. He's at Sloan Kettering (68th and York) room 820A, phone to him is 794-6217. Welcome fone calls, although he's tired now (and sounds dispirited to me). Visiting hours from noon to 8p, but probably best to call first. –0- And he had sautéed chicken livers for dinner. –0- Clare N knows all of above, except possibly the dinner.   marian, Fri, May 22, 1981, 7pm

<u>ALL HANDS:</u> Mal called tonight, sounded a bit under the weather. Says they found and removed a second (benign) tumor from his bladder last week and plan to remove the initial malignant one Tuesday. Sloan-Kettering has him on liquid diet. Doctors envision at least one week of hospital recuperation followed by a 3-4 week stay at

home. I think calls and visits and cards would be rather welcome.   W/5/24/81 pyem

NEWS RADIO EDITORS' LOG/date: Thurs, 5/28/81 –5-5-5
9:15p, Mal called an hour ago to say he'll be operated on Friday morning/may 29/ at 9 o'clock (Sloan Kettering). Says doctors got results of his heart stress tests, and they were good. Mal says doctors think the operation should take about 3 hours (they'll remove the part of gall (?) bladder that is affected) then he should be in recovery another three hours or so. Says doctors tell him they don't think there'll be any problem. He asked, and was told there's no way of knowing if there'll be any recurrence...chances are 30%.
     Mal seemed in very good spirits ... relieved there's a time and date and something will be <u>done</u>. He talked to half the people on the first floor of BC (Broadcast Center), at least, and got regards and blessings from the rest. His main concern is that people not call him Friday or Saturday. (I don't believe they'd let his fone ring anyway), but ... He is obviously pleased at hearing from so many people. ... Says Mrs. will be calling the desk and/or Clare with any news./ marianne g.

☺

42.   Strange Fruit

Diary. Took over editorship of *Union News*. What they expect and what they'll get are two different things. Nobody reads it except the writers. The content is communistic. Everything's "Fraternally Yours". Everybody is your "brother" even your sister. Some sisters look like brothers (cheap shot). Cover to cover, it's a "sempre fi" picnic where nobody's left behind unless their dues aren't paid up. The cover picture is always a brother technician up a utility pole wearing a hard hat, red suspenders, a tool belt, and work boots. His ass is hanging from a pole on a prairie road snaking into the distant Rockies against a blue sky. Below there's tumbleweed, cactus, and road kill. The caption says, "Brother 896999 on the job." Nine is subliminal German meaning *no to give backs.* Same guy on every cover. He's from Central Casting. They just change the ID. A pole poser with a phallic complex. Cuts telegraph lines in war and Indian movies. Never goes home. Sleeps on the pole under an umbrella. Once he was up there in drag to satisfy libbers. I'm not mentioning the union at all. On the cover'll be a white, maintenance guy hanging upside down from a pole with the caption, *Strange Fruit, third party verified.*

☺

43.   We Don't Deliver

Diary: Came in this morning on the run, 45 minutes late-my lower back out of whack. My Santo Domingin friend stops sweeping, says, a bad thing happened, serious, "grande". He couldn't remember the name, but he kept extending his hands in front of his stomach miming "big". I go, "Who? Pete? He's on days now, in maintenance." He shook his head, "No," and kept indicating fat with his arms out, eyeglasses, a pipe. "You sure it's not Pete?" He was sure. "Dead, you say?" He nodded, "Muerto. Over the weekend." Then it hit me. "Mal?" "Yes." The rock of C.B.S. The day, hour, how, didn't matter. Jesus! He's over the roof, I thought, in short sleeve shirt, bowtie askew, holding his attaché case.

With Terkel's exit a demarcation line was drawn between quality news and schlock. Soon after, the line was crossed with the unconscionable mistreatment of Dulles. Time eats everything. Rumor had it, changes were brought about to satisfy affiliates. When Audrey Hepburn was having Breakfast At Tiffany, C.B.S began bellying up to Nathan's and Orange Julius. The word on most everybody's lips was, we've gone from being the Tiffany of fraudcasting to K-Mart of the air. An essential public service had degenerated into comic book programs and hip-hop news.

Like Disraeli's father and Leon Trotsky, Mal was a non-practicing Jew. During Rosh Hashanah I go, "Mal, why're you working?" *I don't observe the Sabbath,* he says, *or go to shule. I don't care to be with people who get righteous from Friday sundown to Saturday and on Monday go back to cutting each other's throats.* Mal had a lot in common with Disraeli's father, who would spend evenings closeted in his library in intellectual pursuit. His housekeeper often turned away synagogue representatives out for donations. Finally, he admitted them, giving a conditional *one-time donation* that *in the future, respect my privacy and do not come back.*

On occasion in the halls I overheard, *the media's full of Jews,* followed by denials from Jews. Frankly, I couldn't care less, but let's be clear. Any time, day or night, shoot a canon ball into *any* newsroom, you'll hit a Jew. The first day of the Writers' strike the picket line looked like B'nai Brith on the march.

Not long after Mal died, Dulles was honored by C.B.S at a ceremonial banquet attended by heads of affiliate stations. Mrs. Dulles gave me the deeper, heart-rending truth at Cholly's New Year's Eve party. *Dulles was honored, given an award for superior contribution to news. But it was a mafia media kiss of death. The worst week of our lives. Subsequently, Dulles was removed from the Roundup, which he had anchored for two decades.* He faded into offbeat hours, retired, and taught journalism. In the late '90's I directed Cholly's eldest son, Weston, as the lead in *Bus Stop,* a TNT community theatre production in New Jersey. During our first meeting in my Englewood driveway he gave me the sad news. *Dulles tripped on a flight of stairs at home, was hospitalized with a concussion, recovered, but the doctors missed a blood clot that ended his life.*

Mal and Dulles were high water marks of excellence and integrity in broadcast journalism- the Edward G. Robinson and Spencer Tracy of news. Last of the Burrow Boys. Now the tail wags the dog.

As noted earlier, Mal came to work carrying an attaché case containing pipes, tobacco, and gourmet cheeses. One day after C.B.S News President Richard Sealant retired at the mandatory age of 65 and then joined NBC, he phoned Mal to say "hello" and tried to get cute.

RS. By the way. Still carrying cheese in your attaché case?
Mal. Yes. But we don't deliver.

☺

44.   Normal Hours

C.B.S RADIO
From: B.K. Director Operations And Business Affairs
Date: September 16, 1983

Dear L__,
We received a letter from Dr. A saying you can only work a 6:30a to 2:30p shift. While it's unlikely that we can assure any employee a particular shift, I asked the Medical Department to investigate your problem. On your return from vacation, please contact Dr. R.G.

Ask for normal hours and your nuts. RG is a psychiatrist. We had a healthy chat. He confided, *I can make a living off one C.B.S office alone.*

☺

45.   No Fingerprints

Firing old-timers is like tearing down churches and historical land- marks and replacing them with efficiency apartments. Old things speak of heritage, and character. If we disrespect them, what are we teaching our children? How we treat our elders and architectural landmarks shapes our dialogue and future thinking. The C.B.S I knew in the '60's had venerable journalists like Dug Edwords, Jorge Hermann, Deric Sevaried, Hairy Breezener, the Kalb brothers, Daniel Offshore, and Charles Colonwud. Hermann, former moderator of *Disgrace the Nation*, lived in Georgetown, DC. To the dismay of neighbors, the Hermanns painted their brownstone a lively pattern of polychromatic colors, with a big daisy and batches of little daisies between the windows. It lasted 10 years. I still see eyeglasses and sparkling eyes looking at me from the studio in 1974 as I record a piece he'd written poking fun at a new word in the Washington lexicon. If one doesn't know about <u>*disinformation,*</u> it can be a <u>grammatical disdemeanor</u>. Ill to <u>discreants</u> who have the <u>disfortune</u> who suffer the <u>disapprehension </u>that no such word exists. It can lead to malicious <u>dischief </u>and no end of <u>disconduct</u>...It's where <u>dis-information</u> is <u>mispensed</u> and gullible types are <u>disled</u>.

In 1981, at age 65, Uncle Woolly, an American news icon, discovered that *fidelity is not earned by position.* After retiring to do a show called *Cosmos,* with promises of future TV specials, Uncle Woolly found himself playing King twisting in the wind. If yee old CEO hadn't been the founder, he'd've been doing the twist himself years earlier. All I know is what I saw in the halls of the old milk barn, people afraid to be seen talking with him lest they incur the enmity of their new bosses. But look, up the hall he is coming down, the once and mighty God of the Evening News. The walls widened to contain the breath of the mighty news icon, always well-dressed, in a Gucci trench coat, suit, pressed shirt, and tie in a Windsor knot, very distinguished in gray hair and mustache, self-composed and dignified. Who would've guessed he was King Lear with a penchant for playing bass in drag, and longing for the companionship of his colleagues, which in the best of times was never more than skin-deep? Their loyalties were to his successor. The Russians have a word, matryoshka, the doll within the doll. What I saw in the halls was the public persona that belied the loneliness of a dethroned king. A matryoshka man within a man wandering about in a house of cards. *A man's reputation is like his shadow, gigantic when it precedes him, and pygmy in proportions when it follows.*

"How come we don't see you on TV, Woolly?" asked the CEO in the hall. He purposely denied Woolly had played a major role in elevating the company to the top of the news junkie heap, and that it was incumbent upon him to honor that achievement. But, as they say, he was not a romantic.

In my mind's eye I see them bumping shoulders in the hallowed halls, two ancient duffers suffering Alzheimer's. *This what old guys do when they retire, wander hallways? Aye, replied the king. And go to concerts in the park when the coon dog can't run no more. Methinks I should know you. Yet I am doubtful: for I am mainly ignorant what hall this is; and all the skill I have remembers not these garments or these walls; nor I know not the pulpit where I delivered the Evening News; nor where I did lodge last night. Do not laugh; for, as I am a man, grown old, yet we'll wear out in a wall'd prison, packs and sects of great ones, that ebb and flow by the moon. Come, let's away...we two alone will sing like birds i'the cage: we'll tell old tales, and laugh at gilded butterflies, and hear poor rogues talk of court news... who loses and who wins; who's in, who's out; - and take upon's the mystery of things as if we were God's spies. There was no respect for youth when I was young, and now that I am old, there is no respect for age- I missed it coming and going.*

In those days they were all preoccupied with saving the company from corporate raiders and a shrinking economy. Meanwhile, replacement anchor Cactus Stan needed room to express his deadpan self with swell, country sayings that cut through the grist: *Let's run it up the flag pole and see if she flies; That dog won't hunt; He could charm a handkerchief out of a silkworm; I feel like I been rode hard and put away wet; Thanks for listening. It's been high cotton. Keep a cow, and the milk won't have to be watered but once.*

In the trenches, Crankcase's presence was like seeing General Macarthur reviewing the ranks. At least that's what I thought then, being a romantic. But in truth, it's no good hanging around when you're retired. He soon discovered that allegiances, policy changes, and old guidelines of integrity shifted disturbingly and rapidly. Crankcase tried to speak up at board meetings, but was outflanked by board members impelled by the need for survival in a changing marketplace.

Uncle harbored the bruised feelings of an outcast. When he started appearing on PBS, I thought he was the elder statesman devoting himself to public service. But in the voice of R. C. Hotpants, *Let's not get maudlin, chum, over a multi-millionaire, who has little compunction about collecting a salary for doing nothing at a time of cutbacks and a strike. Time makes us all irrelevant, chum, except me. I was never relevant. As to loyalty, Mark Twain was right. Pick up a starving dog, make him prosper, he won't bite you. This is the principal difference between a dog and man.*

While wondering where the axe would strike next, many news staffers were dismayed by some on-air colleagues who signed big money contracts and old Uncle Woolly, who collected thousands for doing zero. It was a harsh reminder of the gap between those who kept the company floating, and the "royalty" at the top, who thought they did it by themselves. While the elite feathered their nest, hundreds of their co-workers ended up in the street.

Freethinking scares the establishment. Alienate Madison Avenue, and you can't pay the light bill. So, the pragmatic Moses of fraudcasting led Americans backward, bent over, spread wide the company doors, and let the whores have their way. Oscar Brown Jr, was right when he said in a WLIB interview in 1967, *TV's nothin' but stone comic book.* By the late 1980's the old guard was gone- cast into the Burrow bin of forgotten integrity and scholarship in news.

Sorta Van's lieutenant, Joyless and his aid Stringah, eliminated jobs by cutting a swath through the newsroom with a machete. People were suddenly, callously, and brutally dismissed. Old-timers whose loyalty had often gone beyond the pale were shocked. *Budget cuts were necessary,* they said, *in a shrinking economy. Competition from cable is cutting into the broadcast pie.*

Burrows, even Crankcase, had been against advertisers sponsoring news. When Crankcase saw how *they* destroyed Burrow, he decided *if ya can't beat 'em join 'em,* and went on to make a fortune selling out the Fourth Estate. Sponsors, even the FCC license, come with caveats. An aquiescent press gave rise to produced news, and the Don Hugh-it mentality of *get 'em into the tent.* A former news president said of Hugh-it, *his notion of news is an elephant on water skis in Cypress Garden.*

In 1948 Doug Edwords gave us straightforward TV news reporting. The day he was considered *not dynamic enough* marks the path leading up to the 2004 Tush-Blather debacle. An independent investigation concluded the producers suffered *myopic zeal,* a euphemism for the rush to feed the beast, scoop the competition, and get the ratings, i.e., money. Blather forgot the cardinal rule of news: Do your own digging; trust your own eyes. The only thing TV raises higher is a bar of soap.

Four presidents played *corporate musical chairs,* up to, but not ending with moneybags Lorenzo di Pesce and his scaly Oxford co-hort "Fingahs" Stringah. After the fact, Pesce blamed "Fingahs" for the blitz at Chuckler. He wielded the hatchet into the '90's, but being a smart politician he *left no fingerprints.*

☺

46. Last Plane from Da Nang

Meanwhile, far-east correspondent Spruce Stunning, who had done super reporting from Vietnam, was moved laterally and disappeared.

Spruce was first rate. He never got the credit he deserved for his coverage of those final hours at the airport before the communists swept in; no awards or mentions, no kudos for the drama he so eloquently described, as thousands pushed and shoved in desperation to get out. I'd taken in on-sceners from other reporters, but none surpassed Spruce's heart-wrenching description of those last minutes before the city fell.

Scene: Da Nang airport; sound of airplane. *Hundreds of people are chasing after the plane already overloaded, screaming and falling away as it taxies onto the runway. A woman tries to hand up her child. 'Please! You take. Save my child!' A hand-span away, she slips, falls, trampled under the crowd chasing the plane down the tarmac with no thought of how it could take off if they all got aboard. The plane surges forward. Screams retreat into the engine noise. Several people lose their grip from forearm to wrist to hand to finger and fall away. The more tenacious're dragged along until they drop. Da Nang. The last plane out. A receding tarmac of outstretched arms and pleading voices.*

An audio loop of anguished souls reaching up from Dante's Inferno. The difference between life and death a handgrip away. Was it yesterday, 20 years ago, or today? Murder, pillage, rape, suicide bombers in the name of Christianity without God, Islam without Allah! Disgraceful!

A reporter's duty was implicitly understood based on the Burrow ethic. 'Get it straight! Get it right! Get it objective! And get it on-air!' Last plane from Da Nang was *Spruce's best reporting,* wrote a C.B.S colleague turned author-columnist, *has never been finer.* How was he rewarded? Camera 1, pull back on Spruce, and fade to black.

☺

47.   *The Mee-mo*

Jalanzo. The fuckin' Swan's fah-gotten more than some people know.

Tech. I rarely see him.

Jalanzo. Sound effects man on the resurrected *Mystery Radio Theatre* crosstown in the old Codfrey studios. He never breaks a sweat, which is a bigger mystery than the show. Fastest hands, and inventive. Whaddya doin' back in BOD? Need I ask.

Swan. (walking up) The show's on spring hiatus.

Jalanzo. This whole joint should go on hiatus. It ain't what it used to be.

Swan. Name something that is? I was cleaning out the attic and come across my old tux. I gave it to the Broadcast Museum, along with some sound effects stuff. My God, that place takes you back.

Jalanzo. Tell the kid what it was like. He takes notes, ya know. A fuckin' Gestapo. Tell 'im. So he knows about our glory days.

Swan. Glory, you say? Ha. Jalanzo, me boy. I do hold you dear.

Jalanzo. Not too dear, ya queer.

Swan. Back then, the dress code was suit and tie. We were paid two dollars a show for wearing tuxes on stage with the actors. When things went wrong, an announcer would say, "Now this musical interlude."

Jalanzo. Live organ music.

Swan. "Our program will resume as soon as the trouble is cleared up."

Then, recordings took over.

Jalanzo. It was cheaper. Adios Toscanini. So much for progress.

Swan. Pre-recorded music on 78 RPM discs. Cueing a disc, back timing, it was all new. Technology changed the industry, but fundamentally, we're still tied to the clock, and scripts. Tape revolutionized everything. Now, we can turn around a show in no time from anywhere in the world. Frankly, it was better the old way. We were part of the product.

Jalanzo. Now we're part of the problem.

Swan. Never get carried away, kid. It kills the golden goose. Lay back. Watch the miracle unfold. That's the real show. Like Mae West told me. The score never interested me, only the game.

C.B.S Mamorandum

To: ALL TECHNICIANS   Date: May 20, 1984

DO NOT LEAVE YOUR ASSIGNED STUDIO UNTIL PROPERLY RELIEVED!

☺

Studio B, 9AM. I lean in the door across the hall. The Swan's sitting back at the controls chewing a pencil.

Swan. What's a four letter word for insignificance?

Tech. News. My relief hasn't shown up.

Swan. Who is it?

Tech. Don't know. Where do you go from here?

Swan. Studio E.

Tech. You're my relief and I'm yours.

Swan. But I'm not in dereliction of duty, laddybucks. Like Jalanzo says, You'll go under the lights.

Tech. How are we supposed to relieve each other without leaving the studio? The memo says-

Swan. Memo! Another four letter word for insignificance.

☺

48. Pearls Before Swine

Diary. Oct 26, 1985. Hylton, I'm gonna interview you. *Who?* You. *Me?* Yeah. I'm gonna interview you. *For TV? You got to give some royalty.* No. The 1212 Newsletter. *Say, what?* Circulation 3,000. *I'm going to lunch.* How long you been with C.B.S, 31 years? *Yes.* You've seen a lot of stars come and go: Arthur Codfrey, Ed Sullivan, Lucille Ball, Carol Burnett. You used to ride the freight elevator with Carol Burnett. Was she a regular person? *Yes.* Grace Kelly used to be on the third floor; Andy Warhol was on the sixth with *The Celeste Holm Summer Show;* Patti Page you met in an elevator in L.A. You're lucky in elevators. You once saw Nat King Cole at a water fountain. *Yes.* You worked with Liberace in Radio City. He had black hair then. *Yes.* That's it. Oh, what do you remember most? *That I forgot what you remembered.*

Completed first Newsletter. Nobody at the union office proofed it. Good. Very exciting. Writing, editing, producing a six-page newsletter. Not the usual pap, hardhats wearing tool belts and construction boots on a picnic in Podunk.

The Voice
Vol. 3 No. 1 PUBLISHED FOR RADIO, T.V., AND RECORDING INDUSTRIES June 1985
DIARY OF A MAD TECHNICIAN

Profile: "Tom n' Terry In the Newsroom" by The Mad Tech

How do you like writing news for C.B.S?

People tell me it's great.

What people?

Mostly ones who don't work here. My mother says it's terrific, but to remember that in show business always cash the check right away.

You like MaGoy, your news director?

The job's easy. It's how to deal with him in the hallway.

Hit him with the blarney! It's the only way with the Irish. Then, they love you forever.

It's hard to know when he's kidding or serious.

Just be honest and look for work elsewhere. You're a low-key guy in a brash business.

Sometimes I wonder what I'm doing in it.

Judging by your writing, very well. But what do I know? I'm the janitor. For example, let's take the lead-in that you wrote when Pete Rose made scandalous baseball history.

Oh. What was it?

Don't you keep copies?

Only of my conversations with Tom. The other day – it's two minutes to air, Doug Edwards was waiting on the lead story. I'm typing like mad. MaGoy comes up, kicks my desk, and says, I hear you're hung like a freckle. How about a date? Unbelieveable.

He only dates good writers. I've noticed, you're quiet, efficient, and well-mannered.

Yes. What's wrong with me?

You opened the Pete Rose graph with "The subject is Roses... Pete Rose's-" Very good.

You think so?

What do I know? I'm a technician.

I thought you were the janitor?

I was demoted. I love your piece on the former Newton Minow's "TV is a vast wasteland..." How'd it go?

A survey concluded that young people are getting fat watching television. So I said, what was once a vast wasteland has become a vast waistline. Listen, maybe you can give me with your opinion. I'm thinking of becoming a playwright.

Working on anything?
I'm writing something called "Pun." It's a play on words.

☺

49. Notes From the O'Fey Café

Deer Diary. Tech Yanelli sicked out. It's an annual stomach virus around hunting season. He's northern Italian. I'm southern. He's calm. I'm intense. He's Germanic. I'm Greek. He hunts deer. I object. He calls me a *bambi lover. Venison's healthier than regular meat; leaner, sweeter, easier to chew.* Funny, he's peaceful on the job, but aggressive outdoors. If he flips out it could be open season on the dears of the Fourth Estate.

October. Writers may strike. It'd be like seeing the Kennedy children picketing their parents for a bigger allowance. ***November 3rd.*** On-air screw-up. On cue I hit the tape, the reporter starts, stops, says, " Woops. Again from the top." Later, the tape-ops guy says, *It came in on your shift.* Not mine. *You're the only studio operational. Maybe you rolled dead pot.* I go, You're the only dead pot here. Later, I learn it was taken in by the tech I relieved. He got in a fight with Nervous Nelly, who's always makin' a list and checkin' it twice, and got careless. Who wants to listen two and three times to pieces you don't want to hear in the first place? ***Nov. 9th.*** Air conditioner busted. Hard to breathe, especially with Soviet chain smoking. "Smoke, but don't exhale." More firings. Paranoia is so rampant people're walking around stabbing each other in the chest.

☺

50.   REPORT OF THE BUSINESS MANAGER

February, 1987
IBEW/C.B.S Quarterly Conference
Sanibel Island, Florida

President C.B.S Sports and Broadcast Operation
Executive VP title has been eliminated. The head of Divisions are now line jobs. **Departments have been eliminated**. IBEW has felt little effect by the cut back. Layoffs should stop now and we should prepare ourselves for the reality of the business. TV viewing is about 70%, compared to 90% ten years ago. Cable, Independent TV, VCR's, etc., are draining our viewers. The Company is budgeting for a 1.9% decrease in market growth in 1987. We've **eliminated 1,500 jobs at a savings of $50 million.**

The company thinks the IBEW contract must change. The Staff is unproductive as it **isn't adaptable** enough. Fixed costs are too high, too many penalties, no way to get rid of non-productive employees, scheduling and jurisdiction too rigid.

Sports packaging *among competitors* and growing numbers of non-union producers, daily employees with more flexible conditions, are causing problems. Because of present overheads, the Company can't compete and needs to be able to hire just like them. Under consideration is selling off or leasing some facilities. The Company needs to take strong measures and is determined to survive, and IBEW will play a major role in our future. "As the Stomach Turns" and "Guiding Blight" are in negotiations to continue in-house. If we lose Proctor and Gamble, we'll have to down-size, no question about it.

Company Coalition Meeting: Attendance was high at a joint coalition meeting of WGA, DGA, AFTRA and IBEW, discussing strong proposals of management to the WGA. The **WGA Agreement expired midnight, March 1, and a strike is imminent.**

J.M., Senior Vice President, Operations and Engineering: Goobers and Lysol doing review– main topic was number of people. We will get to our goal by buying out 32 techs and the layoff in New York, Wash., and L.A.

☺

51.   The After 3 Theatre Company

Because Ayn's great with kids, I formed the After 3 Theatre Company, Inc. in 1986. A parent once asked, "How'd you decide on that name? I go, *School's after 3, the kids're after 3, and I teach after 3 drinks.*

One afternoon in drama class a 5-year-old's circling even numbers with a crayon, instead of odd ones indicated by directions. He knew the difference between odd and even. I go, "Did you read the directions?" He nods 'yes'. "Then why don't you circle odd numbers?" He says, "Can't." I go, "Why?" He says, "Because my pencil will turn to dookie."

The excessive need to say 'hello' is a compulsion stemming from the suckling period. 'Hello' is mother's milk. 'Goodbye' is Daddy's weaning. Kids are closer to that milk than adults and tend more readily to let it all hang out. I said to Bernadette, age 6, "You're always talking. You never shut up. You know that?" She goes, "Yes." I go, "Good. Now can you stop talking?" She thinks and says, "Oh, I don't think I could do that."

☺

52.   Workers Unite?

<u>Date: March, 1987</u>

A wave of budget cuts, wholesale firings, and journalistic retrenchment is about to crest over Chuckler News. It not only threatens to diminish the quantity and quality of our journalistic product, but, by "restructuring," to fundamentally alter and diminish the nature of the service we provide the American people.

There is every indication that the future of the news division is in the hands of cost-benefit technicians with little appreciation of traditions of our organization or the responsibilities upon us as messengers in a democratic society.

Therefore, it's time to send a message to the public, to the Chuckler Board of Directors and shareholders, to management and their hired accountants.

For 24 hours of Monday, March 9th we undersigned Chuckler News employees – executives, producers, correspondents, editors,

writers, technicians, researchers, secretaries and news assistant –
will withhold our labor. Our goal on this "No News is Good News" day,
is to kill News on TV and radio in protest against past and pending
cost-reductions that serve corporate profit aims at the expense of
truth in news reporting. Also, let us take this occasion to express
solidarity with striking members of the Writers Guild of America.
Their contract dispute is related to the deliberate retrenchment in
the level of journalism practiced at Chuckler News.

   Signatures: _____ .   _____.   _____.   No signees.

ACT FIVE

END PIECES

1 Prima Donnas On The Line

Winter, 1987. Chuckler's a charnel house, firings, cutbacks, paranoia everywhere. The wrters walked. Management's doing double duty for the same pay. They'll get bonuses afterward. On my break I join the line.

Writer 1. With exceptions when, where, and how strikes happen is less important than why. They're a premeditated, sly balancing of the books, no accident, with the outcome decided in advance by management in collusion with union leaders. Except where individual labor produces perishables companies operate on inventory. When there's surplus, strikes and layoffs are expedient. The company unloads its excess, saves wages, settles, and screw the little guy. It's all pre-calculated to offset deficits, initiate cost cutting, and to find out what it means monetarily to have workers out. They need to cut 20% from a $300 million budget. They knocked off 200 news jobs before we walked.

Writer 2. The stock's performing well.

Tech. Same pattern with us in '72.

Writer 1. The market sees it as saving money. A strike is a forced vacation without pay. Right now they're doing cost comparisons. What's it cost to have us out compared to having us in. Watch. We'll go back when they reach their goal of saving 30 million dollars.

Tech. When NABET struck ABC for six months they saved 19 million.

Writer 1. Every brick in Carnegie Hall contains the agony, blood and sweat of steel workers. It's a testament to greed. While Carnegie was in Europe dedicating libraries, his flunkies put the law on the mill workers. To want decent wages and medical benefits is anarchy. Getting sick from exposure to chemicals and coal dust, toxic materials, and recycled air, don't count. Can you work in a mine?

439

Writer 2. Hey, we go up in elevator shafts to windowless caves in the sky. What's the difference? They have birds down there to warn them.
Writer 1. What if a bird's paranoid?

WGA Negotiating Committee, March 2, 1987
What is the strike about? The company demands:
Discharge: Fire at will. No right to arbitration.
Layoff: 50% of shop exempted from layoff in seniority order.
Temps: Any vacancy can be filled with temp forever. After layoffs, unlimited use of temps. Laid off employees would not have first chance at temp work. 235-day limit a year per temp.
AFTRA WRITING: field reporter with prior story involvement or area expertise or significant individual effort (anything more than a short phone call) can write in studio for anyone.
Managers Writing: News director, assistant news director, managing editor, executive producer, or unlimited supervisors with similar responsibility can write. No limitation on hiring non-union writers as "supervisors".
Successors & Assigns/Transfer of Responsibility: If all or part of the company is sold, union contract does not transfer; contract dies. They can move to new location and contract dies.
Tape coordinator: Two-tiered wage system for radio; 20% of Chicago and New York Network and Local radio shops; salary range $293-$384.
Graphic Artists: The Company willing to move from broader proposals to narrower language.

2.   Look Alike PR

Good News, Bad News: The bad news? The strike's still on. The good news? The writers are talking to each other. Forced civility is un-American. A replacement from accounting entered the newsroom, said, "I'm your scab du jour." A guy from the Atlanta bureau worked the desk, was fired in a new round of cutbacks, and had to pay his own way home. Curmudgeon Prooney declaims the 'barbaric strike' while drawing a salary in his warm office filled with memorabilia, a World War Two bullet from the wall of a latrine, a bronzed Lipton Tea bag, inscribed by Codfrey, *'From one old bag to another.'*

Writer 1. They only understand violence.
Writer 2. Put the pencil away or you'll erase yourself.
Writer 1. They've got to be hurting.
Writer 2. Big companies don't hurt. They're just inconvenienced.
Writer 1. What about public opinion?
Writer 2. Who's sympathizing with an upper middle-class strike?
Writer 1. My mother.
Writer 2. Not mine. She's with her third husband on the Riviera. She says, *the union paying you to walk? Come here and walk on the Riviera. Say you're a lifeguard. Go back when they make up their minds.*

☺

Writer 1. Shakespeare and the bible. Greatest stuff ever written.
Writer 2. Not by one man. Who really wrote those plays?
Writer 1. Shakespeare set the nuts and bolts, but a lot of people contributed, especially actors. He ransacked the Italians for plots. In the book *Trader Horn*, the Trader's in Africa around 1910, tea-totaling with an English lady who asked the same question. "What's that, Ma'am?" says Trader Horn. "Do I believe Shakespeare was written by Bacon? I've heard the idea spoken of in London, but if you'll excuse me sounding harsh, that's one of the most foolhardy notions that the mind of man could conceive. Newspaper talk, I call it. It's well known that the monks wrote Shakespeare. Our astronomy professor at St. Edward's- nice gentleman, I forget his name, but he went out to Australia to study the transit of Venus- how *beit* he always said to me, "Aloysius, my boy, your Shakespeare will carry you wherever you want to go. Read between

the lines. And remember, 'twas not one head, but many that represent Shakespeare. 'Twas the priests, who else? What human man could have learnt so much without the confessional? 'Tis a universal grasp of the genus man never likely to have been wasted on one brain! Of course they kept him supplied! I dare say they were glad enough to earn a regular bit of money ...for the powerful stories they could give him." Who but a monk or priest would be privy to manners and intrigues at court? His genius was putting it all together. Great writers see things on levels in a sweep, and not consciously. Balzac, and de Maupassant had a subliminal connection to the cosmic conscience. I'd love to write news before it happens. Edgar Cayce with Tomorrow's News Today. We're already into subliminal targeted mail. Voters'll receive ads showing candidates with faces resembling them, which will influence their vote. It'll give deeper meaning to 'A Vote For Me Is A Vote For You'. On the other hand, it wouldn't work on people who hate themselves.

☺

3.   An Old pal

Mike Yung came to town for a day on his way to a wedding in Boston. *Two drama teachers died, Trapido and Ernst. The East-West Center is finished. So's George Chun's marriage to Doris. They divorced after their son Bryan died from one rare disease.* Their wedding reception was a Japanese-Chinese luau. Dying young's not so bad. *Even my beautiful Hawaii's dying. High rises in Waikiki cutting down the breeze to Kaimuki.*

☺

4.   Fays at The O'Fey

(during gas shortage)

What're you sniggering at?

I saw someone sneak into the gas line.

How crude.

Yes.

Anyone see him?

I did.

So what's it to you, you playing Red Ryder this morning?

I'd like to give him a piece of my mind.

I'm not going to answer that one.

Lucky I don't have to get on line.

You're not driving?

Sold my car.

You did? When?

Last summer. Remember?

No.

You bought it.

I did? What color is it?

Blue.

Now I remember.

☺

5.   The Demise of C.B.S or Mass Medea

Diary, '81. His name confused me. Was it Van Sorter or Sort Van? First, I thought he was half of the Sauter-Finnegan Orchestra. Then, I'd see his hairy face in the hall, lumbering along on soft feet with a rolling motion- a dancing woolly sucking a Sherlock pipe.

Sorta went from the company's LA sports division to president of C.B.S News. Then, he moved news from its preeminent position as the *Times* of fraudcasting to the Orchard Street of infotainment. He had a tabloid mind and a weird sense of humor. *I had to play detective,* said Horace, a radio writer/producer, *just to figure where we'd meet for an appointment. 'Let's do lunch at 2. We'll talk then about your producing for TV. Meet you at the usual.' I'd call his office, La Biarritz, Armstrong's. Where was he? In the exec dining room cafeteria. One meeting involved clues leading to a Grand Central train to DC. I had to get out at Philadelphia. He was in his office. He's always on the go.* It's harder to hit a moving target. *He hired ex-beauty Queen Phyllis Gorge for the Morning Show. She got a three-year, ironclad contract, which had to be paid in full when the show tanked. Back in peach country, she collected thousands for two and a half years doing nothing.*

In 1983 Sorta Van moved to Black Crock, corporate headquarters, as executive VP of the News Division. Joyless, his lieutenant, became president of C.B.S News. We met in '67 at local when he was a news director. A smooth, syrupy voice in a four-eyed moon face, he was honeyed bitters, a sticky character. His audition card said, 'Voice: Baritone. Quality: Pompous'.

☺

6.   Hello, Mate!

Joyless brought in Stringah to assist him. I'd almost forgotten my ex-newsfeed mate, who suddenly reappeared out of the TV woodwork. His climb up the ladder from a cup of coffee with me to president of Chuckler is unique. Being Oxford educated, he must've had a godfather. Perhaps his English accent faked out the powers-that-be. A good English accent's a sucker punch. After all, it is their language, and when used properly rings like poetry. From Newsfeed Stringah moved to producing, writing, and ingratiating himself wherever it paid off. After Sorta

Van became President of the News Division, Joyless moved up with Stringah as his lieutenant-confidant.

Stringah was a patient, observant guy, and was forever saying 'mate', but at first I had to set his ass straight about newsfeed and me. As soon as he started with the mate crap, I go, "Stringah, read my fingah. We've got more important things to do than worry about a dumb show. It ain't rocket science. When you lock-in the tapes, I'll assemble the show-reel."

He replied calmly without indignation at having a tech wise off. "I shall hold off, mate. May I suggest there is purpose to this madness on behalf of our brethren in the boondocks, where, as you colonials say, it's slim pickings, and I don't mean the actor, mate." I go, thinking fruitcake, "I handle everybody that way." He says, "Well, mate, wouldn't want to be an exception to the rule." I go, "Good. I'll string the cuts together before air, and that way we don't waste time with last minute bullshit."

He gives me a Wally Peepers look, and says, "Wouldn't want to waste time, mate, with last minute bullshit. Time in radio is a commodity."

I go, "Is that accent real or did you study with Stella Adler? I'll be in the lounge. You need to play a tape, do it yourself, but close the door. Tape-ops people operating equipment gets the old timers nervous."

With the crazy overnight hours, who needed arguments at 4a? Not my new mate. He knew that in an argument everybody loses. Newsfeed was the last place to leave a clumsy footprint in the grand scheme of things.

Stringah reminded me of a parrot on a perch, always with the "Hello. Hello, mate!" One time I said, "Enough. I'm gettin' sea sick." Years later, Stringah, the ringah, was knighted by the Queen of England. But I had already knighted him when he asked me to work. I said, "G'night, mate." What do I get by association? Bird calls. "Hello, hello, mate!"

☺

7. *N-yuk, N-yuk, N-yuk!*

Devious Septum. It's not Larry we have to worry about. It's Moe and Curly. They're comin' next week. N-yuk, n-yuk, n-yuk.

In the '80's Chuckler was ailing, and out of touch. Meanwhile, Sorta Van started redefining hard and soft news. Following the Georgia Peach fiasco, he became toast himself, but walked off with enough money to pay 8 tech salaries for 12 months.

Over the years corporate executives dismantled and diminished a solid moneymaking organization by screw-ups, cover-ups, and sell-offs that did not serve the long-range interest of the company, its employees, or its shareholders. One major blunder in '70' s was failure to establish a firm footing in Cable TV, i.e., Vicom, which it had to divest to comply with laws of monopoly. Today, Vicom owns Chuckler. Most sinful of all was the board's decision to sell off parts of the company: Stein Weigh Piano, Inexacto Knives, and the Noo Yawk Yanks, all priced below market value. In the words of the late sports announcer, Mel Allen, *How about that?*

In the '80's a major business mistake derailed the company. President Tailor's decision to buy back company shares to avoid a hostile take-over by corporate raiders, i.e., Ted Turner, put the company in debt during a "listless economy" compounded by a "marked softness in the advertising market-place". Enter opportunist and multimillionaire Lorenzo di Pesce, whose bottom line was profit. After buying up stock, more than the old man held, he became a major shareholder, and was invited by Tailor to join the board. Subsequently, Tailor was ousted and guess who became CEO? Right. Lorenzo di Pesce. *How about that?*

Pesce was short, bald, a pink Spalding with a red tongue. Some called him *a Jewish Yul Brynner. In a turtleneck he looks like a prick.* With the old man's moral suasion juiced out with age, nothing could stop this cost-cutting barracuda. He never heard of the words 'quality', 'class', and 'tradition'. Tell me your cash flow and I'll tell you your name. He took Chuckler to the knackers, selling off the Record Company, interactive television, cable, and the publishing arm. The bank of TV monitors in his office was tuned to Wall Street. Pesce was C.B.S's Judas Iscariot, a usurer guilty of corporate malfeasance.

Tech. (*1980's*) Pesce put out a buy-back of C.B.S stock above market at $190 per share. A year later it was selling for $310 a share. Why?

Jalanzo. A fuck-your-buddy, crony brokerage firm had a sell exclusive and talked it up. Accountants painted a rosy picture to push up the tick. Then, the big guys dump out, and the little guy holdin' his bird. At the top it's all insider trading.

After departing the company in the '90's, Pesce remarked that *Stringah had lots to do with what happened,* and used the *no fingerprints* routine. Probably true. Stringah was in Newsfeed and I forgot he'd been there at all. Then, something written by Svetlana Alliluyeva, Stalin's daughter, came to mind. Lavrenty P. Beria, Stalin's chief of police, she wrote, was the monster behind *the blot on my father's name,* and in *many things they were guilty together.* Heads of state, no less of corporations, depend on the complicity of subordinates.

☺

8.   Strike Impressions n' Scuttlebutt

Writer 1. First we heard Pesce wants to end it, and then Stringah came out and says there's no truth to it.

Writer 2. (*coming up*) The union's ticked. The company broke off talks. (*angry re-act*) Their negotiator went to a birthday party.

All. You're kiddin'? Whose party? We'll picket the house. You took food from the mouths of our kids to feed cake to yours. Boo!

Writer 1. Will time go quicker if we walk faster?

☺

Diary. Saw Stringah in hall; looked glum likewise prez of network news. Told him a joke. He smiles, "First laugh I've had all day." The Director of Tech Services was in the newsroom working the desk. I go, "You found a home as a DA." He goes, "At 3:01 I'm your boss again. Watch out."

(*Heard over the bathroom stall*)

Scab 1. We could be the only two people left.

Scab 2. You're right. And guess what? We're in the shit house.

2ⁿᵈ week out. Weather warmed up, but still nasty. Chilly and rainy with gusty winds. Somebody brought hot coffee from the cafeteria.

Writer 1. Twenty years on the job, suddenly I'm invisible.

Tech. Here's your money, John, and the lotto tickets. No problem from the cashier. What're you reading?

John. The Life of Toscanini. Very interesting. My father played flute in his orchestra. My father auditioned for Stokowski at 16. A lady at a desk verifies the audition in her date book, and asks, *What's wrong?* My father says, *I'm scared to death.* She says, *Oh, don't let that old goat bother you.* He goes in, Stokowski's shuffling music, doesn't look up, points his finger, and says, *Play.* My father does *Evening of a Fawn* near perfect with one tiny smudge. Stokowski says, *Do you know Debussy's?* My father plays it clean. Stokowski says, *Practice more every day.* Outside the lady says, *How'd it go?* My father says, *Badly. I was terrible.* She says, *Wait right there.* Goes into the room, comes back, says, *You did very well.* The lady was Gloria Vanderbilt, his wife. Later she wrote a book and called Stokowski *a big phony.* Stokowski exuded a superior manner to put people off. He created the great conductor image mostly through fear. He'd come in, say, *Stravinsky,* lift the baton, go one-two and they'd play, without a rehearsal. Nothing. That was Stokowski. The musicians he had were the best. Could do anything. One time Stokowski conducted a three-four piece in two-four. But the orchestra knew it and played it in three-four. They'd stopped for some reason and my father, he was young, scratched his head and says, *Excuse me, maestro. Isn't this piece in three-four?* Stokowski says, *Yes.* My father says, *But you're conducting in two-four.* Stokowski says, *It's three-four in two-four.* Nobody talked back or they'd be looking for work in another city. He intimidated musicians, especially novices and old-timers. He would always manage to find something disruptive no matter how picayune. Once, they started an all night session at midnight. Now these were the best musicians around. They finished at 4a without rehearsals. A perfect session, my father said. But Stokowoski points to someone in the rear, a fine musician nearing retirement, and says, *You didn't play loud enough!* Then, he throws down his baton and walks out. It was a sham, my father said. Nobody'd notice one instrument in a group of six playing lower, even if true. Toscanini called Stokowski a clown. He even dressed like one. At home he wore a long robe over a silk shirt with frilly sleeves and a flouncy collar, and his hair was long. One day he answered the door dressed like that. A reporter was there to interview his wife, Gloria Vanderbilt. Stokowski says, *She is not at home. She is at Grri-stede's.* The reporter finds her in the store, identifies himself. Gloria says, *Yes. I remember our appointment. But how did you know where to find me?* He says, *I was at your apartment and your grandmother told me.* One time my father says we were set to perform a children's concert playing music suggesting animals. Stokowski looks out at the audience of children, and says grandly,

We shall musically represent the gir-rahffe. Then points his customary finger at the audience and says, *Who can tell Stokowski what is a gir-rahffe?* A kid raises his hand and says, *A gir-rahffe is a geer-rafe.*

☺

WGA STRIKE: Where We Are Now: Negotiating Committee, 5.15.87

1. DISCHARGE: Manager must critique and warn; Employee must have chance to improve. Arbitration standard same as last contract.
2. LAYOFFS: 30% of shop may be exempted from layoff in seniority order; minimum of one person per shop. All other layoffs in strict inverse seniority order. Employees laid off out of seniority order receive double severance.
3. TEMPORARIES: For one year, after vacancies for discharge or resignation temps can fill job only for 60 days. Laid off staff have first chance at temp work; in cases of equal ability, seniority is considered. 210-day limit a year per temp.
4. AFTRA WRITING: Field reporters with prior story involvement or significant independent effort can write in studio for anchors only.
5. MANAGERS WRITING: Limit to managers writing.
6. SUCCESSORS & ASSIGNS/TRANSFER OFRESPONSIBILITY: Company withdrew proposal. If operation is moved 25 miles or less, union contract still applies.
7. TAPE COORDINATOR – SERVICE AIDE: One individual only; limited to local radio in New York; must be promoted from desk assistant who has one year experience; salary range $311-$407; proposal not effective until January 1, 1988.
8. GRAPHIC ARTS: Company was willing to move from broader proposals to narrower language in: work by managers, over scale, night differential.

Diary. 4a. Steps from the revolving door entrance a dozen picketers trudge along behind police barriers. Illumined by a trash can fire they look like the damned in Dante's Inferno. Joining them is like visiting a sick friend knowing you can split anytime. One guy's reading job listings, another, Kierkaguard, and a woman's hyped over the battle of the sexes.

Writer 1. Beefy hands jumping my bones! Holstein minds ruling the roost. Where's it written that when both partners work, the woman has to do the boring, repetitive, time-consuming, household chores? What law says we're suppose to dust, do dishes, and make beds?

Writer 2. It's the way it is. You're protected like the Queen Bee.

Writer 1. Give me a break, pa-lease! She sits there like a cow spewing milk. Pa-lease! I'd rather live in a monastery. Celibacy's an alternative to the degradation of man's sexual abuse.

Writer 2. Degradation?

Writer 1. Screwing without respect. Who needs it?

Writer 2. That cuts both ways.

Writer 1. Erotic emotion's merely the energy of life. It can be worked off easily doing positive things. Affection, recognition, and love can be gotten from friends who dig you for who you are as a human being, and not for how docile, cuddly, cute, sexy, and ego-building you are for a man.

Writer 2. You're a 60's throwback.

Writer 1. And you're antediluvian. If men had to give birth, guess what? By now they'd've invented a birthing machine. I don't need a man with an overbearing presumptuous prick to clean out my tubes, to relieve the pressure. Until then men will always hold us hostage to the threat of withdrawing their sexual favors.

Writer 2 and 3. What about children? Advancing mankind. Man in the generic sense. Human kind.

Writer 1. I've decided that someone else can have mine, all that're allotted and intended. If I'm going to gain weight it'll be from chocolate fudge and ice cream. Birth is death, stretch marks, wide hips, headaches, nausea, vomiting in the middle of the night. I'm one working woman who is anti-labor.

Writer 2. A guy who marries you'll spend his honeymoon in a test tube. What'll you name your first kid, Pyrex Two? If it were up to libbers, we'd all be jerkin' off.

Writer 3. What's the difference? I'm married and jerkin' off now!

Writer 2. Strikes're a waste of time.

Writer 1. Deeper than that, friend. They touch the root of who we are as a society and as individuals. Strikes bring out our subconscious fear of disconnection, of being rootless. Y'see, amigo, security and uncertainty when challenged take us closer to the great existential abyss, the terror and despair of facing an inconceivable void, a nothingness beyond the imagination. It's fear of poverty; the primal enticing delusion called money. We get so absorbed in superficialities that we become insensitive to the mystery of creation and the miracle of our own existence.

Tech. Does management know all that?

Writer 1. The quest for self in an alien world. To merge with the great overriding universal divinity. The universal sense among men, regardless of religion, that love, morality, compassion, empathy, form the key to unlocking the mind, freeing it from narrow perspectives. Its self-oriented "I-ness," its fear of obliteration, enabling it to merge with the "other" – the collective unconscious- to realizing the oneness of man with nature and the universe. Do you understand separateness? Feeling unique and cut off from an evolving world? *Yes.* Separateness is blown away when the mind is transcended and spirituality takes over. Man has higher human drives and needs than this debasing strike. Man needs meaningful work that's fare, just and moral. Along with the more primitive drives, higher states of consciousness are experiences of unity and eternity. We must, and this is important, we must strive to end duality. *And actuality.* To survive as a species we must develop appreciation of the holistic, unitive and integrated nature of the universe and our relevancy. We must reach a level of consciousness extending beyond insularity. There's too much "I-ness," and not enough "we-ness." Management's "me-ness" wants to destroy labor's "we-ness." Can you lend me 5 for lunch?

Tech. That's an "I-ness" request that leaves me with fear of obliteration and unable to merge with the other, separating the oneness of man with nature and the universe creating a vacuum in me that negates empathy and gives rise to feelings of separateness, destitution, subsequent fear and terror of being impoverished and lost in an alien world which negates personal freedom, personal decision, and travel commitments. Oops. Time to make my exit-stential.

☺

Inside, I flash my ID to security. Down the hall my Santo Domingan friend's sweeping the floor with a lick and a promise. *I'm tired this job.* Buy another house back home. *I got one too many headaches. I just want to disappear. Do nothing. Hit the lotto. Man, the line yesterday goin' down the hall to the next block. Everybody lookin' to get out. You know what I do if I hit that lotto? I goin' to my boss in front of everybody. I goin' to say, "Boss, you always been honest and descent to the workers. A good man. I'm givin' you fifty thousand dollars cash." Cash? "Cash". Well, gee, thank you. I put the money on the table. "It's all yours, boss." Then, I drop my pants and say, "But first, in front of everybody, you have to kiss both cheeks of my motherfuckin' black ass."*

Diary. Studio A, 5a. Paul "Deep Pipes" Lockwood's doing the hourly. He's not on strike because he's AFTRA. I turn to the board tech.

Tech. I could work with Paul all day.
Dilido. Be my guest. I got 'im three more hours.

Tech. He's what C.B.S is all about. If I could rebuild this place, I'd start with Lockwood.

Dilido. And fire yourself.

Tech. He's solid, unpretentious, direct, and never sweats. Owns up to mistakes and doesn't bug us when we make 'em. His scripts are models: double-spaced, cues written out, and clean.

Dilido. Stop. You're givin' me a hard-on. Gimme a sweet management job with a charge card and a golden parachute. Nothin' big. A low six-figure salary I can work out of my home.

(*Lockwood closes, and waves hello*)

Dilido. So when you guys gettin' married?

Tech. After we settle with our wives.

Dilido. Well, I'm not givin' you up without a fight, deary.

Tech. I like loyalty. They teach that up at Fordham, do they?

Dilido. It comes under Morals and Ethics. Classes are across the street in the Bronx Zoo. Same sex meets next door in the Botanical Gardens. (*fay voice*) Any more questions, asshole?

Tech. Yeah. How the fuck did you ever graduate?

Dilido. Straight A's, pal. Still do my rock show on FUV Saturday nights. Workin' on it now. I taped it 'cause I won't be around this weekend. (*edits his tape*) Paul's okay. Not like those creeps outside. Couldn't happen to a nicer bunch. A little humble never hurts. When they settle, they'll be right back at it. Meanwhile, I'm cruisin' and sailin' on paybacks. They're a bitch, ain't they? Ha!

Tech. If Paul were out there, I'd walk with him.

Dilido. Stop jerkin' me off. You don't spring for coffee.

Tech. I think I'll help them by slowing down and stalling work.

Dilido. That's your MO. Try workin'. That'll confuse 'em. I had a thrill comin' in seein' the over-producer walkin'. That hyper, electronic asshole. Comin' in every five minutes to see if the room's still here. He can stay out forever. Only put the fucker on the back door so I don't see 'im when I come in. The tape-ops person would come in here around 6 ayem. He'd be early so he'd schmooze', have coffee and Danish. The over-producer sees 'im through the window and sends in work. One time I go, "Let the man finish his Danish. He's early." The asshole says, "That's the trouble with techs. You go by the clock." He should freeze and shit ice cubes.

Tech. The '60's were better. News ended at midnight and started up at 6.

Dilido. Sweet. I could go for that.

Tech. That's why I took the overnight. But the hours are rough. You drag ass comin' and goin'.

Dilido. I have that all the time. It's called work.

Tech. One second. (*dials phone*) Hello, Desk? Mal Terkel? How's ya pork? (*hangs up*) Tell me, how does a company go bad?

Dilido. Hiring nuts like you. Happens by increments like marriage hittin' the rocks. I'm havin' problems at Fordham. New policy, new creeps trying to establish themselves. They do a little bullshit here, a little there, and next thing you know, it's different ball game. Last month they cut my show to two hours. This month they moved me up an hour. I'm doing this show ten years. Well, what the hell. It's their transmitter. You hear rumors and then, boom, it happens. It's increments. B comes in, followed by X, Y, and Z. New people easily intimidated. Eager beavers. Y'know, high-strung news junkies, electronic assholes with a mission. In a way, writers are lucky. Their job's a career. To me, it's work. One guy says, *I'd go to the moon. Then when I get back my career'll be made.* His career! What's this career bullshit? Pete Robeson, the new guy from AP, says, *the newsroom's like Hollywood full of stars. You don't see it to this extent in print or the wires. There, it's the story not the writer.*

☺

9.   It Ain't the Pajama Game

Diary. That first day the strikers looked like Ivy League yuppies on a cakewalk. *There ought to be an agency where you hire people to walk for you. And maybe they could go to the bathroom for you, too. When you go to the guild, bring back a black forest ham on rye, petitis fours, and a café au lait.* Soon they were dragging ass. Some didn't wear signs, just a button with a line drawn through the company call letters. I checked out the Guild across the street, showed my WGA card, and ate some free food. As time and the strikers marched on, they received less and less media coverage, until they weren't even on the back burner. It embarrasses me to cross the line. So I try the back door but it's covered, too. Next time I'll try the skylight. It reminds me of our strike in '72. I was single then, and didn't feel the pinch, except for the shameful, beggar's parade spectacle. The older strikers with families, mortgages, and fragile health suffered most from lost wages and exposure. You can get pneumonia just taking out the garbage. Striking with no income's a no-brainer. But then nothing's ever black or white unless you're black or white, and maybe not even then if you're hard of seeing. Thirty days out a union driver tossed me a newsletter from a car that said in big headlines, *Techs On Strike!* I'm freezin', my strike sign's giving me neck burns, and they're telling me I'm on strike. Gee. I thought I was rehearsing Pajama Game.

☺

10.   Thumbsucking

Diary: 3a, Studio D. Self-consciousness tightens free flow. Be loose, concentrate on ideas, not grammar. When Mal was alive we took in a piece from a self-smitten reporter in love with his prose. He described a dead body: *Fleas and maggots're developing on decomposing remains.* Gross, says Mal. Cut out the reference to fleas and maggots. He refuses. *Fleas and maggots're integral to the piece.* Mal reiterates. No fleas and maggots. *Why? We get the message without them. What d'ya got against fleas and maggots? Paints a great picture. I'll meet ya halfway n' take out fleas.* No fleas or maggots. It would be terrible for the breakfast audience to hear about fleas and maggots over corn flakes and coffee. Personally, I love 'em on mine. The reporter excises the words, but hangs up pissed over meddling with his prose... Cholly, the news bard, is away. Should've taken the Chink with him. In case you don't know or need reminding, Cholly rhymes news, something dedicated journalists eschew. The Chink's nearby, jerkin' off on the computer, looking for ideas and ways to justify himself. *6:45a.* Correspondent Scott G enters. "I'm Cholly." The Chink starts to talk. "Hold it," says Scott, hands up. "For the record. No goddamn poetry. Now. Waddya got?" Beautiful!

When I talk about my job pressure builds up in my chest like I've just run a 50-yard dash. Ayn's been telling me, slow down. Simple things are hard to do. Right now on TV another basketball player dunks one. Ticks me off. They should raise the basket 5 feet. Turn those giants into midgets. One guy's so tall he uses a bombsight to drop the ball. I hate dunkers who grab the rim and swing on it. Show offs! Socking it to us little guys. Dunkin' and swingin' should be a felony. All six-footers and up should be forced to play with 90 pound back packs on their knees. Their children should be forced to live in a 5-foot high box for the first 15 years to keep us little guys from going Napoleonic. Ayn's a Movement Specialist who also runs a children's after-school program. Today's my day to teach acting and play production. Kids're 4 through 7. Last week, a 5 year old pulls a chair up to the water fountain for a drink, and says, *I have to do it this way 'cause I'm too young to drink.* **Insider strike re-action:** What goes around comes around. Fair-weather creeps! When there's trouble they don't know you. They look for a goat. Cover their asses and head for the hills! Let 'em stew! The air's cleaner. Fewer cigarettes. They're not smoking now. No money. If they get withdrawal pangs they go to the nearby burning ash can and inhale. Let's be fair. We're all expendable. They walked out and the company's still here. I don't like saying it, but let's be fair. Ninety percent of the technicians while sympathetic also say, *Fuck the arrogant bastards! Soon as they walked out everybody's blood pressure dropped, including their own. Writers? Y'mean re-writers! When they stop trying to take jobs away from us then I'll sympathize with 'em. Most of 'em are nothin' but scumbags. I hope they never come back. They think that PRESS card's sacrosanct, like the Red Cross. If you're in a room with two of 'em and one walks out, the other one cuts him to pieces. Now you, for example.* Me? *You're a square peg in a round hole. Like the Over-Producer, you make mountains out of molehills. He thinks popping sound in a piece adds significance. He takes elements recorded at different times in different places and mixes them together in a "production piece." When did news become a production? I'm so hopped up from hyped-up news and commercials, when I watch PBS news I can't come down. I'm a junky looking for a sound bite fix. Starts with hyped-up kid's shows. Every point gets flurries and drum rolls: 2 plus 2 equals 4. Ta-ta-ta-tah! This is the letter A. Boing! Zoom bang. These are the letters A, S, S, H, O, L, E. They spell ASSHOLE! Whiz-bang boom!*

This morning WGA member G.G. Wyneth crossed the line to cat calls.

☺

11.   Policy At The O'Fey Café

Coffee, please.
Milk or cream?
Milk.
Sorry. We're out of milk.

Cream.
We're out of cream, too.
I'll drink it black.
I'll have to make a new pot. We're fresh out.
Don't bother.
It'll only take a sec-
Tea. You got tea?
Sure. Milk or cream?
I thought you were out of milk and cream?
Not with tea. Only with coffee.
That's ridiculous!
Look. I don't make policy. I just work here. It's been a long day. If you're leaving a tip give it to me now. I'm off the clock n' too tired to hang around.

☺

12.　Radio Tech Lounge

Semi-dark, seedy room; lockers line the wall; a broken sliding-door clothes closet; wall telephone; 40 mailbox slots; formica table; mirror; coffee maker; trash can by half refrigerator; spaghetti wiring hanging from dropped ceiling; on the wall a big poster of Roy Rogers holding a gun with a magic marker inscription that says: **Techs Sign Your Charts!**

Two techs doze on couches; one has a napkin over his face, eyeglasses on top; the other is coasting. People come and go, noisily grumbling: *That asshole! Ask me if I give a shit. What's it doin' outside? Tryin' to piss.*

☺

13.　FEE, FICA, FIN

If the following makes sense, maybe you don't.

From: FIN, To: All EMPLOYEES.　Date: December 10, 1986

RE: <u>1987 PAYROLL TAX WITHHOLDINGS</u>

Please note the following pay withholding changes effective with paychecks issued on or after January 1, 1987:

FICA (Social Security): The maximum FICA taxable wage base will increase from $42 to $43,800 in 1987, while the 7.15% rate of withholding will remain the same. As a result, the maximum employees FICA tax will increase from $3,003 .00 to $3,131.70. You could be under or over withheld during 1987 unless you review the appropriateness of your current W-4 withholding allowances and submit a new W-4 Form to payroll as soon as possible.

Federal Income Taxes: As a result of the Tax Reform Act, Federal-withholding rates will decrease within the modified wage bracket. These changes, combined with the elimination of certain deductions under Tax Reform, could render your current level of Federal tax withholding incorrect versus your estimated 1987 tax liability. Consequently, -

FEE, FICA, FIN, FOOEY!

☺

14.   The Sympathizer

(Tech Lounge: Tech1 puts notebook on top of refrigerator, opens door, pops a soda can, drinks, puts it back; stretches out.)

Dilido. *(enter; turns on light; puts lunch bag in refrigerator)* Management workin' the newsroom. Ha. The right hand don't know what the left's doin'. There's a rally out front at noon. You goin'? *(silence)* Try to show less enthusiasm. *(Exits; kills light.)*

Hylton. *(enter pushing trash cart; opens light; goes to wall phone; dials)* It's me. Everything okay? How y'feelin'? Good. Bad. What? So, so. You takin' the pills? The pills. You takin' your pills? Waddya mean, forgot? You don't forget those pills. The pills! Y'suppose to take the pills, mama. The doctor said. The doctor. Did Ronnie call? Ronnie! Did he call? If he calls you tell him I can't meet 'im. Say I can't come! He knows, mama. He knows what about! Y'want me to bring the newspaper, mama? When I come- What? Milk? You want milk? What about the

460

paper, mama? Okay. I'll bring it. Yes, and the milk. I'll bring the milk. Y'goin' to take your pills? The doctor says you have to take 'em. You do it, hear? You take those pills, mama. I'll be home at four. Be good now, mama. I love you. I said, I love you! What? You know? Well, good. Ronnie can't say it. He can't say 'thank you'. Take those pills now, mama. Bye-bye. I love you. I said, I love you. I'm glad you know. Ronnie can't say it. Bye. (*hangs up; waits five seconds, redials.*) It's me again. You take your pills, mama? Ya suppose to take 'em. You take 'em. Hear me, mama? Do like the doctor says. I'll call back to make sure you took 'em! The doctor said for me to do that. Love you, mama. I'm goin'. Bye now. (*hangs up; kills light; exits, returns for trash can; and goes out. Enter Dilido and commander*)

Dilido. (*opening light*)The right hand doesn't know what the left's doin'.

Commander. What else's knew? (*rifling his wall mailbox*)

Dilido. Hugh-it's nosin' around the newsroom in a sharkskin suit. Perfect fit. He knows where the bodies're buried. He buried 'em. They call 'im Smilin' Jack. He looks like a smartly dressed ferret. They're right about one thing, the writers. The company's out to get us all. It's no time for divisiveness.

Commander. Middle class kids with no callouses on their hands. My heart's bleedin'. Where's that letter?

Dilido. Our contract's up next. You gonna walk for them?

Commander. Where's the guarantee they'll reciprocate?

Dilido. We have to trust-

Commander. Get real, Bunky! We supported AFTRA. Then in '72 when we needed 'em, they disappeared. They're all Cut from the same cloth. To them, teching's a dirty word.

Dilido. Times're different. Together we can shut down the whole place.

Commander. Please. The WGA threw our guy out of their office 'cause they couldn't agree on jurisdiction over a paint box. A lousy pen that draws on the screen. How many jobs does it involve, ten? Was it worth losing the support of a thousand techs? We don't need you, she says. It's them against us. One of them wrote in the newsroom log "can't wait for techs to self-destruct. I'll laugh heartily." He ain't laughin' now. I trust 'em as far as I can throw a building. Y'wouldn't want one of 'em in your foxhole. The truth is they'll get more money for doin' our work on the excuse, we had no choice. Let 'em freeze out there. (*opens refrigerator; slams it shut*) Some asshole opened my soda again.

Tech. Can't be a writer. They're out. Only a cheap bastard steals soda. If you were on a ship with a WGA crew, what would ya do?

Commander. Throw 'em overboard. (*ALL exit; Tech meets Mizzie in lobby*)

Mizzie. Gagoots. Where you going? You're my tech.

Tech. Just checkin' the line.

Mizzie. Gagoots-

Tech. I telephoned GG's home.

Mizzie. It's not your business.

Tech. I got a phone company message: *The number's no longer operating.* He must've gotten lots of hate calls. He's an OK guy. Why's he scabbing?

Mizzie. He's from the south. They don't know from unions and city wages. Don't get involved, Gagootz. Those people are hungry and looking for a goat. Don't you be it.

(*SHE goes. Outside HE watches picketers. A cop is nearby*)

Writer 1. I'm going across the street to the WGA roof and piss down.

Writer 2. Y'get your $25 chit from ABC? I'll never sneer at a $20 bill again. How's the wife?

Writer 1. Stopped bein' a pain in the ass. Now she's a thorn in my side.

Editor. (*on his way in shouts*) I hear it's over.

Producer. No. They're at a sensitive and delicate stage. (*Editor mimes jerking off; goes in. G.G. walks up, starts to enter building*)

Producer. Don't do it.

Writer 1. We need solidarity.

GG. Buddy, I'm just trying to keep my head above water.

Writer 2. It'll go against you. The union'll-

GG. Fuck the union, man! Fuck 'em. I resigned. I'm paying them to avoid this kind of thing; not to put me in the street over dumb issues.

Writer 1. We gotta stick together.

GG. I can't afford to be out.

Producer. I'm driving a limo. I can get you a job.

GG. You want me to stay out because of seniority?

Writer 1. There's more to it.

GG. What'll I tell my children? "I can't feed you 'cause I struck for seniority rights, won, and hot dang! The company cut back, Daddy was low man on the totem pole and got fired." You paying my bills?

Producer. They'll fire you anyway.

GG. At least I won't be in a hole.

Writer 2. You're not alone.

GG. We're all alone, buddy.

Writer 1. The WGA offered you money.

GG. On interest. I'm not going into debt to support their crap.

Producer. You want to tell your kids you were a scab?

GG. Better than telling them there's no food in the house. Listen, man. I talked to the Guild, gave them two weeks to get their act together. You don't settle, I'm going in. My heart's with yawl. Two weeks was fair for something that never should've happened. Negotiators can talk all day. They're drawing salaries. Take it away, watch them settle. (*starts to go*)

Tech. (*following*) I see new faces inside. Where're they coming from?

G.G. I don't know. I put in my time and go home.

All: Scab! Rat! Slime bucket!

Tech. Hey. Easy. You talk to the anchors that way?

Prod. They're with us.

Tech. Right. From Martha's Vinyard.

Producer. Mind your business.

Tech. He's a little guy. Yell at the big guys, or are you too scared?

Producer. Everybody! A tech told the scab to cross the line.

Tech. That's ass backwards-

Producer. IBEW scab sympathizer!

Tech. Like you produce!

Cop. Break this up.

Producer. I'm tellin' the Guild.

Tech. I'm a member longer than you. Picketed when you were in diapers.

Producer. Everybody! A scab lover!

Cop. That'll be enough. Keep walking. If you're going in, sir, go ahead.

Tech. In cue, bullshit! Out cue, asshole!

Cop. Sir, please.

Tech. In '67 news pushed out DJ's. Shoe's on the other foot and it hurts.

Tech. (inside; catching up to GG) Did the company try to keep you out?

G.G. Yes. But my lawyer told them I have a right to work. C.B.S saw the point. I'd sue them. I don't like this, but I've gotta feed my kids. Talk about democracy, I joined the WGA because if I didn't I never would've been hired. That's a shake down in my book.

☺

464

15.   The Hasp 1E49

C.B.S MEMORANDUM

From: T.M.   To: ALL TECHS AND AD'S   Date: APRIL 3, 1987

EFFECTIVE A.M. SATURDAY, APRIL 4, 1987

WITHIN THE PAST 48 HOURS, SOMEONE ENTERED THE **TECH LOUNGE**, AND ILLEGALLY REMOVED EQUIPMENT IN THE TELEPHONE FRAME CLOSET. THIS EQUIPMENT CONTAINED WORKINGS NECESSARY FOR MANY PHONES IN THE NEWSROOM. PHONE COMPANY MANAGEMENT PEOPLE REPAIRED THE DAMAGE.

HA! THEY CAN'T EVEN FIND THEIR OWN DICKS!

From: CND, To: Security   Date: April 4, 1987

A hasp and padlock will be installed on the door to 1E49 shortly. Have your guard stay in that room until the lock is installed. Then, the people in the room will move out, taking personal items with them, and the room locked... Security should be the only people who have a key to this room. If a technician needs to re-enter, you'll get a call from a BOD Supervisor, reachable on x. 2021. Your night contact is the CC Supervisor, x. 2017... If Security receives a call from BOD, please dispatch a guard to 1E49. He'll be met by a supervisor and the technician needing entry. Have the guard <u>stay</u> with <u>both</u> men while they are in Room 1E49, record the names of who enters, and what was done... It's imperative that no go near the rear of room 1E49. On the back wall are all telephone frames for Radio News operation, which must <u>not be touched by anyone but a telephone repair person</u> with proper identification. Thank you.

THANKS FOR THE INSIDE INFO! THE HASP ASP!

☺

16.   A Job-Job

Loggers are temp typists in between jobs. Wrapped in earphones tied to a playback machine, they type thankless hours of verbatim garbage. One logger was an arson expert. He could tell *accidental fires from Jewish Lightning- fires started for insurance.* Then came a five-alarm blonde in her 20's, shades of Judy under the Sullivan Marquee 1972.

Logger. The sunrise was beautiful this morning. Golden yellow and red.

Tech. You live high up.

Logger. No. In a basement. I heard it on the radio. How do you stand all this paranoia? I get looks from the strikers. I'm not helping management. If I'm asked, I can't refuse. The one you call the over-producer? The nervy bastard accused me of doing D.A.'s work. When I applied for a research job, he gave me a poor reference, said, *She's not an early person.* Where's he comes off telling me what to do? Temping's a job-job. What I do isn't what I really do. What you see me do in here is not what I do out there. I'm a dancer, and do impressions. The over-producer: *Are you helping management doing Desk Assistant work?* When G crossed the line the over-producer called him a *slime bucket.* I go, look who's talking. Screw that dirt bag. *She's not an early person.* I'm too serious. Tell me a joke.

Tech. A guy says Doctor I don't feel good. The doctor says, You look okay. How's your bowel movement? He says, Like clockwork. Every morning at 7. The doc says, Urine okay? Terrific! Every morning at 8. The doc says, Then what's the problem? The guy says, I get up at 9.

☺

17. The Golden Parachute

Update: Execs Wiman, CEO since 1983, and Sorta Van will each get $400,000 yearly; the former for life, the latter until 1991. With a corn fed face, executives rape a company. In *Treasure of the Sierra Madre,* Walter Huston says, *Let's return the mountain to the way it was. It was good to us. Gave us her treasure. The least we could do is show our respect and appreciation by returning her to the way she was when we first found her.* Not corporate heads. They grab without compunction and bail out with golden parachutes. The price of restoration is layoffs in the trenches. A scientist, whose work on conductors in space rockets is displayed in the Smithsonian, once said to me, *Somebody may be worth 100 thousand more than the next guy, but nobody's worth a million more.*

☺

18.   If We Never Waken

Diary. To go against the majority takes guts, or great ignorance. When the union held up my newsletter, I grabbed 500 copies and distributed them. They got crazy, and our local president tried to fire me. *You printed minutes of a union meeting.* A verbatim. *Parts should've been deleted.* Like a reference to our previous Business Damager. He might run again for office. *Some articles were inappropriate.* I convinced him to keep me on and put out three more issues before the fat lady sang. Nobody ever read the union newsletter before or after me. But they read mine. Well, my mom did. My first issue had a fat turkey cartoon with the caption, *Who Ya Callin' A Turkey? You Turkey!* Writing close to the bone unnerves conformists. In a house organ it's unwise to quote a colleague who says he's pissed and hates his job. I printed an article from a WGA member about Italy; wrote of *the danger in tobacco; the WGA encroaching on tech work.* It scared 'em. They wanted a carbon copy of the *International's* mag: techs in hard hats on telephone poles; weddings; anniversaries; solidarity picnics 'round a B.B.Q. of junk food; and the family singing *God Bless America.* Spaz, a news writer, said, while ripping copy, *And you thought what we do out here is all histrionics. You should be in news.*

I kick back my feet and cogitate. *By God, Stanley, the writers are out but the job gets done! Well, I miss them, Ollie. Oh, posh! Stanley, every day's a holiday! Isn't that the cat's pajamas? The tiddily in the winks. But Ollie, if every day's a holiday, when do we get off? Stanley, don't worry your cranial pan. Leave the details to yours truly. Furthermore, Stanley, life would be just grand if everyone would act in earnest. Ollie, everyone can't act in earnest. Why, pray tell? The joint'd be too crowded. Not if we yell fire, Stanley. Right, Ollie. But we won't worry about that cause we've other fish to fry in our cranial pans. Ex-actly. Life, my dear Stanley, should be a dreamy holiday on a beach sipping lime rickies and mint juleps with balmy breezes and waves lapping the shore. A dream from which we never wake. Ollie? (weepy) If we never wake up, will we still see each other? Of course, Stanley. It'll be like now, only better. There won't be any pain and we'll always love each other and be happy as June bugs. Yes, Ollie, we'll be two rugs snug in a bug.*

☺

19. Clitoris Amaryllis and Caesar, Mighty Anchor!

Equipment checked out for Caesar, I'm at the console reading my Italian verb book. A head looks in and out. Caesar's amanuensis, *He's not here?* I leaf to the A's. Agito, is that a verb? No. It's a noun for C.B.S. Voices murmur and bodies move in the hallway. Advance runners for Caesar. The studio door opens and closes, another head pokes a look and disappears. How can a man read with so many clarions of bullshit? Enter Ms. Clitoris Amaryllis, writer/producer. *You doing Blather?* No. You're doin' him. I'm doin' the show. Clit, a chain smoking egoist, crushes a cigarette underfoot, comes in, sits, takes a No. 2 from her hair, taps it on her knee, her nose, checks her watch, takes out a ciggy, says, *Mind if I smoke?* Yes. Our relationship has improved. Now she asks. She lights up in the doorway, her butt holding the door opened. Cigarette hand out the door, she blows smoke at the ceiling in the hall. The amanuensis turns a corner in a huff, runs into the cigarette. Oh, shit! Sorry.

Brushing ashes from her pantsuit, she says, *He'll be here shortly,* and dashes off. Ms. Clit douses the cig and sits nearby smelling like an ashtray. *He's on his way.* Be still my heart. *What?* Just conjugating a verb. *Got one for chop buster?* Yeah. You and Blather. *We're not verbs.* The hell your'e not. You're both transitive with one object, news. *And you're a predicate looking for a nominative.* I'm a predicate with an objective. I'm looking to go home. She fidgets, presses the No. 2 into her cheek leaving a dimple, gets on the phone. *My contract contains a 'no-strike' clause. Anchors have similar riders.* She hangs up. Ring! *Hi. Gotcha. Thanks.* Hangs up. *He's on his way.* Ring! *Shit! Has he looked at the corrected script? Ring me when he leaves. When he gets here, we should finish in 15, max.* Ring! *Gotcha. He's on his way.* Ring! *The toilet? Near you or us? Go in. Give him the script. Knock first. Okay. Listen for the flush, and then go in. Yes. I've done it. Even zipped him up while he's proofing copy. Hey, that's show biz. (Hangs up) People have no idea how busy he is.* Some don't give a shit. *What?* La mano is hand. *I need three right now.* It's an 'o' ending word that's feminine. Ring! *He's out? Who's he talking to? Stringah? That fuckin' Welsh bullshit artist. Walk by. Point to the script. He'll get the message.* You should do a piece on "La mano morte", what Italian men tell women who object when their hand's on their lap. It's not me, signora. It's my hand. La mano è morte. *The hand is dead.* Right. Door opens. *Jesus! He's not here? He left his script somewhere and can't remember where. He can use mine. Just get him here.* She dials an in-house number. *It's me. I'll be late.* Door opens. *He's on his way.* Door closes. You mind me doing a mic check? *No. Some techs'd be offended. They'd say I was encroaching on their jurisdiction. Hello, 1, 2. Good. You know, you're an obstructionist. I know you don't like us, but writing for Caesar's no picnic. What I do has to fit him like a glove. Before the elephant turns I have to circle him twice. We're the cognoscenti, the pencil paparazzi, demi gods of delineation.* A breathless runner pokes her puss in the door, says, he's behind me. *Hallelujah!* Enter Caesar. *Good to go, folks? Up and ready, boss. Your script. Where was it? It's mine. Bless your pea-pickin' heart.* Caesar goes into the studio by rote, eyes buried in the script. Assuming everything's where he left it three days ago, he sits, and falls flat on his ass. *All set, folks?* Good to go! *That read sucks. One more for the Gipper.* I flag the new top. *That's a keeper.* He exits. I re-rack to the flag, leader the top, give it to the Clit, who says, *I'm fuckin' outa here. Any calls, I'm at Armstrong's.* I open my book. Scrivere- to write: scrivo, scrivi. Clit turns at the door. *What is scrod?* I go, fish. She says, *No. It's the pluperfect subjunctive of "screw".*

☺

20.   Awake and Sing

Associate radio director Sing is a 6'-5", Afro-American artist who paints in the wee hours before coming in. When he pats me on the back, my head registers 9.2 on the Richter Scale!

Sing. My style varies. But on the job I'm a minimalist. Less is more.
Tech. I read blacks are not swimmers. They're not buoyant. That true?
Sing. Don't know any who aren't unless they're dead. You writin'? No? That's cause you "ain't" buoyant, bro. The trick is to float on the job, then go home to your thang. I paint every morning. Then, if anybody gets to me, can't hurt. Dig? You gotta shut out the inconsequentials, bro. Otherwise when you go home you find yourself staring at a blank canvas. You handle them not the other way around. This is a job to earn paint mon-eey. Once the motherfuckers get in on you, you're lost. I put my dee-mons

on canvas. Put yours on paper. Remember, yawl dasn't have to do a classic every time out. Comprendez?

☺

21. O'Fey Café Napkin Notes

Ring! Ring! Hello. *Central Control?* Yes. *How's ya pork?* Posted headline: **HUMPHREY THE WHALE IS DEAD** - Do his wife no? If I let you blow me, does that make me queer too? I'd like to punch him in the mouth, but I hate waitin' on lines. Hello, operator? *Yes.* How's your pork? Hylton, of Janitorial Services, wears natural cologne, Eau di Lui. That asshole news junkie, fuckin' armchair guerilla! Cholly, our poet lariat! A Port Authority biography, For Whom The Booth Tolls. Portrait of the Artist as a Young Idiot. There's a new medical show. *Rebel Without A Gauze.* <u>Names in the news:</u> Yamani and Yafadi, too! Manachin Begin n' Eggs. Live from the Garment District it's *Nightswatch!* On to Pasadena for the Tournament of Noses! She's not feeling well. She's in her right mind. I'll be in the biz-up studio. Ask me if I care? The CIA and reporters have code names for presidents. Jimmy Carter's the Preacher; Rosalynn's the Steel Magnolia; Ronald Reagan's Rawhide, *Hello, desk? It's dead out there.* Bull! Somebody's always eatin' a live chicken. No story gets you thirty days with The Wild Man of the Overnight. *Mercy! Anything but that! Tear out my fingernails! Kill me!* Nights'll do that. I went to college. What'd I learn? Three people'll keep a secret, if two of them are dead. A guy orders two pounds of kielbasa. The salesman says, "You Polack?" The guy says, "Why ask me that? If I order salami, am I Italian? If I order pastrami, am I a Jew? So when I order kielbasa why do ask me if I'm Polish?" The salesman says, "Cause this is a hardware store."

Nine Non-Negotiable Tech Demands
1. Thirty minutes overlap time in shift changes, followed by two 25-minute breaks to run concurrently.
2. Free cafeteria meals, any cafeteria outside C.B.S.
3. Four-day weekends, country of our choice.
4. Lockjaw spray for Anchors.
5. Maintenance uniforms with leather holsters for holding cotton swabs, razors, alcohol, and knockout drops.
6. Monthly supply 500 pounds of tomatoes to throw at news junkies.
7. "No smoking" signs in French, Italian, Spanish, and German, because at Chuckler, English is a second language, i.e., "Non fumare, Stupido!" "Nicht Shmoken, Schmuck!" and "Ne Fumez Pas, Frog!"
8. Self-punching time cards in case we're late.
9. Motorized wheelchairs in all control rooms.

22.   Old School Versus New School

Trash the rest of the interview.
Nuke it!
We lost our connection to the satellite.
One bird down!
There are problems with that piece.
It sucks!
Look for targets of opportunity.
Go fishing!
The western leg missed it. A drop-out west of Chicago.
Zilch west of O'Leary's cow!
Pay attention! I'm going to repeat it again for the west coast.
Read my lips!
Forget the Quinton piece. I'll take a Qaddafy cut.
Kill Q. Bite me a Qaddafy.

His sentences are long, ambiguous, run-on, circuitous, and turgid.

Nuke 'im!

She's been feeding us terrific interviews.

Gives good de-brief.

They've got the goods, but missed the last plane out.

Bird the sucker!

Gimme the crystal ball long-term outlook in a nut shell!

Cut to the chase!

Excise15 seconds somewhere in the middle.

Do an internal!

Gimme the in-cue and out-cue, thank you.

Fuck cue!

Give me something reflective and analytical.

Blue sky it!

The figures were revised upward. Now revise 'em downward.

Kill the stats!

Tapes marked one, two, and three are for the upcoming hourly.

Three suckers for the upchucking!

(shift change)

These are my notes to now, and we're expecting a call-back from a spokes...

Lucy, I'm home! I'm outta here!

23. Ida, *The* Spidah, Tech Schedulah

Ida. Can you work a sixth day?
Tech. I only have clothes for five days.
Ida. Sez you. I'm puttin' you down; 7AM Saturday.
Tech. Make it Friday.
Ida. That's your regular shift.

Tech. So you'll pay me twice.
Ida. Ya lucky we're payin' ya once. Are ya comin' in?
Tech. Let me put it this way-
Ida. Save it fah ya stories. Yes or no? What's that smell?
Tech. I'm taking garlic pills.
Ida. Gawd! Take it some place else.
Tech. I'm supposed to take tenormin, but garlic's safer. No side effects.
Ida. It's chasin' me.
Tech. That's a good side effect.
Ida. It's always somethin' with you. Saturday, 7a. G'bye.

☺

24. A TR to Maintenance

Technical Report.
Maintenance Department.
Time: 1:03p. Place: Studio A. **Equipment:** Ampex #2. **Problem (Be Specific)** The thing-a-ma-jig fell off the what-cha-ma-call-it & I can't crank the whatever.

☺

25. Govnah Goofey

Diary. Covered Governor Rockefeller's Waldorf Astoria luncheon speech to VIP's. He lost his place over the fiscal crises, a slide came on upside down, and he says, *"The budget for the shitty, city-"*

☺

26. More Ribble-Rabble

Tech. I gotta turn my life around.
Dilido. Sit in a swivel chair.
Desk. Where's your tech?
Tape-Ops. In the lounge in a holding pattern.

Desk. Waddya got for me?

Tape Ops. No injuries. A bandit taken to the hospital with a prior heart condition. Scattered flak talk. Hard to follow.

Desk. Dulles wants it for the hourly.

Tape-ops. Okay. I'll piece 'im.

Writer. I'm a doctor of news.

Tech. You should be sued for mal-practice!

Sing. Yeow! What'cha got, ma man? Lay it on. Actuary in da sanctuary! Yeow! How do y'save a whitey from drownin'? Toss 'im a rock. Yeow!

Anchor. I love items that move at 6:50 as advancers for 6:30.

Suicide. Hello, operator? I'm jumpin' off the top of Black Crock.

C.B.S Operator. One moment, please. I'll give you Public Relations.

Ida. How old's your son now?

Tech. Six.

Ida. I remembah when he was in a strollah, or was dat you?

☺

It's my fuckin' Friday. Ask me if I give a shit? Due to budget cuts, the show West 57th is now West 26th. Don't know what I'd do on the outside. *You don't know what you're doing on the inside.* Eat my shorts! The bird's up! Gimme a protective deadpot roll. The bird's down. Forget it. Mal, this is radio. Why the shirt and tie? Who'll know? *I will.* Line 1, a stringer from the Rockies named Cliff Hangar. Put 'im on hold. Switch to you live on cue. One Wash at 40 roll double. We're Birding a Bruno, Tel Aviv straight up. Can he give us a piece or will he be out of pocket until the bar closes? He's efforting it now. Pickup line 10. Hello. I'm sorry. The president can speak to you now. The hourly reads like a thumb-sucker. It's plain as the face on your nose. Listen on the main. I'll listen on the backup. We'll have two sets of ears in case we crash.

Know what I think? *Yes. But tell me anyway.* There's a new pasta diet for quick weight loss. You eat four plates a day. Really? *Instead of olive oil they use castor oil.*

☺

27.   When I'm Calling You, Ooh, Ooh
C.B.S Memorandum
From: Tech-Ops Supervisor   Date: 12.20.89
PHONERS IN STUDIO F
A New PHONE hybrid has been added to Studio F. Please take time to read this.
(is it covered by medical?)
There are 2 new phones, with all numbers. Both phones are identical. One is called PHONE 11, the other, PHONE 12. It's no longer necessary to plug in sports phone 165.

RECORDING
There is no change for recording directly on tape. Press the Phone 11 or Phone 12 button, adjust level, roll tape, and record caller. NOTE: When button is pressed, there is no audio in the phone headset.

TWO-WAYS   (*AGREEMENT ???*)
The audio (*inputs*) for both phones, now *comes* from the mix-minus feed of the console. This mix-minus feed is the ENTIRE board MINUS the last High-Level position. This means ALL phoners should be on the last High-Level position. Please NOTE: If there are two callers, one on phone 11 and the other on phone 12, with both buttons pressed and one on the board, <u>the other caller will hear the board but NOT the other caller.</u> **(???)**

WARNING: DO NOT put the 2nd caller on another High-Level position other than the last one. Feedback will result. If necessary, switch phone 11 and phone 12 on the last position ONLY.
                    Supervisor Tech Ops, **Resident PHD**
Who Caller #1 ? Caller #2 ? Caller #3 ?

☺

28.   Curse of the Wild Man

Swoop. Well, sir, curiosity led us to call an old friend while he was still on the inside in the capacity of assignment editor. We only got half the story because he was dismissed- Please don't fire me, I have a mortgage-"

Editor. I'm only changing your hours, Swoop. (*Thank you.*) Not so fast. You'll be working the lobster shift with the Wild Man of the Overnight. (*The moody guy?*) He's a published playwright, Swoop. Wrote for *Benson*. And guess what? He's a technician. You're a writer. You published? Well, until that day comes, or you find work elsewhere, he's your curse."

☺

29.   The *Rathskeller*

Diary: 5:46AM. The four D's of news: died, dead, deader, deadest. Radio news is not arch. It's the 'KISS' approach: Keep It Simple Stupid. *Tell 'em what you're going to tell 'em, then tell 'em again what you told 'em.* Like the miner who every morning smacks his donkey on the ass with a board and then hits him in the balls with a hammer. When asked, "Why twice?" he says, 'The first one's a wakeup call. The second gets his attention."

Sing shambles in, hands me commercials, sits, and sleeps.

Sing. (*wakes up foggy*) Did I give you the commercials? Man, I would've called in sick, but I did that last week.
Tech. After I call in sick, I feel better.
Sing. 'Cause you're free, bro. I never call in sick when I'm sick. I come to work and give 'em my hang dog look and the fuckers ease off. I been painting all night. Can't wait to get back. I'm working a big piece; ten by ten. The

feel, the colors're just right. I ain't sellin' this baby to no one.

Tech. You told me you were an Artist in Residence. What's that?

Sing. High-larious, bro. It's a hands-on, inner-city program that hires artists to teach kids. The concept came out of a think tank on inner city depravation. The Prince of Wales goes into the inner city to survey the problem of unrest and poverty. I'm there teaching art. Why don't they ask me? Headline: "Prince rides subway to Harlem. Walks on 125th Street" with the limo and chauffeur waitin' on 124th. Headline: "It's not just a royal walk-about." Kiss my black ass! Actuality: "He's not stuck up. Maybe he can do somethin'." Reality check. "How about ten cents for a paint brush for inner-city kids?" "He better not show his ass on my street." He's raising money for inner-city programs. I don't know what he raised, a few hopes. I never saw a penny. God's truth. I 'tended an inner-city convention in the Borscht Circuit. What a laugher! I couldn't get money for a paint brush and they're doing a "think tank" routine at the Concord. That place is so big they've got an indoor golf course. Nobody from the inner-city plays golf. I get there. Don't know anybody. Doesn't matter. I was going to ask for $100 to buy paint brushes. Maybe some erasers and drawing paper, if they could swing it. Know what I'm sayin'? I get there Friday night. The place is in the woods. I say to my roommate, "How do we eat?" He says, "Order up on the phone." So I order up coffee and salad. He orders steak, potatoes au gratin, coffee, two desserts and charges it. I figure the guy's got money. Saturday morning I pass on breakfast. He orders eggs benedict, ham, home fries, a double order of toast, a side of pancakes with coffee, and charges it. I figure he's money. There was a meeting in the dining room at 9. I wrote out my speech. The kids need paint, paint brushes, erasers, drawing paper... bottom line just the brushes. At 9 o'clock four people show up. The convention booked 100 rooms. Where was everybody? Maybe it was too early. At lunch, a 130 people show up. I order coffee n' salad, my roommate orders Chilean bass, and I'm thinking this guy's really loaded. I go, "You always eat like this?" He goes, "No. Only at conventions when they pay." I go, "They?" He goes, "The grant people. Just charge it." "I can't get paint brushes and you're eating Chilean bass." He goes, "Chee-lay-an bass." "Well, excuse my dust, Mr. Chill-lay." At 2PM, the board met over a buffet and open bar, followed by free time, golf, a stage show that night, and a farewell brunch Sunday, where they discussed budget, funds, and gave out applications for the new year. I fill out mine, feeling guilty about my salad. Gimme $100, folks, for the kids. I'll take $50. I'll get a discount. Meanwhile, they're partying and eatin' like it's the Last Supper. It was a long joke, bro, the best show in Monticello. Nothing definitive got solved. Just boozin' and schmoozin'. Sunday morning, I think to hell with brunch. I order up lobster for breakfast. The guy says it's too early for lobster. I go, "It's not too early to get fired. Get me y'biggest lobster." He goes, "Will there be anything else, sir?" I go, "Yes. A side order of 100 paint brushes and charge it."

☺

30.   Bagels, Bacteria and Batteries

Tech. A lounge's for relaxin'. Who relaxes here? The fridge is like a Model T Ford. People in and out, bangin' lockers. It's Grand Central Station!

Jalanzo. Bring it up at the meeting tomorrow. (*exiting; kills lights*)

Tech. I'm not comin' in on my day off.

Ida. (*enter; turn on light*) Gawd, it stinks in here. Keep the door opened. Is there coffee, any milk? Gawd! It's comin' from the refrigeratah. How can you people live with this? Nobody cleans it. This bag stinks and leaks.

Whose is it? A news writer. They're not supposed to use the tech fridge.

Tech. It's revenge.

Ida. Go back to sleep. The milk's rancid.

Tech. It's penicillin.

Ida. This bag says Rickey. He went to TV two years ago. Moldy cheese; expired TV dinners; a rotten egg. What're batteries doin' in here?

Tech. Tech snacks.

Ida. Save it fah ya stories, please. Batteries inna fridge. Ridculous.

Tech. It extends shelf life. They work longer.

Ida. Then you should be in there, too. How d'ya know? Yawe no battery.

Tech. Turn on two flashlights. Keep one on top of the fridge, the other-

Ida. Save it fah y'stories. Gawed! It's a pig pen! A bag, no name, or date. None of you geniuses ever clean it. I gotta do it.

Tech. Write it on the tech schedule. Assignment: Clean fridge. Pick up decontamination suit in BOD. One size fits all.

Ida. Bunchah slobs! Lookit this bag. Nawton? He died last year.

Tech. Eating that lunch.

Ida. Be respectful. Actually, he'd be alive. It was penicillin when he ate it.

(Enter 2 techs; one sits, woofs down food; the other uses wall phone.)

Tech 2. What's with the phone? I keep getting a busy signal.

Soviet. Centrex. Startin' today only in-house calls. (*gulping food*)

Tech 2. Shit! 'Scuse my French. (*slams down phone*) Screw them and their budget cuts. Meanwhile, Cholly gets a million bucks a year.

Soviet. But he brings in a lot more.

Tech 2. The Evening News is 22 minutes, costs $100 million a year and Blather gets 7 mill. The whole news budget's $300 million.

Soviet. Close the fridge, Ida. I'm eating.

Ida. Is that what you cawl it? Slow down. Food ain't goin' outta style.

Tech 2. The White House reporter gets $500 thousand a year workin' one newscast. And we can't phone out.

Tech 2. You call that work reading news?

Ida. I'd call it news if one of you worked cleanin' da fridge.

Tech 2 and Soviet. Please. I just ate. That's disgusting! (*exiting*)

Tech. Along with the depressing yellow, faded décor, the beige mentality-

Ida. Jesus! He's startin'.

Tech. If their cuttin' the news budget how come the bard of news just signed a 10-year multimillion dollar deal? Now he and the Chink'll be all over the place, like goose shit on a Little League outfield.

Ida. Save it for your stories. This is a holdin' pen for disease. A person could get sick just lookin' in this gahbage box.

Tech. Not if you're a technician.

Ida. I'm talkin' *naw-mal people*. I'll clean it now, but I'm not y'scrub lady. Gawd, last week's schedule's inna freezer. I been lookin' all over for it.

Tech. Last week I had five women.

Ida. What idiot- Did you do this?

Tech. I didn't screw 'em all, not yet, but I had five.

Ida. I'm having this fingerprinted.

Tech. I told the broads I work for C.B.S. Turned 'em off. They heard CVS.

Ida. If you ever worked here we'd all get turned on. Who's da prankstah?

Tech. Two I picked up, three picked me up. One we went all the way except actually do it. Took her home and dumped her ass.

Ida. What're you tawkin' about?

Tech. The other two were weird. One treated me like shit. She's history. I took the other one to dinner and didn't even get a goodnight kiss. She picks me up and acts like I don't exist. I shouldn't've said I was a tech.

Ida. Bagels, bacteria, n' green batteries. Dis fridge's awf-limits.

☺

31. *The* Hyphenate

Commander. It's in the contract.

Dilido. We got a contract? That's news.

Commander. World War Two's news to you.

Dilido. Eat my shawts. What's hyphenate mean?

Commander. We'll be doing work that news people do.

Dilido. That's a switch.

Commander. More responsibility means more job security.

Dilido. Will we have to write news?

Jalanzo. Banish the fuckin' thought.

Tech. It's all he says, she says.

Dilido. We'll have to think.

Jalanzo. Perish the fuckin' thought.

Dilido. If we screw-up, can they fire us for incompetence? 'Cause under our present contract we're protected. Maybe we'll join the Writers' Guild.

Jalanzo. NG. They have a work ethic.

Dilido. Hyphenate'll breathe new life in tech work.

Tech. Yours could use some.

Dilido. Eat my shawts.

Tech. You don't wear any.

Dildo. And you love it. Here. Hyphen-eat this.

Tech. We need a letter of marque. (*silence*) Transit letters like Bogey had in *Casablanca*. If we enter Nazi territory, i.e., the newsroom, we want safe passage back.

☺

32.   HATE

Logger. I'm going to the cafeteria. Want coffee? I don't drink it, especially downstairs. Mind if I sit? God. I have cramps in my hands. Type this, type that. Ooh, ahh. That book you gave me by Henry Miller, he wrote it in the '40's, but it's so today. We'd all be happier knowing less. Israel bombs Lebanon; arms to Saudi Arabia and El Salvador; on the Achille Lauro an old man in a wheelchair gets thrown overboard by terrorists. It's all so depressing. Type, type, hype and gripe. It never ends. How can you stand it? I'm only a temp, but I feel the insanity, and my hands react cramping up. Sometimes I think the air stops three feet around me. I never saw so much hate, and not just in the newsroom. Techs hate writers, writers hate techs, management hates everybody, and the feeling is mutual. I hate my computer. It hates me. We hate our jobs and hate ourselves because money forces us to live with that hate. I see all that hate lined up for lotto tickets at the newsstand downstairs. The line goes down the hall beyond the mailroom. There's hate in there, the way they throw the mail around. Even Crankcase was buying a lotto ticket. Why? He's rich. He's doing it out of hate, to screw somebody else. I hate to say it, but under that iconic uncle veneer, there's hate born of all those dumb years reporting worthless news. Negatives, nothing positive, year after year. Miller says, to lose the news would be a great advance. News generates lies and hatred, greed and envy, suspicion and fear. My daddy used to say, behind every 'hello' is fear of being eaten alive. Around here you could believe it. Daddy was never patient with me. He did everything for me. Maybe he thought he was helping, but not letting me do things on my own hurt me. It's like learning to walk. Nobody can walk for you. I don't recall ever seeing anything through and feeling successful, saying to myself, "I did that, mistakes and all. Nobody else." The whole ball of wax's succeeding early. Sometimes I think I'm disappearing, like I took a wrong turn in the road and I'll never get back. It's real bad in November. I emptied out a closet, put in a blue light, and sit there with the door closed. If I'm lucky I'll quietly suffocate.

☺

33.　Barzini and The Italians

Diary. Miz, writer-producer, does the meat and potatoes work for Sticky Face, i.e., interviews, scripting, making sound bites. He just wraps her work. He's an old goat and I'd rather listen to her infectious laugh.

Miz interviewed Luigi Barzini, Italian journalist, novelist, poet and Columbia alumnus, and discussed his book *The Europeans.* I teched and watched through my window, their voices on the overhead speaker a mix of Miz's billowy brown silk dress accented by a delicate yellow neck scarf whispers off-mic as she pours a glass of water. *The rustle of silk,* says Luigi, and their voices melt into mumbling, rustling sensual feathers on my ears. Two silk worms, one laughs robustly, the other smoothes his tie.

Later, I ask Luigi about the origin of "mafia." *In old Sicily when a gentrified man rode horseback he sat straight back in the saddle like un uomo grandioso, and people said, 'Un Mafioso,' - a man of respect.*

Luigi invited me to visit him when next in Roma. Sadly, he died soon afterward. His book *The Italians* is a favorite of mine.

☺

34.   Marie

Diary, 1984. Blather's from the no-denture news school, which *makes him an indentured anchor.* Reporters see themselves as surgeons of news, and shouldn't smile. Weather reporters smile 'cause the joke's on us.

Marie Betzig of BOD payroll was kind, sensitive, single, nearing retirement, and spent weekends caring for her 85-year-old ailing mother. Marie's humor was understated. When she retired, part of the company went, too. She waves me into her office. *What's with Blather?* she says. *He's acting peculiar lately, smiling, saying 'hello'. After years of no 'hello' suddenly I'm getting 'hello' with a smile. That's the scary part, the smile. I don't even know the man. The other day I turn around and he's standing there grinning at me with a big toothy smile. Scared the daylights out of me. Then he says 'hello'. It was scarier than Wally Peepers looking through a window. What's going on?* His ratings slipped and he was told to smile more. *I wish he wouldn't practice on me.*

☺

35.   Kids

Bede After 3, ages 4-7. The movie *Back to the Future* was popular and kids loved the central character Marty McFly. During a play rehearsal a 6-year-old says, "Can I say, Holy Shit?" I go, "Why?" He goes, "Cause Marty says it." A 5-year-old was typing a story on a computer. I go, "What's it about?" He says, "I don't know. I can't read." After jogging around the yard, a 4-year-old says, "It's like going upstairs." Samara, 5, and Ion, 4, were sharing a lollypop. I go, "Where'd you get it?" Samara says, "Found it in the yard." I go, "On the ground? It's dirty." Ion pulls it from his mouth, looks at it, and says, "It's not dirty. It's clean." Samara takes it and sticks it in her mouth.

7-year-old. You know the earth turns and it takes 24 hours to make one complete turn? And it circles the sun as it turns. *Amazing.* It takes 24 hours to rotate, which makes night and day, 'cause at some point half the earth is facing away from the sun. It circles the sun in one year. *How does it do it?* It has a Duracell battery that keeps going and going.

How old are you, Willie? *Six.* When did you turn six? *Next month.*

The kid is ship wrecked on an island, starving. He eats sea weed.
6-yr-old. What's that?
Green linguini.
6-yr-old. No. Silly. He's eating allergy.
Christmas time.
Ion. Good thing Samara's Jewish. Her chimney's too small.

Anon 1. How do you make babies?
Anon 2. Two parents get together, a woman and a man, and make love. Their bodies come together with this. (*points to his crotch*)
Anon 1. Then what?
Anon 2. You pee on her leg.
Anon 1. My mommy carried me in her belly and then one day I walked out of her butt.

During a *Wizard of Oz* rehearsal, suddenly the kids are laughing. An upset Tin Man, age 7, points to Dorothy and says, "She oiled my dick!"

At the end of *Oz* performed for parents, a 7-year-old Dorothy, about to return to Kansas, says, "Oh, Tin Man, don't rust, you'll cry."

☺

36.   Flaws In Da Flaw!

In early 1987 Network Radio began relocating to a room at the far end of the newsroom and brought into the 20th Century with state-of-the-arts high-end technology. It left a gulf between them and the on-air studios where formerly going from one to the other was like falling out of bed. The old 50' by 100' newsroom was gutted and became a dump from soup to nuts. Watts and Lebanon after the fire; a dead zone. Burrow would've been in his element. *I'm high atop a desk, overlooking 'Downtown Beirut', the debris of a once bustling newsroom now a vast, silent wasteland. Salvatore Dali's post-nuclear visions come alive. Stacked desks impaled by broken chairs; a frozen wall clock; rotary phone receivers hanging from cradles; the rubble of crumpled wire releases; spools of inky ribbon from clunky Remingtons bunched in key wells like exposed intestines; wires snake from wall sockets; cables dangle from openings in a dropped ceiling, or protrude from gaping maws in the floor longing to reconnect like fingers on the ceiling of the Sistine Chapel; florescent lights lean meanly against walls ready for loading in rolls of stacked carpet aimed at the on-air studio like canon barrels on a battle ship; defunct teletype machines line a back wall- soldiers dead in the line of duty; one draped in the American flag. I salute you, my fallen comrades. Flights of angels sing thee to thy rest.*

With computers writers and anchors could deliver stories faster with more think time, and read instant updates off a monitor. Sounded great, but old timers fretted. *What if the electricity dies, or the computer- and this was a new word that still haunts us- what if the thing 'crashes'?* Replacing a typewriter with a computer took a leap of faith for those used to hand-held scripts that didn't disappear like a blown light bulb.

Reed Colins walked in at 5a one Monday, couldn't find his trusty typewriter. It had been removed against his wishes and replaced by a computer. In a moment of pique, he dashed the monitor to the floor, and was suspended for a week. Also, computers did not save trees, as advertised. Nervous Nellies backed up everything, including their bowels. There were copies of newscasts, memos, 1040's, merchandise receipts, traffic tickets, birth certificates, cornúti (horns), and hands that were sent off as mafia threats. To limit usage, a secret code was installed on all copiers, which was changed every other day.

The area outside one of my control room windows became the new *60 Shminuets* TV studio, a one-arm bandit for intros, closings, and reverse shots. The window onto the newsroom was the back wall of the new facility. Sealing it gave me the feel of *The Cask of Amontillado.* Then, an acetate based chemical epoxy painted on its floor, gave off toxic fumes, and we cried, *Gas! Downtown Beirut's under chemical attack!* The room was cordoned off with 'Do Not Enter' tape, which I extended across my door. But y'gotta get up early to fox nosies and I was in at midnight.

☺

37. Peter Funk, Piano Tuner

I buried my dad in January. *He folds a long, narrow, red felt strip between the strings.* It's sad, so sad, but there's nothing you can do. It was his general condition. He was senile. Had diabetes. They had to cut off his leg. There was nothing I could do. He was 82. Do you see your father? I nod 'no'. Oh. *He places the tuning hammer on a pin, strikes some notes, and turns the pin gently a hair forward, then back, adjusting for pitch.* I was close to my father. Very close. It makes it worse, when you're close. *Moving up the keyboard he places mute rods between strings adjacent to the one he's tuning, strikes the key, listens, and moves the hammer accordingly.* So how come you haven't seen your dad? *He's a pain in the ass.* Really?

That's odd. In what way was he a pain? *Always fighting. I could never sit down with him and figure things out. My mother was great. But a father's important.* Oh, definitely. Maybe your dad was a loner. Some men are that way. You should visit him. *He plays several chords, listens, then resumes tuning.* How's your son? He must be big now. How old is he? *Seven.* Still going at the piano. *Yes.* That's great. If you remember, we talked last time about buying another piano. I have several I'm working on now in my shop, which I can't get to because I'm too busy with this work. I know of a Chickering for $3,500 from a former teacher. They're good, very good pianos. It's a grand, a little over six feet. I offered 28, but she wanted 32. Well, the problem was it's big. Not everybody has that kind of space. You do. *I'm not sure anymore. C.B.S's having a lot of trouble lately, cut backs, our contract's up in October. We probably won't take a vacation this summer.* Chickering's a good piano. The problem with grand pianos is that they go out of tune easily- most of them, unless you get a Steinway, a good one. They need attention. The pins get loose and then it's really hard to tune. An upright, I'm speaking in general, is sturdier. A tighter piano. This one here is tight. That's good because you can tune it. Somebody buying an upright, even if they didn't know anything about a piano would do okay, because most of them are tightly built. They don't go out so easily like grands. It must be the way grands are designed- the pins laid out- that makes them vulnerable. This one's a good piano, but I'll keep a look out. *Tunes and plays.* Come to think of it I'm going up to Haworth to tune a baby grand. I think they're looking to sell. I'll let you know. *Plays a lovely melody.* You like this song? My dad wrote it back in Germany. He was a composer, you know. He wrote a lot of music. Some well-known pieces, too. *What name?* Funk. Same as mine. Lots of people knew my dad in Germany. He still collects royalties for this one, a waltz.

Plays. Nice, isn't it? I miss my dad. You visit your dad? You only have one. When he's gone, that's it.

☺

38.   A Sojourn at Local
C.B.S Memorandum
From: Director of News. To: Radio News Staff, July 10, 1990

The Facilities folks found flaws in the flooring that was laid for the new TV studio. This will require a new epoxy coating for the flawed areas.

We have no assurance that fumes will be less irritating than before. So this weekend, after the 10 AM hourly, the entire staff will move to AM radio. Broadcasts will resume here at 2:45 PM Sunday. Conditions won't be ideal. But it's better not to chance what we faced before. Everyone working this weekend is being contacted. Thanks.

Getting the floor right became a floorshow in itself.

C.B.S Memorandum
To: ALL TECHNICIANS.   Date: July 11, 1990
The Great Smell Move Part – 2
Once again they will be painting the floor in the new TV studio. This time we'll be moving before the smell gets us. If and when you are assigned to local radio:

- leave the building and take a cab to local. Go to the 16th floor. You must have your ID for entrance to the building.
- Go to the door. Dial the number there to be let in.
- The "AIR" studio is Studio D and the Edit studio is Studio E. Good Luck.

☺

Jalanzo. August and the flaw show's on a fourth curtain call. The good air's going to them. We're boilin', but in there ya can hang meat.

Dilido. Think the smell's bad here? Blow a fart in maintenance and three hours later it's still saying hello.

☺

Miz. The camera dollies and hits a mogul-
Tech. As in anchor?

Miz. And the picture jiggles.

Tech. They're all palsied. Get 'em to jiggle in sync.

Miz. Oh, shush up.

Tech. You're the best, Wally, especially when you killed the Haiti-

Miz. You still harping on that? Pa-leeze.

Tech. My research sauces tell me it was a follow up to Sticky's 1972 piece on the harshness of Duvalier's rule. We've been waitin' 10 years for it. Who's in charge, Baby Doc? The real skinny, you old duffer, is that your wife's cousin Chinette owns an arts and crafts store in Port-au-Prince. Stick your nose in Haitian politics, they'll torch your store. Your wife said kill the piece, or she'd torch you. *There are priorities. A wife's wishes are important.* For mal-feasance of news ethics we're torching 60 Shminutens! Old bones burn like dry leaves.

Miz. Shush. That's him now. He's the best, the best in the business.

Ida. (*entering*) G'mawnin'.

Tech. What brings you into the trenches, sumpin trenchant?

Ida. Listen, trench mouth. They're puttin' anuddah epoxy coat on da flaw. Network'll be outta local. Ya listenin'? But on what planet? It's hard to believe y'beat one million sperm to the egg. When y'come in Sunday cab it to Black Crock, 17th flaw. Ya do the air shows until 2:15PM. Then taxi back here. Get receipts. We'll pay fah da cab.

Tech. AM's on the 16th.

Ida. 17th, Einstein. Look. I should be home havin' cawfee wit my sistah and gettin' dressed fah church. So don't break chops.

Tech. Sunsets're nice from the 17th flaw, but better at the Vin-yahd. Roses in Sconset. Beech trees and wisteria in Gay Head.

Ida. Save it fah y'stories.

Tech. Killies in Squibnocket Pond. Clamming and osprey at Tashmoo. Uncle Woolly aboard his yacht. Barefoot tennis. Rose-tinted sunsets. Quiet nights broken by distant sounds of halyards clinking-

AM was on the 16th floor. I helped Chief Engineer Torchi build the FM on the 17th, but in a minor capacity. "Hand me the wrench. That's a pliers." Torchi did everything with great deliberation; always precise in conversation, and neat. He carried two handkerchiefs for spot checks. He'd spread them on the floor and kneel on them to protect his pants. I asked him, How do you remember which side of the hanky touched the floor? Afterward, he marked them with an X on one side. You wouldn't want to be behind him during a fire alarm. He gave new meaning to rigamortus. In fairness to him, when dealing with electricity, you best go slowly. You don't want to grab the wrong wire.

I went cross-town early to give myself time to check out the control board. Machines have personalities with long memories. Treat them rough they remember you, and will even hold your relatives accountable. I was out to get a feel for the on-air console's temperament. Is she peppy, sluggish, argumentative, or carrying a grudge?

On entering Black Crock, corporate headquarters, I discovered the building was in a weekend austerity mode, no air conditioning. The *industry was in an economic correction cycle.* Yet Crankcase continued drawing his big salary for doing essentially nothing. That's the way it was. The ground floor revolving doors were folded and opened. The lobby was hot. Before I'd gone two feet toward security and the sign in book at the long black table, perspiration dropped from my forehead, sputtered off the stone floor like on a greasy spoon griddle. I felt like Alec Guiness signing in for the steel sweatbox in *River Kwai.* Drops of sweat from my forehead mingled with other droplets smudging the page. I go, "It's the book of sorrows at having to work here. Where's the air?" *Cutbacks,* said the guard, mopping his brow. *Turned off weekends 'cept for working areas.* "This is a working area." *We don't count.*

Elevators are marvels, but I prefer stairs. At elevators I see Paul Muni in the movie where the sidewalk opens up, he steps on an elevator, and descends to hell. The 17th floor was dimly lighted and creepy as a crypt. The eerie cyber creature soda machines were still by the stairwell. Their dyspeptic guts always kicked in angrily, sometimes eating money without belching up a soda. A note on a door said, *AM on 16th floor.* Edging by the soda machines, I opened the stairwell door to walk down a flight, heard a rush of far-off banshees, and stopped. Maybe some nut's lurking in the stairwell? A touchy tech with poisoned cotton swabs? A hapless editor with a sharp No. 2? I remembered the doors locked behind with no re-entry. It meant 17 dark flights down. Who's that? Tony Perkins in his mother's clothes. Julius La Rosa out to stab Godfrey with an ukulele. Stepping from the elevator, I see a shaft of light at a door, held open by a ruler. Network radio was in a studio with a console that was an old pal. The studio looked seedy, but the control board was glad to see me.

☺

39.   Pah-roozin Da Nooze

Ticky-tock-ticky. Page 1. Dumb? How about stupid and costly? Ida, the insidah, the BOD spidah, says, "Da 60 Shminuten flaw's an Earl Schieb job. 'Go with an experienced outfit fah 8 G's,' I go. Instead, they got an Orchard Street special, some guy who puts down garage flaws. They've got ghost cameras dollyin' on their own cause da flaw's not level. A lot's not onna level here. A re-do'll cost 24 grand. The paint'll give you a buzz; if the ratings drop they won't care. The stink doesn't bother Soviet that chain smoker. To him, epoxy acid tone is fresh air. Soviet's the only one I know who eats, smokes, n' talks all at the same time." He goes, *Wrong. I also juggle cartridges and do sound effects. An epoxy on you!"*

Tick-tock-ticky! While the old gang of 60 Shminutens slumbers in the Vinyahd, noses in their wives' snoods; while Ida, the spidah, the BOD insidah, was in *the* Bronx havin' cawfee and toast with huh sistah, another epoxy coat went down delaying Network Radio's *skedded* return from temp quarters at local radio on Sunday at 9 PM. Get a Zamboni to level the flaw! Or turn the reporters upside down and those vacuum mouth, radio-bembas will suck it up only they never exhale. **This just in.** A guy in blue's re-doing the flaw in blue and blends in. He says, "We didn't lay the old flaw. No smell now. We're using pigmented based sea-ment." It's a compound of chopped Desk Assistants, granulated anchors, & coarsely ground pushcart producers. **Radio-bemba Goofs of the Week on the hourly:** "Noted civil whites- rights activist...Some major industrial hypocrisies- democracies." Reading a commercial, one announcer says, "Join us on the cruise. You'll have a eunuch experience, unique..." Then, there was, "This just in..." followed by dead air. The excuse? *Fumes from the epoxy flaw flawed me, and the florescent lights got me florid.* He's on leave in Flaw-rida! Out of the last commercial on an hourly, the anchor loses track of time, backs into a kicker, a frantic director flashes 3 seconds left, and we hear: "On the whole, I'd rather be naked. I'm Mat Krauser." There was an accident in the radio-bemba halls. Cholly was walking along, stopped short, and it took 5 people to remove the Chink's nose from his asshole. A solemn note. They say company lawyers killed writer Tiny Malice by denying her drugs critical to her medical disposition. I weep for this frail and talented lady who had trouble relating to the good old boys. No innocent, Tiny could pitch a bitch with the best. An insider, newly off the Dracula shift, tells us, "In Studio B, I look up from my newspaper. No Tiny. I look again, and she's stretched out under the counter-Nefertiti in a sarcophagus- just resting."

Tiny. You read this? Meg Coonan's on the prez's speech writing staff. Leading into his news conference, she writes, "in the sun-dappled rose garden." Good, hey? She done real good. Think about it.

For Tiny Malice: A rabbi, a priest and a lawyer are stranded on an island. A ship comes by, but they have to swim out and there are sharks. They draw straws. The rabbi swims five feet, a shark eats him. The priest crosses himself, gets ten feet, a shark eats him. The tide's rising so the lawyer decides, better to swim than drown. Halfway out a shark comes up, says, get on my back. I'll take you to the boat. Afterward, the lawyer asks, why didn't you eat me, too? The sharks says, professional courtesy.

☺

40.   Peasant Dreams

Tech. Hey, dildo.

Dilido. Dilido, asshole. The guy you replaced, where'd he retire and why aren't you with him?

Tech. Costa Brava.

Dilido. Nice. After 35 years you'd think he'd send a card.

Tech. Why? You have friends here?

Dilido. Bet in July he goes to Pamplona for the running of the bulls. We got that here, the runnin' of bullshit. I dread comin' in. The wife says, *don't be foolish. We got a mortgage.* You been to California. What's it like? Bet the weather's nicer. What's Hollywood like?

Tech. All actors with speech impediments livin' somebody else's dream.

Dilido. Maybe it's better than their own. I'd go out there. But all I know is this job. Take you, for instance. You do a lot of things. You could survive on the outside. Me, I'm stuck here with my contadini dreams.

☺

41. Save It

Studio A. The air conditioning is out. Large fan going; humid; steamy. Studios have thermostatic controls with three temperature zones; warm, warmer, warmest. "Techs're not supposed to touch the thermostats," says Ida. "It's a jurisdictional mattah. Y'supposed to call air conditioning. But you do what ya want." *It's the writers.* "Is that right, Mr. Technician, par ex-a-lant? If it's writahs, how come cotton swabs are stuck inna thermostats and not pencils?" *They're devious.* "Save it fah ya stories."

☺

42. The Business of Humor

Diary. After eight years on disability, DB was back teching per diem. The week he left I was assigned to observe and back him up before taking over as tech for the News Break, or the Cholly Piles, or whatever it's called. I'd switched from nights to early morning hours, didn't know the turf, but I'd had a modest working relationship with Cholly in '67 at local radio. DB was Sicilian born, had a minor Italian accent, was a good tech, and had two daughters. That first morning I ran into a Sicilian wall of silence with a suspicious, tight-lipped attitude. Little was said beyond *hello* and *they're doing an essay. Speriamo! Let's hope.* I figured he was preoccupied with leaving, and I gave him his space. He'd open up, if he wanted to, but he never did. Later, I learned that his reticence combined a weak heart, domestic trouble, and friction working for the Bruise Bros, vis-à-vis, a self-absorbed anchor and an extremely territorial producer. That morning the show was a breeze. Open and close the mic, and play commercials. Cholly's ability to rhyme news was unique, but for me it was marred by his intensity and his Chinese-American producer- an insecure, sycophantic asshole, who hung on his master's word like the old dog looking into the RCA Victrola. I knew from my comedy experience that the business of humor is not funny. Then, DB's daughters got jobs in television and he came back. That was funny in a strange way.

Tech DB. Retirement, it's-ah boring. I go fishing, then what? Even Sicily, after a couple of weeks, then what? I play handball, then what? My son was right. I should've taken up golf. You meet a better class of people; doctors, lawyers, and executives. Not the kind you meet-ah in the park playing paddleball. Listen. What should I tell people when they ask why I am back? *Be evasive. Say you're watching your daughters in TV. It's a Sicilian custom.* Giusto! To make sure they meet a better class of people. *They're both attractive. Is the brunette-* Not for you. No. Frittellóno. You don't dress right. *What's wrong with my clothes?* That's-ah the second reason. You have-ah to ask. That will tell my daughters who are sharp dressers that you are a man who thinks like he dresses. Indicatívo. Eh? Clothes indicate the man. With you, sono incriminato. They incriminate.

☺

Dilido. I feel bad. Because thinking of him retired on a beach somewhere made me feel good. Coming back after 10 years'd be my worst nightmare. Doesn't he have a life? What possessed him? You're paisans. Talk. *He got bored playing handball in the park. Says he should've taken up golf. Y' meet a better class of people, doctors and lawyers.* Right. Biggest bullshit artists goin'. Know why California has the most lawyers and New Jersey's got the most toxic waste dumps? New Jersey had first choice. This joint's got more balls than the parks department. We'd rather be taken by con artists than bored to death in the park. Know the definition of waste? A bus load of reporters going over a cliff, and there's an empty seat.

☺

43.   The Hysterical Tense

I first met Joe Dembeau in 1967 when he was news director of local radio. He went on to become Rome bureau chief, then president of C.B.S News until he retired in 1982. He was 5'4", had soulful eyes, and a low timbered monotone voice that became even more defused on microphone. At local we'd record his weekly essays with him enclosed by screens to cut down boom and resonance, and used a busted mic that filtered out lows. After he retired, news-writing changed. Past, future, conditional, and subjunctive got distilled into *present tense active.* What was, is, and what happened is happening as I speak, not as I spoke. "I said, he said," and "I heard what you said" are historical tenses. A young editor put it this way. *Ed Burrow's style wouldn't go today. Mood tenses have been streamlined into immigrant speak, modeled after LBJ's speech-writers' guidelines of only five paragraphs. Each paragraph five sentences. Each sentence five words. And every word five letters."* After Dembeau left a logo appeared on the bulletin board- a circle with Mickey Mouse ears encaptioned: FROM DEMBEAU TO DUMBO!

☺

44.   Ida Spidah

Tech. Ida, we're living in the grip of our own demons.
Ida. Check ya schedule, Einstein.
Tech. People are leaches.
Ida. Ya coverin' a sick-out.
Tech. Sick is right. Society is Jekyl and C.B.S is Hyde.
Ida. Hold that thought. Here comes Crankcase. Tell him.
Tech. God, you're insensitive.

☺

45. Never A Disparaging Word

RADIO AND TELEVISION
LOCAL 12.12, BROADCAST ENGINEERS UNION
**INTERNATIONAL BROTHERHOOD OF ELECTRICAL
WORKERS, AFL-CIO**

August 17, 1990

Mr. T, Vice President Broadcast Operations

Dear Mr. T:

Recently, while you were conducting a tour of a studio, a disparaging remark was made and heard by several of our Technicians. While describing the operation of this new facility you said, "This place is designed so that any idiot can sit here and run it!" This remark was made in the presence of members of Local 12.12, and is construed as an attack on our professionalism and talents.

We, Sir, expect a public apology.

While you may have exercised poor choice of words, we feel it was an intentional cheap shot, coming from a man in your position, especially at a time of negotiations.

Respectfully, Pete "Q Tips" Quarantino, Senior Business Damager Rep.

AFFILIATIONS: NY STATE AFL-CIO, NYC CENTRAL LABOR COUNCIL AFL-CIO, NY STATE ASSOC. OF ELECTRICAL WORKERS, UNION LABEL & SERVICE TRADES IN ALL CONTIGUOUS STATES

☺

46. Every Night's New Year's Eve

Diary: 1990. Negative press about C.B.S budget cuts. *Nobody mentions Cholly's new 10-year multimillion-dollar contract. No wonder there's no money. They're giving it to anchors.*

One day, a new Chaplin-eyed writer shows up holding a food tray. Later on I did a Q and A with him for my newsletter. *I was just in the cafeteria. I came off the line and mistakenly sat at a table with several writers and editors for company. I thought it was an opportunity for us to get to know each other informally. I tried introducing myself several times but nobody responded. Amazing! They kept talking a mile a minute with food in their mouths and laughing, mostly when one man spoke. They leaned toward him, talking for his amusement; fast and loud, too, in fragmented sentences and he'd chuckle now and then. I mean, a bedlam of 3-second bites. It was like eating soup while watching a ping-pong match. I like to chew my food then swallow it. Not the other way around... I had the strangest feeling I was in Florida at an alligator pit watching a feeding frenzy. You know, where they throw in meat and the alligators go crazy. They'll even eat each other. I was afraid if I talked they'd eat me alive. And they all had red faces and lots of gas. The loudest one was an amusing little sycophantic Chinese chap with a moon face; rather obsequious, I thought, always chuckling at nothing, playing up to the fellow on his right like he was some sort of mahout. And he had an irritating machine gun laugh that punctuated mostly what this fellow said.* That was Cholly, anchor of *The Cholly Files.* He thinks, says, *Oh, that's him.* Yes. Holding court with his jester. *Take my sandwich. I hardly touched it. I left my soup. God! My stomach's in knots.*

6a. *The Cholly Files,* always delightful. What'll it be today? Cholly a la mode? Tech on the rocks? The Armenian, Cholly's regular writer, is off. The sub's Karol, the libber. One cross gender word and it's a federal case. **6:15a.** Cholly's hot to trot. Karol and the Chink are in rolling chairs by Director Sing who's beside me at the console. We go to air at 6:30a, but if we pre-record now there's time to re-rack, go to air on tape, and Cholly can walk leisurely to TV. Chink's pushin' Karol, and she's pushin' back. He's forever declaring his turf by knit-picking. The writer writes, the director directs, I push buttons, Cholly chats, and the Chink chinks. *The script's visually incorrect.* I think, he's visually incorrect. Looks Neanderthal. Karol replies, *It's readable.* **6:20a.** Cholly's ass's burning. TV's at the other end of the building, a football field away. *What's the holdup? I want natural sound out of the second commercial. That's not what you wrote. Read my lips. Sound first, then the line. We're going to be in deep shit, folks.* Standby, says Sing. Everyday it's Noah's Ark and the impending flood. Deep Shit'll be his epitaph. Suddenly Karol defers to the Chink. Figures. Antagonize him, he rats you out. Cholly's nervous. *Roll tape. I gotta get to TV,* a daily mad dash through Downtown Beirut. I go on TB, *Get roller skates.* He looks up, *We rolling?* I hit record; the Chink grabs a watch; Cholly goofs; we restart; Sing's watch misfires; we go live; out of the last commercial, I hit sound, open the mic; the Chink scowls; I wink at Karol; Cholly closes; splits for TV like he's shot from a canon. Later, when I tell the Armenian, he fumes. *I hate 'im. Absolutely, unequivocally hate the little bastard. God forgive me. He's like a dog with a sock. Holds onto incidentals and doesn't let go. Bush league. That's the censored version.* I go, The best time I ever had was the week we did the show without the Chink. It was no picnic, mind you. You tend to get nervous. He goes, *Me?* I wobble a hand. But you're great. He says, *Thanks. Compliments are rare around here. I'd love to stick the Chink in an armor suit just so I can say there's a Chink in the armor!*

The Chink's perceived generally as a courtier-radio-bemba. *Ha, ha! Hee, hee! Cholly number 1. That make me number 2! Cholly Two Shoe number one Wu Shu. Put dumplin' on my table!* Why would anyone spend their life steppin' and fetchin'? Sinatra's valet was fired after 15 years for dancing with Mia. Asked why he'd stood Sinatra for so long, he replied, *'Cause every night's New Year's Eve.*

☺

47.   Rumination

Diary. Studio E, 4a. No news is good news. I write in my journal. *Invasion of privacy raped the sanctity of individual thought and feeling, and set the stage for the corrosion of the human spirit. The world gave itself body and mind to the deceitful, jackboot mentality of a marauding brotherhood of electronic journalists, and lost-* What? Jesus! You can't write and analyze simultaneously. If you're pregnant you can't open the womb for a look-see. Examine baby afterward. If it's crippled, dump it like a Roman. *Guerilla reporters roam freely; predators everywhere jerking off on misery and misfortune.* Returning from the john, I find the Chink working an ampex- a violation of jurisdiction. I let it ride. Next contract it won't matter. Between give backs, and consolidations, I might end up in TV. The Chink's been polite lately, since getting a slap on the wrist from the producer unit honcho for hording tape when first dibs belonged to NR. Cholly's got the ratings, so his boy got off the hook. Among many techs and writers, Cholly rates thinner than piss on a flat rock. Always with his shirt hanging out and never a thank you. Every day it's the sword of Damocles. I came close to talking with him about it, but decided it's the *Emperor's Clothes.* Le roi il veut! The king wills it.

I liked Cholly. We'd visited each other's homes. But the Chink was insufferable. He shit a turf-conscious brick the day Cholly said, *Come to the house anytime. You don't have to call.* **7a.** Went live, after cutting 12 inserts. Cholly had minutes to write 45 seconds with quick turnarounds. Columnist Russell Baker, a former neighbor of mine on East 58th, says, *Deadlines are deadly. After staring at a blank page all day, the deadline two hours away, I go to the corner newsstand thinking in New York something's bound to give. Nothing. On the way back, while entering my building, I see a neighbor* *unloading his station wagon wearing a spaghetti pot for a hat. Somebody in the Sovereign across the street was throwing potatoes off a balcony. Voila! I had my story. "Potato Mashes Man!"*

Only diehards hold grudges. One anchor shocked a tech who was retiring by saying, "Good riddance. I never liked you." Accusations, especially if false, leave resentment. One Friday I was off. 5a on Monday I find maintenance at work recessing the studio cough button- a handy device in the table next to the mic. When engaged, it kills the mic so a speaker can cough without being heard on air. They said the Friday tech fucked up. *Bullshit,* says GW, a female tech, and member of Mensa. *They cursed him. Called him a fuckin' incompetent! I speak French, German, Italian, Esperanto, and Chinese. That's bullshit in any language. Cholly walks in seconds to air reading a dictionary. When his mic goes on, the asshole inadvertently puts the book down on top of the cough button and shorts his mic. What bothers me is he never apologized for those filthy epitaphs. They should install a cough button up Cholly's ass and one in the Chink's face. Both're recessed!*

☺

Diary, 4a. Murderous non-stop news. Double rolls, clusters of feeds from indefatigable nosies, blood-sucking ego-trippers, leaches on the ass of society, flooding us with tears, guns, and bombs from Brooklyn to Bangladesh. I'm startin' an Anti-<u>Piece</u> Movement. I take a pressure pill; kill the overhead and lean back to ruminate. If you can't ruminate you're in trouble. In an 8-hour day, 5 should be for ruminating with a 3-hour lunch. Ruminations are my ruination. I need a secretary. *Ring! This is the president calling. May I speak to the tech? Sorry. He stepped away from the console to ruminate.* Rumination is somewhere between where you think you ought to be and reality. The biz correspondent comes in, we talk "stock options", and the subject veers. *I noticed your buddies in the newsroom.*

I couldn't help smiling at that Chinese fella following Cholly around like a puppy. Their writer can't stand 'im. Why'd he switch from TV? *The prestige of writing for Cholly and money. You can burn out doing the same thing everyday. In TV you have to answer to a lot more people. With Cholly he's his own boss more or less. He got lucky with that Chinese fella. When he saw him on the horizon he had an orgasm.*

☺

48.   An O'Fey Café Napkin Sketch

Prichard T. Hotfoote was youth and energy incarnate well into his 70's. When not at the UN, he was off on assignment. So it was surprising one summer day to see him hotfooting cross-town from the UN, loose tie, sport coat slung over one shoulder, spry as a spring chicken. Ernie Pyle says in *Brave Men*, November 1943, Hotfoote gave him a *startled hello* in an Algiers airport prior to the invasion of Sicily. Once between planes, he had trouble feeding tape from London. He can't be that inept. Not with 50 years experience. *How do these damn things work, Chum?* The serrated clips were alligators bighting his ass. Unscrew the mouthpiece. *Which end is that? Damn modern contraptions are impossible!* Hotfoote's hot! *Not funny, Chum! I'm out of patience.* Reverse the clips. *I've got a plane to catch. I'm rolling the old fashion way, phone against the recorder speaker. Take it, or nothing.* We took it and he was off leaping tall fire hydrants in a single bound. Wherever he goes, he's there before he arrives.

☺

Diary: I moved on to tech the 8a NR next door. P, its new producer, is a bulldog who records everything, sometimes rolling in two studios at once. Pieces are bumped, updated, or killed for late-breaking news. It's a race against time, deadlines, beat the competition, and pray the content holds until your out. If not, the master copy for re-broadcast to the west coast has to be updated, which means updating or doing it over again. News is unrelenting and thankless. Weaken and the business will eat you alive. It takes 24/7 vigilance. P's in at 2a Monday through Friday and out at 11a, and during that time he's married to a telephone. On his days off he phones in to set-up pieces. His down time is finding me to do work.

We played hyphenate before it was legal. It was expedient. Why stand on ceremony at 5a? Teamwork makes for happy campers. He also recognized that techs were underutilized, languishing talent. In my case, it's a talent for languishing. I had an ear for mixing, good judgment, but a mercurial personality. I'm forever throwing myself overboard. P tried befriending me by inviting me to his health spa in Teaneck. Maybe he wanted to lock me in a steam room and boil out the poisons. Every morning his wife phoned, which gave me a second, unofficial break. When he suggested combining the calls with my real break, I resisted. That's cheating! Why give up two breaks? Tell her to call more often. One time P was out, I picked up the phone, and go, "He's in the cafeteria with a blonde Desk Assistant. The voice on the line says, "Roll on TV." It was P. My fondest memory was putting the screws to the Bruise Brothers over dibs on hot tape. Because they were badgering assholes, I'd hand them out-takes knowing some parts were on the floor. Sooner or later *you get what you give.* After NR I humped around on odd assignments, fell out of the loop, lost my edge to hungrier techs and wound up working weekends. Sometimes, in a fit of loneliness, I miss NR-especially when *the* wife phoned to say, *I love you.*

☺

49. EC

Studio B. Karol's working tape-ops. She steps out with no forwarding address. Usually she plays everything close to the bra. Maybe she told the assignment desk. Twenty minutes later she's back and apologizes. A smidgen of a smile moves across her face. What she says sends her to the top of my Hit Parade. She'd been talking with the Chink. *We had a polite conversation. I expressed my feelings about future commitments to them as a writer. I don't particularly agree with the way the show is run, the subject matter, or the anchor's viewpoint. Working with them had been an unpleasant experience I don't wish repeated. I'm a 43-year-old woman. I know what I think and what I believe. I'm beyond the Emperor's Clothes. I shouldn't have to go along with or accept ideas that are disagreeable to me. Furthermore, I said, your manners leave a lot to be desired. A 'thank you' goes a long way. Right now I feel centered in my thinking. I've worked too long and hard to get where I am to compromise myself writing for a show that's not particularly stimulating or compatible with my philosophy.*

50. Overheard in the Hall

Cholly. There's little Authentic Awareness of Alaska. No igloos. The round sod houses when covered with snow look like igloos. The most north, east, and westerly state? Alaska's all three.

Chink. I've no desire to go there.

Cholly. They say it's really gorgeous.

Chink. I know, but I have no interest.

Because brownie points show up in the snow.

51.   *C.B.S Memorandum*

From: L. Grouper   Date: July 16,1990

Kudos to all who braved the inconvenience of this past weekend and our move to AM radio. Your spirit and determination made it work and represents real pride in your jobs. I must also mention the iron constitution of technician L.C. He finished one shift, turned around to replace a sickout, caught a few hours sleep, and returned for a Monday shift.

I am sure you join me in thanking the folks in BOD, who stayed and endured the odor to keep us on line to affiliates. I owe you another one! So do Hughe-it, and 60 Shminutens.

☺

52.   **The Belles Are Ringing**

Jalanzo. They went down in flames. Y'buddies, *The* Bruise Brothers. *Oh?* Another last-minute job. The new belle of the ball opens her yap at <u>the</u> last minute. <u>The</u> cunt from archives. *Oh, that cunt.* She hears <u>the</u> Bruise Brothers want Christmas bells for *the Cholly Piles,* which is already in <u>the</u> fuckin' barrel- about a maul manager puttin' a sign next to a Salvation Army Santa Clause sayin' *Stop Ringing The Bell!* It disturbs customers. What's Christmas, says Cholly, without the fuckin' bells? Bells go with Christmas like bustin' balls go with him. In comes sorority Jane, <u>the</u> belle of the Last Minute Ball playing *fuckin'* heroine. I got bells on tape. *She's bein' assertive.* She needs an insertion. So they kill the show, set up the bells and go live. I throw 'em the lights. The tech opens the mic. Cholly opens his mouth and gets feedback loud enough to bust his eardrums. Cholly loves his voice, but not at 900 decibels. By switchin' the fuckin' flight plan, the tech got caught with his pants down. He forgot to kill the board key to the master which was rollin' on record. Cholly heard himself in feedback like a banshee with its ass on fire. While they're screamin' fuckin' *epitaphs,* sorority Jane's waltzin' down the hall with a clear head. When I see her, I go, How're ya *bells hangin'?*

☺

507

53.   OT's OK

Diary, '83. For health and family reasons, I switched to days. I figured I'd matured enough to handle people. Frankly, I have trouble interacting with furniture. As a result I almost made the hourly. But first. A tech, the son of a senior TV engineer, was arrested for stealing. Police traced serial numbers on a hocked Nagra back to him at C.B.S. He gambled a $50,000 job for pennies, lost, and was dismissed with no charges.

Obnoxious In the Catbird Seat. A radio tech was fired after security caught him loading his car trunk with old radio shows from the archives. What he left behind he'd scratch and render useless. He'd done it for years wherever he worked. When nostalgia hit big he was in the catbird seat. But he's so obnoxious, I go, who'd buy from him? *It doesn't matter,* says Jalanzo. *He does a mail order business.* Recently, on the *Internet,* I found a lady with a copy of *Lucy and Viv Learn Judo,* dated 1963. She wanted $500! People'll steal your teeth and sell 'em back to you.

Homicide, Pier 57. The day I was parked on the upper deck, Westside Pier at 56th, I accepted OT and missed being an hourly headline. A hit man caught up with a guy on the upper deck, who was trying to get away with a suitcase of jewels belonging to the mob, and shot him. Company employees walking to their cars witnessed it and were killed- one was chased to the end of the pier and shot. OT that day was providential.

☺

54.   The Frozen Boy

The studio door booms open. "Roll, Line 12. (*Editor on phone*) "Sorry to keep you waiting. Tell us what happened." *My husband says-* "Let me speak to him, please. (*Intercom to desk*) Hubby's the eye." *Hi.* "Morning, sir. What happened?" *Fell through the ice. Couldn't be more than eight, poor boy. Hit a patch of thin ice. A neighbor said, they tried reviving the boy, but he was frozen.* "NG. (*on intercom*) Hubby's hearsay."

The hourly opened: Frozen Boy! Dead at Age Eight!

☺

55.   Onion News
WGA to Merge With Longshoremen Maybe
Victor Conspiratorio, Business Damager, gave this speech at a shareholder meeting. One WGA rep attended blindfolded.

Johnny Tillio, Senator Baccala, Mrs. Baccala and all the little Baccalas, our good friend in ab-stencha Jimmy Hoffritz (*crosses self*), distinguished brothers, representatives in legislatin' bodies, fellow dumbocrats, and fellow New Yawkahs. Foist off, a salute to Johnny "Hands In" Di Tillio out-going president, feet first, an old timer, some dirty years inna Brother-hood. Let's hear it for Johnny. (*Claps; signals cut*) I myself personally think that the speech we just heard hizzoner, the mayor, speak was the best-spoken speech he evah spoke, and I know it came from the heart. (*Pats behind, takes out handkerchief, wipes brow*) Ya honor, I must say it's boat a trill and dah-light to see ya here along with many of your cawhorts and aids-de-campies: Tony Brunoleschi, an old friend of unions; Ant-nee Convivio, say Ant-nee?; Patsy "Fishcake" Cicharelli and uddahs too innumerable to mention in a sentence. Pardon the expression. Also, our treasurer, Tommy Intalgio's, doin' a great job lo dese last five years considerin' he's in hidin'. Frankly, Mayah, we're in good company as long as we're close to them. I have a message from out-going Business Damager, Joey Nipples. "Deeply regret dat a special crises, two broken legs, prevents me from joining you. My heart's wit you even if my legs ain't." (*crumples telegram; tosses it*) Too bad he ain't here. I was wit him at the start and I'll be with him at the finish. Election time is just around the corner. I'll be seekin' re-election. I'm honest. Never stole a dime. All I want's a chance.

Before a great guy, an articulate union spokesman, Chairman Abruzzio, ee-meritus, speaks, I'd like to in-jet a prep-a-retory word. Lately, a lotta pilfrin and stealin's onna docks. Dis union don't tolerate stealin'! Pilfrin, but not stealin'. No class! Carelessness is intolerable. You mugs workin' Pier 24. Cut da clownin'! Ya got 24 hours to bring back the pier. Others of you been findin' things before they're lost. And no more drivin' forklifts home. We got 16 violations on one lift parked at a fire hydrant in front of OTB. You know who you are. From now on you're goin' for the tickets, not the union. And watch where ya driven them lifts. Some bozo hit the sandwich guy. Lucky he was on stilts. But he'll be walkin' bow legged the rest of his life. Don't gimme the excuse, y'didn't see 'im, n', "What's he doin' onna dock on stilts?" He's afraid of the piers. Too leaky. He don't trust low tide. Some of you been rammin' forklifts into crates claimin' it was an accident and then coppin' the fallout. Some crates contain fragile, sensitive, micronesian computers, and chips. Those ain't casino chips. Y'know who you are. Keep foolin' round, you'll be wearin' a crate for a kimono and go out on a forklift. Now the speech on da Union's financial position. Ladies and gentlemen, and union members, I give you Chairman Abruzzio.

(*On wide-screen from behind bars*)

Don't be fooled by vertical shadows. They're roll bars in a TV test pattern. There are many reasons our meeting's in Trinidad. Most of our stockholders are in the United States. In sales and earnings for this fiscal period, I note a banner year of substantial improvement over the preceding one. Altho' the first quarter did not look promisin' with 1,898 apprehensions the first week, things firmed up the second quarter with only 899 convictions. All Cubans. *Cheers.* Momentum's carrying into the new year. But final figures won't be available pending the outcome of Senate investigations. These encouraging trends resulted in an optimistic outlook. After preferred stock payments, and considerations, earnings for the second quarter, per share of common Waterfront stock reached a new high of 2 cents. *Cheers.* Non-payable *Boo!* Compared to foist quartah earnings of 1 cent, held in abeyance. How's that for growth? *Hurrah!* We're off to a strong start this "fical year." Expectations for the third quarter are high: 800 brothers will be released. The economy is vigorish. We're planning an advantageous move, a merger with the Supreme Court, in which case we anticipate a year of lazy-fair. *Cheers.* Now here's an important message from our union Tink Tank.

"Convicts, murderers, high-class pilferers, and genteel jewel thieves, are you planning for your retirement? All workers have social security and insurance plans. Wadda you got? Consider Shadynook Farm, a rest home for thieves. By deducting a small amount from each take <u>now,</u> you insure your future at retirement time with an atmosphere you're used to: Penal institutional living at its best. Luxurious split-level cells facing your own walled–in, private promenade. Gold-plated triple-tiered bunk beds with a toilet in the corner. Your own closed-circuit TV featuring all-time famous prison breaks and riots, bombings and leading arsonists of our time. Hot and cold running wardens and isolation rooms with swinging doors. An excellent security system for protection against yourself. Armed doormen 'round the clock and tower guards with 10,000 watt klieg searchlights, and a victory garden for trustee types. Earn ya way in! Four convictions, not just arrests, convictions. To qualify, your arrests must stick. Those with death row complexes: gas and electricity administered free. Your choice. We throw the switch. So live out your insecurity at Shadynook Farm with the customary feeling of being wanted. No lease necessary. You can leave anytime. All you have to do is climb an 80 foot wall. No pole vaulting allowed. Last year 19 accountants vaulted the wall, hit the trampoline and disappeared. Send for our sus-pectus now. On the premise steam rooms and hot baths to burn out mustards and poisons."

Thank you, Chairman Abruzzio. (*Lights dim and up*) That's the news we've been waitin' on. Canary Boy just got his for singing off-key. A great sign for an upswing in business. To kick off the new quarter, encouraging news should dispel fears of a downward business turn. Currently, we enjoy 100 years of business leadership during night hours. Daytime we're a close second to the police. We're now open fah questions. Adjoined. I second da notion. *I'm retired 15 years when do I get my first pension check?* Patience. You know how the mails are. If another 15 years go by and ya still ain't received a check, call me collect. I'll personally go right to work on it.

☺

56.   12.12 *Voice*
Vol. 3 No. 2 PUBLISHED FOR RADIO, T.V. AND RECORDING INDUSTRIES   September 1985

Profile: The Fishin' Technician
Lee O, we go back 20 years to local. You always make things look easy.

Labila, life's difficult enough. Who needs smoke? You want coffee? It's fresh.

I wish I had your attitude.

Labila, we can't all be great. Work on it. You'll get it. Maybe not in this life.

You had a problem on Snoozebreak.

Louie, Louie. Look. I've been around the old elephant, believe me, things like that are better forgotten. We still gotta work together.

What happened?

Louie, it's their show. Let 'em do it their way. It's successful. You can't argue with that. We were comin' up on air. The producer made unnecessary work, which put me behind. We got the show on without a hitch, but it was a hassle. Who needs hassles?

What kind of work?

The producer screwed up by having me edit a master instead of first dubbing it. When the second network wanted the tape back, it was chopped up. To save himself, the producer says, dub the cuts. I say, let's do it after our show, but he insists. I re-set the control board and make a dub. Then he starts sayin', "We've got a system." I go, Fair enough. I hadn't done the show in months. What do I know? He's got a system. Fair enough. It's his show. After a coupla minutes of taking things out, sticking 'em back; put cut three around your neck; hang cut six on the wall; butt one with twelve; I'll hold cut four." I begin to see his system's no system, and I go, you're giving me a headache. So they took me off the show. He's got a rabbi. Who needs it? To work like that everyday. Forget it. Come to Sheepshead Bay. We'll go fishin'. We'll talk, throw out a line, discuss my Hebrew lessons, your Italian classes while pullin' in some blacks. Ya like blackfish? The sweetest fish. Two, three hours out ya got 'em on the table already. Y'never tasted nothin' sweeter in your whole life. We'll go out 10 miles off Jersey, the air's fresh, full of brine. It's a lusty, clean feeling out there, the wind in your hair. Then, there's a tug on the line. Y'pull 'em in fast! Sometimes they argue like a good woman, but ya hold on and reel 'em in! After, we'll cook 'em with white wine. I make a great bouillabaisse. Like bouillabaisse? I got a recipe: garlic salt, salad herbs, pepper, carrots, celery, a couplah onions; cook it over a low flame two hours; take out the bones; drain it off into a blender to a puree. Gets ya through the week. Capish?

We're here 20 years. You takin' the watch or a $500 Tiffany gift certificate?

I'll take a blackfish.

☺

57.   Dual Careers, Studio B.

Sing. It's about emotional time, bro'. Nothin' here's worth upsettin' that. I come to work n' sleepwalk. I don't take the job home. When I'm home, I paint with a clear head. Home's where I get serious about the real shit.

Ring! I pick up the phone. It's Drusilla Randolph, Chairman, Speakers and Friends Committee of the American Cancer Society at West 56th off 5th Avenue. "I'm looking for a guest speaker for the annual 'volunteers thank you luncheon'." Instead of passing her on to the newsroom, I go, "I'll do it. I'll talk about network news and my published play-" *You're published?* "Samuel French." *Oh, what do you do at Chuckler?* "What do I do? Production. I wrote for *Benson* ABC/TV." *That's perfect. What would your theme be?* "Theme?" *The subject? We'd like to put it in our invitation letter.* I turn to Sing, explain the call, and the theme hits me, *Dual Careers.* He agrees to join me. We'll discuss work we do while waiting for the work we really do. The one on the job pays the bills. The one at home feeds the soul. Druscilla loves it. Lecture day, Sing and I rehearse walking along West 57th. Mutt and Jeff gesticulating, and laughing.

Tech. You go first. If you bomb, I'm gone.
Sing. Sing don't bomb. Sing lets it fly.
Tech. Let's enter dueling. You with a paintbrush, me with a pencil.
Sing. They serving food, bro? We got to get some re-munerables. Hep ourselves to the tan-gee-bulls.

Over a hundred women are in the hall. I open first.
Tech. Dual careers are like dual spouses. Y'can only be faithful to one. Network radio's a cross-country spider web linked by phone lines and lately satellites. Chuckler built a satellite in DC to feed New York. Somebody put up a building in front of the dish blocking the signal. I think it was NBC. The stressful part is pulling all the elements

of a program together, knowing where everything and every _body_ is, and getting them on air smoothly. In seconds you can hear talk from New York to Paris to Hong Kong made possible by technicians, the unsung heroes of the industry. You can kiss me anytime. A good tech is like a good cook, everything's in the fingers...now, an excerpt from my play, *Chiaroscuro*...Thank you. Here's my colleague, artist-director Mike Sing.

Sly Sing enters waving a hand that looks like a frond of paintbrushes, says, *I don't want to talk about C.B.S. Only my pictures, which are for sale. (Laughter)* One laugh followed another with a slide show of his "Humanimals" series- various animals in human clothes having cocktails, strap hanging on a subway. Good thing I opened. He'd've been a hard act to follow. Going to work that night was even harder.

☺

58.   An O'Fey Rainy Day

Mal. I knew I was getting old. I was watching Dolly Parton and thinking, Why doesn't she take off that dumb wig?
Tech. Mal, what're you doin' here? You're dead.
Mal. I lied. Read me that list of reporters with odd names.
Tech. How's it feel being weightless?
Mal. The trick is to do it while alive. Read.
Tech. We got Holly Wood in L.A; Irwin Go Bra in Dublin; Helmet Liner in Berlin; Rudy La Pay in Paris. A tech named: Toggle Switches; a cross-eyed director, Lenz Retina. Now the news team of Oz Good and Hughes Bad with Orin G. Groves in Florida; traffic and weather together with Birdie I. View and Breezy Flurries. You miss the desk?
Mal. Only my daughter. Don't know what went wrong. Well, I do. I just wish I could've changed it. She didn't come to my funeral, but neither did I. I hate prolonged anguish. When you arrived I learned to live with it.

Tech. A new Desk Assistant practicing on the phone. "You Kur<u>plotkin</u>, the Russian ballet dancer who defected? Not defective. Defected. You're Kur-<u>plop-kin</u>? Sorry. Thanks for calling." <u>Corporate memo:</u> To improve communication lines and marketing potential, an internal re-structuring is necessary to trim the fat to make us competitive. Peebrain, Pillhead and Mac Boob report to Tanya Cornea, of Braille Books, who reports to Colon Oscopy of Internal Functions. Job Search. Wanted: a vibrant producer to head new non-newsy news show, set for late spring or early autumn of this year or the next, depending. Some Ribble Rabble Lines.

Desk Assistant. How do you relax on TV?

Tech. It's called studied casualness.

Soviet. They took off Dolly Parton's bra and found two Danny DeVitos doing the Salsa.

Cactus Stan. If you're the Arch Bishop of news, what's that make me?

Crankcase. The court jester.

Soviet. Aristotle hit the bottle.

Soviet. You're a gross ignoramus. 144 times worse than an ordinary ignoramus.

Jalanzo. He takes forever to make an indecision.

Mal. Give him a penny for his thoughts, you'll get change.

Writer. He's a repeater reporter!

All. You're out of order! Down with up! Up with down!

Tech. Nothing's more permanent than temporary.

Soviet. Fisch looks taller when sitting.

Producer. Read my lips.

Soviet. Can't. You're nose's in the way.

Tech. Doctor, I have a lot of answers that need questions.

Logger. Writers eat alphabet soup!

Anchor. Sorry I'm late. I was walking behind a slow tech.

Mal. That's redundant. Where are your clothes?

Anchor. Past, present, or future?

Tech. When two guys're talking and one looks bored, he's the other one.

Anchor. I could never leave news. I'm married to it.

Jalanzo. Then sue *the* audience for non-support.

TV Anchor. Lots of fans want locks of my hair.

Mal. How can you keep sending out locks of your hair? You'll go bald.

Anchor. Not me. My dog.

Logger. Just saying hello is too intense.

Writer. You're a good worker when under constant supervision and cornered like a rat.

Tech. Some people drink from the fountain of knowledge, you gargled.

Commander. Call the law department.

Writer. Fisch fired 'em.

Tech. Call security!

Writer. Fisch fired 'em. Call Fisch.

Tech. What should I call him?

Writer. A bottom feeder.

Tech. Operator, give me the company doctor. It's an emergency.

Operator. Wait one. (*Recording*) "In the event of medical emergency requiring an ambulance adhere to the following procedure. In speaking to the person on the other end speak clearly and enunciate. Give them your name, location, social security or medical identification number; indicate if it's an emergency and state the problem concisely. Don't hang up. Your call is important to us. Wait for confirmation. If the line is busy, or you're put on hold, wait 3 minutes and redial. You may begin at the signal."

Bailey and Fisch. (*singing and dancing in top hat and tails*) Is everybody happy? We're permanently temporary. Transitional. Appositional. Always conditional. (*singing*) I'm Philadelphia Bill/I'm the Wall Street shill. You'll find our names on benefactor bills/We smoke cigars always will/We dress to kill/We're the Wall Street shill n' Philadelphia Bill!

☺

59. NOT THE $12.12 *NEWS*

(A broadside w 3 eggs 4 a logo: See No Evil, Hear No Evil, Speak No Evil.)

Decmbr   *Pub Bi T Workg Stiffd*   1986

REPORT FRM T NU BIZ DAMAGR

In anticipatn of a future mergr w t Writers' Guilt (WGA), t distilld minutes of our recnt meetg fol-o n reportr's short hnd. A nu Biz Damagr & Xecutv Bord tuk ovr, institutd draconian budget cuts & *Local $12.12 iz now Locl $3.03>*

1ˢᵗ, I tak ts opportunity t offr belatd greetgs frm our tech famly to our nu temporarily but permanent CEO, Lorenzo di Pesce. Now tt u r "Big Bird," stop actg like "BIG TURD."

Xecutve Bord pasd proposl 4 dues incrz retroactv t 1905. Aprovd purchse Americn auto 4 Biz Damagr + Americn credit card w Americn parkg rites @ home n Amercn ownd parkng lots w foreign privleges on Amercn Militry bases. A 2ⁿᵈ car reqwst 4 t Sr. Biz. Rep. wz put forwrd & passd. A notion by Alfonso Gugootz, ID 327690.02, t bulet-pruf cars, approvd. Notion t giv out-going Biz. Damgr severence pay + OT & paymnt 4 personl daze & sik time not takn, denied. **Nipponese Bros** tenderd plan t computrize office & filing systm. Approvd unilateraly w/a 1-yr Servce Contrct in Japan. **Vision Cabl** declard Chaptr 11 in Braille... PIX pact unrequited... **C.B.S** violates agreemnt Roman Articl 1, XIX, verse VII, St. Jon's Vision. **WSEX:** Mona Bimbo & Joe Zipit came b-4 t bored 4 hanky-pnky. Salutry climx. **Congrats Dpt:** Ts year's *Award 4 Excellence in Fraudcastng* goz t anchor team Oz Goode & Hughes Bad. *Asshole of t Year* went t Mee Ahn Yoo. Unsung Hero Merit Badge wnt t all techs. **Memorabilia:** Rare treas maps to the buried nuz tenets of Ed Burrow on sale @ 99¢ Stor formrly 69¢ wher all items r 99¢ evn 10¢ ones. **Foagy Cornr:** Ts year's retiree party wz @ Spumoni Gardns, Bruklyn. It was a reel suces, considrng there were only 5 deaths, mosly frm ovr-xcitemnt whn desert arrivd. Jim "Cat" Catalona gav a swel spch abot t "gud ole daze" whch lasted 2 secs, about 2 secs too long. Retiree wives dancd; joind by hubbies 2 hours later, evryone doing wild brak dancng whch resultd n severl braks among older senrs. Slo Mo from TV did a great head spin in his wheelchr until Bernie Beanie stuk hz crutch in t wheel. Beanie wz a hit whn he got up t edit tape. He tried t splice 2 ends togethr, his

& a waitres & lost 2 teet inna process. Thn he used a WW II bayonet t cut tape. He leand forwrd, cudn't stop his momentm, kept goin & cut thru 9 tabls, 8 waitreses, 3 cooks, & 2 parkng lot attendnts. We ain't seen him since. Whn we wnt home, evry car had a flat. Beanie wz alwyz on t edge. **Nex Gathrng** in June @ Englwd Cemetry. NG on Feb. T ground is stil frozn. Ts way in June if anybdy hyper-vents or keels ovr we jus shovel hm undr. Bettr yet if it rains, he'll slip undr by himself.

☺

60.　　Bubble Boy

FROM: RADIO TAPE OPERATIONS:
TO: (NR) WORLDNEWS ROUNDUP

From Where: Houston.　　**How:** phone.　　**Quality:** Good.
Time Received: 9/21/Midnite. **Correspondent:** D_.　　**Special instructions:** BUBBLE BOY 8 YEARS OLD TODAY.

Baby D is 8 years old. There'll be a family birthday party. Every day & night for 8 years, D lives inside a large germ-free plastic bubble isolated from the world outside. He is the longest survivor to date of a rare genetic disorder which blocks natural immunity to disease. D travels back & forth from home to hospital in a small transport bubble, and four months a year are spent in an identical bubble at Texas Children's Hospital. What the future holds for the Bubble Boy, no one can say, but for now his family will be singing 'Happy Birthday' from the outside looking in.

☺

61.　　Post-it Post Achille Lauro

European Waters
And the Mediterranean
Chandris Cruise Lines
Achille Lauro

Capacity 900 passengers, 24,000 tons, two outdoor pools, Continental cuisine; in dry dock during the winter. Oct, 28 and March 22 – Eleven-night cruises from Genoa, calling at Naples, Alexandria, Port Said, Ashdod, Limassol, Rhodes, Piraeus, and Capri. From $785 to $1,700....

Entertainment director: Mohammed Abu Abbas. Recreation facilities by the PLO. Makes frequent unscheduled stops. Caftans and Uzis optional.
Bring your own Koloshnikov.
☺

62. God Can't Be Everywhere, So He Made Mothers

In the late '50's tuition at the University of Hawaii was a $105 a semester, new books were in the $20 range, and used ones were about $4. Today, times it by ten. In 1987, one credit at Fairleigh Dickinson University was $203.

My academic transcripts from colleges I'd attended were mailed to FDU Admissions in sealed CIA-like pouches. I submitted documentation of my *life experience*, received 30 credits, maximum allowed, and the accumulated package left me 29 credits shy of an undergraduate degree. So, with Chuckler paying 80% of tuition, I returned to school, and got a BA in 1990 at age 55. Interestingly, the keynote speaker at graduation was an FDU alumna, my former broadcast colleague Ms. Coonan, who'd been writing presidential speeches since 1982. Unfortunately, the week of graduation my mother had been hospitalized with ovarian cancer. On graduation morning I was on my way to visit her in Rivervale Hospital, Red Bank. As I drove by the campus down the Jersey Turnpike, I nodded thanks to FDU, saluted Coonan, who'd come a long way since her own undergrad days, and prayed for my dear mother.

My father knew nothing about Mama's illness. She wanted it that way. To her, he was the ruination of her life and home. For me, it was the sad conclusion to a tumultuous marriage. Certainly there had been love, in the beginning, but fifty-seven years later, it was in shreds, and I had just about managed to save myself. At the time of Mama's illness, my father was in his 80's and agile, but I knew deep down that sooner rather than later I'd have to face the music with him, too, only in his case it was a strange discordant lullaby full of cacophonic old world themes played on a busted cello. For Mama, the family sang psalms, but for him- well, he was the genie in the bottle with no wishes, Stokowski without a baton, and in my heart, I knew one day I'd be conducting his swan song.

Mama lingered in the arms of Morpheus, in a delirium of disjointed memories, calling her children then her own parents. *Mama, where are you? Papa, why did you hit me? What's this in my stomach? Go away, or I'll get mad.* Mad? Mama? Never. That was her problem. She internalized everything, lived in the subjunctive, a non-aggressive opposite of the old man. Where he was active, first person singular, forever full of Sturm und Drang, Mama was Victorian with delicate Ophelian ways. She would give you violets instead of knives. Around two on a May morning, 1990, Mama gave up the ghost, head tilted to the side, Christ-like. "NO!" I scream, ears ringing. "Wake her! Confirm it! Call the doctor!"

Sad, a mother's death and there's nothing you can do. Mother the first Light, the beacon you steer by, dying, fading horribly and there's nothing you can do. You wish you'd become all you'd ever dreamed about. Instead, you kiss the first light that kissed your first tears.

☺

63.   Ecce, Swiss Cheese

Diary: Aug '91. While the wife and son are *down the Jersey Shore,* I fell out with chest pains, and ended up with a bypass. I spent several years under psychiatric care, filling out claims, and fielding phone calls from insurance agents looking to give me a relapse. To them, dead is a benefit. They don't have to pay. Would you consider retraining? *Who wants a man in his 50's who can't lift 10 pounds?* The US Post Office, I thought. The interviews were like the sign on a tenement building. Heart Doctor. Six Flight Walkup. Oh, that was my brother up on a ladder checking the gutters. He was lookin' for money. *Who shovels the snow?* Mother Goose. *Oh?* My wife. *How long has she been Mother Goose?* A few years. She quit teaching and does birthday parties for kids as Mother Goose. Sometimes, going to a party, she has to dig out the car. *Do you help?* Yes. I turn on the ignition and it hurts my fingers.

One day I went to pieces at Dr. A's office. I'm dead inside, Doc, like Montgomery Clift in Judgment at Nuremberg. *Oh?* Nazi's invaded my body. I feel I've been sterilized; half the man I used to be. *The operation added 10 years to your life.* I lost 15 waitin' on disability. When he wrote my claim advisor, it dawned on me that a doctor's word is God inviolate. So, I followed up.

July 9, 1992
Claim Advisor, Rudential, Eastern Disability Claim Division

Dear Ms. V,

Since my heart surgery I still have anginal pain, and take nitroglycerin. I'm depressed over my cardiac condition, and impaired ability to earn a living. The idea of returning to work exacerbates my angina, affects my sleep, outlook, friendships, family, and my marriage...Before my operation I tried several times to go back to work. Each time my condition worsened. I'd like to return to work, but it's physically impossible. Fear of a relapse sends me into panic, and depression... After talks with Dr. A, we agreed on psychiatric guidance from Dr. G. I started therapy, but am reluctant to talk beyond *re-vascularization* and *stress test results.* I broke down in tears. My self-image is weakened. My wife is hesitant in our relationship since seeing me in the hospital with *tubes and I.V.'s sticking out* of me. With help, I hope to improve.

Meanwhile, my parent's home on Homecrest Avenue was sold, and TOM, the family acronym for the old man, came to live with me. My nieces phoned in disbelief. *This one of your jokes, Uncs? He's supposed to be with Aunt Gracie. What happened? Gran'ma wouldn't approve, not in your condition. She's turning in her grave. Flipping's more like it. You left home to get away from Gran'pa. Is he behaving?*

The first morning of Day one.

Pop. You an ungrateful son-ah. You don't love you father. A loving son doesn't act like you.

Me. I only asked you to lower the TV.

Pop. You don't understand-ah. You don't live inna my feet. You don't wear my ears.

Me. I'm upstairs and it's like I'm in bed with the TV.

Pop. You have to consider my position, the situation, the circumstance, but-ah you don't. Why? Because you don't-ah love you father. A loving son has considerazióne, but not you. Why? Because something's wrong upstairs inna the brain. You not right inna the brain.

The rest is commèdia dell'arte; right up to stupid me slamming out the front door. Unfortunately, I forgot it was my house and lock myself out. With his hearing aid, it doesn't take genius to see he'd never hear the doorbell with the TV on. So I go around front and bang on the window, and bang, and bang, until it broke and me with it.

"Son-of-a-bitch!" I shout, spinning around like an idiot, knocking my head against a branch. "Goddamnit!" I grab a rock just as a neighbor walks by. I smile. She smiles. I fake gardening, whistle nonchalantly, turn to see TOM in the window bigger than life, lunatic eyes magnified by thick eyeglasses, tapping his head with a finger and on his lips I read, *You not right inna the brain, filgio mio.*

I sit down on the front lawn, lost and dejected, wondering what is going to become of me. I'm at the end of my rope. I consider suicide, but it's too final. Then it comes to me, the perfect solution for my personality, slow suicide via self-flagellation. I'll dwell on yesterday, wallow in regrets and self-pity, overeat, dress like a bum, compromise every impulse, and encourage doubt and despair. I'll be part Pop, part Mom, a Jeykll and Hyde, no potion necessary. That's me now! Boom! Epiphany struck. All these years it was always Hyde lurking in the shadows waiting to destroy my joy, my need for acceptance. Why? Self-punishment for something I did or didn't do, or couldn't do, and wouldn't accept. What? I hate me. Why? I'm not God. I can't heal the sick, or raise the dead. In short, I'll do what I've always been doing. I'll program myself for failure in the teeth of success. At the moment of success I'll deny it. Blame society, my father, anyone but me. Wonderful! I'll spend my days preoccupied with vengeance against TOM. Where do I start? His teeth. I'll steel a pair from the Southeast Senior Center. Smear cayenne on the uppers, sweet and low on the lowers. I'll stick a chicken feather here and there in his T-shirts and itchy balls in his skivvies. A life devoted to getting even. I'll ask my brothers to help. It'll be a bonding time that we missed as kids. The whole family can join in. Blame him! Hate each other and talk in circles. A real family. Our lives dedicated to needling him and each other. That's the trick! Needle and nurse. Lasagna made with tofu. Soy meatballs. Promise him Italy, give him Siberia!

Suddenly the front door opens, TOM comes out smiling, and I think, What trickery is this? "Bon giorno," he says. "E una bella giornata"

A beautiful day. What, am I cracked? No. He's looking past me.

"Bon giorno, Luigi," says the mailman coming up the drive. Fearful of more bad news concerning my disability status, I go tentatively toward him. As I reach for the mail TOM brushes me aside, arms extended, eyes lit up like the Pope has arrived. To an isolated senior citizen mail is like ice cream, or a trip to the mall. With Tom it's more like getting laid. In all fairness, he's anxious, too – about his pension checks, and because, well frankly, he's a nosy bastard with nothing else to do.

"You know my father?"

"Oh, yes. We had a long talk yesterday."

"He's Luigi, too," says TOM stepping in front of me.

"No," I say, stepping in front of TOM. "I'm two. He's three. Three Luigies in one place. Heavy duty."

As Louie, the mailman, smiles, "That's for sure," TOM moves around me, and reaches for the mail. I push his hand away. He pushes mine. I step forward. He steps forward. The mailman steps back holding the mail out like raw meat before starving lions.

"What-ah you bring me today?" asks TOM, nudging me aside. "The social-ah?"

"Not today," says Louie. "Social Security is always on the third like clockwork."

"Clockwork," I say, snaking my hand over TOM's arm for the mail.

"Luigi," says Louie, "you filled out the address change?" I answer yes for him, while thumbing through the mail with TOM breathing down my neck. "It'll take a few weeks to get straight," says Louie. "This month's check'll go to the old address and get forwarded here. See you tomorrow."

Pop. So, what-ah you got, a check-ah?

Me. A letter. No check! Louie told you.

Pop. No check-ah? What's-ah that letter?

Me. Your draft notice.

Pop. Certo. Read. Who's it from?

Me. The PLO.

Pop. Ro? You sister?

Me. No. Row the boat. Can I read this?

Pop. Certo. What-ah she got to say?

Me. What's the difference? It's addressed to me, not you.

Pop. She send-ah money?

Me. You going to stop talking so I can read the damn letter?

Pop. Don't get mad-ah. Read-ah. You get mad over nothin'.

Me. It's not nothing. It's my letter and you're sticking your nose in.

Pop. What in the devil's the matter with you? You was never like this. You gettin' crazy lately.

Me. Mama was right. With you around you can't hear yourself think. Here. You read it.

Pop. Where's the envelope?

Me. I ate it.

Pop. Always keep the envelope.

Me. Why? The letter's dated. It's from your daughter.

Pop. Makes no difference. Keep-ah the envelope. I like-ah everything together. What-ah she got-ah to say?

Me. I don't know. You got the letter.

Pop. Oh. You mix me up.

There's an oxymoron, I think. How do you mix up minestrone? It comes that way. Other more serious incidences followed that got me thinking it was time to put him in a nursing facility. They had less to do with personality conflicts and more with health and social problems. As Ayn said, he needs to be with people his own age. Breaking the news was not easy, and finding a suitable home was even harder. There'd be days when things were fine, and I'd regret even thinking about it, but Ayn knew better. "Sometimes we want more than the other person can give." She was quoting what Dr. G once told me. "When things are running smoothly-" *We see only the cheese.* "But it's Swiss cheese and it's got holes in it. Sooner or later, you'll fall in." One day I fell in up to my neck. I found myself yelling at TOM in biblical language to make a point because common words were useless. Like, "Be gone thou anal aperture!" "Keep it up and I'll smote thee!" This one, he never failed to hear, "The waters parted, and they crossed into a fuckin' nursing home!" To him, "nursing home" and "smote" meant the same, but he was very curious about the fucking part. So, there I was, Mr. Cinema Paradiso, the Swiss cheese kid, come full circle with the man I ran from at eighteen.

One day TOM says, "You know what's wrong with you, Sonny-boy? Too many things bother you." Yes, I think, and you're one of them. "I gotta more experience than you," he says. "Listen to your father. He knows what he's talking about. Take-ah you pension before it-ah takes you. Waitin' for the extra twenty put lotsa people in the gravy. The dough can't help you once you dead in the gravy. Settle you pension and get the hell out-ah. Let the others kill themselves for the dollar." Suddenly I'm listening; actually following his reasoning. "Meanwhile," he continues, "you sit home-ah in this palazzo and collect-ah you pension. Capisci? And get away from those doctors. You goin' here, there, this doctor, that doctor, and you worse than before. Nobody knows what's goin' to be tomorrow. Take what-ah you got before it's-ah too late. With the check comin' in, you know where you stand. Capisci?" Silence. I wait. More silence. Somehow, somewhere, he has found a period. Wonderful! This could be the start of something big. Then I heard my Mom's voice: *Hold on, Sonny.* But he's right. I should take my pension. *That may be true, but think what it'll mean. Retire; you'll be home more to take care of Him.* Ecce, Mr. Swiss Cheese. The bigger the embrace the deeper the hole.

After looking all around for a nursing home, I found one in my own backyard; and I got him into the Actors' Nursing Home of Englewood. He qualified based on my years in the business. What a relief. At first, I was nervous he might break house regulations and get kicked out. He came close. At 90-years-old, he became the new kid on the block, popular with the women, and the envy of the men. He had a 96-year-old girlfriend, a former singer on the Schubert Circuit, and female admirers. The director said, *Your father's quite the Romeo. Maybe we should get him condoms.*

All that remained now was a decision about disability and retirement. So what do I do while I'm waiting? Ask the wife. *Nothing!* I write.

"You jerk-off! Hang around the house; pretend to be Mr. Fix-it; stick your nose where it doesn't belong. A real pain in the butt. Look. I'm going to ballet at Sandra's; then shopping. Be back at noon. Tonight I go to Gary Null's lecture at the 92^(nd) Street Y."

The wife became a vegetarian, which in Italian is grounds for divorce.

She goes, "You're a victim of your palate."

"What's for supper," our son asks, "sticks and leaves?"

"You're on your own, boys," says Ayn, the eternal student. "Eat greens. No bread, no pasta, and no sugar." *Sticks and leaves.* "Just so you know. Tomorrow I'm Mother Goose, Thursday I'm the Train Lady, Friday, Bonny Bess, Pirate Queen, and this weekend at Citi Corp, I'm Dora-" *The Fedora.* "Explorer." *I've always dreamed of having a wife with multiple personalities.* "I'm keeping up with you, Mr. Down-In-The-Dumps." *That's a good character,*

Mr. Down-In-The-Dumps! "Sometimes you're up in the dumps. I like in between." *I'm not down. I'm thinking. Gogol took 8 years to deliver Dead Souls.* "Get off the pot and deliver live ones."

Now I'm annoyed. "I want receipts for your classes: Gary Dull, ballet, aerobics, guitar, voice, flamenco. I leave out anything?"

"Belly dancing and tap. Come with me and work off that stomach. You can't do it with a pencil." *Big tummies are a children's playground.* "Yours is a national park." Kissing my cheek, she goes out saying, "I'll be back." I go, *If you'll be Bach, I'll be Beethoven. Or, I'll-bee, Edward. You're the terror of my loins, but I love ya, Mudge!* "And I love you, Grudge."

☺

64. Li Shao Long

Chinese New Year: Ayn and I are at Veggie Heaven, Exceptional Oriental Veggie Cuisine, Teaneck. She's been gathering material for a kid's show to celebrate Asian culture. So when manager Gary Wu stops to chat, she peppers him with questions. *Yes, it is the year of the rooster. On the wall there's a rooster, behind the cash register.* A paper cut out of a rooster with outstretched claws. At first the rooster wasn't obvious, but nothing Chinese is obvious. They love puzzles and games that crack the brain.

With Gary I often steer the talk to Kung Fu hoping for tidbits about China. Nothing on the menue, or in China, is what it says except yam fries. In between talk about the Year of the Rooster, I ask Gary about Jet Li, the latest martial arts hero. *Bruce Lee is still the best.*

When Lee died suddenly in '73, age 32, I was dubious about the alleged 'mysterious coma' from which he never woke up. *Yes. He was found in Betti Tang Pei's apartment in Hong Kong.* You think going public with Martial Arts got the elders mad? *I'm not sure.* I suspected jealous rivals, or revenge for teaching the *Lo fun,* foreign devil. Maybe he was caught off guard while taking booze and drugs. *He went to sleep and never woke up.* Maybe it was the Kiss of the Dragon, an acupuncture needle in the neck? His son died, too. *Yes.* On a film set from stomach wounds caused by blank bullets. *Very strange.* The family had dreams of being pursued by a warrior-spirit. *Possibly. Yes. That's why sometimes the old folk dress the boys in girls' clothes, to hide.*

Daemons or negative forces can grip individuals and nations, spawn satanic tyrants who push the world to genocide, and conflagrations like Dresden, Hiroshima, and 9/11. A man seated on a dais behind Hitler during a haranguing speech saw a green light emerge from his back. Man is not up to speed with the devils of his imagination.

In a hundred years of filmmaking, no father and son died from a *mysterious coma* and *blank bullets,* and movies have fired off more rounds than all the wars of human history. Edgar Cayce never went beyond middle school, yet he'd enter a sleep and prescribe medical remedies. In that state he located an herbal cure hidden behind books on a back shelf of a store hundreds of miles away that surprised the owner. Is there a devil, a cosmic mind?

Gary chuckles. *Lately, my 4-year-old son has been making swift arm movements and punching. My wife and I look. What's this, Li Shao Long? We laugh.* Long means dragon, says Ayn. Gary nods. *It's a running joke. We say Li Shao Long and my son swings his arms. Very funny.* Li Shao Lung means Lee Little Dragon. Lee has become a Chinese-American icon.

☺

65. Here They Lie *Even in Death*

Whenever I mention Chuckler or that I wrote and performed on TV, people come on like I just beamed down from the Enterprise. My stuttering Hawaiian friend, a terrific nightclub singer, was right. *One day you're d-d-driving a truck, nobody kn-knows you. Next day you sing Ka-Kamakani, they all want to f-f-fuck you.* Lucy's my Kamakani. *What kind of person was Lucy?* She liked to hurt a man. *Lucy?* When Desi bent over she'd kick him in the balls. Lies leaven life. Truth flattens it. Lucy is the lie we love to adore. She reminds us of our own innocence, which is a lie.

As a 16-year-old family member of the Kannedy clan Maria Chuckles would sometimes fly on the presidential plane. I read that she was *gifted, inquisitive,* and liked to *hang with the press,* which was more *interesting than family talk.* A decade later, at age 26, she was anchoring prime time TV news. Want to be in news? Telephone a network, say you're a gifted ice skater, and inquisitive. It'll be *Hasta la vista!* In under 10.

Resume: Jane Doe; **Age:** 26. **Description:** Attractive, personable. **Extraction:** Polish American. **Position Desired:** TV reporter. Will Travel. **Experience:** 5 years radio news; 1-year Network tape-ops. **References:** None in high places. **Conclusion:** Went west and fell off the map.

Resume: John Barington, Honolulu. **Age:** 24. **Description:** Middling looks; fair sense of humor. **Extraction:** Caucasian. **Position Desired:** Deejay/news. **On-air Experience:** None. **Training:** I gave him one private lesson. **Reference:** Doesn't know a pot from a pan even in the kitchen. **Conclusion:** He got hired. Mama was Hawaii's State Representative.

Ayn and I met Mooshka, wife of Zbiggy, a former national security adviser under Chimney Garter, through her 80-year-old mother who lived in a turn of the century

Englewood Tudor on Brayton back of the Jones Manor. A roadside sign, *Honey 4 Sale*, drew us in. The house and Mamushka were twins set back in time; ghosts of their former selves, grand dames musty from decay and age. Both carried their years with an old world, stoop shouldered elegance. Mamushka's eyes evoked Polish aristocracy and the house was 1870's American Tudor. It rested on two acres over-grown with wild bushes, gnarly trees bent and twisted. The kitchen, plumbing, and heating hadn't been upgraded. The stove worked off butane gas, a water tank stood in a corner, and the wall was lined with glass door, wooden cupboards. Illumination of the house relied on electrified gas sconces and heat was provided by coal burning fireplaces. The bones of the house, smelling of dry wood, showed through broken plaster and mudsling on wire fretting nailed to almond-colored struts.

"They don't make homes like this anymore," says Ayn, dancing ahead of me up the stairs and through deserted bedrooms. "Oh," she cries out, voice reverberating down the hall. "I could sit out here forever." Off the master bedroom a small, screened in porch strewn with dry leaves, hung in space like a nest in the great branches of a linden tree. "Let's sleep here tonight," she says, almost invisible among the leaves. *I see auburn hair in candlelight, hanging down from a wicker divan perched in lilacs, jasmine, and roses; dry leaves golden brown huddle in the corner of her blue eyes while night creatures dance on the sils of her brow.* Leaves crunch underfoot in the lonely bedroom, blown in through broken screens and windows. There was nothing for it but to cry, the way you cry when you see old people whose faces speak of by-gone days, their limbs hanging vines, arms withered branches, their lives rickety wooden stairs, each step a story, jaundiced pocked plaster, funky and crisp as honey toasted walnuts. A horse whinnies below; stomps, champs at the bit tethered to a dream mistakenly called life.

The kitchen was left of the center hall with a winding stairs to upper floors, and to the right, through heavy velour curtains and high double doors reminiscent of Dr. Zhivago's Russia, was a huge ballroom with a walk-in stone fireplace blazing away. On the right a door leads to the dining room. To avoid stairs, and heating a drafty house, Mamushka sleeps like a frugal duchess by the fire on a couch of frayed silk and brocade set among old, musty furnishings, threadbare rugs, a grand piano, and gilt-framed portraits separated by high-valance windows filled by a crush of autumnal hues; orange, yellow, and brown. The fire cracks, spirits pop about, doors above open and close, young, spunky legs bound downstairs in evening dress for late suppers. In the dining room fragrant with roses, a long oak table under a gas-lit brass chandelier, sparkles like treasure, as candles glisten off Lenox place settings on Burano lace, and Italian wine in Murano glass. Liveried domestics skate about clothed in savory odors of baked bread, turkey, and pies. Snow beckons at the windows. Woolly, callow boys glance at gingham girls giggling and clucking coquettishly with furtive whispers. What life once lived now dead and we the living in its afterglow follow too soon.

The house is gone now. Still I see Mamushka, aristocratic in bearing, puttering out back in face gear and gloves tending her bees. The *Honey 4 Sale* sign still leans on what is left of the retaining stonewalls running along Brayton Place. We loved the withered lady, who toiled about the old house and grounds, muttering Polish to bees, bent trees, bricks and mortar, pots in the mudroom, and the earth under her fingernails that would soon cover her eyes forever. *"To every thing there is a time, a time to live and a time to die."* Mamushka was Gaea, Mother Earth, old as the stars, eternal as God almighty. After the house was sold, Ayn and I heard her say to her daughter, Mooshka, *Oh. There was a nice, young couple here several times looking at the house. But they didn't have enough money.* She meant us. She and the bees moved to Florida. *One mustn't cry for days gone or things lost. Crying won't do, but laughter will suffice to fill the void, and death welcomed with opened arms and full heart.*

Mooshka invited us to a New York exhibit of her artwork. Zbiggy was there, too. M's showing was mostly plastic sculpture, which she planned to stop because of dangerous toxic fumes released when cutting and shaping the material. Afterward, we joined them for cocktails and hor d'ouvres at *the* Rubenstein's apartment, Central Park West. Amid the elegant chitchat someone toyed on a grand piano.

Mooshka kept in touch by letter and phone from Silver Springs. I advised her teenage daughter on theatre. Then, one day on the phone I was asked the fatal question that would end our relationship. *You related to the film director?* I said no, heard a click, our conversation faded, and I never heard from them again. I should've said 'yes', arranged a meeting in New York, and not showed up. After all, we get what we deserve.

Voicer: Blaise Pascal. Runs: 24 sec. Place: Paris, 1657
"To be of noble birth is a great advantage. In 18 years it places a man within the select circle, known and respected, as another would've merited in 50 years. It is a gain of 30 years without trouble."

Music: G. Autry. Hear them chuckling along/Out on the air where they belong/Chuckling along with the chuckling chuckleheads.

☺

Closer

Diary: November 1991. There is something exciting and scary about a new job with a prestigious company in a modern building so tall you have to lean back and you still can't see the top shrouded in clouds. Twenty-five years later, I find similar feelings of uncertainty about retirement. The new and the unknown are similar. The end no different than the beginning, except for decrepitude. I look up at what once was my future, this Spartan *Eerie Saracino* stark edifice in tinted glass and black granite, now a tad dog-eared. It's as new as ever to the young who come as I once did; head full of quilted notions looking for answers in a tower of Babel, a bleak media totem pole pointing a cold black finger at heaven. That's what Bailey wanted; awesome feelings going up to Him, otherwise he would've had his office on the ground floor.

One can't see into Black Crock, but the view out from the upper floors is breath taking. Once in the cafeteria, 39 stories up, I came off the line counting change, sat, looked up and *Wo!* A turret at the top of a mast. Drunk in an aerie nest with nothing but sky, birds bigger than people below. A cityscape of spires, roof gardens, a tennis court, a pool, and a blue helicopter pad. A feather landed in my coffee.

In the lobby time is mummified security at long tables and parade rest. Old rock tower of a million indiscretions. You gave me a city home, one in the burbs, put my family and me through school, my father in the Actors' Home. *There are no failures; only experience;* but dreams die hard.

Papers signed and back on the street, jobless but pensioned, sad and glad. If only I'd been born with a pension. Well, hell! I arrived a round peg in a square hole, stayed that way, but depart a horse of a different color. I fight my tears. There was more to give and to get. The cards we hold *are* better than the ones we play. If I had it to do over I'd take better notes.

Hands protecting my chest, I wade into the human river on Avenue of the Americas- *The Wild Man of the Overnight now just a dot in the raster of the Broadcast Museum.* The old man knows what the young man does not, but the young man has what the old man lost.

Weaving between honking, cursing cabs, I take the far curb gently to keep from rattling my chest. A catfish looms up, then a shark, a blowfish, and a tart. *Indian summer. Will it ever be Indian summer again?* A horse in the arms of a hansom cab shakes its withers; champs at the bit; relieves itself. We all leave droppings. Some call it history, others *bull feathers!* Back then we were all young. That's the real story that got away.

The End

PR Fact Sheet

<u>About the story</u>. Here's the scoop, pilgrim. Broadcast gossip from the other side of the window. C.B.S is a fictional insider's look at broadcasting through the eyes of a maverick radio technician who has worked with the top media honchos from the '50's to the '90's. An ersatz story from an airhead who developed into an astute observer of people's characteristics and the demise of the Fourth Estate, Louis A. Coppola seasons his journal with humor and street philosophy: "News is nothin' but the glorification of insignificance." In this fictional autobiographical journey readers are transported from Hawaii to Hollywood to Disneyland, then on to the Big Apple and Big City broadcast journalism- a symphony of off-key characters full of diminuendos and crescendos. There's Uncle Woolly Crankcase, Sue Clueless, Wally Aces, news editor "Roundy"Turkel, Chink and Cholly, technicians Jalanzo, the Commander, and the stentorian announcer Devious Septum.

About the Author

Louis A. Coppola is a produced playwright. He has written for **BENSON**, prime time ABC/Television; performed on **THE LUCILLE BALL SHOW**; and directed for **THE LIEUTENANT**, MGM/Television. He has been published by Samuel French, produced in Equity Showcase, and is a member of the Dramatists and Writers Guilds of America. In 1986 he and his wife Ann, co-founded **The After 3 Theatre Co, Inc**, a not-for-profit children's theatre: website, www.after3theatre.org. Currently, Louis performs for seniors with anecdotal experiences Behind the Scenes. He holes up in Englewood, New Jersey.

<u>Excerpt</u>

Wild Man of the Overnight

(*headshot*)

Ha, ha, ha. I gotta say up front, ha, ha, I got this chuckleheaded habit of talking to strangers. Ha. Why? I don't know. Because most people're tighter than a tick's ass. Ha, ha, ha. Maybe it's an old radio-bemba habit. Everybody chuckles in radio. Hi, Sue. Ha, ha. Hey, Drew. Ha, ha. You can say that again. I can, but I won't. Ha, ha. It's 20 after the hour. What hour? Eisenhower. Ha, ha. In that case, it's 16 hundred and zeros at 3 o'clock. Ha, ha! Ho, ho! There was an accident at a nursing home. What happened? I forget. Ha, ha, ha. What's the time now? Don't know. Took a shower and my waterproof watch drowned. Ha, ha. Hee, hee. (*serious*) Or maybe I'm just reachin' out. I mean the point of going out is contact, but how many people say hello? Hello's a big commitment. It can lead to goodbye, and goodbye's one up on hello. Wave to a passing train and the engineer waves back. Wave to sailors putting out to sea and they wave back. But wave to somebody in the street and you're weird. Sometimes strangers'll talk to me.